TURKEY'S POLITICAL LEADERS

Authoritarian Tendencies in a Democratic State

Tezcan Gümüş

EDINBURGH
University Press

Dedicated to my dad (Karagümrüklü) Ayhan, my mum Ayşe and my sister Selin. It is only through their sacrifices that this book was possible.

Edinburgh University Press is one of the leading university presses in the UK. We publish academic books and journals in our selected subject areas across the humanities and social sciences, combining cutting-edge scholarship with high editorial and production values to produce academic works of lasting importance. For more information visit our website: edinburghuniversitypress.com

© Tezcan Gümüş, 2023

Edinburgh University Press Ltd
The Tun – Holyrood Road
12 (2f) Jackson's Entry
Edinburgh EH8 8PJ

Typeset in 11/15 Adobe Garamond by
IDSUK (DataConnection) Ltd, and
printed and bound in Great Britain

A CIP record for this book is available from the British Library

ISBN 978 1 3995 0008 1 (hardback)
ISBN 978 1 3995 0010 4 (webready PDF)
ISBN 978 1 3995 0011 1 (epub)

CONTENTS

TABLES

TURKISH PRONUNCIATION, STYLE AND SPELLING

Modern Turkish uses the Latin alphabet, modified to ensure that there is a separate letter for each main sound. The spelling thus aims at phonetic consistency. Consonants have more or less the same sound as in English, except for a few letters whose pronunciation is unique to Turkish:

c is *j* as in *j*am
ç is *ch* as in *ch*air
ğ is silent but lengthens the preceding vowel and never begins a word
j as in *su* in clo*su*re or plea*su*re
ş is *sh* as in *sh*ip or bra*sh*

Vowels having the following values:
a as in f*a*ther
e as in t*e*n
i as in t*i*n
ı as *i* in cous*i*n or the *e* in sunk*e*n
o as in *o*ff or cl*o*ck
ö as in f*u*r- without *r* sound
u as in p*u*t
ü as pronounced as the *ew* sound as in f*ew* or st*ew* – without *w* sound

vii

ABBREVIATIONS AND ACRONYMS

AKP	*Adalet ve Kalkınma Partisi* (Justice and Development Party)
ANAP	*Anavatan Partisi* (Motherland Party)
AP	*Adalet Partisi* (Justice Party)
BDP	*Barış ve Demokrasi Partisi* (Peace and Democracy Party)
CHP	*Cumhuriyet Halk Partisi* (Republican People's Party)
CKMP	*Cumhuriyetçi Köylü Millet Partisi* (Republican Peasants' Nation Party)
CP	*Cumhuriyetçi Parti* (Republican Party)
DEP	*Demokrasi Partisi* (Democracy Party)
Dev-Sol	*Devrimci Sol* (Revolutionary Left)
DİSK	*Türkiye Devrimci İşçi Sendikaları Konfederasyonu* (Confederation of Progressive Trade Unions of Turkey)
DP	*Demokrat Parti* (Democrat Party)
	Demokratik Parti (Democratic Party)
DSP	*Demokratik Sol Parti* (Democratic Left Party)
DTP	*Demokrat Türkiye Partisi* (Democratic Turkey Party)
DYP	*Doğru Yol Partisi* (True Path Party)
EU	European Union
FETÖ	*Fethullahçı Terör Örgütü* (Fethullah Terrorist Organisation)
FP	*Fazilet Partisi* (Virtue Party)
GM	Gülen Movement

GRECO   Council of Europe Group of States against Corruption
HDP   *Halkların Demokratik Partisi* (Peoples' Democratic Party)
HP   *Hürriyet Partisi* (Freedom Party)
HRW   Human Rights Watch
HSYK   *Hakimler ve Savcılar Yüksek Kurulu*
        (Supreme Board of Judges and Prosecutors)
MBK   *Millî Birlik Komitesi* (National Unity Committee)
MGK   *Millî Güvenlik Kurulu* (National Security Council)
MHP   *Milliyetçi Hareket Partisi* (Nationalist Movement Party)
MİT   *Millî İstihbarat Teşkilatı* (National Intelligence Organisation)
MNP   *Millî Nizam Partisi* (National Order Party)
MP   *Millet Partisi* (Nation Party)
MSP   *Millî Selamet Partisi* (National Salvation Party)
PKK   *Partiya Karkaren Kürdistan* (Kurdistan Workers' Party)
RP   *Refah Partisi* (Welfare Party)
RSF   *Reporters Sans Frontières* (Reporters Without Borders)
RTÜK   *Radyo ve Televizyon Üst Kurulu*
        (Radio and Television Supreme Council)
SHP   *Sosyaldemokrat Halkçı Parti* (Social Democratic Populist Party)
SODEP   *Sosyal Demokrasi Partisi* (Social Democracy Party)
SP   *Saadet Partisi* (Felicity Party)
TBMM   *Türkiye Büyük Millet Meclisi* (Grand National Assembly
        of Turkey)
TİP   *Türkiye İşci Partisi* (Turkish Workers' Party)
TRT   *Türk Radyo Televizyon Kurumu*
        (Turkish Television and Radio Corporation)
TSK   *Türk Silahlı Kuvvetleri* (Turkish Armed Forces)
YTP   *Yeni Türkiye Partisi* (New Turkey Party)

ACKNOWLEDGEMENTS

Although this book is a work of physical and emotional toil undertaken largely in isolation, I was nonetheless blessed with the support of amazing peers, friends and family that made it all possible.

The first person I must thank is David Tittensor, who showed unwavering support, guidance and belief in this work from the outset. He has been instrumental in its journey from a PhD dissertation to this point. I would also like to thank Shahram Akbarzadeh and Ben Isakhan. Their input made this research that much better. My deepest appreciation also goes to Dara Conduit for her efforts while completing this work in its PhD phase. I must extend my gratitude to Deakin University for accepting me into the doctoral programme and for the resources to undertake this scholarship.

I am endlessly thankful to Sabri Sayarı for both his generosity and input. It was his work on leaders and Turkish politics that formed the genesis for this research, and he was gracious enough to act as my academic host during my fieldwork, which was fundamental to my work and my experience in Turkey. Bahçeşehir University deserves a special mention of gratitude. The university's kindness in providing me with a workspace, a suitable environment and resources was an important reason why my fieldwork was possible at all. My deepest appreciation goes to the Faculty of Political Science and International Relations. Thank you for welcoming me with open arms: Yılmaz Esmer, Figen Türüdüoğlu, Ebru Canan-Sokullu, Selcen Öner, Gaye İlhan,

Alper Ecevit, Arda Kumbaracıbaşı and Ela Ünler. I do not think that there is a warmer, funnier and smarter group of academics.

I cannot go without expressing my sincere gratitude to Nathalie Michel. Her selfless efforts to bring this manuscript to the highest of standards and her passion for this book was remarkable, and I am indebted to her.

I must also thank the EUP editors and anonymous reviewers for their insightful feedback, which helped me improve this work in ways I could not have imagined otherwise.

To everyone who granted me an interview and shared their thoughts, experiences and insights, thank you very much. Your contributions were pivotal to this work, our meetings a highlight of my fieldwork.

Lastly, my endless gratitude goes to my dear family who has put up with everything throughout this journey. Their sacrifices can never be repaid. This book is for them.

In closing, this book could not have been completed without the contributions of the amazing scholarship and research that came before. I hope that it can play a similar role for future scholarship on Turkish politics and studies on democracy.

INTRODUCTION

Turkish political history offers observers a paradoxical mix of profound changes and continuity with the past. Since the introduction of multi-party politics in 1945, the path to democracy in Turkey has been a tenuous and, at times, volatile journey. Throughout its seventy-plus-year history, democracy has endured many disruptions: three direct military coups in 1960, 1971 and 1980, then a 'soft coup' in 1997 and, most recently, an attempted coup in 2016. Along with these developments, the country's citizens have been forced to contend with party closures, periods of political violence and bouts of crippling political instability. Despite its past, the resilience of the multi-party system in Turkey underlines the salience of democratic thought within the political calculations of both the political class and society more broadly.

However, this resilience has not led to the development of a consolidated democracy. The contradictory mix of change and continuity, which could be described as a holding pattern, has persisted. And today, under Prime Minister-*cum*-President Recep Tayyip Erdoğan's rule, Turkey finds itself farther away from democracy, relegated to the category of an authoritarian regime (Özbudun 2015; Esen and Gümüşcü 2016; White 2017). This story, however, is not confined to the Erdoğan era. It speaks directly to a much longer history. The transition to an authoritarian system is another example of the ongoing precarious nature of Turkey's democracy. And so, attempting to diagnose why Turkey has failed to consolidate its democratic gains during its seventy-plus years of multi-party politics is the puzzle that drives and binds the study in this book.

Explaining Turkey's democratic paradox has not been easy. Naturally, whilst a variety of factors have led to this holding pattern, as highlighted by excellent scholarship, the present book takes the position that Turkey's political leaders are a central component to understanding the country's inability to consolidate democracy. The book's exploration reveals how the direction and development of Turkish democracy – including its bouts of crises and instability – have been largely contingent on the behaviour, practices and decisions of its leaders. To put it another way, a key reason for Turkish democracy's precarious existence has rested on the inability of Turkey's leaders to internalise and practice values that are conducive to not only deepening but also sustaining democracy, due to a salient pattern of authoritarianism and undemocratic traits that can be traced among key leaders in Turkey's multi-party history.

Leaders and Democracy in Turkey: The Unexplored Link

The present book does not rule out the social, economic and institutional changes and fluctuations under which leaders operate and which may influence their actions. However, political leaders' actions and choices matter a great deal in the development, sustenance and decay of democratic institutions and processes, especially in Turkey. The use of a longitudinal lens further underscores the reason why a focus on leaders offers a stronger explanatory factor for diagnosing the precarious nature of democracy in Turkey, rather than structuralist, materialist or constitutional explanations, although studies that hold these factors as central to their diagnosis offer important reference points for observers of Turkish politics.

Literature concerned with democratisation and democratic theory assert the important role that leaders play in establishing democratic practice, its breakdowns and consolidation (see Rustow 1970; Diamond, Hartlyn and Linz 1990; Higley and Gunther 1992; O'Donnell and Schmitter 1986; O'Donnell 1996; Alonso, Keane and Merkel 2011; Urbinati 2011; Chou 2012; Keane 2020). This is pertinent, as contemporary Turkish politics has been predominantly shaped by elite initiatives and tensions (Birand, Bila and

Akar 1999; Cemal 1989b; Çağaptay 2017; Heper and Sayarı 2002; Birand and Yıldız 2012; Birand, Dündar and Çaplı 2016b; Frey 1975), which has its genesis in the early republican nature of governance (Heper 1992b, 2000, 2001; Mardin 1973, 1969). Given this unique political character, structured around a strong centralised rule, political decisions have been limited to elite actors, elite institutions and elite settings from the beginning (Özbudun 1993, 2000a; Payaşlıoğlu 1964). Underscoring the importance of studying elites in Turkey, historian Roderic H. Davison has noted (1968, 8–9):

> . . . there always has been an elite in one form of another [in Ottoman and Turkish society]. It has been the ruling element and the moving element throughout Turkish history [. . .] Without the ruling group, Turkish history is inexplicable.

In other words, beyond the multi-party era, the country has a long experience with a highly centralised and personalised form of rule. From the Ottoman Empire to the founder and first president of the modern republic, Mustafa Kemal Atatürk preferred a top-down administrative style and largely lacked tolerance for opponents. Recent works dealing with the multi-party era continue to highlight the patterns of leader-domination within the country's political landscape (Waldman and Calışkan 2017; Karaveli 2014, 2017; Yiğit 2013; White 2015). For example, Waldman and Calışkan have stated (2017, 4):

> Reading Turkish political history is almost akin to reading biographies of its leading figures [. . .] One political figure after another tried to shape and mould Turkey into an image of its liking, and to influence the political and cultural direction of the state.

The authoritarian continuity has meant that 'Turkey has been close to a one-man culture in politics [. . .] since the late Ottoman and early Republican periods', as Ödül Çelep (2014, 6) has surmised. This situation is further accentuated by the fact that leaders wield near-absolute control over their political parties. A point underlined by Metin Heper (2000, 69) is that '[v]irtually all political leaders in Turkey invariably relegated the parties they headed to secondary positions compared to themselves'. This has allowed leaders to personally decide on critical domestic and foreign policy issues

(Sayarı 2002b; Sayarı, Musil and Demirkol 2018; Turan 2011; Kalaycıoğlu 2013). As a result, this class of actors has a greater bearing on political developments in comparison to their counterparts in liberal democratic systems – a fact not lost on Sabri Sayarı (2002, 2–3):

> To a large extent, therefore, political leaders have been responsible for both the achievements and the shortcomings of Turkey's half-century-old experience with democratic politics.

These are not unique observations confined to academic literature. Statements from participants during fieldwork interviews frequently underscored the importance of Turkish leaders to understanding the state of democracy:

> Leadership and personal choices of leaders make a hell of a difference to understanding democracy in this country. This is because Turkish politics and political parties, unlike in Western democracies, do not depend so much on the principles or the issues that they appear to be defending. It is really about the personal choices of leaders that very much dictate developments [. . .] In reality, the choices made by the leadership are critical to understanding developments. And in our political system, what we understand to be leadership is not a whole team, it's the one person. (Interview, May 2016)

This statement by former AKP parliamentarian and political analyst Suat Kınıklıoğlu offers a snapshot of a seemingly uniform response from interview participants. Leader-domination was identified as the norm rather than the exception in Turkish politics, and on a small number of occasions, during my informal discussions with members of the public, it was met with a puzzled 'why should it be any different?' These responses further underscore the importance of leaders to the study of democracy in Turkey and their central position in the eyes of citizens.

Despite the overwhelming role that leaders have played in shaping Turkey's political developments, scholars have rarely chosen to study this specific class of individuals and to trace their effect on democracy.[1] Until recently, there has only been one scholarly contribution that put leaders at the centre of analysis: published in 2002, Metin Heper and Sabri Sayarı's edited volume titled *Political Leaders and Democracy in Turkey* is a collection of biographical accounts on leaders and their influence on Turkey's democratisation. This has ultimately meant that a systematic, historical analysis of leaders' impact on democracy in Turkey has been largely ignored, which is a critical oversight given the power that this class of actors has traditionally wielded.[2]

In filling this paucity of knowledge, this book applies a longitudinal study of leaders to assess changes and detect patterns across the multi-party era. It employs Dankwart Rustow's instruction to political scientists – that is, in the study of political developments elites are 'a concrete island of refuge' because, 'while constitutions and other formal arrangements would project a false image of stability, individuals and groups can be seen as a "binding link" from regime to regime' (1966, 695). Hence, assessing democracy strictly based on the existence of institutions and constitutional arrangements offers little insight, for the obvious reason that the theory might not be matched by actual political conditions determined by the elite's practices, values and choices. Furthermore, not applying a longitudinal study of elites runs the risk of imposing a static image on an otherwise dynamic process and misjudging the problem at hand, by merely studying the snapshot of a historical juncture.

The present book incorporates a study of leaders in their intra- and inter-party context, as well as the symbiotic relationship between these two connected yet independent spheres, so as to offer a thorough understanding of the forces that have shaped political developments in the country. This allows the book to illuminate certain characteristics of Turkish political leaders that have remained unchanged, regardless of the differing political contexts amongst them, carefully highlighting common practices that have not only obstructed democratic consolidation, but also produced major crises, and, at times, brought forward the demise of democracy.

This study, however, does not aim to provide a reason for this recurring pattern in Turkish politics – there are surely varying conditions that might account for this. The discussions here cannot account for reasons to explain this salient character of rule, nor does this study endeavour to do so. Rather, the aim is to reveal how leaders have acted in ways that impeded the consolidation of democracy.

Problematic leaders and democratic backsliding are not limited to Turkey, nor are they unique to its history: there is a growing body of literature, arising

from recent populist authoritarian leaders, as observed in formerly democratising countries, such as Hungary, Brazil, India and Poland. Likewise, a focus
on leadership to better understand the recent anti-democratic trend, as in
the currently weakening democratic practices in consolidated democracies
such as the United States, Britain and Italy attests to this (Levitsky and
Ziblatt 2018b; Norris and Inglehart 2019; Albright 2019; Lendvai 2017;
Keane 2020). This study sits firmly within this larger body of work. By focus-
ing on the leaders' attitudes and approaches to democracy in Turkey, it offers
new insights and extensions to the field of democracy studies, particularly to
scholarship that applies an actor-based approach to democratisation, democratic consolidation and failure, along with serving as a reference for students
of Turkish politics.

Theoretical Approach: Elites and Democracy

The political elite are, by virtue of their authoritative and strategic positions in
powerful organisations and movements, able to affect national political outcomes and the workings of political institutions,[3] regularly and substantially
(Higley and Burton 2012, 247; Best and Higley 2010, 5). They are persons
at or near the top of the 'pyramid of power' (Putnam 1976, 14) with the
'organized capacity to make real and continuing political trouble' (Higley and
Burton 2006, 7). Harold Lasswell similarly affirmed: 'The study of politics is
the study of influence and the influential [. . .] The influential are those who
get the most of what there is to get [. . .] Those who get the most are elite; the
rest are masses [. . .] the elite are the influential' (1958, 1).

It is, therefore, not surprising that theories of democratisation and
comparative studies on political regime transitions routinely underline the
important role that leaders play on the path to consolidation and breakdown
of democracies. In this area, Rustow's framework of democratisation has
affirmed the need for elites to make the required concessions and compromises as a central factor for transition to occur and succeed (1970, 355–62).
Guillermo O'Donnell and Phillipe Schmitter (1986), similarly, have outlined the role of leadership as a vital component for a transition to democracy to occur. Once the move to a democratic system has commenced, the
level of competence, the capacity and the choices of leaders hold central
importance for the new regime's stability and survival (Diamond, Hartlyn

and Linz 1990, 33; Linz 1990, 152). This is because elite attitudes and beliefs have a fundamental bearing on the types of institutions and rules that are crafted once transition has taken place (Diamond 1997, 2; Diamond, Linz and Lipset 1990; Esmer 2010).

This is where elites must agree to rules that organise institutions and their processes (Heper 2002b, 138). These decisions must be premised upon principles of compromise and accommodation rather than conflict. They must set patterns of interaction that foster cooperation in competition and the willingness to compromise (Schmitter and Karl 1991, 79, 82). Political outcomes are valued as positive and not acted out as zero-sum by competing elites (Higley and Gunther 1992); the agreement to make all political changes comes exclusively from within the parameters of the democratic system (Sartori 1995); and self-enforced restraints on the exercise of power exist (Diamond 1999, 70).

We can therefore deduce that the main political actors must exhibit a normative preference for democracy (O'Donnell 1996). The elites must value democracy intrinsically, holding it above all other preferences (Mainwaring and Pérez-Liñán 2013), which ensures that outcomes are achieved through democratic mechanisms, processes and principles. Doing so reduces the likelihood of a democratic breakdown or backsliding, even when the system faces dire challenges (Mainwaring and Pérez-Liñán 2013, 132).

The revolving of elites through the electoral cycle, therefore, must sustain and defend these democratic institutions and uphold processes and norms, thus providing a safeguard from abuse or erosion. Mainwaring and Scully (2010) provide notable examples from Latin America to illustrate this point: elected leaders such as Hugo Chavez undermined liberal democracy in the name of direct democracy in Venezuela; Alberto Fujimori in Peru (1990–2000) and Carlos Menem in Argentina (1989–99) both maintained policies that weakened and eliminated checks and balances on their rule, arguing that this was a necessity to deal with crises swiftly. Steven Levitsky and Daniel Ziblatt have similarly stressed that even the most robust democratic institutions can be eroded due to the undemocratic practices of leaders (2018b, 2018a). This, they argue, can occur in all democracies, and no system can be safeguarded, pointing to the presidency of Donald Trump in the United States as recent evidence.[4] Hungary's transition to an illiberal regime under Victor Orban's rule further highlights the vulnerability of institutions when elected leaders fail to respect democratic norms for sustained periods of time (Kingsley 2018; Lendvai 2017).

These experiences underscore that well-designed constitutions and institutions alone are not enough to oppose democratic backsliding when elected leaders opt not to play by democratic principles and norms. Leaders who simply pay lip-service to democratic values ultimately leave the shell of democratic institutions standing, bare of their pluralist essence (Diamond 2018). In other words, rules and institutions are sustained as long as elite actors follow and reinforce them, but, without this, the democratic regime is weakened and virtually impossible to maintain (Esmer 2010). As there is nothing intrinsic within democracy that immunises it against a breakdown, elite behaviour and choices are imperative to ensure that democracy will even survive (Chou 2014).

What does Consolidation Mean?

It is important to point out that, when we speak of consolidation, it does not signify a complete transition, by conveying a point of 'getting and staying there' (Turan 2015). In fact, reform and improvement in democracy is an endless and constantly evolving process (Diamond 1999). There is no easy way to draw a clear quantitative and dividing line between what is consolidated and democratisation (Walker 2013, 97). Nor does consolidation refer to the mirroring of an 'ideal' system. A consolidated system is ultimately signified through 'the internalization of rules and procedures and the dissemination of democratic values through a "remaking" of the political culture' by the elites (Pridham 2005, 12). In other words, consolidation is achieved when unwritten democratic norms are deeply embedded in the practices of the political elites.

Guillermo O'Donnell's (1996) description of consolidation concisely captures the nature of the matter when he outlines that there needs to be a close match between the formal institutional rules, mechanisms and processes and the informal – namely, the values, behaviours and practices of the political elites and leaders. The institutionalised practices of the formal political sphere must be met by a set of democratic beliefs, values and practices, as adhered to by the political class.

There are a number of key norms, identified by scholars, that elites must value and practice prevalent within a consolidated system. A vital indicator is the political leader's capacity to *concede power gracefully*; 'the politics of retreat' is what democracy requires, and office dependency is a particularly potent obstacle to the healthy sustenance of democratic regimes. The simple distinction between owning or leaving office is a key indicator of whether or not a form of government or particular leadership can be considered democratic, and regimes that allow their leaders to stay on indefinitely potentially compromise the system itself (Keane 2009).

It is therefore essential for the political class to informally agree to the idea that electoral winners will not use their superiority to consolidate their rule by denying the losers from taking office or exerting influence in the future (Schmitter and Karl 1991, 82–83). Doing so clearly declares to the rest of the political elite that the winners of an election can dominate completely or even permanently (Przeworski 2003, 114). The winner imposing high costs on the losing actors can steer the losing side/s to take more reactive measures and resort to non-democratic avenues as a way of preventing major and irreversible costs to their position (Mainwaring and Pérez-Liñán 2013). For this reason, the norm of *institutional forbearance* – which 'can be thought of as avoiding actions that, while respecting the letter of the law, obviously violates its spirit' – is a critical norm existing in consolidated democracies. Where forbearance is strong, even though it might be technically legal to do so, the elites do not use their institutional prerogatives to push the bounds of the system for particularistic gains, or in the effort 'to play for keeps' (Levitsky and Ziblatt 2018b, 106).

To counter this, another fundamental norm is the *institutionalisation of compromise* by the elite (Sunar and Sayarı 1986, 76). This naturally stems from the norm of *mutual toleration*, or the understanding that competing parties view each other as legitimate rivals, and actors accept that all sides have a right to exist, compete for power and govern (Levitsky and Ziblatt 2018, 102). Yet, a leadership that fails to compromise with its opposition, particularly to solve crises, plays an important role in the weakening or breakdown of democracy (Linz and Stepan 1989).

A system that demonstrates a lack of these norms can lead to elites taking more extreme and uncompromising positions (Esmer 2015). When this gulf becomes too wide, it pervades every issue, overrides everything else and obstructs the search for pragmatic solutions to pressing problems faced by the country, which also then seeps into society (Diamond 2008). The polarisation can make conditions impossible to govern or delegitimise opposition by equating them with treason (Erişen and Kubicek 2016, 6–7). Although there are indeed extreme and uncompromising elements in all societies, consolidated democracies are much better equipped to deal with these kinds of developments, owing to the prevalence of key democratic norms as valued and practised by elites.

Consolidation, therefore, is not simply contingent on the mere existence of democratic institutions. Rather, as Diamond notes, there is an intimate connection between elite commitments toward deepening of democracy that is linked to consolidation: 'Deepening makes the formal structures more liberal, accountable, representative, and accessible – in essence, more democratic. Progress toward greater liberty and lawfulness is essential' (1999, 74). In other words, it is one thing to establish formal democracy, but its consolidation is made possible by the elite's adoption of values conducive to deepening democracy. One can speak of democratic consolidation when it becomes routinised and deeply internalised by the elites, which then filters into the social, institutional and political way of life.

Naturally, the intrinsic valuing of democracy and the practice of these norms also have a bearing on institutional arrangements, because the political class values and establishes mechanisms that enforce restraints on the exercise of power and infuse pluralism into the policy arena. Consolidated democracy, therefore, 'offers a variety of competitive processes and channels for the expression of interests and values' (Schmitter and Karl 1991, 78), and these instruments constrain, check and keep rulers accountable (Keane 1999, 11). This is when democracy is its true essence – that is, a 'system of institutional mediation between state and society' (Garretón Merino 2003, 38).

Such institutional arrangements manifest in the existence and robustness of two dimensions: the *horizontal* and *vertical* mechanisms of accountability in consolidated systems. O'Donnell (1994, 2003) has provided a definition of these two categories: vertical accountability constitutes the checks and balances mechanism between ruler and ruled; and horizontal accountability stresses the checks and balances among equals – this includes the executive, legislature and judiciary. From here we can start to infer that the vertical form includes electoral and social mechanisms, which traditionally incorporate elections, media and civil society, while horizontal forms are political and judicial institutions such as political parties, legislature, executive and judiciary.

These above dimensions of accountability see to it that elections are not the sole check and constraint on the exercise of power. Their importance is such that striking a balance between the two dimensions is a sign that a democracy is consolidated (Huntington 1968; Kirchheimer 1965; Dahl 1982). Without them, the mere practice of democracy falls into the fallacy of *electoralism* – the tendency to focus entirely on the existence of elections, no matter how they are conducted or what else constrains the winners (Schmitter and Karl 1991, 6). This tells us that democracy is highly susceptible to a rollback, as the capacity of institutions and legal arrangements are bound to the very group that they are created to monitor.

Leaders, Political Parties and Consolidation

The role of leadership in political parties offers another critical factor linked to democratisation and democratic consolidation (Capoccia and Ziblatt 2010; Bermeo and Yashar 2016). Political parties have instrumental and representative functions, including integrating diverse interests to serve as the bridge between the public and the political regime. This is where intra-party democracy is critical to attain this ideal democratic condition (Garretón Merino 2003, 105; Mainwaring and Scully 1995, 3). Parties with autonomous organisational structures display a key characteristic of an institutionalised party (Mainwaring and Scully 1995). This is because 'institutionalised parties are those that demonstrate consistent patterns of internal organization, mass mobilization, and leadership succession [. . .] such parties stand autonomous from their founding personalities' (Stockton 2001, 97). Institutionalised parties provide greater opportunities for citizens to affect the decisions that shape their lives, which pushes a procedural democracy to move into the realm of a consolidated democracy (Geyikçi 2011).

This is an opposing state-of-affairs in weak or non-institutionalised political parties, which are characterised by a centralised, authoritarian or elitist party leadership and which lack intra-party democracy (Arda Can Kumbaracıbaşı 2016, 17). This in turn strips the party of the freedom and the room to establish vital bonds with society, instead personalising the organisation under the leader (Ostrogorski 1902). In this political environment the leader stands at the centre of the political process (Rahat and Sheafer 2007), playing a role that 'seems to be larger than life', as Kalaycıoğlu (2013, 483) has declared. And in a party system characterised by weak or non-institutionalised parties, the defining feature is competition between individual leaders, rather than organised collective interests.

Under such intra-party conditions, the checks against the slide toward authoritarianism in government is severely compromised, as Levitsky and Ziblatt (2018b, 24–26) have stated. The lack of intra-party democracy may facilitate the implementation of undemocratic policies or the materialisation of undemocratic political behaviour in the inter-party environment or broader political sphere. As Yigal Mersel (2006, 97) has stated, 'it is arguable that a party that is not internally democratic cannot really be externally democratic; in the long run, the internal agenda and predispositions would be bound to influence the party's external attitudes and activities', indicating the organic and symbiotic relationship between the intra-party and the inter-party spheres in democracy.

Whilst this book is not arguing that authoritarian party rule naturally progresses to the party leader's desire to undermine the democratic order, the passage above, as well as this study, demonstrates that a party's internal governance structure is telling of the attitudes and steps it will take vis-à-vis democracy when in government. This is underscored by Cross and Katz (2013, 71): 'Parties that conduct their internal affairs in a "democratic" fashion signal to the public that they have internalised a democratic ethos, arguably adding to their credibility as potential governments or participants in governing coalitions'.

As evidenced by the above discussion, the study of leadership in the intra-party setting offers researchers another vital analytical tool to better understand the factors that shape the nature of a democracy, including its path to failure. This book, for this reason, undertakes a two-tier frame of analysis (intra- and inter-party) to provide a nuanced and substantive study of how leaders play a key role in Turkey's inability to consolidate democracy.

Methods: Navigating Research in a Precarious Climate

This research ultimately demanded methods that left room to detect the nuances and subtleties of political environments over seven decades of multi-party politics. This approach, by its nature, cancelled applying a catch-all-theory-driven analysis, due to the varying political realities experienced throughout Turkish multi-party history. The book employed a problem-driven approach, owing to the character of the research puzzle, as well as the necessity for an informed knowledge of politics, rather than simply immersing the research in normative or abstract theories (Shapiro 2002, 193). Far more important was whether the research could present the dilemma of Turkey's inability to consolidate its democratic gains in a new light, not whether the conclusions of a theory or the assumptions of the author are true.

Therefore, a qualitative method of analysis was chosen, as it demands the scholar's immersion in the research subject and offers opportunities to capture a longitudinal perspective (Conger 1998; Parry 1998). When adequately employed, this method offers opportunities to explore leadership in greater depth longitudinally (Bryman et al. 1988); the flexibility to detect unexpected phenomena during research (Lundberg 1976); a greater chance to explore and be sensitive to contextual factors (Conger 1998); and the ability to reveal deeper and nuanced understandings of the historical experience of politics and the links that it might have to the current political context (Morgan and Smircich 1980).

To further immerse myself, I undertook fieldwork in Turkey from March 2016 to January 2017, with one-on-one semi-structured interviews being the central method of sourcing primary data. Prior to my arrival in the country, the political climate had already been tense, on account of an authoritarian turn by the incumbent government and a slow but steady increase of ISIS and PKK attacks, a common occurrence during my fieldwork. These attacks would ultimately endanger my personal safety.[5] At the same time, public criticism towards the government's policies or President Recep Tayyip Erdoğan came with the high possibility of running afoul of the authorities: it was communicated to me that a study of such nature would not be allowed by a Turkish university, owing to the dangers it posed for the institution, the researcher and the participants.

For this reason, finding participants to discuss political leaders was challenging; following the attempted coup on 15 July 2016, the fieldwork largely stalled. The wide-ranging and seemingly arbitrary purges and incarcerations became a cause of concern for many in Turkish society, resulting in my own growing sense of unease within the volatile political climate in light of the topic of my study. As result, despite countless attempts, it became extremely hard to find willing participants. To give a sense of how significant a roadblock the failed coup and its aftermath was, out of the seventeen semi-structured interviews I obtained, only five were undertaken post-15 July.[6]

This underlined the fact that the social and political context in Turkey would not provide wide-ranging data from one method alone. In order to overcome these shortcomings, multiple qualitative methods were employed to enable a flexible and fluid approach to navigate the complexity of my field research and to acquire more data. Adopting a multi-method approach helped respect the complexity of meaning-making processes and the contradictions of the lived-in world. The combination of multiple methods 'in a single study is best understood as a strategy that adds rigor, breadth, complexity, richness, and depth to any inquiry' (Denzin and Lincoln 2011, 6). This was also a practical necessity given that the research naturally included a strong historical analysis. For this reason, interviews were complemented with an analysis of primary and secondary sources to undertake the triangulation of data.

As part of the triangulation approach, content analysis was employed to provide a critical reading of sources in both Turkish and English. Doing so opened up the opportunity to examine a wider range of available data. It allowed this study to weave together an empirically rich analysis that spans across seven decades. These sources encompassed not only historical news sources, academic literature and audio-visual content, but also human sources drawn from journalistic accounts, personal documents, statements and memoirs. As result, the triangulation approach revealed deeper and more nuanced understandings of political developments. Thus, enriching the scope and range of available sources helped to draw robust conclusions about the role of Turkey's political leaders' inability to consolidate democracy, arriving at findings that were rigorous and rich in contextualised meanings.

Book Overview

The following chapters focus on key leaders who reached the peaks of political power as prime ministers since the transition to the multi-party system and who chronologically defined the periods that they occupied (1950–60; 1961–71; 1971–80; 1983–93; 1993–2002; 2002–15; 2015–current). There were certainly political leaders during these periods, such as Alparslan Türkeş, Deniz Baykal and Devlet Bahçeli, who had a negative impact on democracy;

a focused discussion on their role, however, was not possible given the tight bounds placed on the study.

Time frames were specifically chosen as they represented democratic breakdowns marked by three major coups (1960, 1971 and 1980) and critical political junctures for the following eras (1993 and 2002). These periods offer a clear end point from one democratic era to the next and present defined blocks for a comparative analysis of the prominent civilian leaders that dominated each phase: Adnan Menderes and Celal Bayar; Süleyman Demirel and Bülent Ecevit; Turgut Özal; the turbulent coalitions during the 1990s between Tansu Çiller, Mesut Yılmaz and Necmetin Erbakan; and, finally, Recep Tayyip Erdoğan.

This book will demonstrate that, given the political realities and continuities of leaders across decades, overlaps of these actors between periods are inescapable. Confining individuals to their own chapter would have failed to highlight the persistence of authoritarianism and its binding links regardless of the changed political context and parameters. Thus, a more fluid structure was necessary to uncover these nuances. For example, not every leader – such as Menderes, Özal and Erdoğan – presided over a single-party majority. Furthermore, leaders such as Demirel, Ecevit and Erbakan had long tenures at the pinnacle of their political power, which spanned a variety of political and constitutional contexts. Ultimately, this will illustrate that the characteristics presented are not an accidental collection of tendencies, but rather a point of commonality amongst political leaders in Turkey. Each chapter shows that the failure to internalise democracy is a binding link – a traceable character – between Turkey's leaders, regardless of the political conditions of the time, which is key to diagnosing Turkey's long-troubled democracy.

The present study does not deny that many leaders made contributions that directly or indirectly benefitted democracy. The chapters indeed touch upon them where relevant. Yet, undeniably in their efforts to attain, remain in and govern the seats of political power, the leaders discussed here displayed direct, even brazen, authoritarian actions and characteristics, undermining the democratic regimes they occupied. Many of the leaders consequently even hastened the demise of their parties and of democracy. It is ultimately their authoritarianism and its detrimental impact on democracy that far eclipsed any measures aligning with democratisation, which will be detailed in the chapters of this book.

Notes

1. Indeed, there are works pertaining specifically to individual leaders or periods; yet, these offer a mere snapshot and fail to uncover whether in the history of Turkish politics there exists a unique and salient leadership culture that hinders its consolidation. Furthermore, many of them do not frame their analysis within the democratic framework but act as biographical studies or historical accounts.
2. This lack of engagement with leadership was pointed out by Berk Esen's review of Ergun Özbudun's book on party formations and breakdowns in Turkish politics (2013). Contrary to his notion of a sharp struggle between social and cultural forces as driving force behind the party system, Özbudun was criticised by Esen for overlooking leadership as central to driving developments in Turkey's political party system (2015).
3. The standard definition of institutions to which I refer is the rules (or set of rules) that structure social interaction by shaping and constraining actors' behaviour. Therefore, formal institutions refer to state bodies (courts, legislature, bureaucracy) and state-enforced rules (constitutions, laws, regulations).
4. Freedom House reported one year into Trump's presidency a significant decline in freedoms in the US, because of the president's violations of basic norms of transparency and democracy (Abramowitz 2018).
5. A PKK twin bomb attack occurred only a neighbourhood away, outside the Beşiktaş Soccer Club's stadium, after a game, killing thirty-eight people on 11 December 2016.
6. The interviews spanned four categories of respondents: (1) active politicians; (2) former politicians; (3) political analysts including academics and journalists; (4) civil society actors.

1

1950–60: DEMOCRACY UNDER THE DEMOCRATS, A NEW GAME BUILT ON PAST RULES

Introduction

Following its foundation in 1923, Turkey was subject to single-party rule for twenty-two years under the *Cumhuriyet Halk Partisi* (Republican People's Party, CHP). Following pressure from intra-party opposition in 1945, President İsmet İnönü transitioned the politics of the country to a multi-party system. It took another five years before the first free and fair elections of 1950 led to a change in government, giving a decisive victory to the main opposition *Demokrat Parti* (Democrat Party, DP).[1] As part of CHP's internal opposition, which had split from the ruling party to form the DP, its leading figures Adnan Menderes and Celal Bayar were central to forcing open the doors to multi-party politics,[2] and in doing so, they provided hope for greater liberalisation and ultimately institutionalising democracy. Yet, this was an era that failed to deliver greater political plurality to the country. Developments during the period stood in stark contrast to the progressive steps needed not only for democratic consolidation but also to sustain the new political system. Consequently, after ten years, Turkey's first experience with a competitive system was brought to an end in 1960 with a military intervention.

This chapter demonstrates that the leadership of Menderes and Bayar was a key factor in this outcome. To illustrate this, I begin by outlining Menderes's capture of the *Demokrat Parti* following Bayar's move to the presidency. Acquiring control of a large parliamentary majority allowed him to amass great political power at the expense of organisational autonomy. Along with this, the close working relationship between Menderes and Bayar enabled the leaders to centralise political power. Through a chronologically unfolding discussion, the proceeding sections outline how this state of affairs was used to embark on a majoritarian strategy to erode already weak democratic institutions, with the aim to consolidate the leaders' hold on power. The outcomes of this caused an ongoing point of paralysis between government and opposition, became problematic for maintaining the autonomy of state institutions and later spilled into society. Chapter 1 ultimately shows that, although Menderes and Bayar were instrumental in opening the doors to multi-party politics, they largely shaped the unfortunate state of affairs that befell the democratic system, carrying it to its demise in 1960.

Menderes and Bayar

The 1950 electoral results created a political environment in complete contrast to the preceding twenty-seven-year single-party rule of the CHP. Almost 90 percent of the electorate had voted to give the Democrats 52.7 percent of the vote, while the CHP won 39.5 percent (Sayarı 1978, 42). The winner-take-all electoral system provided an overwhelming parliamentary majority to the DP, with nearly 84 percent of the Assembly seats, as opposed to the CHP's 14 percent (Kalaycıoğlu 1990, 57; Sayarı 1978, 42) (see Table 1.1). With an 80-percent turnover of deputies from the previous parliament, the Assembly could not have been in a configuration more starkly different from the twenty-seven-year rule of the CHP.

Table 1.1 1950 Election Results

Political Party	Percentage of Votes	Parliamentary Seats (Total 487)
Demokrat Parti (DP)	52.7	416
Cumhuriyet Halk Partisi (CHP)	39.5	69
Independents	4.76	1
Millet Partisi (MP)	3.1	1

Source: https://www.tbmm.gov.tr/develop/owa/secim_sorgu.genel_secimler

The DP-dominated parliament elected Celal Bayar as President of the Republic, who, in turn, chose to appoint Adnan Menderes as Prime Minister.[3] In a step that would enable Menderes to consolidate his rule over the ruling party, the Democrat Party's General Administrative Council elected him as the new chairman to fill the position that Bayar had left vacant. Along with Bayar's presidency, Menderes's dual role as both head of government and leader of the governing party with an overwhelming majority guaranteed the pair political power unrivalled by their opponents.

Before moving further, it is important to explain the rationale for dealing with both men, not simply Adnan Menderes alone. Although the role of President was required to be neutral without involvement in the day-to-day politics of the country, Bayar nonetheless continued to have very close ties to the DP, and he regularly played the role of counsel to guide his younger colleague on matters of government and intra-party management (Birand, Dündar and Çaplı 1994). Underlining the symbiotic relationship between the two men, Feroz Ahmad, a leading scholar of Turkey's political history, has observed that, in fact, 'Bayar as the grand old man of the party was there to guide Menderes along' (Interview, October 2016). Many government decisions show Bayar as the instigator of stronger measures against the opposition, particularly against İnönü. Sabri Sayarı, an expert on contemporary Turkish politics, has affirmed:

> Though Bayar was perhaps not involved in day-to-day politics, he was certainly very important. Many people believe that he was the one who was advising Menderes, especially towards the end of the decade. What came out in later developments showed that Bayar had regularly encouraged Menderes to take stronger measures against İnönü. (Interview, July 2016)

Sources closer to Bayar, including Refik Tulga, the presidential aide-de-camp, highlighted the personal animosity towards İnönü. In later developments, Tulga testified that Bayar even stated that he would not hesitate to have İnönü hung. This was also corroborated by former cabinet member Ethem Menderes who recalled that he would 'proclaim dictatorship if necessary' to block İnönü from power (Harris 2002, 50). For this reason, it is very hard to separate the chain of responsibility, particularly for hard-line measures against political opposition.

Bayar's Apollonian stature loomed large over the party. Without the permission granted by his position as President, Menderes would surely have had a hard time pushing forward his wishes. Bayar, along with İnönü, was one of the founding elites of the republic and enjoyed significant political influence within the DP. Few aspiring leaders had the confidence or support to challenge him during his party leadership (Ahmad 1977, 77–78). Menderes knew that Bayar was essential to his own political survival and for this reason cultivated close relations with him (Sayarı 2002a, 77). In fact, Bayar personally appointed his younger and politically inexperienced deputy to the party leadership once he rose to the presidency (Taşyürek 2009, 49). Menderes's son Aydın underlined this point in a 1991 documentary: 'This, frankly, was Bayar's idea. It was Bayar's decision [. . .] because he thought of himself as the father of the party' (Birand, Dündar and Çaplı 2016b, 73). Bayar felt that his young colleague had the political acumen to take care of the Democrats after he became President.

It was also a strategic move by Bayar to influence and direct the governing party from the presidential post (see Ahmad 1977; Harris 2002; Sayarı 2002a). For example, despite his ascendancy to the presidency, he presided over the first meeting of the government to remind the DP of his presence in the party and took back the reigns as Menderes struggled to cope with the growing unrest at the end of the decade (Birand, Dündar and Çaplı 2016b, 84; Sayarı 2002a). Ahmad also underlined this point when he explained that 'many people believe Bayar was the one that was advising Menderes, especially towards the end of their government' (Interview, October 2016).

Undoubtedly, these two central figures were instrumental in the transition to democracy and the expansion of political participation. Both Bayar and Menderes displayed strong commitment to breaking the tutelary single-party rule during the intra-party opposition that pushed İnönü to allow multi-party politics (Harris 2002; Sayarı 2002a; Sarıbay 1991; Sütçü 2011b). In many ways their efforts and the early years of their governance did increase the level of political and economic modernisation (see Mango 2004, 46–47).

The ideas of popular sovereignty and engagement with the people were central to their discourse in early campaigns (Birand, Dündar and Çaplı 1991). These efforts sparked democratic ideals within a society accustomed to elite-driven top-down governance. They became the champions of the 'little man' rallying against the 'tyranny of the state' (Ahmad 1993, 106), and the party became an advocate for private enterprise and individual initiative, which won the support of business, the liberal intelligentsia and the media. The establishment of local party organisations, visits by DP politicians to small towns and villages, and holding open-air meetings contributed to rousing citizens to their own political importance and stake in government (Payaşlıoğlu 1964, 423).

The competition and success of the DP, furthermore, impacted the internal liberalisation of the CHP. In 1946, İnönü gave up his title as *Milli Şef* (National Leader) and his role as the party's permanent chairman in order to usher in intra-party elections every four years (Ahmad 1993, 105).[4] The inter-party electoral struggle forced the CHP to extend its local organisations to thousands of villages across the country (Payaşlıoğlu 1964, 423). Owing to the DP, the CHP was forced to engage with Turkish society to an extent greater than ever before (Ahmad 1977, 105–7). Outside of liberalising the political sphere, the economy began to expand rapidly in the first few years of Menderes and Bayar's rule (Mango 2004, 47).

While the transition to democratic politics marked a break with the past, it did not represent a revolution in leadership culture. Even though Bayar was the party founder and enjoyed wide support as its leader, the DP was not known as a 'personality party' in the style of the CHP under Atatürk and then İnönü (see Mango 2002; Heper 1998). In its initial years, the DP was akin to a political movement set up to end the single-party tutelage; it was not yet a cohesive political organisation, which would have made it hard for Bayar, had he harboured such tendencies. This changed once Menderes replaced Bayar as party leader, as he was forced to shape it into a cohesive political organisation to govern effectively. Menderes was not a leader who enjoyed compromises to his rule. Unwilling (and, in fact, unable) to receive advice, he had an absolute belief in his own intelligence and craftsmanship (Karpat 2011, 126). The position of both Prime Minister and party leader transferred all powers of the government and party administration to Menderes's office (Ahmad 1977, 78), which he very quickly exploited to consolidate his rule through both autocratic measures and political patronage.

It might be assumed that Bayar would have been threatened by Menderes's attempts to personalise the party under his rule. This was not the case.

Indeed, it was unusual among Turkish leaders to share the limelight with another top political leader, but Bayar was secure in his prestige and displayed remarkable pragmatism (Harris 2002). Menderes's unfaltering compliance with the elder Bayar allowed him to share power over the party (Harris 2002, 57). Bayar also knew that his younger colleague's dynamism served his own personal vision for Turkey and that he would act as a bulwark against his long-time adversary İnönü. During their rule, their partnership paid rich dividends, allowing them to impose their will on the political landscape.

Menderes and the Democrat Party

After the first electoral victory, Menderes set out to mould the government to support his position. He immediately selected individuals with no independent standing in the party to the first cabinet. Of the fifteen ministers, only six (including Menderes) were party-men.[5] The other eleven were former technocrats and bureaucrats who had joined the party ranks only recently (Ahmad 1977, 79). These new ministers lacked the popularity and support in their constituencies that would otherwise enable them to be elected without the support of the party. This strategy ensured their absolute loyalty to the Prime Minister as their patron. The alternative was to be banished to the political wilderness (Harris 2002, 50). However, before the year ended, Avni Başman and Nihat Reşat Belger resigned from the cabinet, citing Menderes's regular interference in their work (Aslan 2014, 48).[6] Menderes's conduct against the men was intended to force them to resign, as the Prime Minister used these vacant cabinet positions to co-opt prominent dissenters such as Samet Ağoğlu, Lütfi Karaosmanoğlu and Hulusi Köymen, figures who could mount a challenge against his leadership (Ahmad 1977, 79). Others whom he knew to lack the political acumen or power to pose a threat were removed or forced from positions when it suited his needs, such as Başman and Belger (Ahmad 1977, 79–80). From the outset, these steps countered the possibility of a unified opposition and neutralised influential and politically independent figures who might have hindered his leadership. In doing so, Menderes showed himself to be a shrewdly tactical leader from the very beginning.[7]

In the lead-up to the 1954 general election, he abandoned any pretence of compromise or consensus to fortify his position. This was demonstrated when he warned of the consequences for those party members whose actions, ideas and opinions did not coincide with his own (Ahmad 1977, 86). He dealt with 'troublesome' provincial branches by creating a group of party inspectors, such as Hüsnü Yaman, who directly reported to his office, and he gave the power to investigate and purge local branches of anti-Menderes factions, replacing these posts with Menderes's supporters (*Milliyet* 1954; Yaşar 2014, 514). In some cases, he broke the hold of anti-Menderes factions by completely abolishing the central organisation of the provincial branch and replacing it with a totally new body made up of compliant members, as happened in Seyhan, Adana (Ahmad 1977, 86). Under the guise of party 'reform', local organisations were cleared of anti-Menderes factions, including various Istanbul branches which experienced a purge of around fifty members (*Milliyet* 1954, 1953). And by the general elections of 1954, Menderes was confident enough to disregard the candidate lists prepared by the provincial bodies and put up his personal candidates, whilst filling the central party apparatuses with loyalists (Ahmad 1977, 89, 94–95).

To further illustrate this, the composition of the DP Assembly Group after the 1954 electoral victory was substantially different from that of the previous parliament. Although the DP increased their parliamentary representation, more than 150 out of the 416 Democrat parliamentarians elected in 1950 were left off Menderes's candidature list and replaced with compliant individuals (Yaşar 2014, 519). Men of local standing were replaced with ex-state officials. As many as 50 percent of these local notables were not in parliament after the 1954 election (Ahmad 1977, 87).

The DP's subservience to Menderes's personal decisions was consolidated by amendments to the party regulations, granting him greater powers to expel or force the resignation of internal challengers and veto powers over candidate lists composed by the local bodies (Yalman 1970b, 242; Yaşar 2014, 511).[8] He immediately expelled four Assembly members who had been critical of his authoritarian policies, with reports of regular expulsions throughout the year (Ahmad 1977, 87).

In the lead-up to the 1957 elections, Menderes continued his attack on provincial organisations by disbanding entire party executive committees in areas such as Manisa, İskenderun, Balıkesir and Salihli, at one point proposing that the party entirely abolish its village- and sub-district-level establishments because he viewed them as undermining the efficiency of his decisions (Ahmad 1977, 97). Provincial congresses were prevented from taking place in many areas so as to negate the possibility of vocal and organised protests at a grassroots level.[9] Menderes and Bayar worked in tandem to force the resignations of or dismiss many parliamentarians, including prominent Democrats. This allowed them to increase the number of compliant individuals on the candidature lists in the upcoming election (Yaşar 2014, 534).[10] By this stage, if Menderes had to deal with dissent, it was largely at the individual level, as the continual purges at the central and provincial levels negated the possibility of a strong faction against him.

However, Menderes's dominance over the DP was highly problematic for democracy. As outlined in the Introduction, authoritarianism inside the political party allows the leader to hold largely unrestrained power over political developments: we see the exact manner in which this manifested itself in this period, with Menderes consulting only a handful of aides that resembled 'yes-men' as opposed to objective and independent advisors (Sayarı 2002a, 77). From the late 1950s onwards, the party's *Genel İdare Kurulu* (General Executive Committee) ceased to function as an inclusive policy-making body, as Menderes had filled it entirely with loyalists (Yaşar 2014, 535). In doing so, he single-handedly directed the committee's agenda. Decisions taken at this level were then relayed to the rest of the parliamentary group as government policy (*Milliyet* 1955). Similarly, Menderes replaced old ministers with new faces to prevent the possibility of challenges to his leadership, to deflect criticism by the public and to reward his supporters inside the party (Ahmad 1977, 87). Isolated from the party, he could arbitrarily push policies that stood in contrast to the political realities.

Long-serving journalist Cengiz Çandar has underlined that 'these developments demonstrated that Menderes was the uncontested leader of his party, which allowed him to rule with a strong grip' (Interview, October 2016b). This was, perhaps, best expressed by the veteran journalist Ahmet Emin Yalman in his assessment during the period:

> Nothing has changed [in Turkey's politics]. Premier Adnan Menderes, confident in his native intelligence, intuitive power, fine eloquence, and all his other qualities, has taken the road to monopolising power. (quoted in Ahmad 1977, 81–82)

It also needs to be noted that his electoral popularity and success in elections was a key reason why he was able to take these actions and consolidate his position over the party. His success granted Menderes strong political capital and prestige. While there were dissenters throughout his reign, any serious challenge or attempt at overthrowing him would have been a politically damaging decision for the Democrats. Furthermore, given their close working relationship, any such move would likely have been blocked by Bayar as well.

The Mirroring of Single-party Rule

While the Democrats professed democracy, their understanding was rather rudimentary, manifesting itself in a practice that failed to shed the anti-democratic mentality of the single-party era. Winning government brought with it an irresistible urge to replicate the authoritarian behaviour of the CHP, effectively engaging in a 'mirroring' of the single-party rule (Turan 2015). Ersin Kalaycıoğlu, a prominent scholar of Turkish politics, has noted that this was largely due to the early measures that the CHP meted out against the Democrats, which ultimately influenced the character of their rule against the former rulers:

> The animosity started out in the 1946 elections, which were not free and fair and ultimately poisoned relations from the beginning. It created a bad odour between the two leading parties and elites in the 1940s. When the Democrats won in 1950, with an overwhelming majority, they obviously assumed that they could also act with the same kind of policies and behaviours toward their opposition as they had received. (Interview, April 2016)

Here it can be seen that the single-party character of rule came to inform the government-opposition relations when the Democrats climbed to power. The new government emulated the same methods to stifle the opposition's right to reply in key debates, something they had suffered in the preceding years under the CHP's tutelage (Ahmad 1977, 36). The fundamental problem was that the same kind of political imbalance carried forward into the multi-party period:

> I think part of the reason why this happened was that the *Demokrat Parti* had a huge electoral showing, especially in the 1954 election. Due to the electoral system, the opposition, the CHP, ended with a very small parliamentary

representation, so the asymmetry in parliament carried into politics. Menderes's government felt itself much more empowered than had it been closer in terms of seats in the parliament. (Interview with Sabri Sayarı, July 2016)

In other words, the overwhelming parliamentary majority provided Bayar and Menderes with an avenue to deny the legitimacy of the opposition, in character similar to that of the single-party era. Yet, as Diamond, Levitsky and Ziblatt have argued (see Introduction), this was contradictory and inconsistent with the principle of compromise and self-enforced restraint on the exercise of power, as required from leaders not only for consolidation, but also for the survival of the democratic system. Their power was exploited to constrain the opposition in 'playing for keeps'.

The hostility towards the CHP was perhaps also complicated by the fact that Turkish politics had no real experience with legitimate opposition or open politics, and these men had no reference points for political rule other than the single-party era. Given their overwhelming majority, they could simply mirror a system and a culture that sat in antithesis to the understanding of pluralism, political competition and norms required in a democratic setting, revealing a rather plebiscitarian view of democracy.

A Democracy Built on Single-party Rules

The slide toward authoritarianism was also made possible by the reality that the move to an open political system had not entailed the required structural changes needed to support a healthy plural system with strong checks on political power. Nor did it provide society with the space and opportunity to penetrate politics, beyond the vote. It was a system unresponsive to the institutionalisation of open dialogue and compromise (Sunar and Sayarı 1986, 73–76). This meant that the institutional arrangements which should provide an accountable and representative system were largely lacking in the transition to multi-party politics.

The most critical example of this continuity was that there was no significant revision to the constitution, which had been created in 1924 during the single-party tutelage (Sütçü 2011a, 204; Özbudun 2000b). The 1924 Constitution was shaped by a majoritarian interpretation of government, as opposed to a democracy underpinned by a system of rigorous checks and balances. It held that sovereignty was the 'general will' of the nation, which was absolute and indivisible. The true representation of the public will was embodied in the National Assembly (Özbudun and Gençkaya 2009, 12). This meant that any attempts to limit or curb the powers of the legislature would be equal to restricting the national will, which, in turn, would limit the sovereignty of the nation. In other words, the constitution failed to provide strong checks and balances to curb the power of elected majorities by society and the judiciary (Özbudun 2000, 6).[11] The President alone had the power to veto laws, but he was intimately associated with the governing party, rendering null and void a central mechanism of horizontal accountability (Sütçü 2011a, 205). This left a strong opposition in the Assembly as the only possibility to check the government. Yet, this was also lacking.

Once in power, Menderes, with Bayar as head of state, took advantage of the majority rule that the 1924 Constitution offered. As Diamond stated, elites must commit to making formal structures more liberal and representative to consolidate democracy (1999). However, 'Menderes, with Bayar, made no effort to change the constitution because keeping it as it was served their majoritarian purposes. And so, without constitutional checks and balances it enabled the authoritarian drift of the Menderes government', declared Ergun Özbudun, a leading expert on Turkish constitutional law (Interview, April 2016).

The unwillingness to democratise the constitution demonstrated three factors about Menderes's rule: (1) that neither Menderes nor Bayar were genuine about liberalising the political arena; (2) that the elected government was keen to take advantage of its majoritarian character to unilaterally administer the country and sideline political opposition; and (3) that it demonstrated an understanding of democracy which cared little beyond the ballot-box.

Democrats and the CHP: A Politics of Personal Animosity

Adding to the authoritarian character of the government was the animosity that existed between Menderes and Bayar, on one side, and İnönü, on the other. The political rivalries came to shape the contours of the government's relations with the CHP (Ahmad 1977, 37–38). While campaigning, the Democrats kept reminding society that nothing could change while that 'cunning fox', Ismet Paşa, remained at the helm. This was an effective strategy to play on the schisms in society for electoral benefit, because a large segment of the Turkish population equated the 'despised' single-party rule with İnönü personally (Ahmad 1993, 108).

The acrimony towards İnönü failed to cease when Menderes came to power. This was largely due to the deep-founded fear that the former President was determined to undermine the Democrats' rule. As such, Bayar and Menderes felt insecure as long as İnönü remained active in politics (Ahmad 1977). They were uncertain about their hold over the state institutions, which they thought remained loyal to the old regime and İnönü, particularly the military. This anxiety led to a harassment campaign against İnönü until he would exit politics. For example, at the opening of the Assembly, Menderes targeted İnönü and declared: 'Look in my eyes *paşa*, look in my eyes. No one is going to tolerate your ageing reputation here [. . .] you will pay for all your crimes in the 1946 [elections]' (Birand, Dündar and Çaplı 1991).[12] Menderes's words were ominous and signalled efforts to remove İnönü's legacy to consign it to the annals of Turkish history. To this end, the DP group passed legislation that personally targeted İnönü's prestige. His portrait was removed from bank notes, and his personal train taken away and made available for public use (Birand, Dündar and Çaplı 2016b, 87).

The ill feeling towards İnönü only served to intensify the harassment of the CHP. This was symptomatic of a political system where parties are personalised under their leaders, as was the case in Turkey. In turn, the CHP increased attacks against the Democrats, thus resulting in a bitter and adversarial atmosphere in parliament (Ahmad 1977, 41; Albayrak 2004; Sütçü 2011a). However, it is important to note that the intolerance and antagonism cut through on both sides:

> When things got heated, İnönü became the number-one person who Menderes and Bayar thought was going to cause problems for the government, so they began attacking İnönü. İnönü also responded in a very harsh way. The polarised climate wasn't just due to Menderes and the Democrats, the opposition had a part in causing the dysfunction. (Interview with Sabri Sayarı, July 2016)

Menderes regularly imposed high costs on the CHP as electoral losers, and the reaction that this elicited from the CHP trapped the government and the opposition in a cycle of hostility. These were dangerous divergences from the rules of democratic politics and contrary to the required norms of tolerance and restraint needed to sustain a democracy, which weakened the hope for any form of a consensus-driven and inclusive government.

This set of unique circumstances and Menderes's overwhelming contempt towards his opponent, in a political system that had little, if any, checks on majoritarian rule, created a grave situation for the opposition (Özbudun 2000b). With an overwhelming majority Menderes could rule without taking the opposition's demands and considerations into account (Heper 2002, 228). One remark accurately reveals Menderes's views toward his political opposition and doing politics: 'This', Menderes shouted in response to a series of political attacks, 'is not democracy; it is a blood feud!' (*Time* 1958b). In 1953 the Menderes government demonstrated a clear rejection of democratic norms, by making the decision to confiscate the CHP's material possessions and assets under the *Haksız İktisap Yasası* (Usurpation Law), on the basis that it had been amassed illegally during the single-party period (Mango 2004, 48).

Undoubtedly, during the single-party period, when the CHP and the state constituted one entity, public funds had been used to acquire real estate for the party. The government in this sense was justified to insist that these properties be returned to the state, but in a way this did not diminish the capacity of the opposition to function. Yet, the timing and the severity with which the law was implemented suggest that the move was clearly intended to deal a severe blow to the CHP. This was acknowledged by Fethi Çelikbaş, DP parliamentarian of the period: 'Unfortunately, the DP's policies were characterised with the simple aim to eliminate the CHP' (Birand, Dündar and Çaplı 2016a, 101). The outcome of the law led to considerable material loss for the party, ensuring the closure of the CHP's regional offices, including the confiscation of the party's general headquarters, and it significantly diminished the capacity of the CHP to campaign for the upcoming 1954 general election (Ahmad 1977, 48–49). Similar actions against an opposition party would be repeated by incumbents in the following decades, as will be shown.

What the government could not do against its main rival, it was able to undertake against the minor opposition parties. In the lead-up to the general election of 1954, the *Millet Partisi* (Nation Party, MP) was temporarily ordered to cease activities, and its 2,927 local branches were forced to stop operating when the state prosecutor opened an investigation into the party for anti-secular aims. On 24 January, after a seven-month-long proceeding backed by a DP parliamentary vote, the party was permanently closed (Aslan 2014, 59).[13] When the CHP criticised the action as undemocratic, the government looked to be preparing steps to investigate the main opposition under similar charges. Although the issue was not pursued further, when taken together with the confiscation of CHP resources, it was perceived as a signal of the government's intentions.

Table 1.2 1954 Election Results

Political Party	Percentage of Votes	Parliamentary Seats (Total 541)
DP	57.6	503
CHP	35.4	31
Cumhuriyetçi Millet Partisi (CMP)	4.8	5
Independents	1.5	2
Türkiye Köylü Partisi (TKP)	0.6	0

Source: https://www.tbmm.gov.tr/develop/owa/secim_sorgu.genel_secimler

If Menderes was heading down a dictatorial route, the opportunity arising from a landslide victory in 1954 flagged this ever more (see Table 1.2). While one in three voters had cast their ballot in favour of the CHP, the winner-take-all electoral system resulted in the opposition being further weakened legislatively, dropping from sixty-nine to thirty-one seats in parliament (Kalaycıoğlu 2002a, 58), while the Democrats raised their parliamentary hold to 503 or 91.6 percent (Sayarı 1978, 42). This extreme asymmetry meant that the CHP could not mount any meaningful obstruction against Menderes's measures (Kalaycıoğlu 2002a, 59).

The electorates that the Democrats had failed to win were punished by Menderes: the government took to the task of gerrymandering non-Democrat provinces (*Time* 1954).[14] The traditional hometown of İnönü, Malatya, was broken up into two separate districts. The *Cumhuriyetçi Millet Partisi* (Republican Nation Party, CMP), which had won all five of its seats from the hometown of party leader Osman Bölükbaşı, Kırşehir, was also re-classified from a province to a district, to block the opposition's chances of winning these areas outright again and as a warning to the people in other cities (Sütçü 2011a, 165).

Emboldened by the landslide victory, Menderes increased his intent to rid the opposition altogether. He declared at a public rally in Gaziantep that, 'if the current laws aren't supressing the opposition and their activities then we will introduce laws that will do a better job' (quoted in Birand, Dündar and Çaplı 2016b, 133–34). The overwhelming victory 'had caused the Democrats to become intoxicated by power. This intoxication changed everything for everyone after the elections', observed journalist Mehmet Ali Birand (2016b, 104). Indeed, although democratic institutions continued to exist, democratic norms such as mutual tolerance and institutional forbearance, necessary to maintain their capacity, had largely been abandoned by this stage. And, by the end of 1954, the stark lesson being learnt by the Turks was that liberalising a regime was not the same as transforming it into a liberal regime. To do so, its elected leaders, as such, needed to rule within the spirit of democracy.

Silencing the Press

When Menderes was met with growing criticism of his actions and of the general character of his rule by the media, the press drew his personal ire and suffered under a barrage of regulations that dramatically curbed their freedom (Yıldız 1996; Kaya 2010). Originally, Menderes viewed the press as an ally during his time in opposition (Yıldız 1996, 482–86). Once he began getting criticised for his government's authoritarian policies (Yıldız 1996; Kaya 2010), he publicly displayed disappointment at himself for providing the press with freedoms after his first electoral victory: 'I made a big mistake by providing the Press with greater freedoms in 1950', he remarked and vowed to reign them in (Birand, Dündar and Çaplı 1991).

Staying true to his words, repealing the freedom of the press became a major issue of the period. It demonstrated that Menderes and Bayar failed to realise that a free press was a critical requirement of democracy. As outlined by key democratic thinkers (Keane 1992; O'Donnell 1996), critical and free media are a vital component of the vertical form of accountability, but Menderes viewed critical media like his political opposition and treated them in the same manner. In February 1954, an amendment further tightened the already oppressive press law titled *Neşir Yoluyla veya Radyo İle İşlenecek Bazı Cürümler Hakkında Kanun* (Law on Some Criminal Offences Committed Through Publication or Radio Broadcasts) (Aslan 2014, 61; Yıldız 1996, 492). Media outlets, editors and journalists faced heavy fines and prison sentences, from six months up to three years, for writings that could be deemed 'harmful to the political or financial prestige of the state' or guilty of damaging 'the morals of Turkish society'; that 'agitated the population'; that 'insulted' a public official, or simply 'incited negative thoughts against the Turkish state' (Ahmad 1977, 49; Kaya 2010, 103). Moreover, the changes opened the path for prosecutors to file charges based on personal discretion (Aslan 2014, 61).

Additional amendments to the law in 1956 entirely muzzled the press by broadening its scope (Yıldız 1996, 494–96). The changes opened every news article to persecution, to such an extent that even 'newsboys [were] forbidden to shout any news that indirectly caused "doubts" about the government' (*Time* 1956d). Even criticism of a DP municipality for not having running water was forcefully censored by authorities under the law (Birand, Dündar and Çaplı 1991). Menderes's personal intolerance for any shade of criticism was demonstrated when Metin Toker penned the piece '*Kedi Olmayınca Fareler Cirit Atar*' (While the cat is away, the mice will play), pointing out the tensions within the governing party. In response, the editor in charge of the daily, Cüneyt Arcayürek, was arrested on charges of insulting the Prime Minister and taken into custody (Birand, Dündar and Çaplı 2016b, 121). Other journalists were financially penalised or imprisoned for writing stories such as the retelling of a joke, criticism of Menderes's financial policies and suggesting that the Premier had married for money (*Time* 1956b, 1958a).

When corruption allegations against the government were made in the media, the *İspat Hakkı* (Right of Proof) law was passed to intimidate the press further (Sütçü 2011a, 168). The law ultimately denied journalists and media outlets the right to legally defend the integrity and truthfulness of their published work (Turan 2015, 92; Kaya 2010, 101–2). Without the right to defend themselves against accusations, the press was gagged, not only in regard to what they could say about the government, but also about the growing economic downturn endured by society. In short, a newspaper or a journalist could easily be charged, even if what was published was correct, leaving the interpretation of a news piece by the government virtually all that mattered.

Under this regulation, prominent people, such as Bedi Faik, were arrested. Hüseyin Cahit Yalçın, eighty years of age at the time, and İnönü's son-in-law, Toker, were jailed, and a number of newspapers were closed (Kaya 2010, 101). Between the years 1954 and 1958, 1,161 journalists were investigated, 900 found guilty and 238 of these given prison sentences (Yıldız 1996, 502). Some journalists were imprisoned on two or three occasions, with terms ranging up to three years (*Time* 1960d). Sayarı provides insight into the period:

> Freedom of the press became a major issue of the period. Menderes, Bayar and others did not realise that press freedom is a very key element of democracy. There were some very nasty things that occurred. You saw old journalists like Hüseyin Cahit Yalçın, who had been in the newspaper business stemming back to the Ottoman era, penalised. He was a particularly important columnist and member of the *İttihat ve Terakki Partisi* (Committee of Union and Progress). This man in his eighties was brought to trial. İnönü's son-in-law Metin Toker, who was publishing the most important political weekly of the period, called *Akis*, was thrown in jail. You could not get any closer to İnönü than imprisoning his son-in-law. At the same time, you had the official state radio (TRT) transformed into the government's propaganda machine. (Interview, July 2016)

This statement shows that the press was treated with arbitrary measures to silence any criticism of the government. Furthermore, the administration targeted individuals specifically, such as Toker, to intimidate the leader of the main opposition, İnönü. Since the press had fewer protective measures, the Menderes government exploited the conditions to deny the political opposition a voice in the press.

In the last years of the decade, more newspapers were closed down and more journalists jailed than in any preceding period, including the single-party era (Ahmad 1977, 62). By the beginning of 1960, 2,300 criminal investigations had been launched against journalists and 867 jailed, and in the last four years of Menderes's rule sentences totalling fifty-seven years were meted out to this group (Yıldız 1996, 504). Such was the number of journalists in Ankara's Central Prison that it was referred to as the 'Ankara Hilton' (*Time* 1958a).

This slide into authoritarianism made other founding DP members extremely uneasy. The *İspat Hakkı Yasası* sparked a nineteen-man internal opposition against Menderes during 1955 (*Milliyet* 1955) and became the catalyst for the liberal party wing's long-festering animosity towards his authoritarian style. Subsequently, Menderes had nine members of the faction expelled by the party's *Merkez Disiplin Kurulu* (Central Disciplinary Committee), in which Bayar and Menderes had the final word,[15] while the remaining ten resigned in protest (Ahmad 1977, 89; *Milliyet* 1955). Unable to influence the direction of the party or the government from within, the nineteen dissidents established the *Hürriyet Partisi* (Freedom Party) to openly compete against their former leader (Kaya 2010, 102–3; Turan 2015, 92). This would become the only means to express intra-party dissent.

The other party elites became incensed at Menderes's authoritarianism with one of the founders of the party, Refik Koraltan, privately lamenting to the President: 'Bayar, we are heading towards a cliff edge with great speed' (Birand, Dündar and Çaplı 1991). Yet, the President did not heed this warning or counsel Menderes. Bayar remained in favour of maintaining the government's hard line and supported the law which denied the press the right of proof (Sütçü 2011a, 168). As a result, Fuat Köprülü, another one of the founding members,[16] resigned on the grounds that he no longer could recognise the party which he had helped create; he joined the ranks of the newly established opposition, *Hürriyet Partisi*, with the other DP dissidents. The ill feeling towards his former comrade and the direction in which the government had taken the country compelled Köprülü, upon leaving, to exclaim:

> I am withdrawing from the DP as it is impossible for me to reconcile with its current mentality. Today's DP has separated from its [original] programme and has completely moved away from its founding identity [. . . Therefore] it is the patriotic duty of every Turkish citizen who has faith in the democratic order to put aside all differences and to cooperate in order to achieve this aim [to remove Menderes]. (quoted in Birand, Dündar and Çaplı 2016b, 130, 137)

The public plea for all citizens to unite against Menderes demonstrates how far the country had strayed from democracy under his rule. Following Köprülü, more high-profile resignations from the party took place in response to Menderes's authoritarianism. Two representatives from Konya, Rüştü Özal and Muharrem Obüz, were even more critical of Menderes than Köprülü:

> Today, the Democrat Party has succeeded in making people forget its past services because of the ambitions [of its leader] and the uncontrolled and arbitrary rule. There exists a situation in which very great and mortal damage could be done, first to the existence of the party and secondly, to the country. (quoted in Ahmad 1977, 94)

Rather than weakening Menderes's hold over power, the resignations strengthened his position. He was able to insulate himself further from his party and to surrounded himself more and more with sycophants (*Time* 1956a). With his decisions subjected to little criticism and restraint, he was able to gain total control of the Executive Committee and became bolder in the pursuit of his ambitions.

Majoritarian Democracy and the Authoritarian Slide

The anti-democratic measures against opponents and critics were in large part legitimised due to the majoritarian interpretation of democracy by Menderes, Bayar and other party elites. Unlike the way in which it is customarily perceived in a consolidated democracy, both men rather held the belief that the ballot box was the only form of democratic accountability and that a freely elected government should operate with no restrictions over its rule (Ahmad 1977; Kalaycıoğlu 1990; Tachau 2000; Heper 2002a). This was consistent with Schmitter and Karl, who considered this the fallacy of *electoralism*; accordingly, democracy is based on electoral outcomes regardless of how they are conducted or what else constrains the winners (1991). This view was clearly articulated by Deputy Premier Samet Ağaoğlu:

> Democracy is the regime of numbers. In this regime the wishes of the masses are carried out. We, as the responsible ones in power are obliged to the consideration of the mass of the people and not the shouts of and criticisms of a handful of intellectuals. (quoted in Yalman 1970a, 238–39)

Here it can be seen that the party espoused an interpretation of democracy according to which simply obtaining the majority was enough to exercise unchecked power. This denied acknowledgement of the need to build stronger horizontal and vertical institutions of accountability and preference for creating democratic norms. Therefore, the overwhelming victories fuelled the perception of these men as the architects of contemporary Turkey, the perception that they alone understood what was best for the country. It accentuated and eroded what little tolerance for opposition Menderes had. A prominent scholar of contemporary Turkish politics, İlter Turan noted:

> When the Democrats got into power, they displayed all the pathologies that are associated with majoritarianism [. . .] Any time there were limitations on what they could do, they justified their rejection of these limitations on the basis of representing the majority [. . .] Menderes basically did not want limitations on his power. He tried to use instruments of the state for partisan advantage, and he justified all this in the name of having the people's backing. (Interview, April 2016)

In other words, Menderes's majoritarian interpretation was used to legitimise his attempts at single-handed rule, which he personally acknowledged after his sweeping victory in 1954 in an interview: 'Now the people's lively confidence makes it obvious that there is no further need for such consultations [with other parties]. I am going to have the final word and use aspirin or optalidon as I please' (quoted in Ahmad 1977, 50).[17] The DP's overwhelming success at the ballot box placed the CHP as an illegitimate actor in the eyes of Menderes (Tachau 2000, 133, 136), and the Prime Minister therefore felt no need to appease or consult the opposition (Heper 2002a, 228), as Menderes declared to Mükerrem Sarol, a DP colleague:

> Maybe I am forced to talk [with the CHP] in the parliament. Willing to accept the rights of the opposition under the law. Outside of that, we will not accept any of their suggestions or their attempts to engage with us. (quoted in Birand, Dündar and Çaplı 2016b, 110–11)

As worrying for democracy as those words were, it outlined the contempt for opposition and the zero-sum view of electoral victory. Menderes was unwilling to respect the parliament as a representative body, or to act according to the institution's principles. Measures taken against the opposition were assumed to serve the people's interests. Any opposition to the government's decree simply amounted to, as he termed it, obstruction of the *milli irade* (national will) to which they alone held themselves accountable (Özbudun 1993, 303; Heper 2002a, 228). This created an atmosphere whereby inter-elite relations resembled a war against their political opponents. It also denied the possibility that Menderes would use his overwhelming majority to further democratise the country; rather, this advantage was instrumentalised to seize critical institutions.

Relations between the Bureaucracy and the Government

The mandate which they had received from the people led the Democrats to conclude that they had the right to monopolise and use the state for their own purposes, as an arm of the government (Ahmad 1977, 44–45). To achieve a healthy democracy, state apparatuses need to remain neutral and distanced from the ruling party, as it performs a public service (Turan 2015, 197). However, Menderes acted in the belief that the party in government had to utilise state agencies as partisan agents. This philosophy continued to operate under future leaders.

There were more serious attempts to bring state institutions under direct control of the government. Discarding institutional forbearance, the DP, from the beginning, took an aggressive policy towards these institutions. For example, Menderes's earliest action was to personally retire many high-ranking officers from the military, which he made a habit of boasting about to his party (Birand, Dündar and Çaplı 2016b, 79–80), setting the early tone for relations between the government and the state.[18]

After the 1954 elections, two pivotal laws were passed that gave the government expanded powers over critical institutions. The first allowed the forced retirement of state employees after twenty-five years of service. Previous to this amendment, these positions were legally protected from forced retirement in order to safeguard the autonomy of the institutions for which they worked, such as the *Yargıtay* (Supreme Court of Appeals), the *Danıştay* (Council of State) and university faculties. In the following month, the second amendment entirely removed the minimum years of service before forceful retirement of all government employees without recourse to justice (Turan 2015, 92–93).

The unchecked authority allowed Menderes's government to discharge civil servants whenever it 'deem[ed] it to be necessary' (*Time* 1954). This was most apparent in academia and in the judiciary. Judges and prosecutors were removed from their posts or demoted if verdicts were deemed against the interests of the government (Szyliowicz 1975, 47; Turan 2015, 197). Commenting on these developments, Özbudun asserts: 'They retired many judges whose decisions they did not like. This highlighted the fact that there was no independence of the judiciary under the Menderes administration' (Interview, April 2016). Illustrative of this is the fact that, once the law had been passed, a total of twenty-three judicial officers were forced into retirement, including the *Danıştay Başkanı* (President of the Council of State) and the *Cumhuriyet Başsavcısı* (Chief Public Prosecutor) (Birand, Dündar and Çaplı 1991).

Further legislative steps were taken after Menderes persuaded the Assembly to prevent state employees from involving themselves in the country's politics (*Time* 1958b). The broadly defined expression 'involving themselves in the country's politics' acted as a measure to stop public servants from voicing criticism against Menderes and his government. Academics were the primary targets of this law, as the government did not appreciate their criticism. In particular, professors of law who frequently criticised the legality of the government's policies and actions, bore the brunt of the government's wrath (Ahmad 1977).[19] The actions sparked wide unrest across academia against the growing repression. The student population began to hold regular anti-Menderes demonstrations and boycotted classes, and academics resigned in support of their sacked colleagues (Birand, Dündar and Çaplı 2016b, 135).

The decisions were shaped by the fear that these institutions were undermining Menderes's government, due to a lingering loyalty for the CHP and İnönü (Birand, Dündar and Çaplı 1994, 2016a; Ahmad 1977, 1993). As such, the widening measures against the state institutions hastened the crisis in democracy:

Menderes and Bayar never believed in the motives of the military and civilian bureaucracy; they were always suspicious that the opposition would find a way of getting back at them. This made them act with a tremendous amount of bias against these institutions and bully them around. Doing so stressed and strained the relations between key state organs and the executive branch of government [. . .] which eventually resulted in some kind of breakdown of democracy by 1959. (Interview with Ersin Kalaycıoğlu, April 2016)

It is hard to evaluate how realistic and rational Bayar and Menderes's fears of the state institutions were; nonetheless, as the above statement attests, it generated animosity and aggravated and increased anti-Menderes feelings within these institutions, leading to a paralysis in government–state relations and ultimately creating a political crisis, as will be shown.

Returning to Single-party Tutelage

The increasing economic downturn in the second half of the 1950s made Menderes feel less secure about his ability to sustain his position. Unable to halt the economic crisis, Menderes instead opted to silence criticism about the economy from reaching the public (Ahmad 1977, 53–55). The introduction of further restrictive legislation to an already repressive regime, by this stage, made political activity outside the Assembly virtually impossible. The Electoral Law was amended in 1956 to make campaigning extremely difficult for political opponents. The argument provided by Menderes was based on the notion that opposition political rallies were damaging, not only to himself, but also to the 'New Turkey' he was building (*Time* 1956a). The law forbade political meetings or demonstrations except in the forty-five days immediately preceding elections (Sarıbay 1991, 352). Since Turkey held elections once every four years, Menderes was effectively denying the opposition the right of freedom of assembly and the possibility to engage with the public. These measures forced the CHP to hold meetings in secret to continue their work and avoid the ire of authorities (Birand, Dündar and Çaplı 2016b, 136–37).

In the lead-up to the 1957 election, another legislative act was passed, this time aimed at restricting all demonstrations (Ahmad 1977, 53). The *Toplantı ve Gösteri Yürüyüşleri Yasası* (Meeting and Demonstration Law) banned public gatherings and meetings deemed a political protest. Yet, the power to determine what constituted 'political protest' was left to the authorities.[20] In the case of people attempting to hold 'unauthorised' meetings, the law provided the police with the right to discharge their weapons into the air to disperse protestors, and if the meeting failed to dissolve, they were permitted to fire

into the crowd (Birand, Dündar and Çaplı 2016b, 137–38; *Time* 1956a).
When Fevzi Karaosmanoğlu, leader of a minor opposition party *Hürriyet Partisi*, called this law the work of a dictator, he was suspended from parliament for a period of time, for using what was deemed defamatory language against the Prime Minister (*Time* 1956a). With these laws, the opposition was finding their access to the public slowly closed off.

Despite these efforts, the result of the 1957 elections was a major setback for the Prime Minister and his party (see Table 1.3). The CHP won victories in a third of the country's provinces and lifted its parliamentary share. The Prime Minister still held the majority, but the win was not without major controversy. The outcome was marred by the opposition's accusations of vote-rigging in remote provinces, such as Gaziantep. The government refused to release the final tally, which according to unofficial counts gave the opposition 51.6 percent of the vote (*Time* 1957). Any further investigation was denied when the election records were lost in a mysterious fire (Harris 2002, 50). The dispute led to violent skirmishes between members of both camps, ending with the death of two people (*Time* 1957).

Table 1.3 1957 Election Results

Political Party	Percentage of Votes	Parliamentary Seats (Total 610)
DP	47.9	424
CHP	41.1	178
CMP	7.1	4
Hürriyet Partisi (HP)	3.8	4
Independents	0.5	0

Source: https://www.tbmm.gov.tr/develop/owa/secim_sorgu.genel_secimler

The momentum of the CHP drove Menderes to take greater measures against them. The government requested that the parliament investigate the opposition's activities before and after the election to see whether they had been subversive (Ahmad 1977). The following December, the DP majority amended the Assembly by-law that curtailed the opposition's right to probe and interrogate the government. The changes allowed DP ministers to avoid questions from the parliamentary opposition (Albayrak 2004). The other amendments included: opposition parliamentarians could be thrown out of the Assembly if the government deemed their conduct as disruptive (Aslan 2014, 93); reports of parliamentary proceedings were prevented from reaching the public (Gülsevin 2009, 64); and parties that occupied less than one percent of the Assembly seats were banned from forming a parliamentary group. This was clearly aimed at both the *Cumhuriyetçi Millet Partisi* and the *Hürriyet Partisi*, which sat below the threshold (Aslan 2014, 93). As a result of these successive laws, the right to opposition in the legislature became increasingly difficult, if not virtually removed.

To hold off the CHP's momentum, Menderes created the *Vatan Cephesi* (Motherland Front) in 1958, to further besiege the opposition and its supporters. The Motherland Front was created to counter so-called 'subversion and destruction which endangers national unity' (Ahmad 1977, 61). The state broadcaster, TRT, by this stage used as the government's propaganda machine (Sarıbay 1991, 127),[21] publicly listed the names of those individuals who had joined the Motherland Front on a nightly basis. The government promised to punish those who did not join and to reward those who did: villages that demonstrated support were promised much needed resources, while those that displayed allegiance to the CHP had their electricity cut (Ahmad 1977, 61). In a country that was still largely agrarian, this was an extremely intimidating prospect and a rather crude demonstration of the government's willingness to curtail their opponents' access to resources. Those working for the state did not receive the chance to decide, as the government forced bureaucrats into joining the Motherland Front (Turan 2013, 48). This exercise, however, merely exacerbated the growing polarisation in society and further drove a wedge between supporters of the DP and the opposition, thus accentuating the growing unrest (Uyar 2012; Sarı 2012).

The increasing authoritarianism signalled a leadership that had abandoned what little tolerance for democracy they had had in order to remain in power. The continuity of authoritarian rule in Turkish politics was best captured by *Time* magazine (1958b) in an article on Menderes:

> Only seven years after Turkey won its graduation certificate as a democracy by peacefully voting out of office a regime of a quarter of a century's standing, the Turks again live in a society characterized by the over-the-shoulder glance to see who may be listening.

The levels of repression soon brought the political regime to a breaking point. Society had grown restless, and demonstrations began to flare up in major cities. President Bayar chose to oppose any rapprochement with İnönü or the CHP to solve the crisis, and he scolded the Democrats who made such suggestions to ease tensions (Birand, Dündar and Çaplı 2016b, 154–55). To a Western diplomat he uttered: 'We are going to crush the opposition' (quoted in *Time* 1960c). Thus, the government's encouragement of violence against their opponents became increasingly apparent.

The military was ushered in to quash anti-government demonstrations and also to prevent İnönü from holding a speaking tour of the country. Evidence suggests that Bayar personally ordered the military to block the CHP leader's tour of the country. A key example of this was when the armed forces prevented İnönü's tour of the Aegean region in 1959. It was also during this tour that İnönü survived a stoning in Uşak; with claims that the President had organised the attack on the opposition leader. Bayar later ordered governors and other authorities to use violence to prevent İnönü from speaking in Istanbul. In that incident, the CHP leader barely survived an attack by a lynch mob. Although Bayar denied these allegations, the evidence given by Menderes and other Democrats during the Yassıada military trials in the aftermath of the 1960 coup directly implicated him as the instigator of these actions against İnönü (Harris 2002, 50–51).

This created even greater friction, with a military incensed at being used for the leadership's political purposes, in particular to oppress a former military hero such as İnönü. In one incident, Major Selahattin Çetiner, who had been ordered to halt İnönü's train, resigned in protest (Birand, Dündar and Çaplı 2016b, 161).[22] The police promptly arrested the major, along with two other officers, who then also resigned from their positions in protest. General Gürsel, Commander-in-Chief of Turkey's ground forces, protested the use of troops for political purposes – and was summarily 'retired' (*Time* 1960b).

If the unease of the military was not yet visible, the unrest against the authoritarianism was unmistakable across Turkey: in major cities, communities were polarised along pro- and anti-Menderes lines, and the methods employed to suppress anti-government demonstrations increased the violence. İnönü's motorcades were often violently targeted by groups loyal to Menderes and, in one incident, he was struck in the face by a stone, while another time his car was set upon by thugs, only to be saved by a passing military unit. Menderes also endured his share of incidents when his car was violently set upon by protestors in Ankara on more than one occasion (Birand, Dündar and Çaplı 2016b, 160–77).

The suppression of political opponents reached its zenith on 18 April 1960, with a *Tahkikat Komisyonu* (Parliamentary Investigation Committee). As with the majority of decisions of the government by this stage, the decision to establish the committee was ordered by Menderes and Bayar (Yaşar 2014, 535; Harris 2002). Made up entirely of fifteen DP deputies, the committee was formed to investigate whether the opposition had transgressed legal limits, which, at the same time, ushered in an end to the existing transparency of government. The committee was bestowed with extraordinary judicial, almost 'dictatorial' powers that superseded those of the Assembly and the courts (*Time* 1960c); even more troublesome was that their decisions were exempt from any form of appeal. Placing such powers in the hands of a political body was a clear violation of democratic ideals.

Menderes's legal advisor, Professor Ali Fuat Başgil, warned him that the law to set up the committee carried unconstitutional provisions, which could also be misused to close down the CHP, and he urged that it be sent back to the Assembly to correct its unconstitutional aspects (Albayrak 2004). Menderes ignored this advice and allowed the committee to push forward in its role. When Başgil took his concerns to Bayar, the President backed the committee's powers because he wanted to 'destroy (the opposition) root and branch' (Harris 2002, 51).

The committee's first act was to enforce a ban on all-political assemblies, and over time its powers were increased to include the authority to censor newspapers from reporting anything to do with the committee and its work, to issue subpoenas and to impose prison sentences on individuals who were seen to obstruct or resist its work (Ahmad 1977, 64). By the end of April 1960, the parliament was virtually closed off to the opposition and the media completely muzzled. It looked as though the closure of the CHP was perhaps open for consideration when the committee found the CHP's acts as '*yıkıcı, gayri meşru ve kanun dışı*' – subversive, illegitimate and illegal (quoted in Albayrak 2004). The latest development marked a government on the verge of undertaking a civilian coup.

Reporting on the developments, *Time* (1960c) declared:

. . . since his Democrats wrested office from President İsmet İnönü's Republicans in 1950, they have gagged newspapers, jailed more than 200 journalists, and cuffed the opposition about with barbarous disregard for civil rights [. . .] Menderes knows what his followers are doing, and in fact dictates the laws that they enact.

From *Time* magazine's commentary we can again deduce, firstly, the acute level that Menderes's authoritarian leadership had reached by 1960 and, secondly, the central role that Menderes played in making decisions that closed off politics to voices other than that of the government. His government had abandoned any trace of upholding key democratic institutions.

Societal tension was further strained by these developments. The country witnessed mass anti-government demonstrations by students at Istanbul University, with shouts of 'down to all dictators' directed against Menderes. When the police were unable to disperse the crowd with force, they 'began shooting in earnest, and some twenty students dropped' (*Time* 1960c). The government proclaimed martial law. All of Istanbul's cafés, bars and nightclubs were closed. The university was shut down, and the dean of Istanbul University was arrested when he tried to intervene. The military governor banned any mention of the events in the press, denying that anybody had been killed. A media blackout prohibited reports of all news on the unrests growing across the country and on the resulting deaths. Yet, on a day that came to be infamously known as *Kanlı Perşembe* (Bloody Thursday), hospitals reported five dead and forty wounded (*Time* 1960c). The next day, solidarity demonstrations spread to Ankara and Izmir, which were aggressively contained with the imposition of martial law in these cities. In the end, at least a dozen students were killed by the police in the course of the protests (*Time* 1960b).

Enraged by the growing opposition, Menderes and Bayar took an even harder line: the students, so Menderes remarked, were the 'tools of conspirators', 'fanatic party followers' and 'plots against the country's security', thereby legitimising the use of violence against the student protestors. This was shown when Menderes angrily announced: 'They will soon learn what it means to stand against the state' (quoted in *Time* 1960c). For his part, Bayar ignored the urging and advice of his close confidant, Başgil, to remedy the polarisation in the country by forcing Menderes to resign and then to form an all-party government with the CHP. He angrily replied: 'No! The time for threats has passed. Now is the time to get tough' (Birand, Dündar and Çaplı 1991). These words signalled the abandonment of hope for moderation by the government.

Bayar instructed the creation of a law that provided the military with the authority to open fire in order to disperse protestors (Harris 2002, 51). At other times, the President was direct in his instructions, encouraging deadly force. Whilst riding alongside Menderes, he ordered one of the Prime Minister's aides, Ercüment Yavuzalp, to disperse the large crowd of protestors who descended on the unsuspecting PM in the heart of Ankara, explaining that, if they failed to do so, they would be fired at (Birand, Dündar and Çaplı 2016b, 176). On another occasion, when he and Menderes encountered demonstrators on their return to the Prime Ministry, Bayar ordered security forces to separate demonstrators from the spectators and 'do what was necessary', which implied that the President wanted to 'destroy them' (Harris 2002, 51). Fortunately, no shots were fired, but these developments indicate Bayar taking back the reigns in the face of Menderes losing his grip and the growing willingness to use violence to hang on to power (Sayarı 2002a, 77).

For his role, Menderes refused to take advice from within his party to moderate his actions and, rather, organised counter-demonstrations, which further hastened the fragmentation of society (Birand, Dündar and Çaplı 2016b, 180–82). In Eskişehir, he denounced anyone who had criticised his most recent efforts to repress opposition and told cheering supporters: 'They think they can bring us down, but they cannot. We are too strong. We will fix them' (quoted in *Time* 1960b). Yet, there was no way of slowing down the speed with which societal cohesion seemed to be disintegrating in the face of the government's arbitrary and violent measures.

A demonstration by 500 officer cadets, later joined by close to one-hundred captains, majors and lieutenants, was harder to ignore or suppress. When the Defence Minister called on them to disperse, the cadets shouted: 'Why don't you resign?' (quoted in *Time* 1960a). Demonstrations by students could be ignored or put down by force, but not those by future officers.

The military's discontent with Menderes and Bayar's activities came to a head with the coup on 27 May 1960. The leader of the coup, General Cemal

Gürsel, proclaimed himself head of government and the armed forces. He squarely put the blame for the coup on the leadership. 'I tried to reason with the politicians, but they were blinded by ambition. We had to act', Gürsel announced on radio. 'They ignored my advice. They thought the Turkish nation was a senseless herd'. The intervention, he insisted, was 'for the purpose of having just and free elections as soon as possible', which he alluded was not possible under the direction in which Menderes's government had taken the country (quoted in *Time* 1960b). Thus came Turkey's first experience with democracy, resulting in a tragic ending.

In the following developments, many of the leading names of the DP were put on trial by the junta on the island of Yassıada. Along with Menderes, Minister of Foreign Affairs Fatih Rüştü Zorlu and Minister of Finance Hasan Polatkan were given the death penalty for a number of charges. The most serious of these was the crime of violating the constitution. All three were executed by hanging on 17 September 1961.[23]

At the time of the coup, many Turks felt that the army had snatched the country from the hands of the privileged few and restored it to the people. Describing the mood, the *Time* reported that, 'across the country, soldiers on the streets were greeted by many Turks like liberators with cries of *freedom, freedom*' (*Time* 1960b). The initial reaction across the country reported by the *Time* is telling of a government that had fallen quite far in the eyes of its weary public.

Deliberating over the authoritarianism and breakdown of the Menderes era, Sayarı noted: 'Why did Menderes resort to stronger methods and eventually greater authoritarianism? That's a big question. I mean, why would you do that if you were winning the elections? But again, we go back to political history, the political culture' (Interview, July 2016). And the political culture, in terms of leadership, was one that continued to embody the authoritarian character of the previous era, which stood in opposition to the requirements of leadership, not only for democratisation, but also to sustain the new multi-party system.

Conclusion

The transition from single-party to multi-party politics marked an opportunity to liberalise the political system and make it responsive to society; yet the Bayar-Menderes era carried the single-party character of rule over into a democratic system. Therefore, when diagnosing not only the inability to consolidate but also the rollback of democracy in this period, assessing the role of Menderes with the support of Bayar is key. Their partnership ensured that they brooked no opposition from any quarter, including within the party itself. Menderes slowly consolidated the DP under his rule, with purges, dismissals, the co-option of his critics and a general erosion of the democratic structure becoming common practice. Doing so allowed him to direct the government's overwhelming majority in the manner he desired. Unfortunately, this did not entail liberalising the political system.

Legislative power was exploited to reinforce the repressive character of the government rather than upholding or strengthening the institutions of democracy necessary for consolidation. Menderes used his position to undermine the newly established democratic system. Valuing norms that built robust democratic institutions and practices was not a policy that he pursued: the media were muzzled, while the independence of the bureaucracy, the judiciary and academia were brought under the influence of the government. From the beginning, the leadership exhibited an obvious intolerance for actors and institutions that could provide a check on their power, particularly the right to opposition. This was a critical factor in denying the development of harmonious relations, a *sine qua non* of democratic politics. Overall, there was a fundamental lack of democratic understanding by the two leaders, which ultimately was expressed in the nature of the political developments.

When it was finally ended by the military, Menderes and Bayar, who had been critical for ushering in democracy, ironically were the central actors in its demise. Their inability to discard the single-party characteristics continued the legacy of autocratic attitude towards political interactions and the rule of the country, justified under the veneer of serving the will of the people. By the end, Menderes's government resembled a regime taking great strides at re-instituting single-party tutelage. From a historical perspective, the era stands as both a watershed moment and an example of continuity in regard to Turkish politics and leadership – the paradox of irreconcilable and opposing drives trying to exist on the same plain. And as a result, it was effectively a democracy without democrats.

In the next chapter, I will show that the military junta's attempt to avert another democratic crisis by liberalising the regime did not markedly alter the leadership culture. Rather, the continuity of authoritarianism re-emerged, this time couched within the ideological undercurrents of the time, which once again hindered the deepening of the democratic system and eroded the democratic order.

Notes

1. Soon after the transition to a multi-party system, the CHP called general elections in July 1946 to purposefully catch the opposition off-guard, all while the political environment was deemed to be repressive and heavily skewed to the advantage of the ruling party itself. The outcome, unsurprisingly, was a victory for the ruling CHP, winning 390 of the 465 seats (84 percent), with the DP winning 65 (14 percent) and Independents 7 (1.5 percent) (Ahmad 1993).
2. More than twenty political parties were created after 1945, but only a handful were able to survive (Payaşlıoğlu 1964, 423).
3. The other party founder, Refik Koraltan, was elected as *Meclis Başkanı* (Speaker of the Grand National Assembly).
4. In reality, this change made little difference to İnönü's position in the party, as demonstrated by the fact that he continued to be elected as party chairman until 1972. Nonetheless, it opened up a path that ultimately led to a peaceful transition in party leadership between İnönü and Bülent Ecevit in 1972.
5. These were Adnan Menderes, Fuat Köprülü, Hasan Polatkan, Ahmet Tevfik İleri, Zühtü Hilmi Velibeşe and Nuri Özsan (Ahmad 1977, 79).
6. Fahri Belen also resigned around this period due to health concerns (Aslan 2014, 48).
7. During the early years Menderes had to deal with dissent, particularly from the grassroots of the party. Much of the dissent from below had to do with criticism of Menderes's policies towards the CHP, which were seen as 'lenient'. However, the centralised party structure ensured that criticisms from provincial bodies held no direct threat and helped Menderes deal with them easily (Ahmad 1977, 82–85).
8. Immediately after he received the vote of confidence for his cabinet in 1954, he set up a commission made up of loyalists, with the sole purpose of amending party regulations in order to control the party more easily. The commission was made up of Atıf Benderelioğlu, Zühtü Velibeşe, Osman Kavrak, Hüsnü Yaman, Samet Ağaoğlu, Kamil Gündeş and Rauf Onursal.
9. For example, the Istanbul branch failed to hold a conference for close to two years.

10. These included the likes of Rüştü Ozal, Muammer Obuz, Cihad Baban, Orhan Köprülü, Fuat Köprülü and İsmail Selçuk Çakıroğlu (Yaşar 2014, 511).
11. The document legislated a restricted political arena to hold society and political opposition at bay. The supremacy given to the legislature diminished the standing of the citizen and rendered them without protection from government decisions. The constitution declared the basic rights of Turkish citizens, but it stated that such rights would be enjoyed only 'within the limits stipulated by law'. Hence, the Assembly was constitutionally empowered to restrict basic rights almost at will (Özbudun and Gençkaya 2009). It lacked efficient judicial review of governmental actions and blocked any attempts by society to act against majoritarian rule.
12. *Paşa* is a term used to refer to a General of the Turkish armed forces.
13. The party founders reformed in time for the general elections to establish the *Cumhuriyetçi Millet Partisi* (Republican Nation Party, CMP).
14. This is the redrawing of the boundaries of electoral districts in a way that gives one party an unfair advantage over its rivals.
15. Feroz Ahmad stated that the Disciplinary Committee was controlled by Menderes and Bayar to effectively deal with intra-party opponents (1977, 89).
16. Köprülü also served as Foreign Minister from 1950 until his resignation.
17. Optalidon is a medication used for short-term pain relief.
18. The conditions for workers and organised labour also suffered. The central concern was material outcomes for the country, but the government provided little time for other concerns, such as workers' rights (Ahmad 1993, 110). For example, when Menderes was reminded that he had promised Turkish workers the right to strike, his response was: 'Stop this nonsense. Is Turkey to have strikers? Let's have economic development first and then we'll think about this matter' (quoted in Ahmad 1993, 110). By the mid-1950s, Menderes had completely reneged his promise regarding the right to strike (Beşeli 2002, 204–7). As the economy turned for the worse, he moved to suppress working class associations altogether (Koç 2003, 37).
19. The dismissed academics were also prohibited from taking up positions in foreign institutions, which could only be seen as an attempt to block criticism that might diminish the prestige of Menderes's government internationally (*Time* 1958c).
20. CHP General Secretary Kasım Gülek was one high-profile opposition member who was jailed for six months for breaking this law. In his attempt to test the legislation, he announced that he would go on a country-wide campaign. During his tour, local governors not only refused him permission to hold public meetings, but also decreed that he could not even hold closed meetings

with the local party branches. Gülek was subsequently arrested after waving and shaking hands whilst walking through a crowd, which was deemed a political address by the authorities (*Time* 1956c).

21. During this period, the right to use the state radio broadcaster was legislatively denied to all opposition parties, although no such restrictions were forced upon the ruling Democrats. In justification of the measure, Menderes (as quoted in Sarıbay 1991, 127) stated that 'this practice was completely democratic, because the controlling authority of the radio, which was the organ of the state, was [his] government'. Furthermore, Menderes added: 'The [state] radio was not common property, and it would not be shared with the opposition parties'.

22. Çetiner served as a cabinet member in the military government following the 1980 coup.

23. Although fifteen DP politicians were initially sentenced to death, twelve of the sentences were commuted, except for those of Menderes, Zorlu and Polatkan. Bayar's death penalty was commuted to life imprisonment due to his age. At seventy-eight years of age, he was older than what the law allowed for execution.

2

1961–71: THE RISE OF SÜLEYMAN DEMIREL

Introduction

The coup and execution of Adnan Menderes in 1960 brought down
the curtain on Turkey's first experiment with democracy. After a short
period, democratic politics was allowed to resume, albeit with altered parameters. Officers of the coup created a new constitution granting greater rights
to society, as well as scrutiny of the executive to prevent a repeat of the
authoritarian actions of Menderes and Bayar's government. The break from
the previous era was further marked by the rise of a new leader who ascended
to the prime ministerial seat – Süleyman Demirel.

Despite major efforts by the military to engineer a liberal political system,
the 1960s was yet another tumultuous period in Turkish history: politics, on
account of a society polarised along opposing lines, became marked by paralysis. The conditions ensured that within a decade, in 1971, the military took it
upon itself to force civilian rule to an acrimonious end. The implementation
of a liberal constitution and stronger mechanisms to restrain power could not
ensure steps towards a consolidation of democracy or a stable political order.

The central focus of this chapter is on Süleyman Demirel's leadership as
Prime Minister from 1965 to 1971. Chapter 2 demonstrates that, despite
the military's attempts to create a democratic order through constitutional
restructuring, democracy faced much deeper problems. Demirel was different from Menderes and Bayar in placating the military; nonetheless, in terms

of civilian politics, he struggled to respect demands from the opposition and checks on his authority. This was first reflected inside his party and subsequently carried over into the inter-party environment which impacted the democratic order, particularly when Demirel headed the government. In the concluding section, I explore the leadership style of Demirel and how the inter-play between the intra- and inter-party was the causal factor, hastening the deterioration of the political and social order. Demirel did not govern based on tolerance, institutional forbearance, or politics based on compromise and consensus. Ultimately, Demirel failed to heed the lessons of the Menderes and Bayar era, and his leadership was similarly problematic for sustaining democracy.

Background: The Military as a Political Overseer

Before delving further into substantive analysis, I want to stress that post-1960 was a political environment markedly different from the first multi-party era. The intervening officers aimed to remove any of the influence that the former leaders of the country might have had in the new era. The DP was outlawed, its leaders imprisoned, tried and executed. The military had become an autonomous institution, constitutionally placing itself as guardian and partner of the new regime that it helped create. The new constitution that the military wrote in 1961 was radically different from its predecessor and infused with liberal ideals; thus, the executive had to contend with greater oversight and checks, while state institutions were provided with autonomy, immunity from governmental interference and a civil society able to connect with politics thanks to expanded civil liberties and the social rights of citizens, which also included greater freedoms for labour union activity (Özbudun 2000b, 2011a). The aim was to safeguard against another slide toward authoritarianism.

One of the checks consisted of the formation of a bicameral parliament with the National Assembly and Senate (Landau 1970), where all the members of the military's *Millî Birlik Komitesi* (National Unity Committee, MBK) were made life senators.[1] It also provided the military high command a role in the country's governance. Article 3 established the *Millî Güvenlik Kurulu* (National Security Council, MGK), with the function to assist civilian politicians 'in the making of decisions related to national security and coordination' (quoted in Kars Kaynar 2017, 17). The term 'national security' was loosely defined, thereby giving the military a say in every area before the cabinet. In 1962, a bill was passed that effectively allowed for interference in the deliberations of the cabinet and increased the power of the MGK. These changes positioned the High Command as a central actor in the political and social life of the country in the post-1960 era (see Kars Kaynar 2017). As a result, the control of the armed forces under civilian tutelage became a less likely scenario. For example, in order to appease the military, party leaders issued a communiqué swearing fidelity to the 1960 coup and promised to abstain from acts likely to provoke the army. The fragile state of the newly established political system left itself open to tensions within the armed forces, an institution trying to find stability in its own right (see Birand, Dündar and Çaplı 2016a, 19–115; Ahmad 1977).

With certain military ranks buoyed by the 1960 revolution, the ensuing return to civilian politics posed a major challenge for the political class. After the day of the coup on 27 May, the 'Turkish military had almost become accustomed to interfering in politics' (Birand, Dündar and Çaplı 2016a, 155). This resulted in a decade where the threat of intervention hung over the political arena like a spectre; a situation that was summed up neatly by Emin Aytekin, a colonel of the period:

> The military was completely integrated into politics. To escape this situation, and realign the military with its core function had become a major problem [. . . it was at such a point that] During the military rule every six months in the lower ranks a new junta was being created and preparing to command over the direction of the [Turkish] state. (quoted in Birand, Dündar and Çaplı 2016a, 90)

This was the tense reality that civilian politics faced in the return to elections in 1961, one week after the execution of Adnan Menderes. The elections held on 15 October 1961 ended as a four-party split: a coalition between İsmet İnönü's CHP and the newly formed *Adalet Partisi* (Justice Party, AP).[2] However, this triggered another crisis between the military and civilian politics. The immediate rise of the AP meant that a party made up of former Democrats and sympathisers, who were naturally hostile to the 27 May coup, could capture political power and immediately roll back the military's restructuring.

The risk aroused the ire of radicals within the armed forces. The pressure against the civilian regime brought the coalition to an end after six months. In order to appease the radical elements in the lower ranks and safeguard the legacy of the 27 May coup, the subsequent two coalitions were negotiated by the generals to ensure that İnönü would head the government (Payaşlıoğlu 1964, 426; Ahmad 1977, 179).[3]

The foresight by the High Command to engineer İnönü to lead the governments helped save the democratic system. İnönü's unquestioned prestige among the armed forces was pivotal to soothe the relations between the civilian government and the revolutionary elements within the military. He personally safeguarded democracy in those highly precarious years against two efforts made by radical mid-ranking officers led by Colonel Talat Aydemir to overthrow the government; the first on 22 February 1962 and the second between 20 and 21 May 1963.[4] The attempted coups were unsuccessful largely due to İnönü's personal intervention and efforts in both cases to counter the moves of the instigators and the military from being torn within (see Birand, Dündar and Çaplı 1994, 2016a, 52–115).

It also demonstrated that İnönü was a leader who continued to command loyalty from the upper echelons of the military (Birand, Dündar and Çaplı 2016a; Karpat 1972). Instead of using this to his advantage, he single-handedly saved the system from returning to a military rule that would have been more radical than 1960; a rule similar to a 'rightist dictatorship' (Karpat 1972, 364) under the control of a radical officer described as the 'Turkish Nasser' (Ahmad 1977, 219). And from this point on, the chances of democracy's survival appeared brighter, even if only momentarily.

The Rise of Süleyman Demirel

Despite İnönü's continued leadership over the CHP, the political landscape was changing rapidly. In the void created by the Democrat's closure, the *Adalet Partisi* emerged in 1961 as its natural successor (Sherwood 1967, 55–56; Levi 1991, 136–37; Ahmad 1977, 237). The political vacuum resulting from the coup created a space for people who would otherwise have remained outside of politics. The ranks of political elites, traditionally drawn from the military-bureaucratic class, were changing to include more diverse sections of society, demonstrated by the ascendance of the AP's new leader.

When the AP's founding chairman, Ragıp Gümüşpala, passed away on 5 June 1964, a young[5] successful technocrat, Süleyman Demirel, was elected as his replacement (see Birand, Dündar and Çaplı 2016a, 128–34).[6] Demirel typified the new Turkish politician: he was not from the tradition of the military-bureaucratic intelligentsia that had dominated Turkish politics since the Ottoman *Tanzimat* (reform) period (1839–76).[7] Born to a lower-class family in İsparta, Demirel had changed his status through education and professional acumen. During the 1950s, he had headed the State Water Works and was one of the few bureaucrats whom Menderes trusted (Arat 2002, 88). Demirel was a leader with cultural and historical affinities to the 'ordinary Turk' and seen 'as a man of the people', which ultimately proved a great asset in elections. Nonetheless, he was very much an outsider within the political arena.

Upon his rise to the chairmanship, Demirel came to lead a party with factions.[8] The main division was largely between his camp of moderates and a 'neo-Democratic Party' group that held both extreme anti-military and anti-CHP positions (Levi 1991, 137; Ahmad 1981, 234–35). As leader, he needed to unite the party within a short period of time, or he ran the risk of the party tearing itself apart. For this reason, he looked to quickly stamp his authority over the AP; however, unlike with Menderes and his brazen efforts with the backing of Bayar, Demirel was careful.

He could not possibly have acted, from such an early point, in the same overt authoritarian manner as had Menderes or Bayar. As the architects of the DP, their strong partnership allowed the two men to consolidate power and rule single-handedly. Demirel, however, was a young leader of a party with older politicians; with opposing factions[9] that were problematic for attaining party discipline and unity (Ahmad 1977, 236–37); and a suspicious military prone to reactionary tendencies (Karpat 1972, 364; Cizre 1993). He had to act with prudence, particularly in the early years. To stave off the ire of the military, he played a more cautious hand when dealing with the factions at the start of his tenure.[10] The pathway to total control of the party was a lengthy and arduous affair, as will be shown.

Nonetheless, from the start, Demirel undertook measures to diminish the power of his main rivals and the pockets of resistance within the party. For those who stood in his path, he proved himself to be a formidable force. As a former minister from Demirel's later government, Köksal Toptan, recalled, this was in the traditional leadership mould:

> Like all the leaders before him, Demirel vied to be the strongman leader, and therefore he undertook measures to block and keep at a distance capable and ambitious individuals who could mount a challenge to his rule [. . .] this was very much in the pattern of other Turkish leaders. They won't tolerate an *ikinici adam* (a number two), and Demirel was no different. (Interview, April 2016)

Reflective of this, immediately after Demirel had been elected to head the party, he was quick to distance his main rival Sadettin Bilgiç from the central party organs (Bektaş 1993, 155) and to block Bilgiç's brother Sait from being elected as his deputy chairman, in another strategy to counter Sadettin Bilgiç's potential to encroach on his power (Ahmad 1977, 237).[11]

Unlike Menderes, who did not heed the advice of others, Demirel was a political pragmatist tempered by self-discipline. He consulted others to decide on issues about which he lacked knowledge, but final decisions were always Demirel's, as Toptan recalled:

> As a leader he was happy to seek the counsel and input of other party members. He listened to information and advice; however, it was ultimately him who would make the final call on decisions and direction of the party. (Interview, April 2016)

İhsan Sabri Çağlayangil, who also served as minister in Demirel's governments, substantiated Toptan's observations: '[Through consultations] he figures out how each move will lead to different situations, and if one move leads to a solution what the next will be' (1990, 107). The net result of all this was that, while the party decision-making was not entirely a one-man endeavour, Demirel's own intuitions and proclivities played an important role in shaping policies. He was ultimately the arbiter of party policy, but also aware that he required the help of his subordinates to consult and implement his directives.

To actualise his control, Demirel employed a patronage policy that slowly increased his control inside the AP (Arat 2002, 93). This was most notable through his appointment of ministerial positions, which paralleled Menderes's methods in his early leadership over the DP. For example, when the AP won the elections in 1965, Demirel selected a cabinet comprised of loyalists, or used appointments to co-opt some of his critics in the party. His main rival Bilgiç and his faction were denied roles in the cabinet (Bektaş 1993, 156). Others, such as Aydın Yalçın, Ahmet Dallı, Ertuğrul Akça and Cevdet Önder, did not receive posts, as they were seen as too independently-minded for Demirel (Ahmad 1977, 239). Critics argued that the cabinet lacked the political acumen and personnel to lead Turkey to stability (Ahmad 1977, 239–40). The country faced major political and economic crises, and a cabinet with experienced politicians would have been better qualified to devise and undertake needed reforms. Yet, the configuration of an inexperienced cabinet was driven by Demirel's ambition to remain unchallenged as leader of the party and of government (Bektaş 1993, 156). The experience illustrates that, while Demirel was a pragmatist, there was a limit to his political rationality when devising the steps needed to hold on to the seat of power.

Members within his party were vocal in their criticism against both the weakness of the cabinet and his unilateral approach. Cevat Önder warned that Demirel's 'dictator-like behaviour' would not be tolerated. In a much more revealing insight into Demirel's leadership style and its anti-democratic outcome, Bilgiç, frustrated by the leader's unilateral measures, cautioned him: 'You must not have the ambition to be the sole person with the mentality "I know everything and I'll do everything", you cannot have this in a democracy' (quoted in Ahmad 1977, 239).

Demirel's increasing control negated his opponents the ability to act upon their criticism. The potential for challenge was removed altogether following the third party congress in 1966, when the opposing intra-party faction suffered an overwhelming loss (Bektaş 1993, 158). Demirel was re-elected with 1,239 votes opposed to his rival's 175 (Ahmad 1977, 242). The margin of victory emboldened him to undertake measures to capture greater control, by stacking the AP's Central Committee with loyalists (Bektaş 1993, 158). Operating under his direction, the committee became a mechanism to marginalise and expel his vocal critics (Ahmad 1977, 243), exemplified by the way in which Demirel dealt with Professor Osman Turan. Turan was expelled from the party for violating party discipline after his accusation against Demirel of 'sliding to the left' and serving his particular interests rather than the needs of the country (*Milliyet* 1967d, 1967b). By the end of 1966, the AP's central body was largely populated by the leader's personal clique. His control over party headquarters became strong enough to expel opponents with increased ease and silence his main rival Sadettin Bilgiç (Bektaş 1993, 159).

Unlike the CHP, the AP did not have an established tradition of strong centralised rule. Under Demirel, it was fast acquiring an oligarchic model mirroring that of its predecessors. Consistent with the views of Rahat and Sheafer, the stifling of intra-party democracy ran counter to the conditions necessary for a consolidated system (see Introduction). The absence of checks against Demirel's rule over the governing party severely undermined scrutiny of his political power.

The Re-emergence of Antagonistic and Confrontational Politics

The rise of a young leader in Demirel, coupled with an ageing İnönü and the military's efforts to promote a liberal regime, did not herald the emergence of harmonious politics between actors required for democratic consolidation, especially in an environment as volatile as Turkey's post-coup. Adding to this, the indecisive results of the 1961 election ended with a coalition between the AP, under leadership of its founding leader Gümüşpala, and İnönü's CHP (see Table 2.1). This first government survived six months before collapsing under pressure from the armed forces, for reasons discussed earlier. The following coalition, engineered by the High Command and once again led by İnönü, dissolved in 1963 due to the poor showing of the two minor parties in local elections. İnönü was forced to cobble together his third coalition, this time with independents.

Table 2.1 1961 Election Results

Political Party	Percentage of Votes	Parliamentary Seats (Total 450)
CHP	36.7	173
Adalet Partisi (AP)	34.8	158
Cumhuriyetçi Köylü Millet Partisi (CKMP)	14	54
Yeni Türkiye Partisi (YTP)	13.7	65
Independents	0.8	0

Source: https://www.tbmm.gov.tr/develop/owa/secim_sorgu.genel_secimler

This political instability was playing out as Turkey witnessed a major economic downturn and needed urgent fiscal reforms, while tensions over Cyprus left the country internationally isolated. Turkey's precarious situation required stability to navigate the country out of its financial woes and external predicaments. İnönü, although a cornerstone of strength and stability, was also a source of conservatism, which led to political inertia. The regular dilution of reforms, to which the party was committed, also undermined the CHP's electoral support (Ahmad 1977, 248–49).

This period also coincided with Demirel's ascendancy to AP leadership. Immediately after taking over the party, he undertook an aggressive approach towards the CHP-led government. He issued a direct warning that he would overturn the government as soon as possible, then openly planned to engineer the fall of İnönü with his famous order to his political party: 'Find the 226 (votes in parliament) to dispose the government' (Birand, Dündar and Çaplı 2016a, 136–37). Demirel's efforts succeeded, as İnönü's fiscal reforms were voted down in parliament, leading the former President to tender his resignation from the prime ministerial post.

Demirel's move further destabilised an already fragile regime and faltering economy. Turkish politics had now experienced the collapse of three coalitions between 1961 and 1965, and Demirel himself did not offer any sound or practical reforms (Ahmad 1977, 245). His strategy was largely about attaining control of the government, and the opportunity to implement much needed reforms was wasted due to the wrangling for political power, thus perpetuating Turkey's politically tenuous condition (Birand, Dündar and Çaplı 2016a).

This time around, however, the High Command decided against forcing İnönü into power for a fourth time. A caretaker government was selected to take the country to the elections of 1965, in the hope that results would solve the political impasse. It was comprised of members from four parties, with the AP as the senior partner and Demirel acting as Deputy Prime Minister.[12] The favourable composition meant that he was able to direct policy by leading cabinet meetings, ensuring that the government became his proxy (Ahmad 1993, 138).

This was soon evident when the interim government took Demirel's hard stance against his main political opposition. The government was quick to attack socialist elements, which Demirel publicly denounced as 'groups of perverted minds' (quoted in Ahmad 1977, 190). Stringent and repressive steps were taken against the political Left, and the government prepared an electoral law to prevent Leftist political parties from contesting the next general elections (Ahmad 1977, 191).

Similar to the way in which he was unable to tolerate challenges to his rule in the party, Demirel was likewise unwilling to accept a strong competitor in the multi-party arena. He understood that İnönü and the CHP would continue to mount the greatest challenge for the upcoming elections. The need to limit the CHP marked a return of hostility and conflict that had once defined the politics of the Bayar-Menderes era, further moving away from consensus and compromise-driven politics as well as eroding the hope for consolidation and political stability.

Reflective of this was Demirel's invasion of İnönü's home constituency of Malatya, with a mass of supporters, during the campaign trail of 1965. When he ran into a crowd of hostile pro-İnönü supporters unhappy with his pugnacious attitude, it caused a dangerous stand-off between the two large groups. Demirel's decision to campaign with an anti-İnönü crowd in the former leader's hometown was an extremely provocative move, given the already volatile atmosphere in the country and the animosity that existed between former Democrats and the CHP.

When met with resistance, rather than calming the crowds, Demirel declared to his supporters: 'If they want to kill me, let them. I shall die for the nation'. This heightened the potential for violence even further (*Time* 1965). Such regular displays of belligerence against his political opponents prompted President Cemal Gürsel to caution Demirel against following strong-arm tactics: 'We are not a mature nation. We take many roads, legal and illegal and sometimes dangerous, to exploit the people. I promise that no one ever again will have enough power to make the country turn back to the dark past' (*Time* 1965). This was a clear warning and reminder to Demirel of the dangers for Turkey in pursuing such an aggressive policy against the opposition. İnönü, having learnt his lessons from the past, also forewarned of the danger awaiting: 'The second grey horse is taking from the first and will no doubt follow the same path to destruction' (*Time* 1965).[13]

Demirel did not, however, heed the warning signs and made a habit of antagonising his main opposition, thus exploiting political and social divisions. In later interviews, he remarked that he was happy to link the CHP to the military and the 1960 coup in order to benefit electorally. He agitated public animosity against his opposition with statements such as: 'Whose army is it? The army is not the CHP's, it is the people's army'. He did so to draw direct links between the CHP and military tutelage. He concluded, in a gloating manner, doing so was indeed a good strategy to increase support for the AP (Birand, Dündar and Çaplı 2016a, 149).

These developments showed a leader not averse to making populist and false accusations to delegitimise his opponents for greater electoral gains. By linking the CHP with the military, Demirel was clearly portraying the main opposition as a threat to the political order. This was because Demirel 'had a much greater sense of how politics was going to shape up, how the nation "felt"; how people were going to react to events' (Interview with Sabri Sayarı, July 2016). Demirel was comfortable profiting from tensions in society for political gain, regardless of the deeper impact on the social fabric and democratic order. These early signs began to reveal a leader unwilling to exercise restraint to attain the seat of power.

During this period, the CHP officially adopted a socialist policy, the *merkez sol* or *ortanın solu* (left-of-centre or centre-left), as its official platform. This began to shed the party's elite image, marked by a slide towards the intelligentsia, workers, labour unions and Leftist student organisations (Akar and Dündar 2008). The party of state elites had transformed itself, now championing the rights of workers, new classes of urban poor and rural peasants. The already existing animosity between the major parties AP and CHP, which now adopted opposing political ideologies, infused greater distance between them.

It was therefore unsurprising that, when the CHP shifted to the centre-Left, Demirel, in his opportunism, was quick to declare a war between his centre-Right and individuals adhering to the Left. His attack against the Left now incorporated the CHP, allowing him to depict his main opponents as the subversive source of wide-spread unrest and a 'communist threat' to the nation (Ahmad 1977, 225). Drawing on society's inability to differentiate between socialist thought and communism, he often grouped anything and anyone of the Left as a communist and enemy of the Turkish state and people (Ahmad 1977, 191).

Demirel framed his electoral strategy largely upon a polarising anti-communist narrative to create an almost hysteria-like climate about the 'red threat', whilst also playing upon Turkish society's Islamic sentiment to delegitimise the CHP's embrace of the Left and ultimately attract the conservative and religious vote (Birand, Dündar and Çaplı 1994). For instance, during a campaign speech he declared that '[w]e are the enemies of communists [. . .] Communism will not enter Turkey because our population is 98 percent Muslim. We must be able to call ourselves a Muslim Nation' (quoted in Ahmad 1977, 191). His divisive campaign painted the entire Left, including the CHP and its supporter base, as atheists or non-Muslims. Inconsistent with the norms of tolerance and respect for pluralism required to uphold democracy, this exclusionary form of identity politics posed a danger to Turkey's democracy. Taking these extreme positions – that is, treating his opponents as an 'enemy of the people' and an existential threat – stood in direct opposition to the democratic norms necessary to not only consolidate but also safeguard democracy (Levitsky and Ziblatt 2018b). For this reason, his discourse was mirrored by the Right-wing's depiction of the struggle with the Left as a religious duty (Birand, Dündar and Çaplı 2016a, 180–81). Teasing out these divisive attitudes and engaging in partisanship increased polarisation to alarming levels, threatening the democratic order.

This began to worry even Demirel's caretaker coalition partner, Prime Minister Hayri Ürgüplü. In a fax to President Gürsel, Ürgüplü urged the President to intervene on the grounds that his coalition partner's campaign was having detrimental outcomes for Turkish society: 'The charges of leftism and communism which the Adalet Party leader and Deputy Prime Minister Demirel was throwing around in an irresponsible way are dividing the people into hostile camps. I urge you to intervene in order to save the country from being dragged into a civil war' (quoted in Ahmad 1977, 191).

Ürgüplü's warning came to fruition in Bursa, when the socialist party *Türkiye İşçi Partisi* (Workers' Party of Turkey, TİP) congress was besieged by a mob of 500 chanting 'death to the communists', resulting in physical assaults on the delegates (*Milliyet* 1965b). Subsequent investigations into the attack implicated Demirel's party. The state prosecutor accused the *Komünizmle Mücadele Derneği* (Association to Combat Communism), a reactionary organisation with ties to the AP, of organising the attack. The outcome of the investigation linked the command of the attack back to the AP hierarchy (*Milliyet* 1965a). Although attacks against socialists were not new in Turkey, under the caretaker coalition they had become bolder and more frequent (Ahmad 1977, 226). This episode further illustrated that Demirel was not averse to using extra-parliamentary measures and violence against both political and ideological opponents.

It was becoming apparent that the same hostility which had characterised the CHP-DP relationship in the previous decade was once again exhibited in inter-party relations, albeit now with an ideological dimension. The political climate was aptly summed up by journalist Mehmet Ali Birand: 'The Turkish political arena now had replaced the old CHP-Democrat conflict with a new conflict. A hostility that would occupy the country for years to come, between the Left and Right' (quoted in Birand, Dündar and Çaplı 2016a, 149).

The significance of Demirel's style of leadership for undermining political and social harmony cannot be understated. It was similar to Menderes in the way in which it sat opposed to key norms of tolerance, compromise and forbearance. As the lure of the prime-ministerial post became stronger, it naturally brought Demirel's understanding of democratic politics and inter-elite relations to the fore, even if it was to the harm of democracy. This early period was telling of the authoritarian leadership style that he would embody when he was able to form a government in his own right.

Demirel in Power

Under the growing tension, the elections of 1965 were won decisively by Demirel, with the AP receiving close to 53 percent of the vote, in comparison to the 28.7 percent of İnönü's CHP (see Table 2.2). The public had become weary of the unstable coalition governments, and the turn to the Left could not offset the CHP's loss of popularity. Under Demirel the AP assumed power for the first time after only a handful of years since its inception.

Table 2.2 1965 Election Results

Political Party	Percentage of Votes	Parliamentary Seats (Total 450)
AP	52.9	240
CHP	28.7	134
MP	6.3	31
YTP	3.7	19
Independent	3.2	1
Türkiye Işçi Partisi (TIP)	3.0	14
CKMP	2.2	11

Source: https://www.tbmm.gov.tr/develop/owa/secim_sorgu.genel_secimler

Although Demirel was willing to stoke popular unrest for political gain, he was mindful of the military. If he had taken the same stance as Menderes had against the military, the democratic system would not have lasted as long as it did. Demirel, in this sense, exhibited greater awareness of his limits *vis-à-vis* the armed forces (Cizre 1993). Along with İnönü, Demirel was instrumental to balancing the military-civilian relationship, acting with sensitivity to the political reality. Demirel's pragmatic and steady nature helped build positive relations with the generals, which alleviated much of the unease emanating from the military (Cizre 1993). The political leaders operated in a tense environment throughout this period in order to appease certain ranks in the armed forces who believed that the institution was outside of civilian control. To this, Demirel declared in later years:

> This was always our problem [with the military], and they felt comfortable with relaying their dissatisfaction. Yet, if the officers were unhappy with the direction of the country they should have taken off their uniforms and joined a party. (Birand, Dündar and Çaplı 2016a, 211)

Demirel's pragmatism in handling the military was the central reason why the AP was able to form a government without interference of the armed forces (Ahmad 1977, 192), and in this sense he showed himself to be prudent.

In terms of civilian opposition, his intolerance was like that of his predecessors in the 1950s. Demirel's strongman nature over the AP was evidence of his style of governance. At the head of a single-party government, his uncompromising stance against the opposition persisted unabated, much like that experienced during the Menderes period. The CHP continued to be presented as a communist threat to Turkey with the use of his slogan *Ortanın solu, Moskova yolu* (Left of centre is the road to Moscow), purposefully used to provoke an anti-communist climate and arouse Islamic sentiment in the community, against the party and its supporters (Ahmad 1977, 251; Tachau 1991, 108).

Exploiting religion for political gain began to fuel the rise of religious reactionism, which became a concern for state authorities, particularly Turkey's intelligence agency. An article published by the socialist magazine *Ant* in 1968 (see Özkan 2017) declared that '[n]ational intelligence reports on the threat of [Islamist] reactionism' had been provided to Demirel. The report from the intelligence agency noted that Demirel continued to 'deceive the ignorant masses by exploiting religion to gain votes' and that he remained indifferent to 'the danger of [religious] reactionism which is threatening our constitutional regime'. Effectively, Demirel was forewarned of the danger of his actions by the intelligence services, yet he was unwilling to cease exploiting religious sentiment for political gain.

Relations with the opposition were also returning to the dysfunction experienced under Menderes. The AP's parliamentary majority, through harassment and physical intimidation, made it extremely difficult for minor opposition parties to undertake their representative role. For example, Behice Boran, a parliamentarian from the Workers' Party, TİP, attempting to give a speech in the Assembly, was drowned out by Demirel's parliamentarians' cries: 'Throw her out of the country to Moscow, to Moscow' (Ahmad 1977, 198). On other occasions, this manifested itself as physical attacks against parliamentarians of the TİP: Çetin Altan, a journalist and legislator for the party, was attacked and severely beaten, and another TİP colleague was pistol-whipped whilst trying to defend himself from an attack by AP representatives for voicing his support for and defence of Nazım Hikmet, one of Turkey's most renowned Leftist poets (Birand, Dündar and Çaplı 2016a, 171).

Along with physical attacks, legislative developments of the period demonstrated that Demirel seemed to abandon institutional forbearance by using his majority in the Assembly to pass laws designed to remove his critics on the Left, in an effort to consolidate his electoral position. Testament to this, an Amnesty Law was passed to ensure the release of all political prisoners, including imprisoned Democrats such as former president Celal Bayar. However, the amnesty was not extended to prisoners charged under Articles 141 and 142 of the penal code for disseminating 'communist propaganda' (Ahmad 1977, 196). Countless artists, academics, writers and journalists were persecuted for violating these laws and remained in prison, whilst those from the Right were released under the amnesty (Frey 1975, 52). Further indication of the growing hysteria against the Left was the prosecution of a fifteen-year-old student for writing an essay on Atatürk and Lenin. The government's policy against the Left was as though 'the country was faced with an imminent threat of subversion and revolution', yet 'nothing could have been further from reality', as Ahmad revealed (1977, 196–97). Although they were not a breach of the law, these actions illustrate Demirel's exploitation of prerogatives for ideological and partisan purposes.

This was further underlined when the TİP's capacity to enter the legislative body was radically reduced with the amendment to the Electoral Law's 'national remainder system'. The law was originally created to increase representation and block a single-party monopoly of parliament, and it became the main reason why the TİP was able to enter parliament with fourteen seats in the 1965 elections (Dodd 1969, 183). The act did, in fact, increase the pluralism of the representative body by strengthening the opportunity for minor parties to get into the Assembly (Karpat 1972, 364), making it more democratic. However, after the amendment to the Electoral Law, the TİP was only able to gain two Assembly seats after the 1969 elections, although it received a similar percentage of votes at the 1965 election (see Tables 2.2 and 2.3). The changes engineered the opposite outcome for Demirel: the AP's overall vote had dropped in the 1969 election; nevertheless, the adjustment to the law allowed Demirel to increase his number of seats in the Assembly (see Table 2.3).

Demirel's efforts were a key illustration that he did not prefer deepening democracy, which, as Diamond notes, is making structures more liberal, representative and accessible (1999, 2008). He utilised his majority in the Assembly as a political weapon against his ideological opposition, but also to increase his legislative hold. The frustration that this caused within the Left threatened to increase the growth of violent and extremist socialist movements, as *The Economist* warned in 1968 (32):

> By abolishing the 'the national remainder system' [. . . he] will severely cut down the four smaller parties and perhaps exclude them from parliament altogether [. . .] The main target of this law is the extreme left-wing Turkish Workers Party [. . .] the Workers Party [TİP] is indeed the only legal home for extreme left-wingers. Subversion thrives in political frustration, and whether the Workers Party is subversive now, it is much more likely to be tempted in that direction if its parliamentary outlet is largely stopped [. . .] Moreover the Justice Party already has an absolute majority in parliament [. . .] Mr İnönü has opposed this new electoral law because at the moment he fears Mr Demirel's intentions [. . .] He alleged the Justice Party intends to use the new law to maintain itself in power indefinitely.

The passage captures the outcome that the new electoral law would have for democracy, with a telling prediction of the tensions that it would stir inside the country. This warning was also expressed in parliament by the leader of the TİP, Aybar: 'If this law passes, unrest in the country will rise to another level'. He urged Demirel to repeal the government's decision by stating: 'Otherwise you will be responsible for whatever befalls our democracy' (quoted in Ahmad 1993, 145). Thus, the electoral changes, in the eyes of the Left, were viewed as symptomatic of an illiberal government closing the system to socialism whilst using its anti-communist crusade to tighten its grip on the country. This suspicion was expressed by the TİP and the main opposition leader İnönü, as noted in the quote from *The Economist*.

This pushed Leftist elements to pursue undemocratic means to influence political developments. Some former TİP parliamentarians argued that, since the Assembly no longer was a true representation of Turkish society, only a revolution would cure the country's problems (Landau 1970, 159). In response, radical factions of students who supported the TİP and advocated direct revolution began to set up the *Türkiye Devrimci Gençlik Federasyonu* (Revolutionary Youth Federation of Turkey, Dev-Genç) and various other splinter groups, beginning to partake in violent action (Mango 2004, 66–67).

As mentioned in the Introduction, Linz and Stepan have noted that extreme elements exist in all systems, but the prevalence of key democratic norms in consolidated systems alleviates the possibility of them posing a threat to the democratic order. In fact, 'extreme polarisation can kill', as differences become viewed as irreconcilable (Levitsky and Ziblatt 2018a). Therefore, Demirel imposing high political costs on the Left steered it to take more reactive measures and to resort to violence.

Reflective of this, the situation in the country was dire: street politics slowly transformed into revolutionary, guerrilla-like activities against the government and the state (Bal and Laçiner 2001; Mardin 1978; Sayarı 2010). Leftist groups engaged in occupying university buildings, bank holdups and kidnappings, which quickly spread across the country, thereby putting greater pressure on an already fragile regime. In response, students on the Right mobilised to physically counter the activities of the Left. The government established a riot squad named *Toplum Polisi* (Community Police), which specifically was used to target Leftist activism in universities (Zarakolu 2013). Emboldened by Demirel's use of religious sentiment against the Left, the Right-wing papers openly urged militants to 'be ready for jihad', and street battles began to erupt with cries from the Right to 'attack in the name of Allah' against Leftist demonstrators (Birand, Dündar and Çaplı 2016a, 180–81).

The level of street activism in the late 1960s created a permanent atmosphere of crisis and an element of instability, with both sides caught in a retributive cycle (Ahmad 1977, 199–201). The parliament was rejected as a solution, largely due to the polarisation that existed amongst the politicians themselves. The Assembly and Demirel were seen as instigators, partners to the ever-increasing societal tensions in the eyes of the Left (Birand, Dündar and Çaplı 1994).

Demirel, however, failed to acknowledge the violence from his end of the political spectrum. Rather, he turned his attack against the constitution, which he deemed to be the central problem behind the Left's militancy (Özbudun and Gençkaya 2009, 17). According to Demirel, the existence of social unrest and radicalism was the result of a constitution that provided 'too much freedom' (Ahmad 1977, 199). He proposed to repeal many civil and political rights; to increase the powers of the executive, namely his position;

and to repeal the autonomy given to civil society and state institutions (Arat 2002; Özbudun and Gençkaya 2009, 17).

Demirel's plans to amend the constitution were criticised by the political establishment for the potential to cause more instability:

> It would mean the Constitution and today's Republic will be left without a foundation. The amendments are proposed in the full knowledge that it will open the doors to crisis in the regime [. . .] taking the Turkish nation backwards. (*Milliyet* 1968)

For Demirel, the wide-ranging checks and balances on an elected government were against the *milli irade* (national will) (Arat 2002, 99). The constitutional order stood opposed to his majoritarian views of democracy, as Ersin Kalaycıoğlu asserted in an interview with the author:

> In 1961, Turkey came up with one of the better constitutions of the twentieth century, but it was not accepted as a legitimate document by some and resulted in the ongoing problem of the government of the period acting extra-constitutionally on most occasions. This is despite the fact that it was a constitution that kept them in power [. . .] The argument against the constitution was simply because it was made by the military, it was not legitimate. Yet, the same constitution allowed Demirel to come to power, and his government expected everybody else to act within the constitutional limits except for themselves [. . .] This was the behaviour of the *Adalet Partisi* during the 1960s [. . .] The 1961 Constitution stipulated that the popular will was to be shared with the agents of civil society, bureaucracy and the state, which was unacceptable to Demirel owing to his majoritarian views of democracy. This was despite the fact that the 1961 Constitution was in line with the rule of the law and the liberal ideals that were practiced in Germany, Italy and Austria and other countries. Still, Turkey's centre-Right rejected it because they enjoyed the majority and therefore assumed they were the only party who should promote the interests of the nation, unobstructed. (Interview, April 2016)

As Kalaycıoğlu pointed out, Demirel did not believe that an elected government should be forced to govern with impediments. Demirel opposed the norms required to uphold mechanisms of accountability and attacked the constitution to reduce the checks on his government. This is the reason why 'there was resentment against the constitution by Demirel. He regularly complained about the excessive checks and balances on his power and looked to erode its legitimacy', as Ergun Özbudun asserted (Interview, April 2016).

Unable to make the required constitutional changes – as he did not have the required number of parliamentary representatives – Demirel instead exploited the rising 'danger' posed by Leftist groups to justify instrumentalising his legislative prerogatives to repress the rising opposition. The government took to constraining labour union activism, which had become an effective opposition against Demirel; in turn, it bolstered the legislative support of civil society groups aligned with his administration. The law was aimed at strengthening the pro-government Right-wing union confederation of *Türkiye İşçi Sendikaları Konfederasyonu* (Confederation of Turkish Trade Unions, Türk-İş) and curtailing the activities of the TİP-aligned union confederation of *Türkiye Devrimci İşçi Sendikaları Konfederasyonu* (Confederation of Progressive Trade Unions of Turkey, DİSK) (Ahmad 1993, 146; Birand, Dündar and Çaplı 1994, 2016a, 198). The objective was to eliminate smaller unions and dramatically reduce the resistance of DİSK:

> [The law] prohibited the existence of unions unless they represented at least one third of those working in a particular workplace. Most important, however, was the explicit and public admission by the government spokesmen that the amendment was going to be used to wipe DİSK out of existence. (Işıklı 1987, 320)

Supporting one group of unions over the other sowed greater discord in a country already experiencing polarisation between supporters of Right and Left. The DİSK's heightened militancy and the government's decision to directly support Türk-İş caused the union sector to experience a rapid rise in political activism (Cizre-Sakallıoğlu 1992, 59–60; Mello 2007, 221; Toprak 1996, 95). Open rivalry amongst pro-government and Leftist union confederations further entrenched organised labour and its supporters in an uncompromising cycle of animosity towards each other as well as the state (Sural 2007, 974).

In direct response against the law, the DİSK staged a vast and spontaneous demonstration on 15 and 16 June 1970, which succeeded in paralysing the entire Istanbul-Marmara region. Demirel, unable to restore order, turned to the military to stop the workers and swiftly imposed martial law. By the end, four people were dead, over one-hundred had suffered injuries, and 150 protestors had been arrested (Birand, Dündar and Çaplı 2016a, 198). The unwillingness to compromise with the opposition had created stronger disharmony. Similar to Menderes and Bayar's strategy to repress anti-government protests, Demirel's reliance on the military also invited the institution to take a more active role in the politics of the country (see Ahmad 1977, 176–211). His growing hardline decisions exposed his unwillingness to work through the democratic processes or foster a climate of compromise and consensus, as was necessary to stabilise the crisis. In failing to do so, Demirel ultimately brought military intervention one step closer.

İnönü, in contrast to Demirel, demonstrated behaviour more in line with democratic norms of compromise to contain the violence. He issued a fiat to his party to contain the polarisation and the spectre of a major political crisis. The communiqué stressed avoiding speeches that could be interpreted as against the national will, as well as contentious phrases. Rather, the party was instructed to shape their campaign discourse around 'reform from the economic and social point of view', describing their opponents on the Right as 'social conservatives' instead of 'anti-Atatürk' and 'reactionary' (Ahmad 1977, 259–60).

Polarisation and the Increasing Spectre of Military Intervention

Despite İnönü's efforts, running tensions between the two opposing groups continued unabated. Under a disintegrating political climate, Demirel was victorious in the 1969 elections, delivering his second victory, albeit with a 6.4 percent drop in the AP vote. Yet, while Demirel received a reduced number of votes, the parliamentary majority increased, owing to the amendment to the electoral law, as discussed earlier. For example, in 1969 the AP received 46.5 percent, which resulted in 256 of the 450 parliamentary seats (see Table 2.3). This was a substantial drop from the 52.9 percent that the party had achieved in 1965, which had provided it with 240 parliamentarians.

Table 2.3 1969 Election Results

Political Party	Percentage of Votes	Parliamentary Seats (Total 450)
AP	46.5	256
CHP	27.4	143
Güven Partisi (GV)	6.6	15
Independents	5.6	13
MP	3.2	6
Milliyetçi Hareket Partisi (MHP)	3.0	1
Birlik Partisi (BP)	2.8	8
TIP	2.7	2
YTP	2.2	6

Source: https://www.tbmm.gov.tr/develop/owa/secim_sorgu.genel_secimler

The increased majority did not shore up Demirel's position or provide stability. Turkey continued to suffer increasing levels of economic and political instability due to the Prime Minister and brought his government under further siege. Within this paralysis, the opposition was not in a mood to compromise in order to help him – an attitude that aggravated conditions (Ahmad 1977, 201). The general economic decline continued rapidly, and he lost the confidence of businesses (Ahmad 1977, 245).

At this point, Demirel was also forced to deal with tensions in his own party (Szyliowicz 1975, 195–97; Birand, Dündar and Çaplı 2016a), with the mounting political crisis mirrored inside the AP. After his 1969 electoral victory, Demirel took bolder steps against his intra-party opponents, resulting in a purge of Bilgiç's supporters in local party organisations (Bektaş 1993, 163). He denied all opponents positions in the new cabinet and filled it entirely with loyalists. This sparked a major revolt, whereby Demirel was sent a memorandum signed by seventy-two AP parliamentarians, criticising his authoritarianism inside the party (*Milliyet* 1970c). Instead of compromising, he brought members of the dissenting faction before the party's disciplinary board. Within the month, two leading names of the intra-party opposition, Ethem Kılıçoglu and Cevat Önder, were expelled (*Milliyet* 1970g). This was followed by the dismissal of another four AP lawmakers,[14] triggering the resignation of eight politicians from the party's *Genel İdare Kurulu* (General Board of Directors) in protest (*Milliyet* 1970a).[15]

The growing crisis resulted in a forty-one-member group, led by Bilgiç, to mount a challenge by bringing a motion in the Assembly, accusing Demirel of peddling his influence in government for corrupt practices (Ahmad 1977, 247). The dissenting faction in a formal declaration outlined that their decision was in response to Demirel installing a single-man rule and exploiting the AP for personal interest and gain (Bektaş 1993, 162). Their inability to inform policy or challenge Demirel forced members of his own government to bring on a vote of no confidence against him. By allying with the main opposition, the CHP, the dissenters gathered enough votes to bring down Demirel's government – an unprecedented event in Turkish political history. However, President Cevdet Sunay was quick to manage the crisis and provided Demirel with the right to form a government again, with a coalition of independents and five parliamentarians from *Birlik Partisi* (Unity Party, BP) (Bektaş 1993, 162).[16]

After regaining his prime ministerial post, twenty-six AP parliamentarians from the dissenting faction were purged by Demirel before the Fifth General Congress, this time including Bilgiç (*Milliyet* 1970b). The remaining opposition, frustrated and without an avenue to challenge their leader, resigned and joined their twenty-six former colleagues who established the *Demokratik Parti* (Democratic Party, DP) (Mango 2004, 66; Ahmad 1977, 246–48).[17] This development is yet another example of the birth of a political party due to a rupture resulting from the party leader's autocratic character, displaying parallels to the DP under Menderes.

The removal of his challengers solidified Demirel's hegemony, underscored by his re-election, with an overwhelming 98 percent of votes, in the 1970 party congress (Arat 2002, 89).[18] The disproportionate result was an opportunity to carry out additional expulsions of members charged for damaging party unity. However, it was Demirel who came to suffer accusations that he was 'liquidating honourable members' from the AP (*Milliyet* 1970d). As a result of the large number of defections and removals, Demirel was without a majority in parliament, which became the leading cause of instability for his government (Ahmad 1977, 247).

The crisis inside the AP reflected the increasing volatility of the broader political environment. Weakened, the Prime Minister was eclipsed by events, forcing him into the political background. Mainstream media was directly calling for his resignation, stating that he 'didn't have the ability to lead Turkey' (*Milliyet* 1970h). Sensing Demirel's precarious position, revolutionary groups increased their activity in the hope to bring down his government. This placed the democratic regime in a dire position and increased the spectre of a military intervention to contain the growing crisis.

Fakih Özfakih, a CHP parliamentarian at the time, acknowledged that during this period . . .

> Turkey needed a saving force. Who was going to do this? In the middle there was the Assembly. Yet the Assembly couldn't get to the bottom of these incidents. The police? The police response would usually be, 'It was members from this side, that side. . .' But they could not respond to questions of 'Why isn't there a stop to the spilling of blood?' And in time certain individuals from the very top rungs of the state with whom we had close relations started remarking that Turkey truly needed an intervention and that the spilling of blood on the streets had to be stopped. (Birand, Dündar and Çaplı 2016a, 206)

Similarly, politician Nihat Erim charged:

> Professional agents, trained, armed and directed from outside Turkey, were able to transform some leftist student organizations into urban guerrilla units which carried out kidnappings, bombings and political killings. Openly proclaiming that they were Marxist-Leninist and Maoist, young terrorists managed to turn some of the universities into communist arsenals and strongholds, preparing for the establishment of a Communist People's Republic in Turkey. With extreme rightists, on the other hand, forming paramilitary organizations modeled after Hitler's stormtroopers and preparing for a Holy War against 'communists' and the government unable to control the situation, the country was on the brink of civil war and/or a communist takeover. (1972, 249)

As Erim highlighted, by January 1971 Turkey was in a state of growing chaos: universities were prevented from functioning, students robbed banks and attacked American targets, and factories were increasingly paralysed by ongoing strikes. In return, Rightist militants bombed the homes of university professors critical of the government, with certain Islamist groups openly attacking Atatürk and Kemalism. By the beginning of March 1971, Demirel was incapable of dealing with the civil unrest. His lack of tolerance for opposition both internally and in government, as well as his steps to repress or marginalise opponents, slowly brought democracy to a breaking point. It was clear that, rather than consolidate his rule, he created conditions which made governing impossible.

In light of this, President Cevdet Sunay lost confidence in Demirel and personally expressed his desire for him to withdraw from politics, 'for he [Demirel] had brought the entire establishment against him' (quoted in Ahmad 1977, 247). Sunay, frustrated by Demirel's refusal to acknowledge his failings, conspired with the military generals to end the instability (Birand, Dündar and Çaplı 2016a, 219–21). While the President could only insist, it was the military that finally brought Demirel's reign to an end. Sunay's corroboration with the armed forces against the civilian government would also have direct parallels to Demirel's conduct as President in the coming decades – a point to be discussed in Chapter 5.

On 12 March 1971, Demirel received a strongly worded memorandum from the military that held his government and the Assembly responsible for the political crises plaguing the country. The memorandum declared:

> The Parliament and Government through their sustained policies, views and actions, have driven our country into anarchy, fratricidal strife, and social and economic unrest [. . .] The future of the Turkish Republic is therefore threatened. (quoted in Özbudun 2000a, 33)

The military's letter had ultimately placed the political situation squarely on the shoulders of Demirel and the parliament. With no alternative, the Prime Minister resigned from his post to allow the military to administer the country (see Birand, Dündar and Çaplı 2016a, 223–90).

Demirel protested against the armed forces' actions and deemed them as contrary to the national will and as an attack on democracy. This was true in many respects; yet, after six years of running the government, it also showed that he was unwilling to take responsibility for the role that his illiberal and authoritarian policies towards his opponents had played in bringing the country to its crisis point. Demirel's authoritarian leadership achieved the opposite: it helped disintegrate both his rule and the democratic regime.

His reliance on polarising statements, his measures to physically intimidate opposition and his legislation to restrict the opposition was keeping in line with Menderes and Bayar before him. The parallels, however, should not only be confined to those leaders. Demirel was couched firmly within the broader culture of Turkish leadership:

> Menderes was the uncontested leader of his party. When he was removed and executed, the *Adalet Partisi* led by Demirel filled his political base. Demirel was an unknown bureaucrat at the time, but in time this all changed, and he later came to be referred to as *baba* (father). So what we end up with is this direct line of strongmen leaders in Turkish politics from the *Eternal Chief* (Atatürk) to the *National Chief* with İnönü, and then we ended with Demirel becoming *baba*, the father [of the nation] following them. (Interview with Cengiz Çandar, October 2016b)

Demirel filled the void left by Menderes's execution, as a representation of the centre-Right, with a domineering leadership style. His attempts to be the grand leader, the self-anointed patriarch of the nation as *baba*, propelled Turkish democracy down a similar path. He represented a continuity anchored by the undercurrent of authoritarian style of rule played out in a democratic system. This should not be merely restricted to Menderes and Bayar, as identified in the above quote. Demirel's attitude to leadership was representative of leaders such as Atatürk and İnönü before him. Yet, the unopposed grand leader within a multi-party context could not be sustained without shunning norms including tolerance toward opponents, compromise and consensus-driven politics and respecting the institutions of democracy. His leadership contrasted with the principles and processes of democracy that were designed to protect and sustain these institutions.

Conclusion

The political climate of the 1960s was, in many ways, different from the years under the Menderes and Bayar administration. The military provided itself with tutelary powers over politics to prevent a repeat of the Democrat era. The resulting constitution also instilled liberal ideals complemented with greater checks to counter any authoritarian tendencies of a future government. New political actors replaced the vacuum left empty by the Democrat Party's closure, and class-based political ideologies permeated both politics and society.

Yet, this chapter underlined how the continuity of authoritarian leadership culture once again shaped the political outcomes of the post-1960 era. Like the leaders before, Demirel was not interested in inclusive plural politics or the practice of tolerance in his party. He took steps to consolidate his rule, with dismissals becoming a common feature. Towards the end of the decade, the AP, once a broad umbrella of interests, resembled a party that was run by Demirel and his loyal clique. He was no Menderes or Bayar, but his leadership style became a repeat of the DP experience.

Authoritarian traits came to define also his rule as Prime Minister from 1965 to 1971. As far as the new parameters allowed, Demirel mirrored the same intolerance against his opposition in the Assembly and in society, similar to Menderes and Bayar. For Demirel, government should not be obstructed by autonomous institutions and civil society. As a result, he regularly abandoned forbearance to exploit his prerogatives in order to attack political and societal opposition. Similarly, his attempts to delegitimise the constitutionally imposed constraints on his power portrayed a leader with an understanding of democracy limited to the ballot box. Yet, this was also questionable. The change to electoral laws should draw queries into his respect for a fair electoral process.

These measures and his divisive discourse inflamed an already tense atmosphere, and he persisted in exploiting this atmosphere for his personal electoral gain, which then spilled over into society. The streets came to be coloured with a permanent atmosphere of crisis. Over time, this developed into running battles between opposing groups, which Demirel encouraged, none more evident than in the links between his party and Right-wing groups such as *Komünizmle Mücadele Derneği* or his exploitation of religious sentiments against his opponents.

Indeed, Demirel's positive contribution to democracy was small; his negative impact was considerable. The nature of his rule fragmented his party, paralysed government and divided Turkish society. The era demonstrated that a leadership failing to act in a responsible democratic manner could not simply be overcome with constitutional engineering or military tutelage. Leadership was once again a key factor for democracy failing to gain a deeper foothold, and also for the crisis that befell Turkey. In the following chapter, I will illustrate that the developments after the coup of 1971 followed a similar trajectory. To understand the reasons for the re-emergence of this pattern, I will show that the central responsibility once again remained with the leaders of the period.

Notes

1. The MBK was dissolved after the 1961 elections, but its members retained their permanent positions in the Senate (Ahmad 1993, 129).
2. For a detailed discussion of the *Adalet Partisi*, see Ahmad (1977), Levi (1991).
3. İnönü was favoured and chosen to lead the government, as he was a respected former military figure, which proved key to stemming the support within the military for another coup.
4. Forced from the military after his first effort, Talat was given the death penalty after his second failed attempt at a coup.
5. Demirel was forty years of age when he became Chairman of the AP.
6. Demirel was elected chairman of the AP, with 1,072 votes while his main rival, Sadettin Bilgiç, received 552 votes (Ahmad 1977, 235).
7. The *Tanzimat* was a period of wide-sweeping reforms guided by European ideals and systems introduced into the Ottoman Empire to bring forth a fundamental change. This naturally included the modernisation of the Ottoman state, most notably in the bureaucracy and the military (Tittensor 2014, 29–34).
8. The party came to include a wide variety of individuals: secularist intellectuals and reactionary Islamists, officers and the anti-military, former Democrats and those new to politics. This all resulted in instability and factionalism.
9. The three major factions in the party were made up of retired officers led by Party Secretary General Şinasi Osma and the members of the *Cumhuriyetçi Köylü Millet Partisi* (Republican Peasants' Nation Party) who had merged with the AP and former Democrats (Ahmad 1977, 234).
10. Demirel was pragmatic enough to realise that the military could not be brought under civilian rule and opted for the virtual autonomy of the armed forces. Although these measures ensured military oversight in decisions, it also allowed the AP to win the confidence of the high command and relative autonomy in government.

11. Sadettin Bilgiç was a former hardline Democrat who had served in Menderes's Parliamentary Investigation Committee in 1960 and had acted as chairman after Gümüşpala's death, until the general congress.

12. The other three parties which contributed to the government were *Yeni Türkiye Partisi* (New Turkey Party, YTP), *Cumhuriyetçi Köylü* (Republican Peasants' Nation Party, CKMP) and *Millet Partisi* (Nation Party, MP).

13. This was a clear reference to the AP's emblem of the horse, which had been taken from the Democrats to illustrate that the former was a direct inheritor of the latter's legacy.

14. The expelled lawmakers included the following: Ahmet Hikmet Yurtsever, a senator from Bingöl; Ekrem Dikmen, a representative from Trabzon; Vedat Önsai, a representative from Sakarya; and Kadri Erdoğan, a representative from Sivas (*Milliyet* 1970a).

15. Sadettin Bilgiç, Faruk Sükan, Talat Asal, Cihat Bilgehan, Mehmet Turgut, Yüksel Menderes, Ali Naili Erdem and Ömer Lütfü Hocaoğlu (*Milliyet* 1970a).

16. The *Birlik Partisi* amended its name in 1973, to *Türkiye Birlik Partisi* (Unity Party of Turkey).

17. In the 1973 elections, the *Demokratik Parti* received 11.9 percent of votes, and this provided the party with forty-five representatives in the Lower House. It was the third party in terms of the vote percentage and the fourth party in terms of the number of representatives. The party disbanded in 1980 due to defections and poor electoral results in the subsequent elections (Ateş 2012).

18. Demirel received 1,425 votes to 28.

3

1971–80: YEARS OF STRIFE – THE BATTLE BETWEEN SÜLEYMAN DEMIREL AND BÜLENT ECEVIT

Introduction

After Demirel was forced to resign in 1971, the military restructured the political arena in order to prevent a recurrence of the political and societal dysfunction of the late 1960s. The junta-backed 'above-party' government made wide-ranging changes to the constitution, which repealed much of its liberal character. It was hoped that the amendments would foster political stability by providing greater powers to the executive, as a safeguard against a repeat of the previous period.

During these years Demirel maintained his role as the head of the AP while, on the other side of the political divide, changes were taking place inside the CHP. A young social democrat, Bülent Ecevit, replaced the ageing İsmet İnönü and brought with him hope that there could be a liberalisation within the party. As the leaders of the two most dominant parties of the era, Demirel and Ecevit alternated six times as Prime Minister between 1974 and 1980. This was a significant indicator of the electoral popularity of both men and the competitiveness of the party system. In this sense, it was a break from the single-party governments that Turkey had largely experienced up to this point. Nonetheless, constitutional restructuring and changes in the political landscape did not resolve government paralysis and political violence, which accelerated between 1976 and 1980 and saw more than 5,000 people lose their lives. The generals determined that the situation had totally

escaped the control of the leaders and undertook another military intervention on 12 September 1980.

This chapter will demonstrate that the political developments of the period
were largely in response to both Ecevit and Demirel's leadership and a critical
reason for understanding the democratic failure of this period. Although the
military maintained its tutelary position, it could not exert substantive influence over civilian politics and determine political outcomes: if it had, civilian
rule might not have slowly resulted in the 'complete erosion of governmental
authority' between 1973 and 1980 (Tachua and Heper 1983, 25).

I begin the chapter by highlighting Demirel's opportunism in exploiting
the draconian conditions of the military rule between 1971 and 1973 against
the Left and his unwillingness to acknowledge his role in the crisis of the
1960s had led to the country's impasse in the preceding decade. This chapter will also broach how Ecevit's capture of the CHP after removing İnönü
through an intra-party democratic process failed to offer a break in Turkey's
traditional leadership style. The remainder of the chapter then demonstrates
the competition between the two leaders, in their race to seize power, and
their reluctance to value democratic norms worsened the growing paralysis
and enflamed the violence between their supporters. Evidence of this were
their attempts to control the branches of the state to wield against each other,
thereby acutely reducing the institutional capacity of the system to deal with
political problems. The leaders' unwillingness to make democracy a normative
preference in their competition further weakened an already fragile democratic system, while revealing that constitutional engineering alone would not
necessarily lead to democratic stability or consolidation.

Background

The military intervention of 1971 did not carry out a total restructuring of
the multi-party regime, as was the experience of the 1960 coup. The changes
repealed many of the civil liberties afforded by the 1961 Constitution and
strengthened the power of the executive (Özbudun 2000b, 9). Priority was
given to the 'restoration of law and order', which led to the repression of
groups, organisations and individuals viewed as Leftist. Writers, academics
and activists, including politicians, were rounded up, jailed and tortured, and
organisations on the Left were prohibited, whereas activists from the Right

were allowed to persist. During this period, the military junta tried over 10,000 individuals, overwhelmingly activists from the Left (Birand, Dündar and Çaplı 1994).

With the country under martial law, the generals engineered an 'above-party' government, drawn from an Assembly dominated by conservative, Right-wing and anti-reformist actors, who were tasked with carrying out the legal and political restructuring (Ahmad 1993, 1977). The forty constitutional articles amended were targeted for their liberal nature and viewed as generating the country's ills (Birand, Dündar and Çaplı 1994). Özbudun and Gençkaya (2009, 27) placed the amendments into three categories:

> (1) Curtailing certain civil liberties in conjunction with restrictions of the review power of the courts; (2) strengthening the executive, particularly by allowing the legislature to grant it law-making powers; and (3) increasing the institutional autonomy of the military by excluding it from review by civilian administrative courts and the Court of Account.

The scope of amendments covered nearly every institution of the state: the unions, the press, radio and television, the universities, the Council of State, the Constitutional Court, the National Assembly and the Court of Appeals. The regressive nature of the changes ensured 'that there is no going back to the period before 12 March' (Ahmad 1993, 152).

Demirel during the Military Rule (1971–73)

Demirel had declared that the coup was against the will of the nation; yet, ever the pragmatic politician, he seized upon the opportunity presented by the military's anti-Left crusade. He showed no hesitation in applauding or collaborating with the commanders to bring about the political and constitutional changes he desired (Cizre 1993, 113). For Demirel, as outlined in the preceding chapter, the autonomy of civil society and state institutions as a counterweight to the Assembly and executive were against the 'national will'. He was quick to side with the junta so as to repeal the checks on the executive by autonomous agencies in order to 'place democracy on a secure foundation' (Arat 2002, 99).

This came about because the military regime did not go so far as to dissolve the parliament and assume power directly, which enabled Demirel's party to maintain its large representation and the Assembly to maintain its pre-coup composition (see Table 2.3). The above-party government, under veteran CHP politician Nihat Erim,[1] was tasked with making amendments to the constitution: Demirel's AP provided five of the ministers, with most of the other cabinet roles filled by technocrats and independents.

Nonetheless, Erim made his rule dependent on Demirel's support.[2] This was surprising given that Erim did not need to have conciliatory relations with parties, as the backing of the generals would ensure that his government was protected and that policies would be implemented. Erim's appeasement ensured Demirel a high level of influence from the beginning (see Ahmad 1977, 290–92) and allowed Demirel to direct the above–party government from the outside, which had a large bearing on the nature of the constitutional amendments that the government was tasked to undertake. As such, the repeal of the liberal articles of the constitution were in line with Demirel's wishes (Ahmad 1977, 117–19; Cizre 1993; Özbudun and Gençkaya 2009, 27–28). When presented to parliament, the repressive political climate meant that there was no public discussion and that parties such as the CHP were pressured to vote in favour. This gave Demirel the ability to impose favoured solutions on the politic, by taking advantage of the threat of force by the military (Özbudun and Gençkaya 2009, 28). Thus, constitutional change was accomplished with no genuine negotiation or compromise among the political parties.

Demirel continued to exploit these conditions to ascertain advantages and to disadvantage his opposition.[3] The most critical illustration of his anti-democratic measures was marked by the military court trial of three Left-wing activists – Deniz Gezmiş, Yusuf Aslan and Hüseyin İnan – during the military junta. The death penalty given to the three young activists was vastly disproportionate to their alleged crime and politically motivated (Sayarı 2010, 201). When the Assembly was given an opportunity to overturn the ruling of the military court, both İnönü and Bülent Ecevit rallied the CHP to vote against the ruling, whereas Demirel mobilised the AP and other parties on the Right to vote for the men's execution, refusing İnönü's personal pleas (Ünlü et al. 1998). As the vote was being taken, he turned to face the members of his party and shouted: 'Raise your hands! Raise them!' Then he and his colleagues began shouting: 'Three from us, three from them!' This was in reference to the execution of Adnan Menderes and two of the other *Demokrat Parti* politicians (Temelkuran 2006).

This course of action brought about greater tension between Demirel and a large segment of Turkish society, which would ultimately fester with the return to civilian politics:

> Their [Gezmiş, Aslan and İnan's] deaths failed to have the deterrent effect which it was supposed to create. Instead, capital punishment only served to create *heroes* and *martyrs* of such prominent radicals as Deniz Gezmiş for future generations of Leftist militants. (Sayarı 2010, 201)

Nonetheless, Demirel viewed it as an opportunity to 'get even' with the Left and to provide another significant blow to his political and ideological opposition.[4] As a result, the period of military rule from 1971 to 1973 was a triumph for a man who insisted that political reforms had to have priority over socio-economic ones. Reform simply denoted the marginalisation of the Left and repealing the autonomy given to civil society and state institutions.

With Demirel at the centre of political developments, the commitment to deepen democracy by making formal structures more liberal, accountable and representative, as necessary for consolidating a system, was not a priority (see Introduction). In fact, Demirel and the military's efforts ensured once again that Turkish society was placed at an arms' length of politics. Although he declared the military's decision to intervene as undemocratic, Demirel overall was more than happy to manipulate the conditions to gain an advantage over his rivals – namely, by bypassing democratic processes to impede checks and balances and by pushing reforms devoid of democratic ideals.

The Rise of Bülent Ecevit: The Left's Mirror to Demirel

After the transitional period under the army's tutelage, general elections were allowed to resume in 1973. The electoral result was a blow to Demirel, as he failed to win back his position. It was his bitter rival, the CHP, which came out first. Its *merkez-sol* (centre-Left) ideology – revitalised by a young new leader, Bülent Ecevit, who had replaced the long-serving İnönü in 1972 after an intra-party vote – secured the CHP's win. The peaceful transition in leadership from İnönü to Ecevit, it must be noted, was an extraordinary development in Turkish political history. The decision displayed İnönü's democratic spirit at the time, as office dependency is a potent obstacle to democracy: the distinction between owning and leaving office is a critical determinant of whether a political leader is democratic, as Keane observed (2009). İnönü held elections, then conceded power gracefully after losing, thus showing his values by abiding by the democratic process. This was a point of exceptionalism within the prevailing culture of political leadership in Turkey. He oversaw the transition to party politics and the experience of intra-party leadership renewal through a democratic process, an anomaly when assessing leaders and democracy in Turkey. For this reason, he effectively stands above the rest when assessing the multi-party period.

In stark contrast, Demirel continued his heavy-handed rule over the AP, despite the disarray within his party before the intervention, the indignation of being forced from office by the military and losing an election. In fact, his actions during the post-memorandum period strengthened his position over his party (Ahmad 1977, 316–17). Demirel ensured that the same tried and tested loyal subordinates continued to occupy the AP's executive body, which insulated him from any challenge (Bektaş 1993, 163–67).[5] His monopoly on power was so great that Demirel was the sole nominee for the AP's leadership elections. This tight control was observable throughout the decade, manifesting in results that were highly disproportionate. In one example, he received a resounding 1,358 out of 1,376 votes in the 1976 party congress (*Milliyet* 1976a).[6] This is consistent with the observation of Isakhan that, in the absence of free and fair competition, democracy becomes a façade for those in power (2012). The internal party elections were essentially a sham, as Demirel believed that his rule had to be absolute, according to former minister Ali Naili Erdem:

> Süleyman Demirel could never accept a challenger to his leadership. There was never a consideration to produce a second, nor third, nor even fourth person in charge. He always wanted to be the one and only person at the top. (quoted in Bektaş 1993, 166)

In other words, Demirel was a leader very much in the mould of his past and current contemporaries in Turkish politics, who endeavoured to retain their seats at whatever the cost to their party, and even the country. His grip on party leadership in the face of electoral losses, party disaffections and resignations demonstrated Demirel's lack of deep conviction for democratic values.

The backgrounds of Demirel and Ecevit could not have been more contrasting: Ecevit came from a prominent and well-educated family, and his father had served as CHP parliamentarian (see Tachau 2002). In this sense, he was part of the republican establishment. After having served both as journalist and as İnönü's interpreter, he was selected as the CHP candidate for Ankara in the 1957 general elections (Dündar and Akar 2015, 58) and chosen to serve as a minister in all three coalition governments between 1961 and 1965.

Despite his prestigious political and intellectual background, Ecevit was very much a man of the working and lower classes and staunchly against appeasing the military during the 1971 coup, which led to the intra-party rift with the ageing İnönü (Gaytancıoğlu 2014, 164–66).[7] He demonstrated remarkable empathy for the working masses and peasants in the country. In some ways, his role in the cabinet eroded the traditional distance between politics and society, which endeared him to the Turkish masses. Serving as the Minister for Labour, he piloted through parliament a bill which legalised workers' strikes, a first in Turkish history, and he later engineered his party's turn to the left-of-centre, socialist platform (Mango 2004, 68–69). This unwavering backing of the labour movement, unfortunately, also directly implicated him in the polarisation that was to come (Akar, Dündar and Özcan 2004). Nonetheless, more so than the leaders before him, Ecevit did make concerted efforts to liberalise Turkish society. The workers and citizens occupying the lower classes in Turkish society were never far from his politics of social equality.

However, Ecevit's empathy towards the working class did not translate into strong democratic tendencies inside the party. Upon his ascendancy to the post of General Secretary, Ecevit displayed the traditional model of Turkish political leadership. His rise to the number-two position and the CHP's adoption of a centre-left direction, which he engineered, caused a major rift with the conservative faction within the CHP. A seventy-six-person bloc, led by Turhan Feyzioğlu, denounced the direction as anti-Kemalist and attacked Ecevit (Ahmad 1977, 256). In what was seen as the battle to succeed İnönü, Ecevit utilised the powers of his position to harass Feyzioğlu and his supporters and blocked their activities, which included meeting their local constituents (*Milliyet* 1967c). With İnönü's support the party statute was amended to accord complete control to the party executive, thus making it easier to deal with critics (*Milliyet* 1967a).[8] This drew accusations that Ecevit was employing the same autocratic practice as Menderes over the DP and that the changes constituted a clear violation of the Political Parties Law (Ahmad 1977, 257).[9] Feyzioğlu and seven others from the anti-Ecevit faction resigned immediately after the statute was changed (Ahmad 1977, 257). In parting ways, Coşkun Kırca, a member of the resigning group, warned that those who had helped Ecevit dispose of the opposing faction would pay a similar price: 'One day you will be purged also' (quoted in Akar and Dündar 2008, 124). Proving to be a prescient statement, others, like Celal Kargılı, were later hauled in front of the CHP's disciplinary board and dismissed for criticising Ecevit and the party's direction (*Milliyet* 1970f, e).[10]

Early on there were rumblings that Ecevit would not tolerate opposition to his decisions and that the actions against his main opponent Feyzioğlu were symptomatic of the broader party leadership culture:

> The CHP went through an internal struggle; this internal factionalism between who was going to succeed İnönü had really reached extreme heights. Ecevit won, Feyzioğlu lost and resigned to form his own party [. . .] This was the character of factionalism inside the CHP. Ecevit was from the Left, whereas Feyzioğlu was from the Right-wing faction. This episode exposes another characteristic of Turkish politics. In healthier democratic settings, Left-wing and Right-wing factions can and do co-exist within a party. In Turkey, they don't, they are expelled by the winning faction. (Interview with Sabri Sayarı, July 2016)

This underscores that Ecevit, despite his democratic overtures and measures to provide greater rights to workers, was not willing to tolerate threats to his aspirations to lead the party. The treatment meted out to the Feyzioğlu faction was a reminder that authoritarian tendencies continued to shape understandings of leadership, despite the generational change coming through the CHP.

This period led to a total of forty-eight lawmakers resigning in retaliation against Ecevit and the centre-Left direction of the party (*Milliyet* 1967e).[11] The departing members announced that they had formed the *Güven Partisi*

(Reliance Party, GP) and unanimously elected Feyzioğlu as the party leader.[12] Again, Turkish politics witnessed the formation of a political party from the fallout of party-elite dysfunction and autocratic party leadership. In 1945, critical opposition within the CHP had led to fragmentation and the formation of the DP. Almost a generation later, the same experience brought virtually the same response, which suggested that little had changed in the practices of leaders.

The resignations also weakened CHP's power in parliament, with its numbers in the Lower House reduced from 135 to 102 and in the Senate decreased from 47 to 32 (*Milliyet* 1967e). The CHP's representation in government dropped to 22 percent in the Lower House and 21 percent in the Senate. In turn, it increased the leverage of Demirel, whose *Adalet Partisi* held 240 seats in the 450-seat Assembly and 66 out of the 150-seat Senate.

Nonetheless, this weaker position in parliament did not diminish Ecevit's standing inside the party. With Feyzioğlu and his faction forced to abandon the CHP, Ecevit was the undisputed number two, and his faction became a dominant force. He personally initiated an Extraordinary Congress in 1970, where his supporters won the majority of the critical posts, which ensured that only İnönü stood between Ecevit and complete control over the party (Ahmad 1977, 260).

As General Secretary, he enabled the local party organisations to have greater influence in the party decision-making processes. This slowly shifted the power from the central apparatuses to the peripheral regional bodies (Ayan 2010, 203; Güneş-Ayata 2002, 105; Bektaş 1993, 86). On the surface it was seen as the democratisation of the party, yet it was merely a political manoeuvre to erode the power base of the old guard, as Ecevit's appeal and popularity at the grassroots was substantial (Bektaş 1993, 85).

The strategy went a long way in helping him ascend to the seat of party leadership and end the thirty-four-year reign of İnönü in an intra-party vote in 1972 (Bektaş 1993, 85–86). The removal of İnönü marked the first time in the CHP's history that the dominance of the party leader was broken. At the age of forty-two, Ecevit captured the seat that had once been occupied by Atatürk. Although a watershed for intra-party politics in the CHP, Ecevit's leadership style did not mark a change in how the party was run, as it essentially retained its authoritarian structure.

Despite a display of democratic overtures after winning the leadership (Bektaş 1993, 87), Ecevit showed himself to be a leader extremely uncomfortable with the fact that he had to work with others to pass decisions. According to Sabri Sayarı, he 'did not get along with others in the party and was not an agreeable person as the leader' (Interview, July 2016). Those who did not provide unquestioned loyalty were forced to move on. This was made apparent by the resignation of his close ally, Kamil Kırıkoğlu, who was central to Ecevit defeating İnönü. Kırıkoğlu resigned from the position of General Secretary along with twelve members of the *Merkez Yürütme Kurulu* (Central Executive Board, MYK) in response to Ecevit's management style (*Milliyet* 1973b). A journalist who had close ties to the CHP, Cengiz Çandar, substantiated Sayarı's assessment that Kırıkoğlu had difficulty working alongside Ecevit:

> Despite Kırıkoğlu being the architect of the strategy that helped remove İnönü, he fell out with Ecevit because there was no teamwork to Ecevit's leadership, because Ecevit wanted to control all the decisions and the direction of the party once he was in power. (Interview, October 2016b)

Orhan Tokatlı's observations as a political analyst of the period substantiated this assessment further:

> Ecevit is very suspicious. He always keeps people at a distance. In fact, he does not view people favourably [. . .] no one can work alongside him for long. They will work for a little period then leave and others will come. (quoted in Akar and Dündar 2008, 294)

Much like the leaders who had come before him, he did not want to accommodate potential challengers or tolerate criticism, and the 'regular change of people around him was to lessen the possibility of open criticism and consolidate his control', as Ersin Kalaycıoğlu asserted (Interview, April 2016).

Ecevit's aloof style and desire for supremacy ensured that high-profile resignations continued apace, illustrated by the resignation of Kemal Satır after thirty-six years of service.[13] Following Feyzioğlu, Ecevit was quick to oust potential challengers such as Satır to protect his position. In a letter to İnönü, Satır described a sustained campaign by Ecevit to expel him, which culminated in disciplinary proceedings against Satır for speeches that he had given at the CHP congress. This forced his resignation, as he was unwilling to work in the party under repressive conditions (*Milliyet* 1972b). Like Feyzioğlu, upon leaving the CHP Satır announced that he was forming a new political party under the name of *Cumhuriyetçi Parti* (Republican Party, CP). Following these high-profile departures, 500 CHP members also resigned to join Demirel's AP by the end of 1972 (*Milliyet* 1972a).

Watching the developments in this early period, İnönü, in an extremely telling assessment of his former protégé, lamented to his close colleagues:

> He [Ecevit] is identical to Menderes. When emotion and ambition are mixed together, it will drag a person to disaster. May Allah protect this nation. (quoted in Dündar and Akar 2015, 88)

İnönü's concerns were well-justified. Changes made to the party constitution in 1976 enabled Ecevit to institutionalise his control. The amendments eroded the autonomy of the local party branches by centralising power in the party headquarters. This was a reversal of his earlier supposed democratisation of the CHP, which allowed regional branches greater input in the party's decisions; a move that had ultimately helped him unseat İnönü. Since the central body existed largely under the tutelage of Ecevit, decisions taken by the leader were no longer subject to debate, paving the way for their direct implementation. In doing so, the amendments provided Ecevit with greater powers to silence dissent (Bektaş 1993, 93). It was yet another important amendment which blocked the avenue that Ecevit himself had used to climb from the seat of General Secretary to party leader. The change reduced the significance and power of the General Secretary in the party (Musil 2011, 35); thus, the position became subordinate to Ecevit and removed any spectre of a challenge to the leader by the party's second-in-command (Bektaş 1993, 93).[14] As a result, Ecevit was able to maintain a tighter grip over the party and stay in a position to reject any checks on his decisions (Tachau 2002, 115).

Through these increased powers, Ecevit dominated intra-party appointments. Those whom he viewed as potential challengers – such as Deniz Baykal, Besim Üstunel and Ahmet Yücekök – were marginalised or purged from the party's Executive Council (Akar and Dündar 2008, 294; Bektaş 1993, 91). Others whom he suspected to conspire against him – such as Orhan Eyüboğlu,

Ali Topuz and Hasan Esat Işık – were co-opted into his cabinet so that he could keep a closer eye on them (Akar and Dündar 2008, 294).

The party's Disciplinary Board was utilised to dismiss parliamentarians and local mayors who refused to demonstrate total obedience to Ecevit or his vision. Lawmakers such as Necati Aksoy, Çetin Şenses and the mayor of Ankara, Vedat Dalokay, were dismissed during their terms, accused of breaking party discipline (*Milliyet* 1975, 1977, 1979a). Others, such as Hamdi Özer, who was summoned in front of the board, quit before he could be dismissed, citing Ecevit's authoritarianism as the basis for his resignation (*Milliyet* 1979b). Ecevit's control also caused major tensions inside the party: during the CHP Congress in 1976, a group incensed by the highly centralised way in which the party was being directed and by the inability to influence delegations disrupted the meeting with violence (*Milliyet* 1976b).

In response to these incidents, Ecevit's autocratic character became more pronounced. Against party protocol, he began preparing the Executive Council's list without consulting the provincial chairmen of the party (Kınıklıoğlu 2000; Bektaş 1993, 96). Important figures, such as İnönü's son Erdal, noted the hardening of Ecevit's character the longer his leadership lasted:

> When I met him again in the late 1970s, I realised how much Ecevit had changed. After the battle that he had endured during that period [the Güneş Motel incident in 1977] and in government, I realised at that moment he had become an entirely different person [. . .] How had he changed? He was more determined. He spoke with certainty. His treatment of others was more severe. (quoted in Akar and Dündar 2008, 253)

As the decade wore on, his experiences had made him increasingly determined to remain the head of the CHP and transformed him into an outwardly authoritarian leader. By the end of the decade, any discussion against his leadership was completely muzzled (Akar and Dündar 2008, 294). These experiences sadly revealed that, instead of providing a break from the traditional character of rule, Ecevit continued his predecessor's leadership style over the CHP, as poignantly noted by Çandar:

> İnönü was the uncontested leader of the CHP for a very long period, but when Ecevit replaced him, it did not mean that he brought a change in leadership or

intra-party democracy, or greater democratic institutionalisation. He replaced İnönü and became another İnönü. He became the *şef* [chief] of the party. (Interview, October 2016b)

Naturally, this also caused unrest against his rule (Bektaş 1993, 97); as a result, he began to take even harsher measures to seek out potential areas of dissent. Ecevit ordered surveillance on branches suspected of fostering intra-party opposition against him, which were then written up as reports provided to him and dealt with accordingly (see Akar and Dündar 2008, 287–94).

Although there was a generational change, in the end he continued the authoritarian structure of the party that enabled him to counter opposition and criticism and hold on to leadership (Bektaş 1993, 100–3). Ecevit's leadership style, which tended to hinder intra-party democratisation, was an indication that he was not a leader with a democratic character. In fact, the authoritarianism of his rule resembled, according to Kalaycıoğlu, a 'one-man Führer type of party leader' (Interview, April 2016).

This was evident in the way in which the CHP was personalised under Ecevit. From Atatürk to İnönü, the party had always resembled a 'personality party', and under Ecevit's leadership this tradition was repeated. His personal image and persona, rather than the party itself, was emphasised with the slogans *Umudumuz Ecevit* (Ecevit is our hope) and *Halkçı Ecevit* (the people's Ecevit), as well as the fabled heroic image of *Karaoğlan* (a kind of Robin Hood folk hero) that was attached to him (Sayarı and Esmer 2002, 53; Tachau 2002, 115).[15] The party's supporters began describing themselves as *Ecevitçi* (Ecevist), which was very much in line with identifying oneself as an *Atatürkçü* (Ataturkist or Kemalist) during Mustafa Kemal's reign over the party. After the Cyprus incursion in 1974, he was transformed into a patriotic and military hero, with official images adorning him as *Kıbrıs Fatihi Mücahit Ecevit* (Ecevit the Mujahedeen, the Conqueror of Cyprus) (Dündar and Akar 2015, 96).

Ecevit's capture of the CHP meant that the two most popular parties of Turkey were ruled by ambitious and authoritarian leaders. As Ecevit stood for the Left and Demirel represented the Right, the authoritarian nature of their leadership was also couched within a polarised ideological dimension, which would have serious repercussions for Turkey's democracy. Their struggle was symbolic of Turkish political parties, and politics in general, which continued to operate largely autonomously from the public sphere, acting in the interests of their leaders rather than on behalf of national interest. The lack of intra-party democracy ensured that political developments would remain largely hinged on the authoritarian personalities of leaders, made evident by the return to competitive politics.

The Return to Civilian Politics

The 1973 election results marked Ecevit's rise from party leader to political leader. The CHP won the largest number of votes with 33.3 percent of the tally, yet the 185 Assembly seats fell short of the 220 required to govern as a single party (see Table 3.1). Demirel's AP was the second-largest party with 29.8 percent of the popular vote, resulting in 149 seats. However, the 16.7-percent swing against Demirel marked his continued decline since the 1969 elections. In the words of DP parliamentarian Cevat Önder, 'the people had eliminated Demirel' (*Milliyet* 1973a). In a democratic party culture, this outcome would have meant a change in leadership; not so in the Turkish context. The AP was Demirel's, and he had no desire to remove himself from the seat of leadership. Rather, it spurred him on to take an even more aggressive stance towards the other parties in order to safeguard his diminished political power. This meant that he would continue to take an uncompromising position towards his main political rival, Ecevit. Hence, Demirel moved further to the Right.

Table 3.1 1973 Election Results

Political Party	Percentage of Votes	Parliamentary Seats (Total 450)
CHP	33.3	185
AP	29.8	149
Demokratik Parti (DP)	11.9	45
Millî Selamet Partisi (MSP)	11.8	48
Cumhuriyetçi Güven Partisi (CGP)	5.26	13
MHP	3.4	3
Independents	2.8	6
Türkiye Birlik Partisi	1.1	1

Source: https://www.tbmm.gov.tr/develop/owa/secim_sorgu.genel_secimler

The persisting economic instability and growing societal tensions of the time drove interest groups, journalists and academia to push for a grand coalition between the two major parties. Despite the practical necessity and appeals from the public, both men resisted forming a partnership due to their competing political ambitions.[16]

As the leader of the party that received the most votes, Ecevit had the power to form the government. In the absence of obvious parliamentary allies and facing a hostile, conservative Assembly, Ecevit managed to build an unlikely coalition with Necmettin Erbakan's Islamist-oriented *Millî Selamet Partisi* (National Salvation Party, MSP).[17] Although a highly surprising choice, this was done out of necessity due to his isolation in parliament:

> Ecevit, in 1973, after finishing first, could not find a natural coalition partner, so he formed a coalition with an Islamist like Erbakan. That was an interesting decision by Ecevit. Why would you do that? If you look at coalition theories, you are supposed to form a coalition with your neighbouring parties, not with those at the other end of the extreme. But that was the only party that was willing to form a coalition with the CHP. If Demirel had shown interest, that would have been a good solution for the country. Yet, we ended up with an unnatural partnership. It also showed that Erbakan was an opportunistic politician, driven to grab at any chance to come to power, and he grabbed that. (Interview with Sabri Sayarı, July 2016)

Yet, the coalition ended abruptly, as sharing power was not in Ecevit's nature. Ecevit's 1974 decision to send troops to intervene in Cyprus lifted the Prime Minister's prestige. To capitalise on this sudden surge in his popularity, he dissolved the coalition with Erbakan on 18 September to call early elections. However, the CHP did not have the allies in the Assembly to vote in favour of early elections. Politically isolated and out of government, the decision to end the partnership underscored the acuteness of his desire to rule single-handedly, made even more irrational because Ecevit dominated the coalition with Erbakan (Ahmad 1977, 340). Ali Topuz, a former CHP parliamentarian of the period, asserted that this pursuit for dominance ultimately drove Ecevit to make one his greatest political mistakes (Akar and Dündar 2008, 212).

By December 1974, Ecevit had exhausted all avenues to go to an early poll, and Demirel was given the right to form a government and looked for anybody who would deliver him the majority. He forged a partnership with Erbakan – who once again demonstrated his opportunist character – in an 'anti-Left' union of Right-wing parties called the *Milliyetçi Cephe Hükümeti* (National Front, MC).[18] The coalition was rounded out by Feyzioğlu's *Cumhuriyetçi Güven Partisi* (Republican Reliance Party, CGP) and the ultra-nationalist *Milliyetçi Hareket Partisi* (Nationalist Movement Party, MHP) led by Alparslan Türkeş, one of the officers who had instigated the 1960 coup.

Demirel's attainment of the seat of power emphasised the scale of Ecevit's isolation in parliament. It further highlighted that the decision to go to early elections was rooted in his blind ambition to govern as a single party, despite the political realities:

> Ecevit became too full of himself after the Cyprus incursion. There were posters of him on buses depicting him as *Karaoğlan* and *Kıbrıs Fatihi*, and so he made this very strategic mistake of dissolving the coalition and going back to new elections. Why would you do that if you were already in power? He ultimately thought that the electoral momentum was with him, but Demirel was a politically very shrewd actor. He saw what was happening and thwarted Ecevit's aims by not going to new elections. Ecevit as a result was left standing naked. Demirel took this opportunity to form a coalition with Erbakan [Feyzioğlu and Türkeş]. In the end, it was a very critical mistake by Ecevit in 1974, costing him the prime ministership. (Interview with Sabri Sayarı, July, 2016)

Ecevit's impatience paved the way for Demirel to return to power and regain the advantage over Ecevit. However, the National Front coalition did not bring any stability to the country. It served to inject more tension into an already polarised society along the Left-Right political spectrum. The coalition was created as a *Sola Karşı Sağ Cephesi* (A Rightist Front against the Left) and to stop the rise of Ecevit (Ahmad 1977, 346). The name chosen for this political union reminded observers of Menderes's *Vatan Cephesi* (Motherland Front) of 1958, which was Demirel's attempt to isolate his main political rival. A member of the MHP's Central Body at the time, Taha Akyol, further underlined this:

> The National Front coalition was created, not with the rationale to become an inclusive government or to lower the tensions in the country. It was purely

formed to counter and stop Ecevit and the rise of the Left. It was based simply on a sentiment to create a barrier against the Left. The outcome of this saw those millions of citizens who supported the Left and Ecevit view us as their enemy [. . .] The National Front's principal mistake was that it was a front, acting with the [particularistic and defensive] rationale of a front. (quoted in Birand, Bila and Akar 1999, 47)

The guiding reason for Demirel to create the National Front was to restrict the Left's participation in politics. Its narrow and reactionary character made it incapable of stabilising the tense political climate and implement much-needed reforms, illustrating that the Demirel-led government had little tolerance for its main opposition and no desire to interact with them as legitimate political actors. This flagged a coalition that was not going to act in a manner consistent with measures to deepen the practice of democracy or respect pluralistic and liberal principles.

For this reason, Ecevit and the supporters on the Left were once again forced to operate under a repressive government. Demirel during the late 1960s had already proven his hostility towards the Left (see Chapter 2) and during the military-sponsored governments. In power again, he boldly declared that he and his party were 'opposed to every type of left (meaning the left of centre CHP)', and the reason to 'form a government was in order to fight against the Left and communism' (quoted in Ahmad 1977, 346). Such developments were dangerous, not only because of their anti-democratic character, but also for casting a wide and ambiguous net 'in which anything or anybody the Right described as Leftist was open to physical attack' (Ahmad 1981, 18; Birand, Bila and Akar 1999).

Demirel openly legitimised repression by framing the conflict between Left and Right as 'a struggle between traitors and (his) patriots' (quoted in Ahmad 1981, 19). When street violence between the Leftist and Rightist militants resulted in daily killings, it was therefore not surprising to hear Demirel declare: 'You will never make me say that nationalists (Rightists) are killing people' (quoted in Mango 2004, 76). The slogan popularised by pro-government media – 'Demirel in Parliament, Türkeş in the streets' – aptly described the division of labour between Demirel and his junior coalition partner against their political opponents (Ahmad 1981, 20).

The coalition's populist narrative couched in the division between the 'virtuous people' versus 'the dangerous other', whereby the other could be anyone that did not agree or support the Right-wing coalition, showcased a leadership that operated against the required democratic norm of tolerance, which was mirrored by their supporters. Since the battle against the Left was portrayed as protecting the country from a 'communist threat', the Front's actions emboldened the conservatives and religious reactionaries against anyone whom they deemed Leftist. It was therefore no accident that the upsurge of Right-wing violence correlated with Demirel forming the coalition government, as experienced in the previous era. This would not be the only period in which Turkey experienced a government regularly creating a climate of fear among the opposition, as will be discussed further in Chapters 6 and 7.

The State as a Partisan Instrument

The relatively even representation in parliament created an environment where neither leader could dominate. This, nonetheless, did not discourage the practice of governments attempting to control the state and the bureaucracy for political gains, similar to Menderes (see Chapter 1). The sitting government's marginalisation, discrimination and purge of postings inside the state organs became a regular occurrence (see Gourisse 2013). Officials who did not support Demirel's coalition, or were seen to harbour sympathy for the Left, were dismissed and replaced with supporters (Ahmad 1981, 19; Gourisse 2013). The lack of institutional restraint was not unique to Demirel-led coalitions. When in government, Ecevit, too, distributed bureaucratic posts to CHP supporters and other members of small Left-wing groups (Gourisse 2013).

Under Demirel this appeared to be more systematic. The state and government were partitioned between the coalition partners to centralise political power and exercise against political opponents (Ahmad 1993, 165; Gourisse 2013). Demirel took over the *Anadolu Ajansı* (Anatolian Agency) and *Türk Radyo ve Televizyon* (Turkish Radio and Television, TRT). This ensured a monopoly and total control of all media,[19] which he did not hesitate to exploit in his personal 'anti-communist' and anti-Ecevit crusade (Ahmad 1977, 351). The Ministry of Education was transformed into an instrument of the Right-wing MHP, which allowed it to extend control over schools and universities. As a result, 'the minor parties exerted a political influence totally out of proportion to their electoral support and representation in the Assembly' (Interview with Sabri Sayarı, July 2016). Partitioning the state and ministries in line with the patronage networks of the coalition partners contributed to significant government dysfunction. İlter Turan has noted (Interview, April 2016):

> The government looked like a confederation of ministries. Each partner had their own domain, and the others did not interfere. For example, if a ministry were in the Nationalists [MHP] hands, they would just fill it up with Nationalists. The other coalition partners would tolerate that. The ministries in the hands of *Millî Selamet* would be filled up with their people, and on it went. So, you ended up with a highly fragmented government. It was no different with the state apparatuses, which were treated accordingly, in the same manner. This led to the rapid exhaustion of public resources and essentially worsened the violence.

As Turan's interview reveals, while the fear of Ecevit kept the Front coalition together, the mobilisation of ministries and state institutions for partisan interests rendered it impossible for the government to function in a cohesive and efficient manner. In this sense, like Menderes and Bayar, the political leaders of the period also identified the state's institutions as areas that should equally fall under their control (see Chapter 1). Their seizure reveals how the state was slowly entrenched in the political crisis and transformed into a site for radicalised mobilisation.

Demirel was also complicit in placing sympathisers in critical positions within Turkey's national intelligence agency, the *Millî İstihbarat Teşkilatı* (National Intelligence Organization, MİT). Throughout this period, the MİT hired AP and MHP followers, while those identified with Left-leaning views, or those who were critics of Demirel's conservative-nationalist ideology were marginalised or purged from the organisation. Under AP-coalition governments, MİT officers were used as an extension of the Front to sabotage the activities of the CHP and its leadership (see Akar and Dündar 2008, 228–36).

In preparation for the battle with Leftist groups, 'commando camps' were established by the Ministry of Youth and Sports, as well as the Ministry of National Education, to provide training to the MHP-aligned militants on the Right in order to combat the Left's revolutionaries (Ahmad 1981, 20–21; Birand, Bila and Akar 1999, 47–48). Benefitting from access to the Customs and Monopolies Ministry, supplies of medicine, arms, ammunition and explosives were brought into the country to assist with the illegal operations of the Right-wing militants (Gourisse 2013, 134).

The influence over institutions also allowed the coalition government to shield the Right from prosecution (Gourisse 2013, 133). With most political murders of Leftists, the police never seemed to make arrests, and if arrests were made, perpetrators often escaped from prison, creating an atmosphere of immunity suggesting that elements within the Turkish state were colluding with the government (Birand, Bila and Akar 1999; Ahmad 1993, 172).[20] Giving insight into this troubled state of affairs, Çetin Yetkin, a public prosecutor of the period, reflects on his experiences:

> In cases where Right-wing militants were investigated for murders of Leftists individuals, the accused individuals would normally have alibis provided to them from numerous state hospitals. For example, at the date and time of the murder the certificates would indicate they were undergoing an operation, or they were giving blood and things of this nature. There were health reports of this kind, and every time we attempted to investigate whether these reports were authentic, all our attempts were blocked and hampered [by the authorities]. (quoted in Birand, Bila and Akar 1999, 48)

It became clear that the increasing number of assassinations and acts of violence from the Right could not be addressed without exposing the government, which would mean ceding power, something that Demirel refused to entertain. The zero-sum view of politics pushed the government to abandon restraint and encourage violence so as to stave off challenges to its authority. The protection of militants provided these groups and individuals with greater confidence to create a climate of terror and intimidate opponents (Ahmad 1993, 168; GSNSC 1982, 147).[21]

This is not to deny that elements of the Left also played a role in the violence. In fact, during his short-lived coalition with the MSP, Ecevit provided amnesty to all political prisoners from the 1971 coup. This was specifically devised to free vast numbers of Leftists incarcerated during the military junta. Many former Leftist prisoners subsequently regrouped, establishing new and highly efficient revolutionary organisations, while others fled to the guerilla camps in Jordan and Syria, run by the Palestine Liberation Organization (PLO), to undertake further training in the use of explosives and weapons. By the mid-1970s, nearly thirty-five different Leftist militant groups were active in Turkey. These groups were responsible for various criminal acts, including a systematic campaign of assassinations directed at officials whom they held responsible for the deaths of other Leftists. The most significant of these murders was former Prime Minister Nihat Erim in 1980 by the *Devrimci Sol* (Revolutionary Left), in retaliation for the death penalty received by Deniz Gezmiş and his two colleagues in 1971, as discussed earlier in this chapter (see Bal and Laçiner 2001; Sayarı 1985, 2010).

In fact, many CHP deputies harboured sympathy for the radical Left and formed links with Leftist revolutionaries. Çandar illustrated this with the revelation that Kamil Kırıkoğlu, when he had been the CHP's General Secretary, gave him refuge in his house while Çandar was on the run from the authorities. This enabled him to escape, attend PLO guerrilla training camps in the Middle East and then make his way back to Turkey:

> Kamil Kırıkoğlu was a very close friend to us [Leftist activists]. When I was a political fugitive in the early 1970s, I hid in his house. Nobody thought that I would hide in such a high-profile person's house. That is how I saved my skin and fled the country to the Middle East. After the amnesty, when I went back to Turkey, until Kırıkoğlu's death we regularly would see each other. He saw me as his confidant, who I was of course, and I saw him as mine. He hid and protected me. We had a very special relationship. (Interview, October 2016b)

While the CHP did not have formal operational ties to Leftist revolutionary groups, in the manner of Demirel and his junior coalition partner MHP to Right-wing militants, there were nonetheless established links and sympathies between these actors within the CHP hierarchy, and presumably also at the lower rungs of the party.

Yet, as the Front government grew more authoritarian and as he was backed into a corner, Ecevit also pushed for further support from Leftist movements. Although never official up to that point, the ties with the Left were formalised in the late 1970s. The CHP and Turkey's largest and most powerful union confederation, the socialist and radical, DİSK announced a working alliance. The purpose of their partnership was to topple Demirel's coalition and bring Ecevit back to power (Ünlü et al. 1998). The strategy of using the DİSK to mobilise on the streets and the CHP in the Assembly became a successful movement against Demirel (Birand, Bila and Akar 1999). This, however, was not only controversial, but also anti-democratic, as members of the DİSK and their networks were regularly implicated in violence and as DİSK rallies were known for carrying the anti-system chant *Tek yol devrim* (The only way is revolution). This further deepened tensions and drew the ire of the military (Ünlü et al. 1998).

Like Demirel, the decision to form an alliance with such politicised groups had endowed the Left's criminal activity with an air of legitimacy and immunity, just as their opponents would enjoy under the coalition governments.[22] Ecevit's act served to drive political tensions higher, and the extra-parliamentary measures moved the competition for power outside the realm of politics. At no time in Turkish history was the political arena so divided and polarised as it was in the 1970s. As Sayarı explained, the leaders were ultimately exploiting violence for their benefit:

> The thing is that political violence became a political football during this era. The leaders were playing with it. Whenever the Leftist groups did something, and somebody asked Ecevit who was responsible, he would try to cover this up. If a Right-wing group did something, killed somebody, then Demirel would say he was not sure who did it. It was obvious that they were trying to cover it up. The police force was divided. The judiciary was divided. None of that helped overcome any of these problems [. . .] I think what Turkey lacked at the time were responsible political leaders who could do something about this state of affairs. (Interview, July 2016)

The fight to dominate the political arena resulted in increased frustration, political paralysis and violence in the country (Tachau 2000, 137–38). Their choices entrenched the state in a political crisis, hindering any hope that parliament would be an interlocutor and arbiter to stabilise conditions (Tilly 1978). This was because, as Sayarı has noted, violence was exploited for political point-scoring. Consequently, the extremist groups were able to capitalise and provoke further conflicts, which established a cycle of revenge killings. The leaders' intolerance for each other came to play an important role in undermining democracy and stability across the country.

1977–80: The Loss of Political Legitimacy and Authority

Within this climate of increasing violence and near government paralysis, Turkey went to elections on 5 June 1977. The outcome saw Ecevit gain his best result, capturing 41.4 percent by winning 213 seats, but fell short of the absolute majority by thirteen. Demirel, on the other hand, received 36.9 percent, which converted into 189 parliamentarians (see Table 3.2). A grand coalition between Demirel and Ecevit might have been strong enough to create stability. Ecevit, in fact, looked at this option favourably; however, Demirel continued to oppose any such partnership (Tachau 2000, 138; 2002; Akar, Dündar and Özcan 2004; Birand, Bila and Akar 1999, 32). Hence, the continuing hostility between the two leaders rendered the chance for a democratic rescue operation impossible (Tachau 2002, 122; Heper 2002a, 234). Ecevit, again unable to find a coalition partner, allowed Demirel to establish another National Front with Erbakan and Türkeş. As had previously been the case, Demirel had to pay a cost for his desire to rule, enabling his junior coalition partners to attain a political power that was out of proportion with their electoral support:

> After the 1977 election, Demirel again looked for anyone that would give him the majority in parliament. Erbakan, as the opportunist politician, grabbed the chance to control certain ministries. Yet, when you look at these coalition pay-offs, the amount of seats that the smaller parties received in parliament in proportion to their votes, for Erbakan and Türkeş, was, in fact, much more than what they had to offer in terms of electoral support. (Interview with Sabri Sayarı, July 2016)

Hence, Demirel was willing to make these politically irrational compromises to deny Ecevit power. In an interview decades later, Demirel retained this uncompromising view of Ecevit, blaming him for Turkey's ills during the period, further adding that he had formed the second National Front because a coalition with Ecevit would have been against the national will (see Birand, Bila and Akar 1999, 75; Dündar and Akar 2015, 108).

Table 3.2: 1977 Election Results

Political Party	Percentage of Votes	Parliamentary Seats (Total 450)
CHP	41.4	213
AP	36.9	189
MSP	8.6	24
MHP	6.4	16
Independents	2.5	4
CGP	1.9	3

Source: https://www.tbmm.gov.tr/develop/owa/secim_sorgu.genel_secimler

The closeness of the contest gave them enough support to retain their political zones, but not sufficient incentive to cooperate. Driven by the fear of losing political ground in such a competitive environment ensured that tensions reached new heights:

> In a sense the competitiveness made the stakes even higher, made it more difficult for these two leaders to come to some sort of agreement and form a grand coalition, because they thought that, by pursuing hardline policies and strategies, they would hold on to their own group in the parliament – this is a common tactic employed in Turkish politics. You attack the opposition to hold on to your own base, but this entirely undermined the chances for a coalition [between them] and consequently for any hope of stabilising the situation inside the country. (Interview with Sabri Sayarı, July 2016)

In order to delineate their political territories, the leaders stuck to their intransigent positions and continued to blame each other personally for the country's problems. The instability culminated in the collapse of the government:

> It must have been ego, plus political miscalculations. Ecevit pushed for new elections after the 1977 electoral result, pointing to the reason that the elections did not produce a majority. He knew that he could increase his votes due to his popularity. However, Demirel, the old fox, saw what was going to happen and refused to vote in favour of early elections. That's how they got deadlocked, Ecevit pushing for elections, whilst Demirel opposed it. And

since the CHP didn't have any other allies on the Left, Demirel ended up coming to power again [through the second National Front coalition]. This turned into a point of extreme resentment for Ecevit. The competitiveness of the party system contributed greatly to this situation. (Interview with Sabri Sayarı, July 2016)

Ecevit, frustrated about not occupying the seat of Prime Minister and politically isolated despite attaining the highest percentage of votes, orchestrated the downfall of Demirel's seven-month-old government. In a deal made at the Güneş Motel, he enticed ten AP parliamentarians to quit the party. These parliamentarians then helped Ecevit with the numbers he needed to form a government (*Milliyet* 1977).[23] However, this act served a major blow to Ecevit's reputation and deepened the paralysis in government (Mango 2004, 76). The ensuing scandal, combined with an acute economic crisis, proved disastrous for Ecevit in the mid-term by-elections. He resigned in November 1979 after twenty-two months (Mango 2004, 72–78), leaving Demirel to form another Right-wing coalition.

The bitterness between the two men was heightened after the Güneş Motel episode: the resulting political discourse consisted of accusations and counter-accusations. Other parliamentarians, in the example of their leaders, followed suit with regular fistfights in the Assembly (Ünlü et al. 1998). As a result, 'the parliament, as a place to get things done, became an arena where the parties could howl at each other but not get much done', concluded Turan (Interview, April 2016), indicating that the legislature had essentially stopped operating.

The paralysis forced the President of the National Assembly, Cahit Karakaş, to publicly declare: 'I would sincerely like to express that all the laws in conformity with the needs of our citizens have not been enacted yet' (quoted in GSNSC 1982, 107). Providing statistics for the 1978–79 legislative year, he announced that, from 138 draft laws and 178 legislative proposals, only seventy-nine had been passed as law; among the forty-nine censure motions submitted, fifteen had been discussed and reached a decision, while twenty-eight had been withdrawn; and fifteen draft laws urgently needed to combat the violence were suspended due to the political impasse (GSNSC 1982, 107). The total figures for the decade further underline the level of dysfunction in government: only one-fifth of draft laws submitted to the Assembly had been enacted, and only ten percent of all questions had been addressed by the sitting government during parliamentary question times (GSNSC 1982, 107).

Despite the widening crises in the country, the ongoing hostility between the two sides made stability improbable. This was unlike in consolidated settings, where political leaders with sharp differences often work hand-in-hand during times of crisis, because of a culture of compromise, as outlined by Przeworski (1988). In Turkey, however, there was no sign of rapprochement, consensus, or compromise, despite the severe stresses befalling the country. 'The concept of loyal opposition is incomprehensible to the Turks,' remarked a European diplomat, further adding: 'If one party takes the position, the other is sure to oppose it, no matter what the cost to the country' (Gage 1979). This accurately summed up the nature of the leaders' strategy of 'doing politics'. For instance, when Ecevit was back in the seat of power on 5 January 1978, he had to move the budget through the Assembly by the constitutional deadline, the night of 28 February. He found himself sponsoring a bill prepared by the previous government of Demirel (GSNSC 1982, 38), but Demirel, in opposition, voted against the bill which his government had prepared earlier. Likewise, Ecevit was now defending and promoting a budget that he had declared just weeks earlier as 'lacking any basis'. The leaders took up positions opposite to those they had held just a few weeks earlier. There was simply an unwillingness to act through democratic norms in the zero-sum political climate, which they had helped entrench.

The personal tirades of Turkey's two central political leaders further fuelled the political paralysis. Demirel lambasted the CHP as an 'illegitimate' government, and he even refused to refer to Ecevit by name or as the Prime Minister (Gunter 1989, 65). Ecevit described Demirel as '[a] party leader who has resorted to the most shameful methods in our political history, who has collaborated with criminals, the person who has secured personal benefits from others' (quoted in Gunter 1989, 65). When Ecevit was attacked at a political rally, he blamed Demirel and yelled out to the crowd: 'Demirel, you coward, don't take refuge behind bandits and thugs' (Ünlü et al. 1998). Both had little regard for the other's political position.

Turkey's unfortunate ongoing political crisis was described by *Time* as follows:

> In no small measure, Turkey's fruitless search for stability can be traced to lurching shifts in leadership that involves the country's two top politicians, Bülent Ecevit, head of the Republican People's Party, and Süleyman Demirel, leader of the Justice Party [. . .] Since January 1974, Ecevit and Demirel have alternated as Premier half a dozen times. The two-man game of musical chairs has done nothing to resolve the country's protracted economic woes, which include 70 percent inflation rate, 20 percent unemployment and shortages of everything. (1979b)

Other articles directly implicated their personalities: 'For all their parliamentary squabbling, Ecevit and Demirel are divided more by personal animosity than by ideology' (*Time* 1979a). For example, Demirel, knowing that a partnership with Ecevit would have constituted a solution to overturning the country's fortunes, remarked: 'Ecevit's Government is crumbling, why should I save it by joining in a coalition when all I have to do is wait?' (quoted in Gage 1979). This personal acknowledgement provides an insight into Demirel's drive to re-attain the seat of power, whatever the cost to the democratic order.

Unsurprisingly, as the decade came to a close, conditions had become dire. In addition to the severe economic crisis, the escalating street battles between Leftist and Rightist armed groups, as well as the ever-mounting death toll left Turkey divided between Left- and Right-controlled neighbourhoods and regions.[24] The country was fraught with regular political and targeted assassinations, outbreaks of sectarian violence resulting in mass murders between Sunni and Alevi citizens,[25] a rise in religious fundamentalism and armed attacks by the *Partiya Karkerên Kurdistanê* (Kurdistan Workers' Party, PKK) in the Southeast. There was also the emergence of *serbest bölgeler* (liberated zones), including in Istanbul. These were neighbourhoods or regional towns under the control of revolutionary groups with their own 'people's court', brandishing their own forms of justice outside the control of the state (see Ünlü et al. 1998; Birand, Bila and Akar 1999). It appeared as though anarchy had spread to the most remote parts of the country (Gunter 1989). Years later, in an interview, even Ecevit acknowledged that the atmosphere in the country 'was, in fact, a war zone' (quoted in Birand, Bila and Akar 1999, 71). All the while, he and Demirel were too busy quarrelling, unwilling to move beyond their personal interests. *Time* wrote:

> Today, Turkey is gradually nearing disintegration. An average of 25 people are being killed in a week, the State constantly in a state of bankruptcy and people cannot find the most basic commodities of consumption as a result of foreign exchange shortage [. . .] Demirel once said he would cooperate with Ecevit only in a case of war. The situation facing Turkey at present is more serious than a state of war. It is now a time to give priority to the interests of the country rather than political interests. (1980)

As noted previously, it would have been logical for Ecevit and Demirel to team up in a 'grand coalition' of their two parties, which together polled more than 75 percent of the vote (see Table 3.2); however, their bitter rivalry transformed multi-party politics and the state into a personal battleground that was amply matched by their supporters.[26] Had they demonstrated values such as moderation, necessary for democratic politics, perhaps stability might have been achieved. Instead, they persisted in finger-pointing, blaming the other for the ills of the country and its spiralling political crisis:

> The leadership tried to blame the other side for having incited the clashes. There was a clear lack of determination on the part of the leadership to treat these clashes as a national problem in which all parties should unite to bring under control [. . .] the natural thing would have been for the two major parties to treat the situation as a national emergency and come together. But the polarised politics was confounded by the two stubborn leaders who did not trust each other [. . .] In the end things got worse whilst their stubborn personalities fuelled the polarised political climate even more. (Interview with İlter Turan, April 2016)

This tension was playing out against a backdrop of mounting pressure from the generals to stabilise the climate. Throughout the last years of the decade, the MGK's regular calls for the government to pass stronger legislation so as to combat the rising tide of political violence had become more frequent and vocal. However, the civilian politicians remained inert (Birand, Bila and Akar 1999). Similarly, regular warnings to resolve ideological divisions within the police force and the intelligence agency, key to overcoming the violence, never came to fruition (Cizre 1993, 191). And in December 1979, in a last attempt, the generals addressed a stern letter to the two leaders, condemning the widespread politicisation of the bureaucracy and calling on them to collaborate to restore order and immediately bring the political violence to an end (Birand, Bila and Akar 1999, 135). Yet, as Turan recalled, both leaders remained unmoved:

> In response to the letter, both Demirel and Ecevit said that the warning was not addressed to them, but to the other party. They remarkably did not want to accept the idea that this was a systemic problem and continued to blame the other for the ills of the country. (Interview, April 2016)

Demirel argued that the message was not for him because it came at a time when he was in power only for a short period:

> We received the letter fifteen days after we formed the government. There is no reason for this letter to warn us. This letter has nothing to do with my government. Why should I take responsibility? [. . .] I am neither responsible for the bloodshed until this point, nor the state of the economy, nor poverty. (quoted in Birand, Bila and Akar 1999, 136–37)

Similarly, Ecevit concluded that, since he was no longer in government, the warning was not intended for him, but rather aimed at Demirel (Ünlü et al. 1998). Effectively, 'it was as if this opinion [of the military] was directed at a vacuum', so concluded a member of the military High Command (quoted in Gunter 1989, 68), and the letter was all but forgotten in a couple of weeks (Demirel 2003, 344). By this stage, so Cizre noted, the generals seemed to have exhausted all hope that their recommendations would be fulfilled by any of the governments, as the leaders 'lacked the goodwill or were driven simply by electoral opportunism' (1993, 171).

The unwillingness of Demirel and Ecevit to come together on any issue was further illustrated by their failure to elect a President following the end of Fahri Korutürk's term on 6 April 1980, which left the country without a chief of state. Commenting on the political inertia, one of Turkey's leading journalists at the time, Mehmet Ali Birand, observed: 'In short, the rules of the game no longer existed in this free for all, which has dispensed with the principal tenet of democracy, namely, consensus. The people of Turkey watch on as passive spectators at this deadlock in the political party system' (1987, 48). Sayarı recalled similar feelings of exasperation towards both leaders and the increasingly likely spectre of a military intervention:

> The fact that the military had already intervened twice in Turkey by that time clearly indicated that there was this history. Couldn't they see what was going to happen? They couldn't elect a President, the parliament was deadlocked, the economic crisis was building, people were being killed in Left-Right clashes, and the PKK had just emerged. When journalists had posed this question to them over and over and they kept blaming each other, they refused to acknowledge their part in what had befallen the country. (Interview, July 2016)

As both leaders persisted in their accusations and worked to ensure the failure of the other, the generals decided to intervene on 12 September 1980. The constitution was suspended, parliament and all political parties dissolved, and democracy was brought to another end; an outcome that William Hale (1994, 232), neatly summed up: 'In retrospect what is surprising about the coup of 12 September 1980 is not that it happened, but that it took so long, and that politicians did so little to prevent it'. The leader of the coup, General Kenan Evren, in a later interview, similarly stated that, had the two men formed a coalition, the army would never have been able to mount a coup (Ünlü et al. 1998). Many years later, with the benefit of hindsight, Ecevit lamented: 'I wasn't even surprised by the coup because everything had gotten so out of hand' (quoted in Dündar and Akar 2015, 109). The zero-sum politics of both men unfortunately 'ended up as zero for everyone', and for this reason, support for the military intervention was overwhelming:

> Especially in the period from 1977 to 1980, the two major parties needed to unite behind a common platform against terrorism, because that was the major reason for the military intervention. The military did not intervene for the economic crisis [and] it might have been disgruntled by the inability of parliament to vote in a new president. The main reason for the intervention was the killing of hundreds of people [. . .] The public reaction was sup-

portive of the coup, at first. Society had reached a point where the thought was along the line of 'let's have somebody do something about this'. I think people had a sense that, if the military intervened, then the killings and violence would come to an end, and in fact this is what did happen. You saw an illustration of this public support in the referendum results, which was a very high percentage in favour of the military. But when it became evident that there was torture in the prisons, hundreds of thousands taken into custody, these unfortunate events decreased the popularity of the junta drastically. However, if you asked the average man and woman on the street at the initial time in September 1980, they were in favour of the junta due to the pervasive conditions. (Interview with Sabri Sayarı, July 2016)

Conclusion

The nature of leadership of the period impeded not only the opportunity to deepen democracy after the reset to civilian politics in 1973, but also dragged it down the path to its third termination seven years later. Ecevit and Demirel's rivalry, seemingly based on a winner-take-all mentality, ran counter to the democratic ideals of inclusivity, self-restraint and politics centered on compromise and consensus between political actors. Neither man expressed an outward wish to entirely dismantle democracy; yet, their continued behaviour, fuelled by political ambition and personal animosity, caused ruinous damage to the democratic system and the political order.

Demirel's zero-sum view of politics was in discord with democratic values, apparent before the recommencement of civilian politics. He utilised martial law conditions to the advantage of his own political position and to repress his ideological opponents, to such an extent that he facilitated the execution of Leftist activists. Given his influence over the military-sponsored government during this period and the illiberal character of the constitutional amendments, it clearly demonstrated that he was not in favour of deepening democracy, but rather pursuing undemocratic reforms.

On the other side of politics, Bülent Ecevit ended İnönü's thirty-four-year reign and ascended to the party leadership of the CHP. However, the generational change in leadership did not provide a break in the character of the rule over the party. Ecevit very quickly took hold of the party to become another İnönü. He marginalised, harassed and purged his opponents and amended the party constitution to broaden his powers. As a result, the character of the rule of both men over their parties mirrored each other, one on the Left, the other on the Right.

The political power that this afforded them was not utilised to strengthen the rule of law, the parliament or democratic processes, but rather resulted in a political arena characterised by the clash of personal ambitions. The resulting paralysis prevented the formulation of strong reforms, including anti-terror legislation, which were urgently needed to regain order. In abandoning institutional forbearance, what they could bring under their political control was used as a political weapon to counter the influence of the other. Over time, critical state institutions were rendered incapable of acting as a neutral interlocutor and at times became a facilitator of criminal activity against each side of the political divide. The competition for political power was pushed beyond democratic processes and institutions, eventually setting an example that shaped the manner in which politics and society resolved differences, which paved the way for violence to spill into the major urban areas and later spread to the countryside.[27]

This was a pattern in total accord with the historical pattern of elite interactions in Turkey's history. Again, leaders wasted an opportunity to salvage the situation, rather opting to push, bend and break already weak institutions for their own particularistic goals. Their competing authoritarianism resulted in a 'complete erosion of governmental authority'. The generals saw that the leaders had allowed developments to go well beyond political control and considered an intervention as a solution. Although the coup brought the violence and political dysfunction to an end, it created another troubling chapter in the country's history. In the following chapter, I will show how, despite the wide-sweeping efforts of the military junta and the lessons to be drawn from this era, the leadership through the 1980s and 1990s displayed characteristics that again posed great challenges to consolidation.

Notes

1. Erim was chosen, as he was seen as the least controversial person in the political ranks and thus the most likely candidate acceptable to all parties (Ahmad 1977, 290).
2. The reasons for placating Demirel and his party seem to have confused politicians and political observers, as there was no explanation for Erim to do so. It rather was interpreted as a sign of his weakness as a leader who had been tasked with implementing neccessary fiscal reforms, yet had chosen to appease the anti-reformists led by Demirel (Ahmad 1977, 290–91).

3. Throughout this period, the influence that Demirel wielded over Erim ensured that cabinets could not be formed without his approval; he engineered an AP parliamentarian, Mesut Erez, to become Vice Prime Minister, which provided him further control over the military-backed government (Ünlü et al. 1998). When the acting Erim government drew up reforms not to his liking, Demirel was quick to withdraw AP ministers from the cabinet to create a crisis, until he got his way (Ahmad 1993, 153–54). On other occasions, his influence was used to wield measures designed to pass legislation in order to purge known liberals from universities and the bureaucracy, and he failed to permit measures with which he did not agree. For example, he refused to give Erim the power of decree that would carry the force of law, as he could not entertain another person holding such power (Ahmad 1993, 154).

4. Also illustrative of Demirel's proximity to the military rule is the fact that Chief Justice Ali Elverdi, who handed down the young men's sentence, later became a parliamentarian for the AP and the leading prosecutor in the case; Baki Tuğ was made a parliamentarian for Demirel's party after the 1980 coup (Birand, Dündar and Çaplı 1994).

5. Due to the drop in votes after the 1974 election, there was a challenge against Demirel from Orhan Oğuz. Yet, in the intra-party vote Oğuz lost to Demirel by a landslide margin, 1,038 to 76 votes. The only other challenge came in 1978, by Kamran İnan. The date of election was cancelled by Demirel on a number of occasions, in a ploy to thwart İnan's supporter base from attending the vote. In the end, Demirel was easily able to defeat the challenge with 1,439 votes to İnan's 88 (Ünlü et al. 1998).

6. Six ballot papers were empty, and twelve were deemed invalid.

7. Ecevit disagreed with İnönü's appeasement of the military's incursion into politics on 12 March 1971. He advocated a non-compromising stance against the military, which saw him resign from his position as General Secretary.

8. İnönü had thrown his support behind Ecevit in his battle with Feyzioğlu (Bektaş 1993, 163).

9. Articles 45, 46 and 50 were amended. These changes provided the Party Executive complete control over all members, including representatives and senators, as well as giving the Disciplinary Committee power to expel members of the Assembly.

10. Celal Kargılı accused Ecevit of 'dragging the party into its grave' with his leadership (*Milliyet* 1970f).

11. The numbers were comprised of fifteen senators and thirty-three members of the Lower House.

12. Kemal Satır served in various positions including as the Vice Prime Minister, as well as the party's General Secretary before Ecevit.

13. On 28 February 1973, the party merged with Feyzioğlu's *Güven Partisi* (Reliance Party), which was renamed the *Cumhuriyetçi Güven Partisi* (Republican Reliance Party, CGP).

14. Under İnönü's rule, the Secretary General always retained a level of autonomy and power in the party.

15. So much so was the CHP personified by Ecevit that an English journalist who came to report the elections wrote back to his paper: 'The Turkish election has been one by a party called Ecevit' (Ahmad 1977, 330).

16. According to Demirel the reason for his decision was the following: 'There was no way we could. Neither our parliamentary group, nor at the grass roots level were we ready for it. Besides both the CHP and us [the AP] had organised our parties in opposition to one another. We would not have been able to make such a move' (quoted in Birand, Bila and Akar 1999, 32).

17. Ecevit stated in later years that the coalition with the religious MSP had been formed to demonstrate that secularism and religion were not at odds. Also, it was thought that the cooperation between the two parties would help to improve relations within Turkish society (see Dündar and Akar 2015, 92; Akar and Dündar 2008, 177).

18. The idea was first proposed by Celal Bayar and Ferruh Bozbeyli in 1974, but it was rejected by Demirel at that time.

19. One of the first changes that Demirel made was to replace the head of the state broadcaster, İsmail Cem, with the stridently conservative Nevzat Yalçıntaş.

20. For example, when Abdi İpekçi, the editor-in-chief of one of the main newspapers, *Milliyet*, was assassinated and his killer caught, it turned out to be Mehmed Ali Ağca, who later came to global notoriety in 1981 for his attempt on Pope John Paul II's life in Rome. He succeeded in escaping from a high-security prison in Istanbul with the complicity of some of his guards (Ahmad 1993, 172).

21. It has been noted that Ecevit suffered a number of attempts on his life during the 1970s. Depending on the literature, the numbers vary between three and eight, with credible sources counting three (see Birand, Bila and Akar 1999; Dündar and Akar 2015).

22. Neither Ecevit nor his party displayed the same level of formal patron-client links and rhetorical support as did Demirel for the Right wing. In reality, the Left could never be brought under centralised control, as it was a movement divided into a variety of political organisations and violent revolutionary groups

who also competed against each other (Ünlü et al. 1998). This was unlike the Right, which acted under one banner, making it easier to command.

23. Since the eleven seats fell short of the thirteen required for majority rule, he also coerced Turhan Feyzioğlu and Salih Yıldız from the CGP along with Faruk Sükan from the DP to join his coalition (*Milliyet* 1977).

24. For instance, an unidentified gunman opened fire into the crowd from the buildings surrounding Taksim Square where an estimated 500,000 had gathered to celebrate 1 May in 1977. In the commotion, the police threw sound bombs from their armoured personnel carriers, creating further panic, then drove their vehicles over demonstrators that had lain down to escape the bullets, or into panicked crowds looking to escape. In addition, strategically placed vehicles blocked off escape routes, causing more injuries, as large numbers crushed those that had fallen. Hundreds were injured and thirty-four killed in the incident. The perpetrators of the incident have never been identified, nor has anyone been held responsible in a court of law (*Cumhuriyet* 2009).

25. For example, on 26 December 1978, 126 deaths resulted from violence between the Sunni and Alevi community in Kahramanmaraş. Between May and July 1980, fifty-five deaths occurred when Sunni groups mounted sustained attacks against Çorum's Alevi community (Birand, Bila and Akar 1999, 100–9, 148–54).

26. This is reflected in the dramatic rise in the number of people who lost their lives in terrorist incidents between 1976 and 1980: 108 in 1976, 319 in 1977, 1,095 in 1978, 1,362 in 1979, and 1,928 during the first nine months in 1980 (Sayarı 2010, 202).

27. Communal violence along sectarian divisions (Sunni and Alevi) accounted for the second-largest number of fatalities in this period (Sayarı 2010, 204). Turkey's dramatic drift into political violence after 1976 claimed the lives of numerous politicians (including former Prime Minister Erim), journalists, academics, jurists and union officials (Sayarı 2010, 204). By 1980, thirty-one of Turkey's sixty-seven provinces reportedly contained so-called 'liberated-zones', areas under exclusive control of one ideological faction or another and closed off to state security forces (Gunter 1989, 72).

4

1983–93: TURGUT ÖZAL AND THE PENCHANT FOR ONE-MAN RULE

Introduction

In the immediate aftermath of the 1980 coup, the military undertook a major restructuring of the political system. Mass arrests and trials ensued,[1] newspapers were shut down, the parliament was abolished, all political parties were closed down, and party leaders – including Süleyman Demirel, Necmettin Erbakan, Alparsan Türkeş and Bülent Ecevit – were arrested and tried for their roles in the breakdown of the regime. They were subsequently banned from participating in politics.[2]

It is against this backdrop that Turgut Özal, a US-educated technocrat, stepped into politics to fill the breach. Although a confidant of Demirel during the 1970s, Özal was nonetheless removed from partisan politics and its devastating outcomes of the previous era. His pleasant demeanour and successful management of the economy during the years of military rule helped fuel his popularity amongst an electorate fatigued by years of political polarisation, violence and military rule. With the return to electoral politics on 6 November 1983, the generals controlled the election process and engineered two parties that would act in line with their wishes. This was extended to three on Özal's insistence, resulting in the participation of his *Anavatan Partisi* (Motherland Party, ANAP) and his surprise win.

This victory led to Özal's ten years in power, whereby he was able to further liberalise the country's economy. Yet, Özal's approach to leadership was a significant impediment to the democratic system: much like the leaders before him, he did not display a style of rule that was in line with the concepts and norms required for consolidated systems; rather, he reflected a majoritarian understanding of democracy. Liberalisation, for Özal, was limited to opening the economy to market competition, and even this, at times, was contradicted by his policies.

In this chapter, I will begin by tracing Demirel's attempt to use his relationship with Özal to direct the political outcomes from behind the scenes, and by showing how Özal's unwillingness to abide by Demirel's wishes fractured their relationship, as it would play out in later developments. Also analysed are the changes made to the *Siyasi Partiler Kanunu* (Political Parties Law, SPK) by the military junta, which demonstrate that the changes to the SPK regulated the already standard practice of authoritarian leadership and benefitted Özal's leadership style. The discussion then outlines that the experiences of Özal's rule over the ANAP were consistent with those of Menderes, Demirel and Ecevit over their parties. As Prime Minister presiding over a single-party government between 1983 and 1989, Özal maintained the military-imposed parameters, removing hope for increased pluralism. In the final section, I will illustrate the outcomes that Özal's rule posed for the government during his presidency from 1989 to 1993. Juxtaposing his time as Prime Minister and as President underscores his unwillingness to respect norms or institutional processes in order to achieve his aims, regardless of the altered political and legal realities. Ultimately, Özal's ten years at the pinnacle of power proved to be another problematic period for democracy in Turkey.

Demirel's Özal Gambit

During the military intervention in 1980, Özal, at Demirel's urging, became the chief economic reform architect of the coup era. Cengiz Çandar, who later acted as Özal's foreign policy advisor, recalled that Özal had not been part of the political establishment before going into civilian politics:

> Özal came out of nowhere in the 1983 elections. He was a well-known bureaucrat from the former Demirel government and then became the economic architect of the coup period. During the military rule, when pre-coup politicians were banned from the political sphere, Demirel endorsed and pushed Özal to become Deputy Prime Minister. This was in order for Demirel to have someone on the inside, to be able to influence political

decisions through Özal. Demirel always wanted to have his fingers in the political configuration. It was his cunning style. Then Özal ran the economy, with which the generals were satisfied. They then let him run for government at the resumption of civilian politics because they saw him as harmless, and they also figured that an election with three parties would provide more legitimacy to the elections. In the end, Özal won the elections to become Prime Minister. (Interview, October 2016b)

Özal's position enabled Demirel to keep his hands in policy-making, which Demirel tried to exploit. Their relationship, until then, had resembled an *abi-kardeş* (siblings) dynamic, in which Özal referred to Demirel as *abi* (an endearing term used for an older brother). Demirel believed that his former protégé would enable him to circumvent his political ban and act as a proxy; however, the two men's ties were ruptured when Özal formed the ANAP, an action that Demirel viewed as Özal taking advantage of his forced absence. Demirel regarded this as Özal undermining his political ambitions, as he too was busy establishing a new party behind the scenes (Birand and Yalçın 2001, 154–58). Deeming this as an act of betrayal, it became a source of hostility when Demirel re-entered politics years later as a rival.

Nonetheless, the electoral victory facilitated Özal's transition from bureaucrat to democratically elected Prime Minister. The economy continued to take precedence, and he immediately acted to delimit the powers of the state – a reflection of his neoliberal economic philosophy, which would be his principal concern throughout his reign (see Sayarı 1990) and which ensured economic growth, taking primacy over all other areas. This was outlined with declarations such as 'I am going to give the economy more importance than the political', as recalled by one of the founders of the ANAP, Mehmet Keçeciler (quoted in Birand and Yalçın 2001, 215).

Backed by a large parliamentary majority and taking advantage of the ban on experienced and popular pre-coup politicians,[3] Özal was able to implement policies largely unhindered. The military's efforts, in addition, had created a space that lacked a robust labour movement and was void of any social groups that could form strong political and societal opposition to his economic programs. Society remained in a political straitjacket, unable to impose pressure on policies. The environment enabled Özal to revolutionise the economy by bringing an 'end to the protectionist and paternalistic state' and to embrace the global liberal market (Acar 2002, 172; Kalaycıoğlu 2002b, 46; Mango 2004, 85).

Table 4.1 1983 Election Results

Political Party	Percentage of Votes[4]	Parliamentary Seats (Total 400)
Anavatan Partisi (ANAP)	45.1	211
Halkçı Parti (HP)	30.5	117
Milliyetçi Demokrasi Partisi (MDP)	23.3	71
Independents	1.1	0

Source: https://www.tbmm.gov.tr/develop/owa/secim_sorgu.genel_secimler

A New Political Parties Law

The new *Siyasi Partiler Kanunu* (Political Parties Law, SPK), a key legacy left over from the military rule, allowed Özal the room to undertake his endeavours in a unilateral manner. The amended SPK was vital as it informed party leadership practices and intra-party democracy. The *Dernekler Kanunu* (Law of Associations) regulated the activities of political parties until the mid-1960s, but in 1965 the SPK was adopted as a specific code of regulation for political parties, in line with the 1961 Constitution. It was not until the SPK's major overhaul during the 1980 coup that it had a critical impact on intra-party structures (Bayraktar and Altan 2013; Çelep 2014; Ayan 2010; Musil 2011). It regulated a structure that subordinated the political party to the wishes of its leader. Pelin Ayan Musil has identified the three ways in which the SPK gave rise to an authoritarian party structure (2011, 43–45). Firstly, it made the parties dependant on state revenues, creating a cartelisation effect. Secondly, it fostered the centralisation of candidate selection processes in political parties. Thirdly, the SPK enforced a hierarchical structure to which all parties became subject. This left very little opportunity for organisational decentralisation conducive to intra-party democratisation. Former Deputy Prime Minister Murat Karayalçın lamented that the SPK placed an undemocratic constraint on all parties from this point onward:

> After the changes to the *Siyasi Partiler Kanunu*, we were forced to have a vertical and highly centralised hierarchical organisational structure, which had to be implemented according to legislation based on the constitution of the 12 September junta, and, in fact, still today political parties have to be organised accordingly to the law, unfortunately. (Interview, May 2016)

Whilst the architects of a political party might attempt to institute a democratic structure, the regulations, as İlter Turan recalled, made such attempts impossible:

> In the late 1990s a liberal-leaning party called the *New Democracy Movement* was created. They had to hand in their party statute to the Ministry of Interior to formally enter politics. The ministry rejected their application because the *New Democracy Movement* statute asserted that the central organs of the party did not have the authority to remove local officials of the party. The ministry ruled that this statute was against the Political Parties Law and had to be amended. In other words, even if a small party through its own rules attempted to challenge the imposed centralised structure of the Party Law and have a more democratic structure, it was charged with not conforming to the law. (Interview, June 2016)[5]

The SPK was not devised with a view to advancing participatory politics. The junta undertook these amendments to provide state institutions with oversight over parties so as to block a recurrence of political elites exploiting divisions in Turkish society, as they had done in the 1960s and 1970s (Kınıklıoğlu 2002, 20). However, its unintended consequences were that it facilitated leadership domination:

> When you look at what was behind the Political Parties Law, basically it was an inexpensive way of exercising state control over political parties themselves, by rendering the central organs of the party responsible for everything the party does. If someone in some provincial organisation does something wrong, the central organs are responsible for tending and removing the people from their positions. Otherwise, the central party organisation shall be held responsible by state authorities [. . .] The law was changed because the aim of the 1982 Constitution was to de-politicise society. Laws were created to introduce limitations on parties establishing linkages with civil society organisations or establishing their own linkages in society [. . .] This has been somewhat changed over time, but the basic structure to support a highly centralised party structure, empowering the central organs of the party for everything, remained, including candidate designation.
>
> The constitution and the [Political Parties] Law allowed holding primary elections. The initial spirit was that primary elections would be the

rule; candidate designation by the central organs of the party would be the exception. However, the reverse has become the norm. Basically, the central organs of the party became the basic agency in which candidate designation was implemented. As a result, holding primaries has decreased over time. (Interview with İlter Turan, June 2016)

Therefore, according to Turan, while the SPK does not regulate against intra-party democracy, by its nature it supports the authoritarian characteristics of party leaders. The resulting power to select candidates has meant that leaders are much harder to remove from their posts because political careers are dependent on the leader.

Controlling candidature lists ultimately created a culture of obedience, which is one of the reasons why leaders do not favour an open process. The consequences of the SPK allowing leaders to override the intra-democratic process of pre-selection has largely blocked the development of a party body that can hold leaders accountable. Reflecting on his own experience, former parliamentarian Onur Kumbaracıbaşı highlighted these tensions:[6]

> The [Political Parties] Law unfortunately bestows too much authority on the central party apparatus. Many party candidate lists are dictated from the party headquarters. Meaning, they don't ask the local organisation, or the grassroots members, and at times they don't even ask some parts of the central administrative body. The leaders can prepare the list that he or she wants [. . .] When I say the headquarters, I am largely referring to the party leader, whose personal preference will have a large say on the list. They will absolutely include whomever they want [. . .] Since the leader controls the political careers of their parliamentarians, this has meant everything is now in the control of the leaders. (Interview, April 2016)

The SPK, in many ways, paved the way for the normalisation of intra-party authoritarianism. Political parties became subject to the character and wishes of the party leader, restricting the party from establishing strong links with the public. This, in turn, is a large factor behind the lack of institutionalisation of political parties in Turkey. In the introductory discussion, scholars – including Mainwaring, Torcal and Kumbaracıbaşı – found that party institutionalisation is a key component to democratic consolidation. We can therefore begin to understand how this set of circumstances in Turkey not only allowed for leader-domination, but also increased the divide between the party and the public.

The SPK also marked a stark shift from the previous periods under Menderes, Demirel and Ecevit's intra-party rule, whereby leaders had to expend their energies devising strategies to maintain their position over the party. Although the SPK in theory does not block intra-party democracy, it does allow leaders with substantial power and flexibility to interpret the law as they see fit. As a result, in the post-1980 coup environment, the domination of political parties by their leadership became much more straightforward whilst supporting the institutional weakness of party organisations.

Özal, the Party Leader

It was within this space that Özal formed his party. In creating the *Anavatan Partisi* (ANAP), Özal recruited inexperienced individuals who belonged to the Left, Right and religious-conservative camps (Ahmad 1993, 193; Ergüder 1991, 155). Özal calculated that this coalition had the best chance of helping him achieve his vision, while not raising the ire of the military, as General Kenan Evren held veto power over the party lists and gave permission to compete in the elections (Cemal 1989b, 41–42; Birand, Bila and Akar 1999, 258–59).

Despite the propensity to emphasise liberal ideals, this philosophy was essentially fiscal in nature. Özal's leadership of the ANAP was as autocratic as those who had come before him (Kalaycıoğlu 2002b; Acar 2002; Özen 2013); however, unlike the leaders discussed above, Özal did not have to contend with opposition or strong party factions. The ANAP was built by one man, according to his own image (Kalaycıoğlu 2002b, 46). And, in doing so, he gave power to a collection of actors who would otherwise have remained in the political periphery, reminiscent of Menderes's leadership. ANAP politicians owed their careers to Özal's patronage, allowing him absolute authority over the party:

> When somebody like Özal with only bureaucratic credentials emerged to form a party, nobody with experience would join him, nobody would dare. Only some individuals from Muslim fraternities, some bureaucratic colleagues he had, and third-, fourth-, fifth-tier politicians from the Justice Party

[*Adalet Partisi*] would dare to step into politics alongside him. These individuals were in that sense political nobodies. Then they became men of power upon ANAP's electoral victory. Since Özal had hand-picked them, because Özal had provided electoral success, identity and political power to them, he therefore exercised power over ANAP politicians accordingly. (Interview with Cengiz Çandar, October 2016b)

Indeed, under the junta, Özal was forced to pick political unknowns. These factors, combined with the SPK, placed absolute authority in Özal's hands and provided little, if any, opportunity for intra-party democracy, denying the party's local bodies any input in ANAP policy or direction. The party, infantilised from the outset, established a political culture in which total obedience to Özal's leadership was pivotal to a deputy's survival and dismissal the response to challengers or those who did not meet his wishes (Birand and Yalçın 2001, 379–80, 386).

It became common for Özal to disregard the party statute; his decision would be implemented and the statute amended to fit the outcome (Cemal 1989b, 130). For instance, Mehmet Keçeciler was removed from his position by Özal, then given a new position inside the ANAP, a position that did not exist in the official party statute, but the latter was immediately amended to accommodate Özal's decision (Cemal 1989b, 130; *Milliyet* 1987).

Mirroring the intra-party strategy of leaders before him, Özal controlled ANAP candidature lists to maintain the unquestioned obedience of his politicians (Cemal 1989b, 126–27), often making sweeping changes, such as assembling the names of 1,300 candidates to contest the 1989 municipal elections (Cemal 1989b, 130). All decisions regarding the ANAP (and later the government) were crafted from his personal residence, with the counsel of his family instead of ANAP officials (see Cemal 1989b, 125–53).

Aware of the power he wielded over their political careers, deputies were forced to act in compliance with Özal's wishes. Haydar Özalp, an ANAP representative for Niğde, in an interview with journalist Emin Çölaşan that appeared in *Hürriyet*, provided a first-hand account of Özal's relationship with party politicians (1988). When Çölaşan posed the question whether Özalp or other ANAP parliamentarians provided Özal with any critical feedback, he responded with a definitive 'no'. When Çölaşan asked why not, Özalp responded:

As you know, in the past, parliamentarians were selected through primaries and by citizens. Those who were chosen through primaries had a certain character. Today, we don't have this. This is simply the general way in which things operate in the ANAP.

Çölaşan: Namely, what you are saying is that, to a certain point, you have all been selected and put on the candidate list personally by Turgut Özal. Everyone has been selected and chosen by him personally . . .

Özalp: That is clearly the case.

The exchange between Özalp and Çölaşan underlines the power that Özal held over his parliamentarians. Chosen at Özal's discretion, they had little ability to question decisions or shape policy, which resulted in unquestioned obedience to Özal and led to the ANAP being labelled the 'Turgut Özal fan club' (Ahmad 1993, 193). In a similar assessment of Özal's leadership, the late journalist Mehmet Ali Birand asserted in his ten-part series on the leader: 'Whatever he said went [. . .] Outside of him, nobody else had much of an idea of the decisions that were going to be taken' (Birand and Yalçın 2000). Özal went so far as to publicly declare: 'Nobody knows what I will do' (quoted in Cemal 1989b, 124) – a deliberate message about his power to those around him.

The few who dared display dissent were treated with little patience and were condemned to the outer periphery or purged. The ANAP's more liberal members, such as the Minister of Finance Vural Arıkan and the Minister of State Kaya Erdem,[7] were removed from their cabinet positions because they questioned conservative policies and challenged Özal's decisions (Ahmad 1993, 192). Others, like Türkan Arıkan, a parliamentarian for Edirne who resigned after one year due to Özal's authoritarian rule, stated: 'The rule of Turgut Özal has gotten to such a state inside the party that he cannot bear to listen to another voice but his own' (*Milliyet* 1984b). Vural Arıkan, after being removed from cabinet for his indiscretion, resigned, citing Özal's autocratic leadership (*Milliyet* 1985). Özal's brother, Korkut, offered a similar criticism in an interview with *Nokta* magazine:

There is one party; at its head is Turgut *bey*. Turgut *bey* is the only one who can lay a claim to all the rewards and ills from everything that has been done until today. No other person has a right to the rewards or ills of the party

[. . .] Turgut *bey* is responsible for everything that the party does. This is how he leads the party as well. Namely, he has the last word [. . .] Besides, there is no party in Turkey that is democratised. This is where Turkey's troubles arise from. (quoted in Cemal 1989a, 15)

This bleak assessment indicates that the leadership style of his brother was absolute and consistent with the political culture of Turkey. Özal's authoritarianism reflected the typical practices of past leaders and was a key component in Turkey's ongoing struggles to achieve democratic consolidation.

Prime Minister Özal

Early into his first term as Prime Minister, Özal's public character appeared increasingly rigid and overly confident. The inclusive demeanour of his speeches coloured with the word 'we', in the lead-up to the elections, was replaced by the constant use of 'me' or 'I' after securing his electoral victory (Cemal 1989b, 84–85). Individuals in opposition were publicly belittled; criticism was not tolerated, but received with public contempt and ridicule, indicative of a leader who saw himself as the only person capable of solving the country's problems (Cemal 1989b).

Özal's intra-party leadership as the *tek adam* (the single leader) was mirrored in the way in which he managed the government. This allowed Özal to impose his authority on the government, as Mesut Yılmaz, a minister of the period, recalled:

What was going to happen, how it was going to be done and with whom, was generally devised by Özal himself [. . .] I can comfortably say the government was Özal's government. (quoted in Birand and Yalçın 2001, 208)

Yılmaz's observation demonstrates direct parallels between Özal's rule over the ANAP and the management of the government. Accordingly, ministerial posts were assigned without consulting the individuals or considering their competency in their chosen ministries; rather, government officials were selected for their ability to follow his orders (Birand and Yalçın 2001, 208). This lack of transparency and dialogue led to most in the party being taken by surprise at new ministerial appointments, with some only becoming aware of their roles while sitting in the Assembly or from media reports (Cemal 1989b, 124–25, 193; Ahmad 1993). Zeki Yavuztürk, Özal's choice for Minister of National Defence, recalled:

> My appointment as the National Defence Minister baffled many people. I was taken by complete surprise because my profession had nothing to do with defence. I was an engineer. I was only made aware of my appointment when it was announced in parliament [. . .] In fact, in general, many others in the cabinet were put in ministerial positions which were not their profession. (quoted in Birand and Yalçın 2001, 209)

Selecting inexperienced deputies for the cabinet provided Özal greater control over government, rendering his leadership unaccountable to his party and his decisions absolute. Lacking political know-how, inexperienced ministers were unable to offer informed and knowledgeable counter-proposals to his decisions (Birand and Yalçın 2001, 204–10).

All that was expected of ANAP parliamentarians was to rubber-stamp and implement Özal's decisions (Cemal 1989b, 128; Acar 2002, 170–72). One of the ANAP founders, Adnan Kahveci, recalled: 'To be honest we only needed seventeen technocrats for ministerial positions [. . .] The remaining deputies were only there to lift their fingers [to provide the required parliamentary votes]' (quoted in Cemal 1989b, 128). ANAP deputies were not viewed as autonomous political agents; rather, they were seen as legislatures of the Prime Minister's goals.

Since ministerial appointments took place solely at Özal's discretion, decisions to remove and appoint cabinet members were often hastily made, and cabinets were regularly interrupted by sudden changes – a pattern that was in line with the leaders discussed earlier. For instance, following the ANAP's poor showing in the local elections of 1989, Özal dismissed twelve members of his cabinet and took personal control of the economic portfolios (*LA Times* 1989). As ministers were chosen based not on merit, but on the level of loyalty to Özal, cabinet positions therefore constituted a central source of patronage (Özen 2013, 83). This was reflected in the five new ministries that he created and that were deliberately kept vacant. He told ANAP parliamentarian Yıldırım Aktürk that the empty posts had been established as a source of patronage to maintain competition for his loyalty amongst ANAP deputies (Birand and Yalçın 2001, 336).

Eroding the Parliament's Processes

Party-subservience allowed Özal to rule government by fiat. Former Minister Mükerrem Taşçıoğlu recalled that, before Özal's first government received a vote of confidence in the Assembly, Özal personally prepared and presented close to thirty governmental decrees to be signed without examination by the cabinet (Birand and Yalçın 2001, 208). Özal himself admitted that for six years his government ministers had been asked to sign empty decrees, which he then filled out according to his own wishes (Frankel 1991, 75). This resulted in many ministers finding out about legislative changes made to their portfolios in the *Resmi Gazete* (Official Gazette) (Cemal 1989b, 124–25). The sheer volume of bills passed without parliamentary oversight led Özal's administration to be labelled as 'government by decree' (Acar 2002; Heper and Keyman 1998, 267; Frankel 1991, 75). Many of the decrees provided the Prime Minister with greater powers to directly apply policy, particularly in the economic realm (El-Khider 2000, 241).

Özal's government passed the largest number of decrees by any government, civilian or military, up to that point. The ability to pass laws by decree had been introduced into the constitution during the second military coup of 1971 and was expanded upon by the 1980 junta: until 1980, there had been thirty-four decrees by all governments and ninety-one during the military rule from 1980 to 1983. Over the five years of Özal's administration, this increased exponentially to 161 decrees. When compared to the 354 laws introduced between the end of 1983 and March 1989, the decrees made up close to 50 percent of all laws (Cemal 1989b, 129), setting an unfortunate precedent for future leadership (see Chapter 7). This reliance on decrees demonstrates that Özal essentially abandoned any practice of forbearance due to his aversion to parliamentary procedures and oversight (Kayaalp 2015, 23).

As noted in the Introduction, O'Donnell and Shedler, amongst others, have found that a key component to democratic consolidation is the existence of strong institutions that work to provide constraints on the exercise of power. By exploiting his prerogatives and being without checks and balances,

Özal could bypass parliamentary processes, as the leaders before him had done, thus further weakening the representative capacity of these institutions.

This 'flexible' attitude towards legal parameters was embodied in a comment that he purportedly made to an ANAP deputy: 'The law should not be an impediment to the aims of the government' (Cemal 1989b, 116). On another occasion, he famously professed: 'What does it matter if I violate the constitution for once?' (Heper 1990a, 610–11; Mango 2004, 85). Such comments indicate that Özal, if he could not or did not have the time to amend a law in his favour, was open to simply disobeying the law to attain his agenda.

Özal further undermined parliamentary oversight by creating the *fon* system (extra-budgetary funds). This new system was designed to provide him with unrestrained spending of state finances through a source of expenditure external to the formal budget and therefore beyond the oversight of the Assembly and the bureaucracy (Mango 2004, 87; Ahmad 1993, 190–91). Under the ANAP majority, a bill was passed on 28 May 1986, which provided Özal with the sole power to use these extra-budgetary funds (Ahmad 1993, 191). At the time, not even the officials in charge knew the scope of the external budget, as funds were generated at his will. Subsequent research has estimated that more than 150 separate funds existed, ranging from the *otopark fonu* (parking lots fund) to the *fakir fukara fonu* (helping the poor fund) (Özen 2013, 85). Over time, their use became so rampant that the funds amounted to half of the government's overall budget (Özen 2013, 85; Ahmad 1993, 191) and the primary source of Özal's patronage politics (Öniş 2004, 127),[8] directly financing the ANAP's electoral campaigns (Özen 2013, 85). The *fon* system, as Ahmad has asserted (1993, 191), 'became the private budget of political power, and their purpose was entirely political: to buy elections'. In short, state resources were used to generate the political outcomes that supported Özal's particularistic aims.

The use of these funds eventually normalised corruption within the government. Emin Çölaşan (1987) observed in the mid-1980s that the practice became so prevalent that it had turned into a political norm:

> The ANAP has destroyed all the values we held sacred. Ten years ago, we as a nation used to consider swindling, theft, bribery and corruption as dishonourable. Now they are normal things.

Effectively, Özal's decision to bypass democratic processes to directly govern the country transformed political norms. Instead of strengthening democratic practices during his administration, he demonstrated a lack of regard for law or ethics, which had unfortunate and devastating repercussions for Turkish society:

> Özal introduced economic liberalisation without putting any kind of legal infrastructure or controls in place to regulate and limit its excesses [. . .] His failure to provide ethical references for his new Turkey weakened the public fabric of the nation. Corruption, though always a factor in Turkey, was generally shunned as evil prior to the Özal era. In the last two decades it became more or less an accepted way of life. (Lowry 2000, 27–28)

In addition, Özal extended his control by appointing relatives and close associates in critical roles within the ANAP and the government. His brother Yusuf Özal, his cousin Hüsnü Doğan and his brother-in-law Ali Tanrıyar were appointed to ministerial positions. Yusuf Özal was made Minister of State after serving as the head of the State Planning Organization, while his cousin Doğan was appointed Minister of Agriculture and then Minister of Defence. Tanrıyar served as Minister of Interior, while Adnan Kahveci, who was known as having a father-son-like relationship with Özal, first became Özal's Chief of Staff, later served three terms as Minister of State and then as Minister of Finance. Özal's older brother Korkut was responsible for developing business relations with Saudi Arabia, while Özal's son Ahmet became his closest aide and advisor. Özal's daughter Zeynep was involved in the Istanbul branch of the ANAP, while his wife Semra was an ever-present and dominating influence over party decisions (see Cemal 1989b, 136–54; *Milliyet* 1987, 1984a). Those who found themselves at odds with Semra Özal were either purged from the ranks or marginalised (Acar 2002, 171). The nepotism did not go unnoticed by both local and international media outlets, including the *The Economist* and *Financial Times*, who referred to the Özal government as '*Özal Hanedani*' (Özal Dynasty) (Cemal 1989b, 149; *Milliyet* 1984a; Birand and Yalçın 2001, 379).

The Özal family exploited their position to attain major economic benefits for themselves and close associates. Although Turkish politics had not been immune to corrupt practices, Özal's administration became synonymous with corruption. The Özals and their network amassed substantial personal wealth, which they flaunted, despite Turkey's widespread economic hardship. Under the policy of economic liberalisation and privatisation, the Prime Minister provided lucrative contracts to his family members and close associates (Birand and Yalçın 2001, 386). When the Istanbul Stock Market opened in 1985, Özal's son made a fortune. Yet, Özal was unapologetic to those who criticised his son's wealth, stating: 'He is an ordinary citizen, so why should he be excluded because he happens to be the son of the Prime Minister' (Mango 2004, 87). He also helped his son capitalise on a legal loophole that enabled him to break the state monopoly over television and set up Turkey's first private channel *Star 1* in 1990 (Tittensor 2014, 63). Throughout the period, his family's appetite for material rewards was blatantly flaunted, with open disregard for ethical behaviour (Mango 2004, 86–87).

The Prime Minister actively encouraged the abuse of these newfound privileges: Özal viewed corruption as norm in political life, setting a precedence for similar practices by the leaders who came after him – that is, Tansu Çiller and Recep Tayyip Erdoğan (see Chapters 5, 6 and 7). Turan has argued that Özal's actions significantly damaged the country's political ethics:

> First of all, when we talk about Özal, we have to realise that he was transformed in the process. What you might call the economic missionary gradually became the corrupt politician. His family and their entourage were closely identified with corrupt practices. Furthermore, he almost thought corruption was a normal thing. It's not that corruption had necessarily been lacking in Turkish society earlier, but the elected people did not look at it as something normal. But Özal tended to think that this was part of political life. His family, in particular, did not constitute a very good example of clean politics [. . .] The family acquired an amount of wealth which they had not possessed before his political position. He also pressed businesspeople to act generously to his son in their business relations. Hence, these are not pages to be remembered. (Interview, June 2016)

Indeed, Özal circumvented democratic processes, took shortcuts, exploited loopholes and ignored moral codes whenever they stood in the way of implementing his vision or attaining economic advantages for his personal networks.

Özal and the Bureaucracy

Özal saw the bureaucracy as another critical area to be controlled. Despite being a product of the bureaucracy, Özal became very critical of its autonomy once he became Prime Minister (Öniş 2004). Much like with parliamentary oversight, Özal viewed the bureaucracy as a major obstacle to his plans for the economy and therefore expected bureaucrats to loyally implement his economic vision in much the same manner as he expected from ANAP parliamentarians (Cemal 1989b, 115–18). Özal's declaration to 'restructure the state' in order 'for the state to serve the people' was construed as his intent to wrest control over the state from the state departments and grant their authority to himself (Özbudun 2000a).

By flooding the bureaucracy with loyal technocrats or circumventing it altogether, Özal was able to obtain control over bureaucratic institutions (Heper 1990a). Autonomous units were created to operate within or parallel to the existing agencies, which were then filled with loyal members flown in from the United States. This group, parachuted into pivotal positions at Özal's discretion and bestowed with great powers, soon became known as Özal's 'princes' or 'princelings' (Birand and Yalçın 2001, 304–6). In one example, the Ministry of Finance was left with the sole duty of collecting revenue after the creation of the Under-Secretariat for Treasury and Foreign Trade. The latter, composed chiefly of his princelings, was given the key task of devising and implementing fiscal policies (Öniş 2004, 128).

There was also the policy of bringing semi-autonomous agencies under the influence of Özal's office. As a case in point, he appointed Rüşdü Saraçoğlu, a young US-educated technocrat, to head the Central Reserve Bank (Heper 1989; Birand and Yalçın 2001, 2000). Saraçoğlu recalls that Özal wanted the bank to have limited autonomy, which would thereby give him a say in key decisions (Birand and Yalçın 2001, 332). In this regard, and contrary to Özal's rapid economic liberalisation, legislative mechanisms were kept in place to provide Özal control over the Central Reserve Bank, such as Law Nr 1567 (*Türk Parasının Kıymetini Koruma Kanunu*, Currency Protection Law), which allowed governmental interference and / or power to overturn the bank's decisions (Birand and Yalçın 2001, 333). Despite requests that it be lifted, in line with fiscal reforms, Özal refused, on the grounds that '[o]ne day it would serve the needs of the government' (Kumcu 2003).

Bypassing the traditional bureaucratic processes created a semi-bureaucratic group entirely loyal to Özal, a group that lacked due process or a culture of holding the government to account (Öniş 2004). According to both Cüneyt Ülsever and Emin Çölaşan, this was because the 'princelings' lacked bureaucratic experience and know-how (cited in Birand and Yalçın 2001, 304–5). These decisions weakened the bureaucracy's ability to influence public policy-making and succeeded in centralising decisions under Özal (Heper 1990b). Problems were compounded by internal conflicts within the various layers of the bureaucracy, especially the new layers that were loyal to Özal and the old guard that remained loyal to the state (Öniş 2004). This exposed the state to fraudulent practices and large-scale corruption that were orchestrated by this group of loyal bureaucrats (Birand and Yalçın 2001, 305; Mango 2004, 87).

Furthermore, these developments weakened an already fragile economy, particularly in the second half of the 1980s, as Özal's decisions were neither implemented through robust processes, nor supported by sound economic rationale (Mango 2004, 86–87; Öniş 2004), but rather characterised by his impulse for political gain. He openly admitted as much when questioned by close colleagues (Cemal 1989b, 92–93, 108–9; Birand and Yalçın 2001, 334). For instance, interest rates were changed nineteen times in 1987, with the government regularly amending the rules and determining rates to suit its political needs (Cemal 1989b, 88). It is remarkable how far Özal diverged from the neoliberal economic vision that he had espoused when first entering office. The liberal vision he had once championed was ultimately overtaken by his authoritarian tendencies, often at great expense to the economy, as the above examples have demonstrated.

In his efforts to control the bureaucracy, Özal failed to show restraint in the face of legal parameters (Özen 2013, 85). An ANAP member observed of the period that Özal's 'drive to bring the bureaucracy under his control brought us [the government] to a point at which we were faced with trampling on the rule of law' (quoted in Cemal 1989b, 116). Similarly, Saraçoğlu recalls that Özal, in his rush 'to re-shape Turkey, was happy to bypass legal processes and norms [. . .] he actually made a habit of cutting corners' (quoted in Birand and Yalçın 2001, 331–32). These statements underline Özal's record of redrawing rules that were seen as an obstacle to his economic and political objectives (Buğra 1994, 147–48).

Such actions illustrate Özal's lack of institutional forbearance. He was comfortable deploying his institutional powers as broadly as possible to push the bounds of the system in an effort to attain particularistic aims. This weakened vital state institutions by reducing their autonomy, leaving them vulnerable to appropriation for particularistic ends. Such behaviour demonstrates parallels not only with Menderes, Demirel and Ecevit's attempts to co-opt different arms of the state and bureaucracy, but also with future leadership, which had an even graver outcome, as will be shown in Chapters 6 and 7.

Özal *vis-à-vis* Rights and Freedoms: Maintaining the Junta's Straitjacket

Liberalising the political system was not a preference under Özal. The Prime Minister's overwhelming majority in the Assembly gave him the power to push through democratising legislation, should he have chosen to do so, but he showed little interest in amending the laws inherited from the military government. As shown above, the ANAP's Assembly majority was used to meet Özal's particularistic aims, which were far from a commitment to deepening democracy.

As such, embarking on democratising measures and expanding rights did not appear to be a calculated political strategy, as journalist Emre Kongar noted: 'I don't think Özal gave much weight to democracy in his thinking. Democracy was not a philosophy, a value system, nor an ideal for Özal. Özal's actions were simply concerned with achieving his personal aims' (quoted in Birand and Yalçın 2001, 386). Turan has provided a similar evaluation of Özal's commitment to democracy:

> I'm not persuaded that Özal's primary goal was to build a Turkish democracy. But he did things which essentially transformed society, and maybe made it more suitable for a democratic system to operate, without necessarily having democratisation as his major goal. (Interview, June 2016)

While there was some opening-up in areas, these were largely unintended outcomes. Özal himself had made it clear that his aim was 'first economy, then democracy'. Until Turkey achieved a satisfactory level of economic growth (by his measure), political liberalisation would be sacrificed. Özal had, in fact, acknowledged before the 1980 coup that his economic vision could not be implemented in a liberal democratic setting (Ahmad 1993, 193). Indeed, while some repressive laws were amended, often these clauses were replaced by others just as illiberal in character (Birand and Yalçın 2001, 331).

Maintaining the straitjacket on democracy therefore provided the ideal context to implement his vision. The trade union law, the higher education law, the law on elections and political parties, the penal code and the law governing the operation of Turkey's radio and television remained unaltered. Turkey continued to burn, censor and ban books, and to jail its writers. Torture prevailed, and prisoners, held in abysmal conditions, regularly staged hunger strikes (Ahmad 1993, 193, 197). When confronted in a *BBC* interview with allegations of systematic torture and human rights violations, Özal denied the claims (2018a).

The laws implemented by the military not only persisted but were also utilised to silence criticism. One such example is Özal's reliance on repressive laws to curb criticism by the media and his attempt to bring the press under the influence of the government (Cemal 1989b, 257–58). In some instances, more restrictive legislation was put into place (Cemal 1989b, 318–20; Birand and Yalçın 2001, 2000), including the *Türk Ceza Yasası* (Turkish Penal Code) and *Basın Yasası* (Press Law), which were incorporated into a total of fifty-two legislative acts during Özal's time (Cemal 1989b, 313–14). In the beginning, Özal had regularly signalled hopes for greater freedoms in the post-coup environment (Cemal 1989b, 257); however, the promise to loosen restrictive press laws was quickly forgotten, as Özal failed to make any changes to the legislation that restrained the freedom of the media (Donat 1997, 222).

Özal's attack against press freedoms grew more acute as both the economy and his popularity faltered (Cemal 1989b, 264). The Prime Minister became an outspoken critic of the media, making statements such as the following: 'Not only are we faced with a political struggle, but there is also one against the press', and 'during this election [1986 elections] we have another struggle, one that is with the media'. He painted the media as an obstacle and 'enemy' of democracy and the 'national will' (Cemal 1989b, 258). This was very much in step with Menderes's attitude towards the press, as discussed in Chapter 1. Both men came to power promising friendly relations with the media, but as the economy began to suffer from their policies, the media became a target of the government's attacks and was seemingly portrayed as a threat to the political order. In doing so, Özal and Menderes failed to respect the notion that a healthy democracy requires a flourishing media to act as a mechanism of accountability.

Like Menderes, Özal's verbal attacks went hand in hand with legal proceedings against major dailies such as *Hürriyet*, *Günaydın*, *Cumhuriyet* and *Tempo* in the late 1980s (Cemal 1989b, 267; Donat 1997, 222–23). Owners of newspapers personally bore the brunt of the government assault. The owner of *Tercüman*, Kemal Ilıcak, was targeted with financial penalties and threats, a result of his wife and fellow journalist Nazlı Ilıcak's regular criticisms of Özal (Donat 1997, 223). Headlines such as 'Özal's War with the Press' in *Cumhuriyet* reflected the Prime Minister's relationship with critical media. This was underscored by the statistics of his five-and-half-year rule: 2,792 journalists and writers were tried, twenty-six journalists jailed, 368 individual works censured, 308 book titles banned, thirty-nine tonnes of newspapers confiscated and destroyed, a total of 303 legal cases opened against thirteen different newspapers, and billions of fines were meted out against the media, while newspapers suffered unending price increases to their paper supplies, which were ordered by Özal in response to media criticism (Sarılar 1989; Cemal 1989b, 266–67, 313).[9]

Özal's 'No' Campaign and Lead-up to the Presidency

By 1986, the party structure, designed by the military junta, was faltering. Still banned from politics, prominent leaders of the pre-1980 coup era had established political parties by proxy. The generals' attempt to eliminate the old pattern of politics based on 'leader parties' by permitting political novices to run for office had failed. This was the case for Demirel who was guiding the *Doğru Yol Partisi* (True Path Party, DYP); Ecevit, through his wife Rahşan, had founded the *Demokratik Sol Parti* (Democratic Left Party, DSP); Necmettin Erbakan was directing the new Islamist *Refah Partisi* (Welfare Party, RP); and Alparslan Türkeş led the *Milliyetçi Çalışma Partisi* (Nationalist Labour Party, MCP).[10] In the face of the undemocratic institutions that Özal's government operated and the ever-rising inflation, the public turned to these familiar leaders for a solution (Ahmad 1993, 195).

This public sentiment was highlighted at the 28 September 1986 by-election results. The DYP attained 23.7 percent of the votes to ANAP's 32 percent in a stunning show of support for Demirel (Ahmad 1993, 195). Although Özal's party scored the highest percentage of votes, Demirel became Özal's main rival, particularly for the centre-Right. These developments indicated that the politics of the country was rapidly coming full circle.

Due to the strong showing of the previous leaders' proxy parties, Özal came under popular pressure to overturn the military-imposed bans. Given the ANAP majority, the Prime Minister could have amended the constitution that would have revoked the law (Birand and Yalçın 2001, 290–91). In fact, Mesut Yılmaz noted that two-thirds of ANAP's Central Committee were in favour of overturning the bans in the Assembly (Birand and Yalçın 2001, 291); yet, the Prime Minister did not want to compete against these experienced politicians, aware that he would face greater scrutiny and electoral pressure in doing so (Birand and Yalçın 2001, 295–96).[11] In particular, his apprehension was, as Saraçoğlu described, a 'Demirel-phobia' (Birand and Yalçın 2001, 294):

When Demirel returned to politics in [19]87, it scared Turgut *bey*. The brave individual who didn't have a fear of anyone was fearful of Demirel's return to politics.[12]

This fear saw Özal strategically place the issue before a referendum and personally head the 'no' campaign in order to uphold the political bans. Özal's opportunism overrode any adherence to basic democratic standards, especially when they threatened his position. The chapter ultimately marked a major turning point in Özal's career, costing him the few remaining democratic credentials he possessed. Journalist Hasan Cemal went so far as to declare that it was 'his most undemocratic act of all' (1989b, 309). According to Sabri Sayarı (Interview, July 2016):

Özal handled things quite well, up until 1987. When it became clear that the ANAP was not going to win, he then turned into a different personality. For example, the referendum to bring back pre-coup political party leaders, if you were a democrat, why would you oppose this? This was exactly the same thing that the military had done. He headed the campaign against lifting the political bans, wearing his famous t-shirt that said 'no'. I was personally surprised by that. I thought Özal, though not exactly the perfect democrat, acted in that spirit more than the previous leaders. But he lost that, which was a big deal in his career. I don't think he recovered from that.

Özal's steps to maintain the bans were indicative of a leader who wanted to hold on to the reactionary nature of the post-coup regime, as it provided him with the ideal political space. Despite his efforts, the 6 September 1987 referendum returned a slight majority to the 'yes' vote, enough to rescind one of the junta's most radical measures. For the first time in his political career, Özal would now have to face highly experienced competitors who enjoyed an already strong electoral presence.

A snap general election was then called for 29 November 1987. The ANAP government, in an effort to obstruct the gains of the pre-coup leader parties and to strengthen their advantage, made a late amendment to the Electoral Law (Cemal 1989b, 252; Mango 2004, 88).[13] Özal's party won the election (see Table 4.2), albeit with a smaller margin; however, the new electoral law conversely meant that the ANAP's share of Assembly seats increased. In 1983, 45.1 percent of the votes had provided the ANAP with 211 seats (see Table 4.1), whereas the 36.3 percent of the votes that the party received in 1987 translated into 64.9 percent of Assembly seats. This further diminished the democratic standards in the country, with the result declared to 'constitute one of the least representative elections in Turkish history', as Kalaycıoğlu (2002a, 61) has written. It also created a crisis of legitimacy that engulfed the ANAP government.

Table 4.2 1987 Election Results

Political Party	Percentage of Votes	Parliamentary Seats (Total 450)
ANAP	36.3	292
Sosyaldemokrat Halkçı Parti (SHP)	24.7	99
Doğru Yol Partisi (DYP)	19.1	59
Demokratik Sol Parti (DSP)	8.5	0
Refah Partisi (RP)	7.2	0

Source: https://www.tbmm.gov.tr/develop/owa/secim_sorgu.genel_secimler

While the amendment was successful insofar as it helped retain Özal's position in government, it did not stop Demirel's re-entry to the Assembly. The DYP was the third-largest party after the *Sosyaldemokrat Halkçı Parti* (Social Democratic Populist Party, SHP), led by İsmet İnönü's son Erdal.

President Özal, Bending the Constitutional Bounds

Özal's fortunes continued to wane over the following two years, with the 26 March 1989 municipal elections shining a light on the scale of his prob-lems. The ANAP's overall vote dropped below 22 percent, and the party managed to win only two municipalities out of the sixty-seven (Ergüder 1991, 161), while İnönü's SHP and Demirel's DYP rose to 28.6 and 25.13 percent, respectively. In less than five years, the ANAP's and Özal's popular-ity had more than halved, slipping from near 45 to under 22 percent.

The ever-declining support forced Özal to look for another avenue to hold on to power. His wife Semra recalled that he sensed the inevitability of his electoral slide, but refused to fall into the role of opposition, as such a proposition did not sit well with him. Consequently, Özal nominated him-self for the presidential seat, which was soon to be vacated by Kenan Evren (Birand and Yalçın 2001, 394–95). After a bitter fight in parliament, the ANAP's majority enabled Özal to muster enough votes to assume the presi-dency (Heper 1992a, 110–11).[14]

The presidency would afford him another seven years at the pinnacle of political power, from where he would be able to influence developments. Had he chosen to continue to lead the government until the next general elections, Demirel would have politically relegated him. Thus, the presiden-tial post became a salvation:

> Özal from 1983 to late 1987 operated in very calm waters, in stark contrast to the political landscape of the 1970s. That's why he could accomplish his economic goals easily. He was left alone and went largely unchallenged. But when Demirel and other pre-coup politicians re-entered politics, he couldn't break into the established patterns of party followership and party voting. If he remained as party leader, signs indicated that, in the next election, Demirel would have beaten him easily for control of the centre-Right. He sensed that, and that is why he became President. (Interview with Sabri Sayarı, July 2016)

Indeed, Ülsever noted that this was a retreat rather than a victory: 'Özal did not ascend to the Presidency, he escaped to it' (quoted in Birand and Yalçın 2001, 395). In doing so, he became the second civilian president after Celal Bayar (Ahmad 1993, 217), but the decision should not be interpreted as an attempt to weaken the military tutelage. Özal simply wanted to continue to influence outcomes, just as his predecessors had done.

In office, Özal disregarded the constitutionally neutral and above-party role of the President and exploited legal and political opportunities to convert the presidency into the centre of the executive. He continued to maintain direct links with the ANAP, which he promoted and supported in his capacity as President (Heper 1992a, 111; Mango 2004, 88), staunchly defending this conduct: 'If what I say seems to favour the ANAP, that is not because I discriminate between the political parties but because my views and those of the ANAP coincide [. . .] since I founded [it]' (quoted in Heper 1992a, 112).

Özal also engineered changes in the ANAP to ensure that he would retain control over the government. Most notably, he hand-picked a loyal successor, Yıldırım Akbulut, to be the Prime Minister, a decision that bypassed intra-party democratic processes and took the ANAP and even Akbulut by surprise (Birand and Yalçın 2001, 411). Akbulut maintains that Özal informed him of his decision as they walked side-by-side up the stairs of the Assembly to Özal's swearing-in ceremony as President. Former cabinet member Hasan Celal Güzel explained: 'After becoming President he [Özal] wanted someone that would continue to allow him the same authority and wouldn't pose a challenge to him'. Akbulut was chosen for this reason (Birand and Yalçın 2001, 411). Ever accommodating, Akbulut allowed Özal to govern along the lines of a *de facto* executive presidential system (Heper 2013, 143; Çınar and Özbudun 2002, 183), which permitted him to act as the head of the party and in effect to control the ANAP's parliamentary majority. This was in explicit contravention of the constitutional principle of presidential impartiality and ultimately set a precedent for future presidential conduct (see Chapter 7).

Özal remained unapologetic, having made no secret of his desire to marginalise the parliament and to transition Turkey to an executive presidential system throughout his time as Prime Minister (Acar 2002, 174). As s close colleague noted, Özal preferred a presidential system: '[B]ecause he always wanted to be the first [. . .] He thinks of only what will provide him with the strongest position' (quoted in Cemal 1989b, 122). This said, as Prime Minister Özal did not have the ability to amend the constitution so as to change the governing system, given that the ANAP did not have enough parliamentary numbers (Cemal 1989b, 254–55). Nonetheless, by maintaining his direct control over the ANAP, he could rule in a *de facto* executive presidential manner (Acar 2002, 174; Heper 2013, 145), thus weakening the autonomy of the parliament as the representative body.

In time, the limits to Özal's control over the ANAP and the government began to appear, as he could do little about the simmering tensions among the party deputies, given the continued loss of electoral support under Akbulut and the tensions that this caused. On 15 June 1991, Akbulut was displaced in an intra-party vote by Mesut Yılmaz (Kalaycıoğlu 2002b, 49), with the open backing from Semra Özal (Çınar and Özbudun 2002, 184; Birand and Yalçın 2001).[15] The combination of his wife's approval, the need to change the ANAP's political fortunes and Yılmaz's growing popularity in the electorate were factors that stopped Özal from directly intervening in the intra-party vote. Yılmaz, however, hinted that he would not be as compliant as Akbulut, repeatedly reminding Özal that the President should not step into the realm of government jurisdiction (Gönenç 2008, 508). This jeopardised Özal's control over the parliamentary government:

> He tried to do something, which is being done much more blatantly today [referring to Recep Tayyip Erdoğan]. After Özal became the President, he initially fancied that he could appoint a Prime Minister who would be obedient, and he would appoint a Council of Ministers that would almost be ceremonial and a group of Under-Secretaries working under each ministry whom he would have direct influence over, and he could ultimately control the government like that [. . .] It soon became evident that he was not going to be able to do that. This was signalled when there was a change in the party leadership from Akbulut to Yılmaz. (Interview with İlter Turan, June 2016)

Once Özal realised that Yılmaz was not going to allow the ANAP to remain under his authority, Özal undertook alternative measures which triggered deep fractures in the party and amplified government instability,[16] including the elevation of his wife Semra to the head of the ANAP's Istanbul branch.[17] When Minister of Defence Hüsnü Doğan and other close associates, including his brother Yusuf Bozkurt Özal, voiced their disapproval, they were publicly disparaged (Pope 1991; Acar 2002, 171). In addition to these manoeuvres, Özal began holding secret late-night meetings with loyal ANAP deputies at the presidential residence in order to undermine Yılmaz's leadership (Birand and Yalçın 2000).

When Yılmaz sidelined pro-Özal elements and shut down avenues that enabled the President to influence government, Özal's character turned increasingly hostile. He orchestrated the resignation of ANAP parliamentarians to create a new party which he would control behind the scenes (Birand and Yalçın 2001, 498–513).[18] Çandar has argued that Özal's efforts to split the ANAP stemmed from what he perceived as a betrayal:

> When he moved up to the presidency, his party was taken up by Mesut Yılmaz. Özal didn't want Yılmaz to lead the party at all. Özal was against him rising to ANAP leadership. I know it first-hand because he told me directly. He formed the ANAP, its name, the logo, everything was his idea, everything was his brainchild [. . .] When Yılmaz consolidated his power over the party, he sacked pro-Özal elements or they resigned. In fact, it was my proposal to Özal to let them resign immediately. It was in Özal's mind to form a new party and step down from the presidency. We were discussing all these together in a very confidential way. Semi-jokingly, when we were watching the ANAP congress live on TV, at a certain point I turned to him and said: 'Where did you find all these guys? If there was a reward to find the meanest and most incapacitated people to gather and form a party, you have to be awarded for it. [I mean] Where did you find these guys?' He turned and said: 'You want to know really? From the street, they were nobodies'. (Interview, October 2016b)

Following the 1992 party congress, nineteen members – sixteen of them currently serving parliamentarians, including former Prime Minister Akbulut – resigned from the ANAP under Özal's directive (Birand and Yalçın 2001, 501–7). The resignations decreased the party's Assembly numbers to ninety-six (*Milliyet* 1992a).[19] Mass resignations continued over the following days, with a total of fifty-four former ANAP parliamentarians, including five of the founding members of the party. In addition, Özal's wife Semra and the entire women's branch of the ANAP quit the party (*Milliyet* 1992c). In the context of the party's decreasing electoral support, the resignations threatened its future survival.

There was nothing new about the substance of these acts. Özal's efforts to fracture the ANAP mirrored the lengths to which his predecessors Menderes, Demirel and Ecevit had to go in order to maintain control over their parties. Each leader viewed their parties as their own personal fiefdoms, consequently fracturing their parties and causing dysfunction within the government. Özal had no desire to follow the constitution and democratic norms if his ambitions were jeopardised. Yılmaz's purge of pro-Özal elements from the ANAP in order to consolidate power also mirrored previous authoritarian party leadership patterns. With the struggle between Özal and Yılmaz, Turkey witnessed the split of a party due to competing authoritarian interests.

Özal's efforts to direct the government also saw the establishment of a shadow government operating from the presidential residence. Özal consulted a handful of loyal ministers and high-level bureaucrats, side-stepping relevant ministers and even the Prime Minister to devise and implement unilateral economic and foreign policy decisions (Mango 2004, 90–91; Birand and Yalçın 2001, 494–98; Donat 1997, 199–200).[20] For instance, Prime Minister Akbulut was informed of his government's new foreign policy initiatives (decided by the President) through media reports (Donat 1997, 199–200). Özal's sustained disregard for the lines of responsibility prompted the Minister of Finance and Customs, as well as two Ministers of Foreign Affairs, to resign within the first twelve months of his presidency (Mango 2004, 90; Heper 1992a, 112; Birand and Yalçın 2001, 529–30).

Özal relied on retired General Kemal Yamak to act as his 'shadow chief of staff' in order to develop an adventurist foreign policy during the First Gulf War (Ahmad 1993, 201). This contravened civil-military protocols, prompting the acting Chief of General Staff, General Necip Torumtay, to resign, sparking a major crisis between the President and the military (Mango 2004, 90). Despite overwhelming parliamentary and military opposition, Özal drew Turkey to the brink of entering the First Gulf War (Hale 2013, 160), largely to boost his personal standing domestically and internationally (Acar 2002, 174). Özal bypassed the government and the Assembly to directly engage in secret diplomatic talks with the US administration under Bush, which would have enabled Turkish troops to enter the war. This decision was ultimately averted by forceful opposition from the military (Frankel 1991; Mango 2004, 90–91; Ahmad 1993, 200).

His overall conduct became the source of political dysfunction, creating a crisis of legitimacy within the wider government. Demirel, as the main opposition voice in the Assembly, used every opportunity to snub, attack, discredit and delegitimise Özal (Heper 1992a, 113), accusing the President of violating the constitution with his 'partisan' behaviour (Heper 1992a, 112). The situation between the two leaders deteriorated to the point where Demirel blamed the political crisis on Özal, vowed to remove the President from his post once he had the parliamentary numbers (Heper 1992a, 112) and began a nation-wide campaign to force early elections (McLaren 2008, 168). This only served to intensify an already volatile political climate (Birand and Yalçın 2001, 494).

Existing tensions worsened with the elections held on 20 October 1991. The sharp swing against the ANAP brought Demirel to power as the head of a coalition government with İnönü's SHP (see Table 4.3). With Demirel and Özal occupying the two highest branches of government, Turkey witnessed yet another example of government dysfunction at the hands of avowed political foes.

Demirel used his powers to isolate and weaken Özal, while Özal in turn became more intolerant and vindictive (Birand and Yalçın 2001, 494–95). Demirel warned government parliamentarians to withhold information from Özal (Birand and Yalçın 2001, 494), and in retaliation Özal regularly delayed or refused to sign governmental decrees concerning the appointment of key bureaucrats – by March 1993, forty-seven such decrees were waiting to be signed by the President (Gönenç 2008, 509). In turn, to limit the President's powers and circumvent his oversight, Demirel introduced a series of laws called *baypas yasaları* (bypass laws) (Tanık 2009; Donat 1992).

Table 4.3 1991 Election Results

Political Party	Percentage of Votes	Parliamentary Seats (Total 450)
DYP	27	178
ANAP	24	115
SHP	20.8	88
RP	16.9	62
DSP	10.7	7

Source: https://www.tbmm.gov.tr/develop/owa/secim_sorgu.genel_secimler

Conversely, in order to obtain knowledge of the government's policies, Özal began holding meetings with bureaucrats at the Presidential Palace and established his own team of experts and Under-Secretariats to pursue policies independently from Demirel's government (McLaren 2008, 168; Birand and Yalçın 2001, 497). Özal even sidelined Demirel to chair the Prime Minister's cabinet meeting in March 1993 (Tanık 2009). Although his decision was constitutional, it was an extremely aggressive act that went beyond the norms of government-president relations, further inflaming the political tensions.

The political tit-for-tat, over time, transformed Özal into a frustrated and isolated President (Birand and Yalçın 2001, 546). Demirel leading the government, coupled with the loss of the ANAP, left Özal exposed to an increased level of criticism and limited his pursuit to direct developments (see Frankel 1991; Heper 1992a). His presidential advisor Çandar recalls how Özal became a lonely President due to the changed political landscape:

> Özal was a President under siege in Çankaya. It was a period where Demirel was calling the shots with his coalition partner Erdal İnönü [. . .] His power could not be sustained as President because Demirel became the head of government, and he tried and campaigned to limit Özal's presidential powers [. . .] The only thing that was left to rely on was his own party, but that had a very clear distance to him under Yılmaz's leadership [. . .] He therefore became a lonely man at the top, and so he did not represent the best example of a strongman leader. Indeed, he was a strongman when he was successful, when he introduced success to the Turkish economy and managed the transition of the economy. He was the right person at the right time, which led him to be a powerful man. Therefore, Özal was able to put his stamp on a very important period of political history in Turkey. So, yes, he was the strongman, but under favourable conditions. However, he was not the type of strongman in the mould of Demirel. In fact, when Demirel stepped back into politics, Özal was paralysed, he lost his political footing. Then it was downhill from there for him. (Interview, October 2016b)

Özal became increasingly embittered and dejected, carrying out presidential duties often without consulting Demirel's government (Heper 1992a, 113), including regular trips overseas to pursue a personalised economic and foreign policy agenda parallel to the government (Birand and Yalçın 2001, 506). Frustrated at his growing isolation, Özal planned to resign from the presidency and to step back into politics by forming a new party with former ANAP colleagues (Birand and Yalçın 2001, 538, 543–44; *Milliyet* 1992b).

What Özal failed to see is that his continued overreach and push against democratic rules and institutions had damaged an already fragile multi-party system and created a crisis in government. One of the five generals who led the coup of 1980 commented on the period:

> We think that the country is going down the drain; we intervene, make a new constitution in the hope that we can have a better democracy, and withdraw to our barracks; soon we see that democracy reverts back to its old ways. (quoted in Heper 1992a, 114)

The general's comment highlights that, despite the military's efforts, Özal continued the pattern of authoritarian culture; Özal's presidency, much like his prime ministership, was founded on the premise that a president should not be obstructed. This set a troubling precedent, showing the extent to which constitutional limits could be broken or stretched by a sitting president. However, before he could move forward with his plans, Özal's role in Turkish politics came to sudden end on 17 April 1993, when he died of a heart attack.

Conclusion

The immediate era in the wake of the post-1980 coup was a highly dynamic period in Turkey, but it did not move the country towards consolidation under Özal. His leadership style proved problematic. It failed to deepen democracy and foster democratic practices to attain consolidation.

Like leaders before him, the political party was personalised under Özal. This was accommodated by the new SPK, which regulated leader-dominance over their parties. This was also a natural outcome, given that the ANAP had been specifically created to serve Özal's personal political ambitions. In putting the party together, he made sure that all powers were coalesced in his hands: ANAP politicians had to display complete loyalty for their political survival, a loyalty that Özal was ruthless in exploiting.

The personalisation of the ANAP, along with the single-party majority he enjoyed, allowed Özal to exploit this position in order to gain unchecked power in his office. He freely wielded political power over the Assembly, which was then extended to the bureaucracy; yet, these institutional prerogatives were not used to liberalise the system by granting rights to a society that had been forced into a straitjacket by the laws of the junta. His government made no attempt at expanding democracy, making politics responsive to the needs of the public, nor did he strengthen vertical or horizontal forms of accountability. Rather, he maintained the draconian structures and legislation of the military junta, as this offered him largely unfettered rule. The ANAP's majority was used to bypass parliamentary processes and disregard democratic and state institutions where possible, and he introduced greater levels of corruption to political life. Ultimately, Özal showed little tolerance for obstacles against his decisions, regardless of the constitutional and democratic limits placed on his role, which ultimately altered the bounds of acceptable behaviour by leaders. Similarly, as President, he was able to coalesce the powers of the parliamentary government in his office through a subservient ANAP government. When Özal lost control of the party, he was unwilling to temper this path; instead, he pushed harder against the political realities, which ultimately brought on a higher degree of stagnation between his office and the parliament.

Although a liberal in the economic sense, perhaps his statement of acting 'contrary to the constitution' best encapsulates both his impatience towards democratic checks and his idea of leadership, as a leader who prioritised direct unfettered rule. Indeed, Özal had grand visions for Turkey; yet, his ten-year-long tenure had a detrimental effect on democratic institutions, norms and political ethics. Following Özal's death, a new generation of leaders was ushered in, alongside the established names of Demirel, Ecevit and Erbakan. Despite these shifts in the political landscape and the hope that new leaders brought, Turkey could not break from its leadership culture and take strong steps towards consolidation, as the next chapter will demonstrate.

Notes

1. According to an official government report, 43,140 individuals suspected of 'terrorist' activities were arrested. Of these, 13,749 were convicted and received sentences ranging from one year to more than twenty years of jailtime. Forty-seven of those convicted received the death sentence, the youngest being seventeen years of age; see Sayarı (2010).

2. Similar to the coup in 1960, the intervention engaged in major constitutional engineering of the political sphere. Aiming to depoliticise society, the broad and numerous liberties afforded in the previous constitution were severely curtailed and the political role of the military considerably enhanced as a tutelary institution (see Özbudun 2000b, 2011a).

3. Özal did ask for Demirel's blessing and permission to acquire former AP parliamentarians, such as Necdet Seçkinöz, Mehmet Gölhan, Mehmet Dülger and Atilla Peynircioğlu, to help form the ANAP. According to the sources, Demirel did give his blessings to Özal, but was against any former AP parliamentarians going across to the ANAP. In fact, he refused to provide any assistance to Özal, because he planned to return to the political arena (Birand and Yalçın 2001, 154–58).

4. A ten-percent threshold had been introduced into the constitution by the military junta to block the fragmentation of the party system experienced in the 1970s.

5. The *Yeni Demokrasi Hareketi* (New Democracy Movement) was founded in 1994 by businessman Cem Boyner. The party disbanded in 1996 after it failed to win enough votes to enter parliament.

6. Onur Kumbaracıbaşı served three consecutive terms as representative in the Assembly from late 1987 to late 1995, and acted as a minister in coalition governments.

7. Erdem also served as Deputy Prime Minister, along with his ministerial position.

8. One form of this was to provide credit at preferential rates to those close to the government (Öniş 2004, 127).

9. The Istanbul Second Penal Court's figures concerning hearings against the media are a further testament to the level of repression meted out to journalists: in 1984, 200 cases were opened against a total of 312 defendants; in 1985, 257 cases against 302 defendants; in 1986, 202 trials involving 420 defendants; in 1987, 317 trials against 509 defendants. The statistics from the Istanbul Second High Criminal Court are as follows: in 1983, 90 trials against 121 defendants; in 1984, 266 defendants; in 1985, 135 defendants; in 1986, 56 cases against 89 defendants; in 1987, 23 cases against 32 defendants (*Basın Konseyi Dergisi* 1989).

10. In 1992, the party reverted to its former name, *Milliyetçi Hareket Partisi* (Nationalist Movement Party, MHP).

11. In a later interview, General Kenan Evren – who had led the coup, was the main architect of these bans and served as President of the republic at the time – remarked that he did not oppose the constitutional change and had left Özal's government to make the decision (Birand and Yalçın 2001, 290–91).

12. Özal later acknowledged that he had opposed lifting the bans largely because he was 'mad at Demirel' (Acar 2002, 169).

13. The changes by the ANAP introduced a district level quota over and above the national quota of 10 percent. Therefore, for any candidate to win a seat in parliament, their party needed to gain more than 10 percent of the national vote, and the party list had to obtain more than the district level quota as well (see Kalaycıoğlu 2002a).

14. Most notably, opposition parties harshly criticised Özal on the grounds that, as proven by the local elections of 26 March 1989, the popularity of the ANAP had decreased dramatically. Thus, the election of the President by such a party, enjoying only the support of a small portion of the electorate, was morally and politically unacceptable (Gönenç 2008, 507).

15. In the lead-up to the intra-party vote, Özal had serious reservations about Yılmaz as potential leader. Yet, after warning his wife about Yılmaz's potential flaws, Özal was eventually dissuaded by Semra and did not intervene (Birand and Yalçın 2001, 453–87).

16. The tensions arising from Özal's ambitions to manage the ANAP and Yılmaz's desire to act independently surfaced when Özal stormed out of an ANAP meeting after his former party drew up a list of candidates different from the list of names he had provided (Birand and Yalçın 2001, 489). The final breaking point in their relationship came when Yılmaz refused to abide by Özal's direction during a private meeting at the presidential residence (Birand and Yalçın 2001, 490).

17. The Istanbul office was the most influential and strongest branch; hence, without its support it would have been extremely hard to control the rest of the party.

18. Although the announcement of the new party was close, it did not eventuate due to his untimely death.

19. After the 1991 elections, the ANAP dropped to 115 representatives; however, three parliamentarians defected to the DYP, leaving it with 112 members in the Assembly leading into the party congress.

20. For a good analysis of Özal's foreign policy during his time as Prime Minister and President see Hale (2013).

5

1993–2002: THE 1990S AND THE CRISES OF DEMOCRACY

Introduction

The death of Turgut Özal brought a colourful period in Turkish political history to its end. Yet, this did not signify a change; rather, politics continued its usual pattern despite a changing landscape marked by the arrival of emerging new leaders on the political scene. The 1990s were marred by major political upheavals, economic instability, a violent conflict raging in the southeast of the country and governments collapsing as quickly as they had been established. Mirroring past behaviour patterns, political leaders were responsible for the economic, political and democratic crises that marked this decade. In the midst of these crises, the military intervened once again on 28 February 1997 to decide the fate of the sitting government.

This chapter's opening discussion focuses on the prominent politician Erdal İnönü, an anomaly within the leadership culture at this juncture. Juxtaposing experiences under İnönü exposes the level of authoritarianism of Turkish leaders and its negative impact on political outcomes. The chapter then shifts its focus to Tansu Çiller, as a central political actor throughout this era. Although Çiller symbolised a generational shift in leadership, her conduct in power resembled that of the traditional political culture and shaped anti-democratic political developments of the period. The analysis then extends its focus to the fractious coalition governments between Çiller and Mesut Yılmaz: an unstable period fuelled by the two leaders' clamour for power, at a cost to the country's stability. Next, this chapter will survey Necmet-tin Erbakan's political leadership style to illustrate how his regular demon-stration of Islamist values were a causal factor for the 1997 intervention. Furthermore, it will explore how Süleyman Demirel, as the President, played a critical role behind the scenes in accommodating the military intervention and subsequent breakdown of the government. The chapter ends with Bülent Ecevit, who, despite his political experience, showed that his leadership style was starkly reminiscent of the CHP in the 1970s, as manifested in similarly grave consequences for his government.

Erdal İnönü: An Anomaly amongst Leaders

In 1991 Demirel became Prime Minister by forging an unlikely coalition with Erdal İnönü's social democratic SHP, thereby ending the long-running tensions between the Left and the Right, which had wreaked havoc on the political landscape from the late 1960s to the 1980 coup.[1] Contrasting politi-cal ideologies did not distract the DYP-SHP constellation from forming a harmonious governing coalition, which lasted until 1993, when Demirel vacated his prime ministerial post for the presidency, which had been left empty after Özal's death. It was the first time in Turkish politics that a coali-tion government enjoyed goodwill from both sides. One of the founding members, Korel Göymen, who also served as a ministerial Under-Secretary, recounted Demirel's conciliatory disposition toward İnönü:

> The popular discourse in Turkey has always been that coalitions don't work. However, our coalition with Mr Demirel worked very well. Demirel and İnönü put up a very good example of mutual respect and tolerance between partners. I cannot recall of any significant issue between the two ideologically different partners that previously had confrontational relations during the 1970s.
>
> A crisis emerged just prior to the declaration of the coalition's cabinet. One of the top people in our party wanted the post of Foreign Minister, whereas in the original arrangement we were given the Defence Ministry. This caused a crisis within our party and upset Mr İnönü. I suggested that I speak to Mr Demirel to see if a solution could be found. After I spoke to Mr Demirel, he asked: 'Will this ease the pressure on Mr İnönü?' 'Yes, it would be very much appreciated', I replied. Then he immediately called his aide to change the (cabinet) list: 'Let's give SODEP the Foreign Ministry'.

He then turned to me and said: 'But this is the only time, there won't be any further changes'. I replied: 'There won't be anymore changes'. So he had a great deal of respect for Mr İnönü. This continued throughout their working relationship. This, however, was contrary to our political culture. Here you see two different leaders from two different roots coming together. (Interview, April 2016)

This contrasts markedly with Demirel's character in the 1960s and 1970s, even though, as clearly presented above, he remained the dominant voice over his party and the coalition, continuing to make changes in cabinet without consultation. Nonetheless, the congenial nature of the coalition was unique and atypical of past political experiences of the country.

Demirel's uncharacteristically conciliatory manner may reflect the reality that İnönü did not represent a threat to his leadership of the government. İnönü's character reflected his democratic values and was markedly different to his peers, both past and present, and contributed in no small part to intra-party stability and, ultimately, the stability of government. Onur Kumbaracıbaşı who served as a parliamentary deputy under İnönü, noted:

Erdal İnönü, when he led the party, he was a complete democrat. Everything was done through pre-selections. He wouldn't accept anything that wasn't decided with pre-selection, and he would work with whomever was elected [. . .] Erdal İnönü led the most democratic era in SHP-CHP's history [. . .] He was told that he did not suit politics in Turkey. This is right because of the nature of politics in Turkey. He would have fitted in well in a consolidated system like the British or French context. So politics during his era was prosperous and healthy. (Interview, April 2016)

Kumbaracıbaşı's personal insight reveals that İnönü's leadership offered a contrast to the pervading authoritarian culture. However, his democratic disposition rendered him open to attack by a political culture that demanded aggression:

Mr İnönü had a very democratic way of running the party, which was appreciated by some who came from the same political culture. After some time, he was also criticised for not being a 'strongman', who, when necessary, quite often banged his fist on the table and acted as vulgar as the other political leaders around him. But that was not his personality [. . .] Leaders in Turkey expect total obedience. The only exception I saw to this was Mr İnönü. He had no interest in being the aggressive leader. In fact, people criticised him, which he allowed. He said he learnt from his mistakes, and he meant that. (Interview with Korel Göymen, April 2016)

These comments demonstrate that a leader with a strong democratic nature, such as İnönü, is critical for political stability and was key to the longevity and success of the coalition government:

In many respects, İnönü was an anomaly in Turkish politics. A true democrat and very low-key person [. . .] For example, when Tansu Çiller took over from Demirel and headed the coalition with İnönü, it survived. Çiller was a difficult leader to get along with, and successfully managing his partnership with Çiller, as he did, really showed İnönü's easy-going nature and tolerance as a politician. He was someone that was much more agreeable than you would normally find in Turkish politics. The way he served as Deputy Prime Minister and Foreign Minister showed that he was a type of politician different from the norm in Turkish politics. (Interview with Sabri Sayarı, July 2016)

The insights from Sayarı, Göymen and Kumbaracıbaşı illustrate that political stability demands leaders who can act in a conciliatory manner, in line with the norms required for consolidation. The point is further highlighted by the coalition's collapse soon after İnönü's resignation from his position in government and as leader of the SHP in September 1993,[2] four months after Demirel had become President.[3]

This period can also be used to draw critical lessons to better evaluate the reasons for political instability in Turkey. The 1990s highlighted the importance of political relationships and the fact that a party's survival is principally influenced by leaders' personalities. İnönü's democratic leadership style was markedly different from Turkish political norms, which rendered his position vulnerable to criticism: İnönü was ultimately undermined by those who behaved in a more traditional authoritarian style, a commonplace amongst elites.

Tansu Çiller as Party Leader

Demirel had been elected by parliament to fill the role of President after Özal's death, and he was to follow a path similar to Özal in selecting Tansu Çiller as his successor to lead the *Doğru Yol Partisi* (True Path Party, DYP) (Mango 2004, 94). Although he did not mirror Özal's striking attempts to push the constitutional limits of the presidency (see Arat 2002; Bodgener 1993), he was unwilling to relinquish the leverage that the DYP had in the parliamentary make-up. His rationale was that he would face less resistance and retain the power to influence political developments, if the DYP maintained its strong position in government. Thus, when the time came to fill the newly vacant position, Demirel ordered Hüsamettin Cindoruk to remain Speaker of the Assembly and not contest the party leadership (Birand and Yıldız 2012, 22–23). Cindoruk, Demirel's long-time loyal deputy, was by far the most popular party member and by all accounts would have comfortably won a party leadership vote. However, Demirel's request for him to stand down as a candidate allowed Çiller to accumulate enough votes to win the intra-party ballot (see Birand and Yıldız 2012, 22–25; Cizre 2002b, 201–2).

Given that Çiller had entered the DYP only in 1990, her successorship to Demirel at the June 1993 Extraordinary Congress was a remarkable achievement. DYP parliamentarian Hasan Ekinci attributed Çiller's opportunistic personality and Demirel's support as the principal factors behind her rapid rise within the upper ranks of the party (Birand and Yıldız 2012, 28; Kesgin 2012). Demirel brought Çiller into his party to reenergise DYP ranks and quickly made her the Minister of State responsible for the economy (Cizre 2002b, 201–2). For Demirel, Çiller represented the ideal candidate to revitalise the image of the DYP among the electorate, which at the time was heavily dominated by older men:

> While at Boğaziçi University, Tansu Çiller published a couple of academic articles which helped build her reputation as an economist and then she quickly found herself in the DYP. Around this time, Demirel's advisors kept warning him that the image of the party hierarchy did not appeal to the electorate because it was made up of old men and urged him to bring in some new faces. To modernise the party's image, Demirel brought in Çiller and

gave her a cabinet position almost immediately; she was then helped in her rise to the party leadership. All this happened within a short period of time. (Interview with Sabri Sayarı, July 2016)

The introduction of Çiller worked favourably for the DYP's electoral standing: the public was thrilled by a woman's rise to power in Turkish politics, the first to be elected to the leadership of a party positioned on the Right. Her rise symbolised the country's 'switch to youth and dynamism' of the post-1980 era (Pope 1993) and represented the recognition of women's advances in Turkish society (Bodgener 1993). A political outsider from a modest family in Istanbul, Çiller and her ascent, in the eyes of many voters, embodied the dynamism of modern Turkey. Çiller brought hope to a country that had witnessed little to no political liberalisation since the military rule, ongoing economic bottlenecks and the threat of terrorism by the PKK (İnal 2015, 4, 6).

Nonetheless, Çiller failed to make a break from the well-worn path paved by her predecessors. She had come to power through an intra-party election, espousing democratic values to the party delegates.[4] Yet, like Demirel and Ecevit, Çiller showed that she was unwilling to leave herself open to the possibility of removal from her leadership role through the same internal democratic process and thus behaved in a similar fashion.

The DYP's structure, built on the centralisation of power and accumulation of resources in the hands of its previous leader provided a ready-made powerbase for Çiller to wield, enabling her personal wishes to slowly dominate over the party. Among her colleagues, Çiller quickly earned the reputation of being confrontational and difficult to work with (Kesgin 2012, 39). Under her directives, disciplinary action was taken against intra-party opposition and 'potential challengers' (Cizre 2002b, 207–8). Former Health Minister Rifat Serdaroğlu noted that party decisions were made and implemented arbitrarily and often served particularistic purposes and outcomes (Birand and Yıldız 2012, 48–49). Köksal Toptan, who also served as a parliamentarian with the DYP during this period, recounted:

Out of all the political leaders I was fortunate to work under, Tansu *hanım* [meaning Mrs Tansu] was the least inclusive when it came to running a party. I can say that she wasn't too inclined to consult and take advice from others.

Hence, Tansu *hanım*'s leadership was not conducive to fostering a democratic culture inside the DYP. However, let me also underline that this is not so different from other leaders in Turkey's history. The tradition to run parties single-handedly is part of the political culture of this country. (Interview, March 2016)

First-hand accounts by DYP parliamentarians indicate that Çiller, in keeping with the traditional Turkish leadership style, utilised the existing centralised structure to mould the party to reflect her political ambitions and enact her wishes.

By removing members closely associated with Demirel, Çiller eliminated the risk of any challenge by a faction loyal to the previous leader. During the 1995 party congress, she proclaimed as much: 'The DYP is launching young, dynamic, and storm-like cadres [. . .] we are leaving behind archaic values' (quoted in Cizre 2002b, 203). Party co-founders, including İsmet Sezgin, Hüsamettin Cindoruk and Köksal Toptan, were soon marginalised, and supporters from outside the party's ranks were placed in critical positions (Birand and Yıldız 2012, 28, 50).

Around this period, Çiller's steps to fortify her position became bolder and more audacious, discarding any semblance of democratic practices. She ignored the results of the primaries and personally dictated her preferred candidates to replace defiant serving deputies (Cizre 2002b, 207; 2002a, 91). Many of the candidates for DYP safe seats in the 1996 general election were either individuals with whom she enjoyed close ties or known sympathisers (İşleyen 1999). Çiller excluded fifty incumbent parliamentarians from the list altogether and placed other serving representatives not to her liking in places that the DYP had no likelihood of winning. Conservative-statist candidates consisting of former police chiefs, regional governors from the regions that were living under a state of emergency in the Southeast, former bureaucrats and conservative nationalist figures were placed on the electoral lists of electorally favourable places (Cizre 2002b, 203). This pattern continued in the 1999 elections, whereby Çiller once again disregarded primaries by removing twenty-eight incumbents from the list. Others whom she did not favour were forced to contest for unwinnable seats (Önal 1999). As a result, all names close to Demirel were purged entirely from the DYP's Assembly group within a few years.

Çiller also embarked on a campaign to dismiss any provincial-level party officials who opposed her (Cizre 2002b, 208). In one example, her former Minister of Interior Sezgin noted that Çiller purged more than fifty provincial offices and between 400 to 500 district party offices (Birand and Yıldız 2012, 48). To illustrate this further, Çiller expelled sixty-five out of the eighty existing provincial party heads between the 1996 National Convention and June 1999, and she removed 126,000 registered members of the party from the Istanbul branch alone (Çetin 1999). Owing to these developments, Yeşim Arat concluded that Çiller 'deinstitutionalised the party, turning it into an organisation with an idiosyncratic, personalistic structure; [and] by fall 1995 she had single-handedly left her stamp on the party organs and administration' (1998, 12). Her former Minister of Interior Meral Akşener's comments are particularly revealing of the control that Çiller exercised in the party: 'Decisions were imposed on us [. . .] If you didn't agree with the decision, you would keep silent. The biggest problem of the DYP was insecurity and fear' (quoted in İşleyen 1999). Another former party delegate, Ünal Erkan, labelled Çiller's leadership style as 'sultan-like' (quoted in Cizre 2002a, 96). This resulted in her colleagues realising that the best way to maintain their political careers rested on total obedience to their leader (Cizre 2002b, 207–8).

Çiller's domination of the party became even more pervasive with her husband Özer Çiller's involvement in the DYP and government decision-making, as was the case with a decree tabled under Özer's guidance, to dismiss all ministerial Under-Secretaries and replace them with individuals appointed by the Çillers (Birand and Yıldız 2012, 49–50). With Özer Çiller making decisions about dismissals and appointments, some party officials began to refer decisions to him for approval instead of the relevant minister (Birand and Yıldız 2012, 48–50). In the face of flagrant nepotism, intra-party tensions escalated and led to an *enişte rahatsızlığı* (brother-in-law crisis), which triggered further resignations (Birand and Yıldız 2012, 48). Journalist Nazlı Ilıcak described Çiller's dependence on her husband to govern:

> In an instant she became the Prime Minister. She surrounded herself with yes-men. And all of a sudden, she realised how powerful she had become. On top of this, she is a woman; because she is a woman, she needs her husband. In fact, they ran the country as husband and wife. (quoted in Birand and Yıldız 2012)

Undeniably, the social and cultural practices, resting on a pervasive patriarchy, played an important role in Çiller's decision to rely on her husband's support. Nevertheless, Özer Çiller's role is critical in highlighting the personalising of policy decisions and demonstrates that Tansu Çiller overtly bypassed her party to make critical decisions with an unelected and unaccountable actor, not dissimilar to the part that Turgut Özal's wife Semra had played inside the ANAP (see Chapter 4).

Again, similar to Özal, Çiller frequently conducted party and government business from her official residence in Ankara, surrounded by loyalists and special advisors from outside the party and government (Brown 1994, 60). *Hürriyet* journalist Fatih Altaylı noted that this enabled Çiller to centralise decisions and disregard party oversight, with detrimental consequences to the political culture:

> In relation to the administration of Turkey, Mrs Çiller approved every type of politically unethical act in Turkey. Decisions for bids on government tenders were carried out in the Prime Minister's personal residence. Other members of the Çiller family excessively interfered in politics and the bureaucracy, they were almost embedded in governmental business, acting like a shadow prime ministerial cabinet [. . .] All of this came about during Çiller's era, and like a disease it has infected Turkish politics ever since. (quoted in Birand and Yıldız 2012, 51)

Indeed, conducting government business with unaccountable actors left both party and government susceptible to corrupt practices and entirely bypassed oversight processes. This absence of intra-party democracy, echoing decision-making mechanisms under Prime Minister Özal, further eroded political ethics and maintained undemocratic precedents that would influence the future trajectory of Turkish politics, continuing to act as a key impediment against democratic consolidation.

Çiller's Governance and the Undermining of Democracy

The authoritarian practices and pursuits of the Prime Minister had a disastrous outcome: the economy deteriorated less than a year into Çiller's term, culminating in a major financial breakdown in 1994 (Mango 2004, 94–95; Cizre 2002a, 92–93); bank lending rates reached 1,000 percent, and inflation peaked at 106 percent (Çağaptay 2017, 66); Çiller's lack of political experience resulted in the continual mishandling of policy. The economic and political fallout was further compounded by Çiller making decisions single-handedly:

> Çiller became leader of a political party without any prior political experience. She was the most inexperienced leader that we had in Turkish politics until that point. She came in cold, had no real experience about how things worked in government. The inexperience was problematic for her leadership [. . .] The handling of government work, as far as how she managed the party in parliament, was very weak. (Interview with Sabri Sayarı, July, 2016)

Furthermore, Çiller was unwilling to take the advice of experts and interested parties when making decisions, particularly from members of the bureaucracy. The manner with which she insisted on making economic choices without consulting state agencies, such as the Central Bank or relevant business groups (Heper and Keyman 1998, 268), resembled Özal's conduct. It undermined the bureaucracy's capacity to act not only as check but as impartial arbiter (Dunleavy and O'Leary 1987).

Çiller's interference in the Central Bank's independence saw her fall out with two Central Bank governors in quick succession (Brown 1994, 60). When Çiller became Prime Minister in 1993, Şükrü Saraçoğlu was forced to quit because of his personal conflict with the Prime Minister's monetary policy. The following Central Bank governor, Bülent Gültekin, had an ashtray thrown at his head by Çiller in a meeting because he refused to follow her orders (Münir 1996). Gültekin, upon resigning, put in a formal complaint to President Demirel, citing Çiller's continual obstruction of the Central Bank's autonomy as his reason for stepping down (Doğan 1994). Overall, she worked with three different Central Bank governors and as many Secretary-Generals of Treasury due to her authoritarian behaviour (Münir 1996), which proved to be disastrous for the economy. As a direct result of her policy mistakes and dysfunctional relationship with the bureaucracy, the Central Bank lost half of its reserves, and the economy contracted by 6 percent, culminating in the major economic crisis of 1994 (Celasun 1998).[5]

Faced with an annual inflation of 106 percent and 15 percent currency devaluation, the need to raise quick capital saw Çiller pass illiberal policies. The most striking example of this was a new land-title legislation (Law Nr 4070) introduced on 19 February 1995, which allowed the Treasury to seize and sell the land of anyone who only held an Ottoman title (Anderson 1994). Greeks, Armenians and other minorities who had fled in 1922, as well as Turks who simply did not have modern titles, experienced immediate dispossession of valuable lands which they had occupied for generations.

The Prime Minister and her family benefited greatly from Law Nr 4070, claiming highly prized lands in places such as Kilyos and Kurtköy (Anderson 1994). Çiller employed criminal networks to intimidate occupants attempting to enter their properties or from pursuing the matter further. It was reported that, in cases where land owners refused to yield, they either disappeared, were severely beaten or murdered (Anderson 1994). These stand-over tactics underlined that state resources at the disposal of the government were viewed as possessions to be distributed according to the wishes of Çiller and her family (Heper and Keyman 1998).

Çiller and the Crisis of Democracy

As the economy plummeted, Çiller's electoral support also eroded. Complicating matters further, this period coincided with increased terror attacks by the PKK. The regular news reports, shocking images of dead soldiers in the media and growing influence of the PKK in the Southeast of the country made it the central agenda item both politically and publicly. What Çiller saw, however, was a possible solution to her declining support (Cizre 2002a, 92–93): in the early days of her leadership she had promised to employ a democratic solution to the 'Kurdish question', in contrast to the militaristic option favoured by the previous administration (İnal 2015, 12). However, sensing an electoral opportunity, she aggressively declared that the terror would 'either end, or it will end' (Birand and Yıldız 2012).

Her hardline strategy was the securitisation of the 'Kurdish question', giving the military complete autonomy to handle the issue (Heper 2007, 176; Cizre 2002b, 202). By taking this approach, she abandoned any efforts to utilise political processes to work through issues related to the country's Kurdish community. Süleyman Demirel lamented, in a later interview, that this ultimately 'left the people to suffer between two unyielding forces [between the PKK and the Turkish Armed Forces]' (quoted in Birand and Yıldız 2012, 74).

With the rule of law seemingly suspended to 'fight terrorism', the country experienced its gravest threat yet to the democratic order (Human Rights Watch 1997). The Prime Minister's uncompromising stance fuelled the escalation of human rights violations, an increase in targeted assassinations, the destruction of villages in a bid to undermine rural support for the PKK and the establishment of patron-client relations between Çiller's government and criminal organisations to conduct illegal activities in the fight against the terrorists. Despite countless accusations and evidence of systematic torture and maltreatment of suspects and critics,[6] state prosecutors and Çiller's government rarely pursued investigations (Human Rights Watch 1997) and often turned a blind eye (Mango 2004, 97; Meyer 1998).[7] Çiller's declaration that '[t]hose who shoot a bullet or suffer a bullet for this nation are honourable persons. They are all heroes' was interpreted as an endorsement of the perpetrators of these gross human rights violations (quoted in Birand and Yıldız 2012, 169).

Under loosely defined anti-terror laws, individuals or organisations that did not support the government's narrative were open to persecution. Human rights lawyers and activists were tortured (Birand and Yıldız 2012, 108), critical media subjected to imprisonment and fines, newspapers were closed, books and other publications banned, access to conflict-ridden regions prohibited, and numerous cases of targeted assassinations occurred (Panico 1999, 1). Almost ten years after the 1980 coup, the country was still experiencing oppressive conditions, similar to those imposed by the military junta – a clear indication that Turkey had made little progress towards consolidation under a leadership which permitted wide-spread violations of fundamental rights and civil liberties. Journalist Ahmet Altan outlined the repressive environment to which citizens were subjected during this period:

> You can say there is no freedom of expression, you can say there is press freedom, and you are right in both statements. It's not like in a typical dictatorship – the borders are not clear, you can't know where they are. The application of the law is arbitrary. But in many ways the arbitrariness is worse. You don't know when you will get into trouble. (quoted in Panico 1999)

The climate of authoritarianism that Altan describes was exemplified by the torture of children. In one prominent example, sixteen teenagers, the youngest fourteen years of age, accused of scribbling 'no to paid education' on a wall in Manisa, were charged with being members of a terrorist organisation. During their incarceration they were subjected to physical and sexual torture by security personnel, which came to be described as 'the country's greatest moment of shame' (Birand and Yıldız 2012). The children were initially sentenced to twelve years imprisonment, but this was later overturned on appeal (see Birand and Yıldız 2012, 123–27).

It was within this unstable and volatile environment that Çiller initiated proceedings in early 1994 to remove the immunity of six parliamentarians from the pro-Kurdish-rights *Demokrasi Partisi* (Democracy Party, DEP).[8] The DEP representatives subsequently were tried and sentenced to fifteen-year sentences for incorporating Kurdish into their parliamentary oaths.[9] The developments were condemned by the US Congress and the Council of Europe, who compared it to conditions during the 1980 military junta (Brown 1994, 56). Cindoruk, the parliamentary speaker at the time, recounts that he strongly advised the Assembly against taking this avenue. Doing so damaged the trust in parliament as a representative body:

> What needed to be solved by democratic means was turned into a fight between the parliament and the peoples of the [Southeast] region and became a matter of distrust for the entire political system. (quoted in Birand and Yıldız 2012, 81)

This reflects the crisis in the democratic order that was to follow this episode. Çiller had little to no interest in democratisation or strengthening institutions by making them more liberal, representative and accessible. Her security policy and her approach to dealing with the problems of the country's Kurdish community further eroded democracy and exacerbated the problem. Cengiz Çandar has noted:

> Because she was so weak, had no political background, had no political insight and no intuition, Çiller couldn't control anything. Hence, the period of her rule became a very chaotic period. It was the worst time in terms of the Kurdish issue, because she had no power or foresight. She just transferred

all the responsibility to the military, and then the whole thing became more intractable. (Interview, October 2016b)

Çiller's actions illustrate her lack of interest in political solutions, such as moderation, dialogue, respecting the rights of the opposition and her over-reliance on authoritarian policies. This was damaging, not only to the rule of law and the parliament's role as a representative institution, but it also further destabilised her government.

This came to the fore in 1995, with four days of unrest in the Gazi Mahallesi, a largely Alevi neighbourhood in Istanbul. The demonstrations ended with the death of twenty-five civilians, 500 people wounded and thousands taken into custody as a result of the exceptionally violent police response. The responsible authorities, including Istanbul Police Chief Necdet Menzir and Governor of Istanbul Hayri Kozakçıoğlu, escaped investigation or punishment. Despite overwhelming parliamentary pressure, including from her coalition partner, CHP's Deniz Baykal, Çiller blocked criminal investigations into the role played by the two men. This prompted Baykal, who was incensed at the Prime Minister's decision, to end the DYP-CHP coalition (see Birand 2012; Birand and Yıldız 2012, 97–103). In 1995, Kozakçıoğlu and Menzir were made DYP parliamentary deputies upon Çiller's instruction, which provided them with immunity from any future investigation.

Tansu Çiller and Mesut Yılmaz's Coalition

The dissolution of the DYP-CHP partnership forced the country to early elections on 26 December 1995. Çiller, however, failed to win back favour with the electorate: The parliament was divided between five political parties after the elections (see Table 5.1). Necmettin Erbakan's religiously orientated *Refah Partisi* (RP) won the largest number of seats with 21.4 percent of the vote but fell short of the seats required for single-party majority. Erbakan was unable to find a willing coalition partner, as the military establishment was uneasy with the rise of an Islamist party, pressuring the other four parties against entering into a partnership with the RP. This forced President Demirel to offer the opportunity to Çiller to form a coalition government, as the DYP had the second-largest number of parliamentary seats.

Table 5.1 1995 Election Results

Political Party	Percentage of Votes	Parliamentary Seats (Total 550)
RP	21.4	158
ANAP	19.7	132
DYP	19.2	135
DSP	14.6	76
CHP	10.7	49
MHP	8.2	0

Source: https://www.tbmm.gov.tr/develop/owa/secim_sorgu.genel_secimler

Çiller managed to forge a coalition with Mesut Yılmaz's ANAP. From the outside, the partnership seemed a suitable fit between the two centre-Right parties with similar economic policies. However, the government was quasi-paralysed from the beginning, largely owing to the fact that Çiller and Yılmaz competed for supremacy, which drove them to despise each other (Jackson and Kislali 1996).

The fractured relationship was exposed when corruption charges against both Çiller and Yılmaz were brought to the parliamentary agenda by Erbakan's RP.[10] Rather than vote the motion down with their joint parliamentary majority, both leaders instead backed the investigations against the other (Haque 1996). Each leader's decision to support the legal probes against the other marked an extraordinary development given that they were coalition partners.[11] Yet, as this book has shown, this was a familiar pattern in Turkish political history. Bodgener (1997) concurred, observing:

> For the time being Turkey has a highly personalised, faction-ridden system that is bringing politics into disrepute. An excess of personal leadership ambition makes a compromise almost impossible – except when self-interest is being served [. . .] The personal rivalries on the centre right – between Yılmaz and Çiller, and Özal and Demirel before them – have weakened its traditional grip on Turkish politics. There is almost no difference in policy between ANAP and DYP but the personal dislike between Yılmaz and Çiller is poisonous.

The toxic relationship was largely fuelled by competing political ambitions: Yılmaz aimed to displace Çiller in order to capture the DYP and dominate the centre-Right of politics (Birand and Yıldız 2012, 143), while Çiller could not tolerate Yılmaz holding down the senior position in the coalition government (Birand and Yıldız 2012, 142). Knowing that Turkey sat on a political and economic knife's edge, other experienced political leaders, such as MHP leader Alparsan Türkeş, urged them to resolve their differences (Birand and Yıldız 2012, 146). The bitter inter-elite conflict nonetheless continued and brought the government to an end five months later, in June 1996. This is reflective of Stepan and Linz's observations that a democracy where the leaders regularly fail to demonstrate tolerance towards their rivals will ultimately end in a crisis or breakdown (1996).

Having fallen foul of Yılmaz and facing an imminent legal and parliamentary investigation, Çiller hastily forged an alliance with Erbakan in July 1995 to hold on to power. This decision marked a major reversal, given that Çiller had previously campaigned against Erbakan and promised to never work with Islamists in order to prevent them from coming to power (Cizre 2002b, 205; Mango 2004, 96; Kinzer 1997b). In fact, Çiller had proclaimed that Erbakan and the *Refah Partisi* were trying to lead Turkey 'back to the dark ages' (Meyer 1997), being 'more dangerous than the PKK' (Birand and Yıldız 2012, 113).

Ultimately, the partnership proved mutually beneficial. Çiller needed Erbakan's support to defeat corruption inquiries tabled against her in parliament, whilst Erbakan wanted to reap the material benefits of power for his patronage networks (Cizre 2002a, 94; Mango 1996, 9). Although the RP had drafted resolutions that initiated the investigations against Çiller (Reuters 1996), subsequent parliamentary votes by Erbakan's party helped Çiller defeat the criminal investigation into her personal affairs. This indicated that even so-called pious Islamists were not averse to opportunism and pragmatic politics. The agreement provided Erbakan with the prize that he had sought for his entire political career – that is, the seat of Prime Minister – while Çiller became Foreign Minister, after agreeing to switch positions after two years.

The deal inflicted substantial damage to Çiller's credibility, highlighting her view of democracy as a means to an end. Çiller's Minister of Interior, Meral Akşener, once described her former leader as a 'liar, unfaithful and unreliable' (İşleyen 1999). It was perhaps this moral void which enabled Çiller to preserve power at any cost to democracy. This supposition was captured in comments made by Yılmaz, who declared: 'They haven't formed a government partnership but a partnership in crime' (quoted in Kinzer 1997a). Similarly, James Meyer remarked (1997, 31):

> Çiller's alleged corruption and attempted cover-up have done grievous damage to Turkish democracy by helping fundamentalists reach power, increasing popular mistrust in the leadership, and bringing the military back into politics.

These sentiments were also felt inside her party, with fifteen DYP deputies voting against the coalition in parliament. This was followed by the resignation of several DYP founding members, including Sezgin, Cindoruk and Toptan. The defectors immediately established the *Demokrat Türkiye Partisi* (Democrat Turkey Party, DTP) (Haque 1996). The episode resulted in forty-four parliamentarians resigning from Çiller's DYP to join Cindoruk's DTP in protest and reduced the number of DYP's parliamentary numbers from 135 to ninety-one. The loss of numbers created enough pressure to end the coalition (Birand and Yıldız 2012, 253).

The Rise of Erbakan

Not all of the instability and crises during this period can be blamed on Çiller; Erbakan's leadership was also highly problematic. Like many political leaders, Erbakan sought to shape the direction of the country in accordance with his own vision (Özdalga 2002, 136). He had been active in politics as the head of the Islamist *Millî Görüş* movement (National Outlook, MG), entering parliament as an independent for the religiously conservative city of Konya in 1969. He established Turkey's first Islamist party, the *Millî Nizam Partisi* (National Order Party, MNP), in 1970.[12] Following the 1971 coup and the subsequent closure of the MNP for anti-secular activities, Erbakan founded the *Millî Selâmet Partisi* (National Salvation Party, MSP) (Kepel 2006, 345). The MSP's establishment marked the start of a recurrent pattern for Erbakan: each time the country's Constitutional Court closed down his party, he founded another one.

In fact, in his four decades of active politics, Erbakan's religious agenda and rhetoric consistently invited tension with the secular establishment

(Tittensor 2014, 58). Erbakan was a religious reactionary and a leader predisposed to politically risky behaviour, given that he was overtly Islamist in a strictly secular regime (Özdalga 2002; Poulton 1997; Turam 2012, 47–48; Tittensor 2014, 58; Kepel 2006).[13] This was evident six days before the 1980 coup, when an MSP meeting in Konya to commemorate al-Quds Day for the 'liberation of Jerusalem' turned into a pro-sharia demonstration (Kepel 2006, 346). On that day, a 10,000-strong crowd dressed as militants with replica rifles refused to rise during the national anthem and brandished banners in Arabic text (Birand, Bila and Akar 1999, 164). The generals viewed the events as a threat to the national order, and this ultimately became the trigger point for the coup (Birand, Bila and Akar 1999, 164–65). Like other political parties, the MSP was dissolved, and its leader Erbakan arrested and jailed in April 1981 (*Milliyet* 1981, 1980).

Erbakan's unwavering attitude was principally driven by the belief that his personal vision for Turkey was desired by most Turks and therefore needed to be implemented for the betterment of society (Birand and Yıldız 2012, 56–57). Like most Islamists of his generation, Erbakan blamed the ills of the country on corrupting Western influences: his religiously influenced social programme, *Adil Düzen* (Just Order), sought to structure Turkish society and policy in such as way as to realign Turkey with its 'natural' condition and link its future with the Muslim world (Rabasa and Larrabee 2008). He rarely swayed from the course towards this aim.

Like his political peers, Erbakan exhibited a highly personalised autocratic leadership style throughout his political career. Similar to Özal, Erbakan did not need to compete for party leadership in the way in which Menderes, Demirel and Ecevit had been required, as he was the founder of all the parties he led. Erbakan took sole control of selecting party policy, administrators and candidature lists and insisted that everyone obey his personal authority (Atacan 2005, 190–92). For example, the MSP, which existed from October 1972 until its closure following the 1980 coup, was a broad alliance of religious orders and conservative groups, which had come together in an effort to break the tutelage of secular parties (Rabasa and Larrabee 2008). Despite this plurality, Erbakan suppressed other views and factions in favour of his own loyalists, imposing his version of Islam on party ideology and direction.

His leadership was not without tension. Erbakan's authoritarian style caused friction with other religious factions, such as the Nurcu movement that accused him of dictatorship (Atacan 2005, 190).[14] Erbakan's monopoly of power prevented the dissenting group from seriously threatening his position (Özdalga 2002, 137). Instead, sixteen parliamentarians resigned from the party and withdrew their support for the MSP (Yeşilada 2002, 67).[15] This only served Erbakan's ends, with the defections alleviating any future potential of a united challenge against him. On another occasion, a founding and senior member of the MSP, Korkut Özal,[16] was removed from MSP's Central Administrative Committee for suggesting that the party officials should have input in selecting its members (Atacan 2005, 191).

It became evident that Erbakan had anointed himself the absolute leader of Turkey's Islamist movement, often giving speeches that depicted his leadership as a religious calling. In one example, he summoned people to his party in the name of jihad and warned followers that neglecting their duties to the party was akin to performing one's prayer without ablution (Atacan 2005, 191). In doing so, Erbakan freed himself from criticism and challenges from other religious groups and entrenched his rule within the vernacular of religious legitimacy. The state authorities' repeated sanctions against him only enhanced this standing, making him a martyr figure in the eyes of his supporters (Özdalga 2002, 137). Nazlı Ilıcak, who served as parliamentarian for Erbakan, noted that this strong religious stance was a central reason for the unwavering loyalty:

> Mr Erbakan created a network that was totally loyal to him, and the individuals he selected were based on upholding this system of reverence. I didn't witness anybody object to Erbakan *hoca*. He had absolute authority over the party. They say it is in every party, but here there was a religious element to explain this unquestioned obedience to him. (quoted in Birand and Yıldız 2012, 327)

As a result, Erbakan's followers elevated him to a revered religious figure. References such as *Erbakan Hoca* (Erbakan Hodja) and *Mücahit Erbakan* (Mujahedeen Erbakan) were common names used by Erbakan's followers (Birand and Yıldız 2012, 56). Erbakan's charismatic personality helped foster a unique cohesiveness and uniformity within his parties (Kamrava 1998, 295). Remarks by the *Refah* mayor of Beyoğlu, Nusret Bayraktar, in a 1994 interview further emphasise this point:

Our party is based on two fundamental principles – great ideological strength and very great discipline [. . .] Discipline means absolute obedience to our leader, Necmettin Erbakan. (quoted in Kamrava 1998, 295)

In other words, it was extremely difficult to counter this institutionalised deification of Erbakan and oppose his leadership and decisions. Erbakan was re-elected in the RP's annual congress in 1990, with 551 out of 552 votes (Özdalga 2002, 138), and not a single vote was cast against him at the 1993 party congress (Kepel 2006, Atacan 2005), highlighting the scale of his absolute rule over his parties.

Undisputed loyalty, consolidated by a religious narrative, put Erbakan beyond challenge, despite his many electoral failures. Party members rarely blamed him for continual electoral losses, party closures and poor political fortunes over four decades, even though he single-handedly administered the parties (Atacan 2005, 191). This meant that his parties suffered the same fate regularly. One of his party colleagues described (quoted in Özdalga 2002, 138): 'Imagine a rubber band that you try to stretch as much as possible. *Erbakan Hoca* always does that. He stretches and stretches, without in fact realising that the band may snap. And, sometimes it does!'

Erbakan: An Islamist Prime Minister in a Secular System

His indifference to political realities was once again demonstrated when Erbakan entered a coalition with Çiller. The rigid anti-system and Islamist characteristic was certain to play a much greater role in political developments, now that he was no longer on the margins of the political arena, but rather leading a government. Erbakan's Islamist vision did not incorporate an inclusive and pluralist idea of Turkish society, nor was it premised on the democratisation of the system. In fact, his statements during this period led to doubts about his commitment to secularism and democracy. For example, in 1994, he famously declared: 'Refah Party will come to power, and the *Adil Düzen* will be installed. What is the problem? Is the transition period going to be rough, or is it going to be smooth, sweet or bloody?' (quoted in Birand and Yıldız 2012, 89). Such remarks were a cause of great concern among the military, as well as the secular and political establishment (Turam 2007, 49).

Following Erbakan's lead, *Refah* politicians, emboldened by the party's newfound status, regularly made alarming calls to usher in an Islamist regime (Birand and Yıldız 2012, 188–90). Turkish intelligence recorded the following speech, given by a *Refah* politician at a gathering:

> Just like the Muslims in Iran we will rise up against this bitch of a regime and stomp on it, or we will bring a Muslim party to power and bring this about gently. If you love your God and Prophet follow them. Don't go following the path of Europe's Thessaloniki devil [Mustafa Kemal Atatürk . . .] A Muslim cannot be secular and Muslim. This regime must be cleaned from the roots. This regime will be made to go even if it doesn't want to go. The Turkish Armed Forces cannot protect Turkey. The nation is in danger. This is why we created *Millî Görüş* [. . .] if they try to close down *İmam Hatip* schools whilst *Refah Partisi* is in government, blood will be spilled. It will be worse than Algeria. (quoted in Birand and Yıldız 2012, 190)

Certainly, Erbakan could not control every politician representing *Refah*; nevertheless, the frequency and number of individuals partaking in this type of violent anti-secular rhetoric could not have been unknown to him either. For instance, Şükrü Karatepe, the mayor of Kayseri, Şevki Yılmaz, the deputy for Rize, and Hasan Hüseyin Ceylan, the party spokesperson all gave speeches that were similar in their pushback against the democratic order (see Birand and Yıldız 2012, 187–93).[17]

For a leader who had total control of the party, Erbakan appeared uninterested in exercising his authority when it came to such matters, perhaps because he did not want to lose the support of extreme factions, or he simply agreed with the nature of these statements. Essentially, *Refah* conferences and rallies provided a climate of support for the provocative anti-system politics that seemed to match the rhetoric (see Birand 2012).

Erbakan was also complicit in the increasing political tensions with his Islamist and reactionary pursuits as Prime Minister. When he came to power, he proposed lifting the ban on head veils in universities. Following his proposal, Turkey experienced regular anti-secular protests marked with chants of 'down with the secular dictatorship' and 'long live the sharia' (Birand and Yıldız 2012, 164). Although these were not official party rallies, *Refah* flags and banners accompanying other pro-sharia symbols were symptomatic of

Refah's unstated approval. The rising number of the incidents after Friday prayers and shocking images on television screens began to cause agitation across society.

As Prime Minister, Erbakan made no attempt to alleviate the growing tensions. Erbakan's silence, interpreted as tacit approval, emboldened the pro-sharia movements across the country (see Birand 2012). *Refah* meetings and gatherings continued to use an overtly Islamist tone and visual symbolism. In an already tense political sphere, Köksal Toptan, DYP deputy of the period, acknowledged that Erbakan went out of his way to fuel these tensions unnecessarily:

> During my time as Minister of Education between 1992 and 1993, the headscarf ban was close to being solved. It only remained in one to two universities, so there was no need to bring the headscarf onto the public agenda. Yet, as soon as Erbakan got into power, he started declaring: 'The university rectors will stand in salute to the head veil. The *İmam Hatips* are our backyards'. Statements such as these caused Turkey serious harm. (quoted in Birand and Yıldız 2012, 164)

Indeed, the Prime Minister's antagonistic and bullish remarks toward secular principles fuelled greater polarisation. His single-minded approach stood opposite to democratic norms founded upon tolerance and inclusivity. It demonstrated a leadership attempting to exploit its prerogatives for ideological gains, which, as O'Donnell has noted, when pervasive, is an indication of a weak democracy (see Introduction). In this regard, Erbakan was no different from his opposition counterparts and predecessors. Like Menderes, Demirel and Ecevit, his grand rhetoric represented a binary view of Turkish society, the 'us vs them', ultimately entrenching the electorate into opposing camps. Erbakan, however, was unlike the other leaders, as his rhetoric was in direct opposition to the state's founding principles.

In addition, a number of Islamist national projects were announced, including the creation of an 'Islamic' car, the construction of a Grand Mosque in Taksim Square and the conversion of the Church of Hagia Sophia in Istanbul into a house of worship for Muslims. Erbakan also spoke disapprovingly of Turkey's relations with the West, especially military relations with Israel, and he pledged to withdraw Turkey from NATO and the European Customs Union, and to forge close ties with Muslim countries, which further heightened tensions between his government and the military (Özdalga 2002, 137, 143; Mango 2004, 96–97; Tachau 2000, 142–43; Tittensor 2014, 48).

The military was being drawn further into politics by Erbakan's activities. As noted in the Introduction, Diamond has found that leadership which does not display moderation invites excessive polarisation and destabilises the system, even accelerating democratic breakdown. For this reason, Erbakan's policies, which transgressed the bounds of the secular order, resulted in *Refah Partisi* being labelled a greater threat to the country then the PKK by the members of the military High Command (Birand and Yıldız 2012, 204).[18] This marked a serious change between Erbakan and the military.[19] Erbakan and his party were unwilling to deviate from their politics, which further increased tensions. With Erbakan and *Refah* in power, the polarisation of politics was no longer between rival political leaders, as it had been between Çiller and Yılmaz; rather, it was now between the governing party and the state.

Tensions reached their peak on 31 January 1997 when the *Refah* municipality of Sincan, on the outskirts of Ankara, organised a day of protests to mark al-Quds, the liberation of Jerusalem, which mirrored events in Konya twenty-seven years earlier. Throughout the day, crowds heard violent speeches against Israel and witnessed a strong display of solidarity with radical Islamist organisations such as Hamas, as well as the Iranian Islamist regime. In a more radical departure, the RP mayor, Bekir Yıldız, publicly called for the implementation of sharia law in Turkey (White 2013, 40; Mango 2004, 97), a move that pushed the military to take action.

On 28 February, the military-dominated *Millî Güvenlik Kurulu* (National Security Council, MGK) issued Erbakan's government with a memorandum, demanding that eighteen measures be taken against political Islam. Erbakan ignored most of the recommended measures (Heper 2002b, 139) and attempted to avert their enforcement by instigating a parliamentary debate (Birand and Yıldız 2012, 219–21). The military, growing tired of the Prime Minister's delaying tactics, increased their pressure, mobilising the judiciary, universities, citizens and civil society associations (Çağaptay 2017, 80).

In June 1997, Erbakan resigned in fear that the military might once again directly intervene. This development became known as a 'post-modern coup' or 'soft coup', leading to the dissolution of the RP-DYP government. The military had pressured Erbakan to resign from power without taking over the government. Thereafter, the Constitutional Court closed down the party and banned Erbakan from politics for violating the separation of religion and state; an outcome which he had previously experienced.[20]

Erbakan's persistent desire to enforce his own vision on society and impose on the state a pronounced Islamic identity was a frequent source of his political troubles. Nonetheless, as columnist Ali Bayramoğlu observed, along with *Refah*, the main political actors also carried the blame for the crisis:

> Was *Refah* Party guilty of provocation, it was. I have no doubt about that. *Refah* Party's politics and certain regular outputs were guilty of this. For instance, there were comments made by Şevki Yılmaz in Rize and Şükrü Karatepe's words in Kayseri [. . .] but it wasn't the military's role to correct this. This should have been solved within the political framework [. . .] Yet Çiller and Yılmaz's personal battles didn't allow for this [. . .] But the *Refah* Party management of this period did not help either, it went about it in a provocative character. (Birand and Yıldız 2012)

For a leader who enjoyed unquestioned power over his party, Erbakan was unwilling to lead more responsibly and show better judgement. But, as noted above, he was not solely at fault. Other party leaders refused to act with consensus or beyond their personal interests on even the most urgent of matters. This allowed the military once again to solve the crisis in its own way. The inability and unwillingness of leaders to make concerted efforts to save democracy damaged the democratic system once again.[21]

Looking back, Erbakan may have been the most single-minded politician. Although his desire to reshape Turkey in line with his personal vision does not set him apart from the other political leaders, the regularity of his party closures and bans throughout his career underlines that Erbakan was loyal to the secular democratic system only for as long as it served him. Democracy, for Erbakan, seemed to have been the tool to attain personal rule, as he once declared: 'Democracy, yes, as long as it favours my and my party's interests. If not, it makes no great difference' (quoted in Özdalga 2002, 144). In this respect, he was no more committed to undermining democracy and displaying authoritarian measures than others, yet what set him apart was his opposition to the secular state.

Demirel's Presidency: Steering the Breakdown of Government

Demirel won enough parliamentary votes to ascend to the presidential office on 16 May 1993, which he occupied until 16 May 2000. His decision to become the head of state, a role with traditionally limited executive powers when compared to the prime ministership, might seem puzzling. However, his reverence can be traced back to the founder of the nation, Atatürk, who served as Turkey's first President from 1923 until his death in 1938 (Çağaptay 2010, 140). The presidential office, for this reason, has traditionally held great prestige and attraction, shaped by the politician's desire to be above the state and its institutions:

> Sitting in the presidency has always occupied the minds of Turkish leaders. Although the real power rests in the hands of the Prime Minister, leaders always have in it their mind to move to the Presidential Palace because, throughout history, the presidency represented optimal balance between the military, as the founding institution and the protector of the republic. Since the Commander-in-Chief Mustafa Kemal Atatürk was founder of the republic and the first President it meant real power and prestige. Attaining the presidency is therefore something leaders want to pursue to go into the annals of history [. . .] So Demirel rose to the presidency after Özal, but he promised and campaigned to strip the powers of the President during Özal's time. When he became the President there was no more talk of stripping the powers of the role because he now occupied the post. (Interview with Cengiz Çandar, October 2016b)

As Çandar noted, Demirel maintained the same powers of the presidency, which he had previously campaigned to take away from Özal. Rising to the position of President without the ability to influence political developments would have rendered him ineffective and inconsequential and did not suit his leadership style (see Chapters 2 and 3). Ascending to the coveted position would allow him to truly embody the popularised moniker given to him – that is, *baba* (father) of the nation.

As President, Demirel quickly became uncomfortable with the direction of his former party, the DYP, under Çiller's leadership. Çiller's brash style and problematic decisions ensured that his time in the presidency was marred by growing problems that needed regular attention by the President himself; as Heper states, Çiller 'turned the party she had inherited from Süleyman Demirel into a *pariah*' (2002b, 146). Former DYP Istanbul Branch President Celal Adnan explained that Çiller was unwilling to comply with Demirel and aimed to consolidate power over the party:

> Çiller wanted to manage the party [on her own]. She wanted to re-design the party according to her own desires. By removing Demirel's control, she wanted to give the party a new identity. But Demirel couldn't digest this. Nor could his team [in the party] digest this. (Birand and Yıldız 2012, 28)

In turn, Demirel attempted to regain influence inside the DYP. To Ilıcak, this was because Demirel 'always preferred to work with people he could dominate. Without a need to consult and to be able to direct people – that's how he understood politics' (quoted in Birand 2012). Çiller's management of the DYP caused tensions between her and Demirel, which then spilled into the relations between the two arms of the executive, similar to the experience between Özal and Demirel (see Chapter 4). When Çiller's prime ministership became more controversial and the country slumped into economic crisis, Demirel tried to engineer a new government without Çiller: once her coalition with the CHP had ended, he urged her to go to an early election, in the hope that another political party would win the vote (Birand 2012).

Demirel also undertook an active role behind the scenes to undo the Çiller-Erbakan coalition. He was complicit in weakening the government's position by supporting the military's aims against the *Refah* government (Birand and Yıldız 2012, 244–49). Thanks to the key role that he played in this 'post-modern coup', it was dubbed the *Çankaya Darbesi* (Presidential Coup) (*Milliyet* 1997). Journalist Fehmi Koru recounts that, when the military pressure on politicians increased after the 28 February memorandum, Demirel directed the defection of parliamentarians from the DYP to join Cindoruk's newly formed DTP to speed up the demise of the coalition:

> During that period Demirel played a prominent role. Through phone calls to individual parliamentarians urging them to resign, Demirel helped the downfall

of the [RP-DYP] government. The journalists of the time were witness to this, and the parliamentarians who personally received the phone calls recounted this later. (quoted in Birand and Yıldız 2012, 236)

A *Refah* parliamentarian of the period, Bülent Arınç, corroborates this account, squarely blaming the President for fostering the crisis:

> The President was like a virtuoso conducting developments. Perhaps he was directing the military as well. We [*Refah*] were that suspicious about him [. . .] I think close to forty parliamentarians were removed from the party [DYP]. In all these instances they were instructed [by Demirel]. If you ask them, they wouldn't refute this. Most of those who resigned have stated: 'We received instructions, which is the reason we resigned'. (quoted in Birand and Yıldız 2012, 235)

After Erbakan's removal, Demirel took the opportunity to bestow upon Yılmaz the right to form a coalition. However, the decision was against protocol, as Çiller was the remaining coalition partner and expected to have the opportunity to form another government. Demirel's actions indicated that he would not allow the opportunity to orchestrate Çiller's removal slip from his hands. Celal Adnan claims that the President had organised the necessary parliamentary numbers needed for Yılmaz to form a government:

> When he gave Mesut Yılmaz the permission to form a government [over Çiller], how was Yılmaz to form a government? Yılmaz needed an adequate number of parliamentarians, which he did not have. Hence, there was a plot by the media, the military, and businessmen [along with Demirel] that forced the resignation of forty representatives [from the DYP]. They placed Cindoruk at this faction's head, and then Cindoruk provided Mesut Yılmaz with the parliamentary support, and a weird coalition was formed as a result. Demirel, at the time, was declaring his innocence: 'If I don't intervene, the military will'. So don't do it, and don't let the military intervene either; he was the President after all, and this is the important point. He should have resisted. He had to resist. But such logic didn't exist. What happened? He became the king of the coup. (quoted in Birand and Yıldız 2012, 254)

The President's critical role in bringing down the government is highlighted here, as he opted to support the military instead of looking for parliamentary solutions. He took it upon himself to shape the outcome rather than accept the composition of the parliament elected by the electorate. Thus, the *milli irade* (national will), to which Demirel regularly referred throughout his political career to justify many of his authoritarian and destabilising measures (see Chapters 2 and 3), was virtually ignored when it jeopardised his preference.

In fact, Celal Adnan states that Demirel's decision to overstep the bounds of his role to act as the arbiter of politics ultimately brought an end to the dominance of centre-Right politics in Turkey: 'The centre-Right dissolved due to Demirel's inability to let go, and it never recovered from that. Demirel couldn't remove himself from the 28 February incident, and as a result he sunk the centre-Right' (quoted in Birand and Yıldız 2012, 244). From this point on, the centre-Right ceased to resemble the strong electoral force it had once been, ending a political lineage that stemmed back to the *Demokrat Parti*.

The Re-emergence of Bülent Ecevit, 1999–2002

Yılmaz formed a coalition with Ecevit's *Demokratik Sol Partisi* (Democratic Left Party, DSP) and Cindoruk's DTP on 30 June 1997, in order to take Turkey to the next scheduled general elections. The coalition lasted a mere sixteen months due to Yılmaz's corruption; the latter was forced to resign when the Assembly censured him for his part in a suspect privatisation deal of the *Türk Ticaret Bankası* (Turkish Trade Bank) (Mango 2004, 97; Birand and Yıldız 2012, 285).[22] Bülent Ecevit succeeded him in a caretaker role until the elections in April 1999.

The results of the general election maintained Turkey's fragmented political landscape, with the votes divided amongst a myriad of parties (see Table 5.2). Ecevit's caretaker role coincided with the capture of the PKK leader Abdullah Öcalan by Turkish security forces in Kenya. As acting Prime Minister, Ecevit became the beneficiary of the surge of nationalism stemming from this development (Birand and Yıldız 2012, 292). His popularity and distance from the failings of recent coalition governments enabled Ecevit to win 136 Assembly seats (the largest share). He then partnered with the MHP, which was headed by Devlet Bahçeli after Türkeş's death in 1997. Yılmaz's ANAP completed the three-party coalition.

Table 5.2 1999 Election Results

Political Party	Percentage of Votes	Parliamentary Seats (Total 550)
DSP	22.2	136
MHP	18	129
Fazilet Partisi	15.4	111
ANAP	13.2	86
DYP	12.01	85
CHP	8.7	0
Independents	0.9	3

Source: https://www.tbmm.gov.tr/develop/owa/secim_sorgu.genel_secimler

The DSP–ANAP–MHP partnership provided much needed stability after the crisis-ridden governments from 1993 to 1999. In December 1999, the government remarkably entered accession negotiations with the European Union, which witnessed Ecevit's coalition initiate a number of democratising reforms in order to comply with EU standards (Lagendijk 2012).[23] But a personal feud between the Prime Minister and the new President, Ahmet Necdet Sezer, who replaced Demirel in 2000, triggered a major political crisis. At a meeting of the National Security Council on 19 February 2001, Sezer accused the government of covering up corruption scandals. Ecevit took the accusation as a personal affront, vehemently defending his government. Sezer was then alleged to have thrown a copy of the constitution at the Prime Minister, remarking: 'Either you have not read the Constitution, or you don't understand what you have read' (see Dündar and Akar 2015, 153–54). The Prime Minister immediately left the meeting and walked into a press conference announcing to the waiting media 'the serious crisis' between the two men (Akar and Dündar 2008, 478). Two days later, the already fragile economy collapsed, resulting in the worst economic crisis in the country's history.

Ecevit and the DSP (1985–2002)

Despite much improvement in inter-elite relations, as demonstrated by Ecevit's coalition with two parties from the Right (the MHP and the DYP), his democratic credentials had their limitations: the DSP was created under

Ecevit's personal direction, and he approved the entire cadre of the 612 party founders (Akar and Dündar 2008, 369). Ertuğrul Günay noted that this provided him with near-absolute power over the party:

> The DSP was not provided with a strong legal structure [. . .] it was turned into a closed organisation, and the local bodies and party governance were treated as Bülent Ecevit and his wife Rahşan wished [. . .] There was this unbelievable 'I did it, and it's done' understanding that was introduced into Turkish politics thanks to them. (quoted in Dündar and Akar 2015, 145–46)

From the DSP's inception, power rested solely with Bülent Ecevit and his wife Rahşan. The Ecevits' omnipresence in the DSP was only matched by Özal's and Erbakan's rule over their parties. Like these two leaders, the entire party structure and personnel served to maintain the rule of its leadership, Bülent and Rahşan Ecevit.[24] Any other voice was not tolerated, and dissenters were expelled.[25]

This personalisation of the DSP prevented the party organisation from exercising any influence, with party executives and headquarters merely implementing and administering the leader's wishes (Kınıklıoğlu 2002, 5). The Ecevits handpicked the names on the candidature lists and kept them hidden from party officials, including parliamentarians, in order to prevent questioning or challenge (Özdalga 2005, 92). Loyalty to the Ecevits was therefore paramount for political survival, and any display of political ambition or independent thought was seen as a threat; hence, members were marginalised (Özdalga 2005, 83). Party officials were often put under surveillance by the couple (Özdalga 2005, 94) – a repeat of the measures that Ecevit had undertaken during the 1970s. One of the party founders, Haluk Özdalga, said that the DSP had simply been created to serve Ecevit's political ambitions:

> In the DSP model, the party organisation is reduced to one single feature: for one person's instrument to reach power. To meet this aim, the organisation is kept under complete control. All other features and functions that the organisation must possess are subordinated to this basic goal and are pushed to the background. No legal or ethical rule can obstruct attaining this objective. In the DSP, all practices by the organisation are the result of such an unbridled ambition [. . . Ecevit] does not see himself bound to any law or party statute. (2005, 331)

The frailty of party unity was soon exposed under the weight of the Ecevit's autocratic rule. At the age of seventy-seven, the demands of the prime ministerial role began to take a toll on Ecevit's health, which became most evident when he was forced into hospital for sixty-seven days. When Deputy Prime Minister Hüsamettin Özkan urged Ecevit to step down, he was accused of trying to oust Ecevit and forced out of the DSP (Birand and Yıldız 2012, 350). Özkan promptly formed the *Yeni Türkiye Partisi* (New Turkey Party, YTP), with sixty-three DSP parliamentarians, including six acting ministers.[26] Such was the scale of the defection that it amounted to half of the DSP's parliamentarian group.

This was yet another example of a new party formed due to tensions arising from a leader's authoritarianism. Nor was it the first time that such a development was the cause of instability for a sitting government. After nearly five decades in politics, Ecevit had not learned that subordinating the party to his interests alone worked against the public good. Furthermore, his unwillingness to concede power is a key indicator that he did not embody robust democratic values.

The falling-out between President Sezer and Ecevit resulted in a major economic crisis. Combined with the split within the DSP, MHP leader Bahçeli threatened to pull his party from the coalition, which resulted in the elections scheduled for April 2004 being brought forward to November 2002. The outcome brought the newly created *Adalet ve Kalkınma Partisi* (Justice and Development Party, AKP) to power, while all the leaders of the period – including Ecevit, Çiller, Yılmaz and Bahçeli – and their parties failed to garner enough votes to enter parliament. This highlighted the failure of this entire group of political leaders in the eyes of the electorate. As Çandar has reflected, they were seemingly guilty of all the turmoil that befell the country:

> You know that there is more or less a consensus with many political scientists, politicians and political observers that the period after Özal until the election of the AKP is the lost decade of Turkish politics. Leaders such as Tansu Çiller, Mesut Yılmaz and Necmettin Erbakan all became the main protagonists of this period. Yet, I'm not sure whether you have to attach any importance to these people. They don't deserve any [. . .] In the [19]90s we found ourselves in a political arena where we had leaders that don't deserve to be written down in history books. They just happened to be the leaders during that era. When you look at Mesut Yılmaz, Tansu Çiller, Deniz Baykal, Süleyman Demirel, the game was among them because they held all the power in the political

arena. Nobody could wrestle the leadership from them once they became leaders. You needed to have a game-changer in order to get rid of them. The game-changer of the period was the economic conditions – the financial crisis of 2001–2. As a result, we lost Mesut Yılmaz, Tansu Çiller, Bülent Ecevit and all the others from that period. Not only do we not remember them, but we also don't even miss them. Despite what is going on at the moment [referring to Recep Tayyip Erdoğan], for me at least, it was the worst period I have ever known in Turkey [. . .] None of those names from that period deserve to be remembered in a positive way. (Interview, October 2016)

The observation is a strong and sweeping indictment of the leaders of this era. It further reiterates that the political parties of the period continued with a leader-dominated model; as a result, Turkey witnessed the same political outcomes – a fractious and paralysed political system. Overall, the constant repetition of past mistakes illustrated that consolidation could not be achieved through political and constitutional restructuring, as Ersin Kalaycıoğlu has concluded:

The 1980 military junta tried to insert new elites, who turned out to be fail-ures. They failed to play a game different from the previous elites. At least with the previous elites, they had not made those mistakes before. But the elites from the post-1980 era failed to learn from previous mistakes. They failed to do things differently. These new elites acted more like the previous elites. Özal, Çiller, Yılmaz, they were all dismal failures [. . .] The military should have understood that it is a matter of elite political culture. Not simply a matter of changing characters and constitutions. (Interview, April 2016)

Regardless of the generational change, the leadership pattern remained the same, and so did the political output and outcomes. The experiences post-1980 reveal that leaders failed to heed the lessons of the past, which brought about crises of democracy, in both intra- and inter-party relations.

Conclusion

From Demirel's ascension to the presidency in May 1993 to November 2002, the country lived through a turbulent period, suffering a cycle of largely dys-functional governments led by Çiller, Yılmaz, Erbakan and Ecevit. Outside of Ecevit's short-lived coalition, none exhibited a serious commitment to taking strong democratising measures for the greater public good. Instead, they were largely motivated by their personal, material, or ideological objectives. Under their watch, the political landscape was stagnant and replete with crises, owing to the personalisation of their parties, their intolerance, their abandonment of compromise and moderation in pursuit of personal and political ambitions. This resulted in the violation of the rule of law and the repeal of human rights and civil liberties, as well as corruption at the highest level, with even the parliament undermined.

As Kalaycıoğlu proclaimed, these experiences illustrate that the style of leadership prevalent before the coup was strongly evident in the 1980s and 1990s; as a result, they carried forward. Only Erdal İnönü offered a point of difference with his democratic character. Multi-party politics starved of democratic norms and practices ultimately weakened democracy, rather than moving it towards consolidation. Therefore, the loss of these leaders from the political landscape after the 2002 election brought forth the promise of stability. However, after a brief period of normalisation, politics fell back into familiar themes of leadership, with even graver outcomes for Turkey's democracy, as will be detailed in the next chapter.

Notes

1. The DYP-SHP coalition enjoyed the support of 48 percent of the voters, with 266 seats in the Assembly.
2. Murat Karayalçın replaced İnönü, and he was then replaced by Hikmet Çetin when the SHP merged with the CHP. The latter was soon removed in an intra-party vote by Deniz Baykal on 9 September 1995. Once Baykal ascended to the CHP leadership, Çiller's demeanour and policies in government caused relations to sour and the coalition to dissolve on 5 October 1995 (Birand and Yıldız 2012, 112–13).
3. When Çiller could not receive a vote of confidence as a minority government, the two subsequently decided to once again form a partnership as caretaker coalition government until the elections of 6 March 1996 (Birand and Yıldız 2012, 113).
4. For instance, during the DYP congress to hold the intra-party vote, Çiller's speeches outlined her wish to lead in an inclusive manner and create greater harmony in the party and in government (see Birand 2012).
5. Her personal clashes with high-level bureaucrats ultimately led to her setting the private sector against Çiller. In the face of skyrocketing inflation and plummeting wages, the country lived through its largest labour unrest since the 1970s. Economic confidence retreated, which was detrimental to a country already living through a major economic downturn (Cizre 2002b).

6. The *Türkiye İnsan Hakları Vakfı* (Human Rights Foundation of Turkey, TİHV) documented 124 deaths in custody from torture and ill treatment from January 1991 to September 1995. The majority of the deceased had been detained on terrorism charges. The report also observed that, during the same period, ninety-eight individuals disappeared while in the custody of the security forces or under mysterious circumstances (HRW 1997).

7. Human Rights Watch (1997) noted: 'Either the government is unable to stop the practice because it does not fully control its security apparatus, or it does not wish to do so because it views the tough methods of the security forces as an important asset in the fight against the PKK and various radical armed groups'.

8. The party was later closed down by the Constitutional Court due to the same incident (Kamer 2018).

9. They were found guilty of undermining the unity of the Turkish state (Kamer 2018).

10. Çiller and her husband were accused of tampering with the privatisation of two state companies and the misuse of the prime ministry's discretionary funds.

11. In addition to the ANAP, more than two dozen of DYP parliamentarians voted to have Çiller investigated, indicating how much she had fallen in the eyes of her own party.

12. Erbakan's bold Islamist rhetoric and stance subsequently led to the closure of the party in May 1971 by the country's Constitutional Court (Birand and Yıldız 2012, 329).

13. Until that point Erbakan had seen the closure of two of his parties, had been banned from politics by the 1980 military junta and served time in prison for his political activities.

14. Nurcu is the term commonly used to refer to the community of followers of the Islamic Sunni scholar Said Nursi (1877–1960). Nursi's teachings stressed the need for Islam to engage with modernity. He initially advocated the role of Islam in the newly established Turkish Republic. This brought him into conflict with the new Turkish state. Due to the critical view of religion held by the new Turkish state, Nursi's followers formed underground networks that spread his teachings across the country, later becoming a strong factor in the development of civil society in Turkey (Tittensor 2014, 34–37).

15. After the falling-out, the followers of the Nurcu movement threw their support behind Alparsan Türkeş's MHP and Demirel's AP in the 1977 elections.

16. The older brother of Turgut Özal.

17. These were not single incidents, as at the time countless recordings were leaked to the media and the public, by unknown sources (see Birand 2012).

18. The head of the Turkish Naval Forces, Güven Erkaya, made this remark to newspapers.

19. Pressure was also applied by the authorities that followed the actions of *Refah* to ensure that the party operated within the limits set by the constitution and the Political Parties Law.

20. To highlight Erbakan's continual aims to undermine the secular order, the incident in Sincan was virtually the same as a political rally for Erbakan's MSP, which took place in Konya in 1980 (Kepel 2006, 346). The measures against the party and Erbakan were very much similar to ones taken by the military in 1997.

21. This episode saw the military increase its authority over the political and public domain. To ensure that another Islamist and anti-secular party would not once again rise in politics, the military began the comprehensive application of the 28 February protocols, resulting in a mass purge of bureaucracy and councils. Large-scale operations against business associations suspected to have Islamist leanings were undertaken. The introduction of military attachés into bureaucratic and state institutions brought them under direct military oversight. These included the state broadcaster TRT, the Radio and Television Supreme Council (RTÜK), which is the state body overseeing the broadcast media, and the Council of Higher Education, the body that oversees universities.

22. On July 2004, Yılmaz and Güneş Taner, the Minister of State during the period, were put on trial in the Supreme Court for this matter – thus making Yılmaz the first ever Turkish Prime Minister tried by a civilian judiciary (*Radikal* 2004).

23. The stability during this period was also due to implementing economic reforms after negotiating an aid agreement with the International Monetary Fund (IMF).

24. In 1987, the Ecevits took a short intermission from politics after general elections, when the DSP failed to get into parliament. However, instead of leaving the leadership to an intra-party vote, they selected a compliant leader that would not offer a challenge if they decided to come back to the party. Thus, Necdet Karababa was selected by the couple, but Karababa resigned in 1989 due to the Ecevits regular interference behind the scenes (Akar and Dündar 2008, 375).

25. This was immediately conveyed when Celal Kürkoğlu challenged the leadership of Rahşan, who formally led the party due to the ban on Bülent Ecevit. He was purged along with his entire supporter base, who represented 213 out of the 612 founders of the DSP (Akar and Dündar 2008, 371).

26. The YTP merged with the CHP in 2004, due to poor electoral support and bad party management.

6

2002–15: RECEP TAYYIP ERDOĞAN AND A DEMOCRACY DISMANTLED

One simple man alone could take the entire state because there is no strong politi-
cal and economic force that could hold him back. The only one was the military.
With that gone now, you do not have anything else. Under these circumstances he
can ravage the state. (Interview, April 2016)

Ersin Kalaycıoğlu's statement, made during an hour-long interview in
the early months of 2016, is a particularly cutting summation of Recep
Tayyip Erdoğan's character and eerily offered a glimpse of what was to come.
The quote is especially poignant given that Erdoğan's democratising initiatives in his first term, after sweeping to victory in 2002, resulted in Turkey
being hailed as a model for the rest of the Muslim world and given that, a
decade later, Turkey had incrementally been transformed into a sub-type of
authoritarian regime under Erdoğan's leadership.

Hence, this begs the question: how do we explain Turkey's shift away
from democracy to authoritarian rule? This chapter will show that the grad-
ual reversal of democracy was once again largely due to the political leadership. Erdoğan's leadership style falls in line with the country's political
history, whereby leaders have consistently failed to display a commitment
to democratic norms and institutions. In its most acute manifestation, his
leadership has displayed the same pattern of intolerance, eschewing institutional forbearance, violation of rights and lacking respect for institutions

and processes of democracy, all of which resulted in Turkey's slide towards authoritarian rule.

This chapter will outline the details that led to the creation of Erdoğan's *Adalet ve Kalkınma Partisi* (Justice and Development Party, AKP) and how Erbakan's autocratic rule of his Islamist parties triggered another party split in Turkey. The following sections will move through the steps taken by Erdoğan to remove the military as the arbiter of politics; to erode the independence of the judiciary; and to monopolise the media landscape. The chapter will conclude by outlining Erdoğan's third legislative term from 2011 to 2015 and in what manner the Assembly became an institution to fortify his power against challenge and establish his personalised rule.

From *Fazilet Partisi* to the AKP

When Erbakan's government was brought down by the 28 February 'post-modern coup', the *Refah Partisi* (Welfare Party, RP) was disbanded by the authorities and Erbakan banned from entering politics for five years (*Milliyet* 1998). Although this marked Erbakan's third party closure, the group quickly reorganised to establish the *Fazilet Partisi* (Virtue Party, FP) which, in essence, did not deviate from *Refah*'s *modus operandi*; its membership, structural composition and policies were identical to its predecessor's. Despite his political ban, Erbakan controlled the FP from behind the scenes.

In an attempt to reshape the FP, so as to avoid the cyclical fate of its predecessors, an intra-party opposition, referred to as the *yenilikçiler* (reformists), was formed (Birand and Yıldız 2012, 327). This faction was largely made up of the younger cadres of the party, led by Abdullah Gül, Bülent Arınç, Abdüllatif Şener and the charismatic Istanbul Mayor Recep Tayyip Erdoğan. The *yenilikçiler*'s aim was intra-party democracy, as well as to compel the FP to be more responsive to societal needs and to appeal to a broad cross-segment of the electorate (Birand and Yıldız 2012, 326–30). By promising intra-party democracy they offered hope for party institutionalisation.

In a challenge to Erbakan's authority, the *yenilikçiler* nominated Gül to run against Recai Kutan for the party leadership. The intra-party election on 14 May 2000 was close, with Gül receiving 521 votes to Erbakan-backed Kutan's 633. Following the outcome, members of the *yenilikçiler* were sent to the disciplinary board, a possible precursor to being purged (Birand and Yıldız 2012, 326–30). Before they could be dismissed, the Constitutional Court closed down *Fazilet* for anti-secular activities, marking Erbakan's fourth party closure (*Hürriyet* 2001). In its place, the *Saadet Partisi* (Felicity Party, SP) was formed, and Kutan was again appointed by Erbakan to lead the new party. The *yenilikçiler* group interpreted this as a sign of Erbakan's unwillingness to relinquish control over the party or move towards reform. The group broke away from the *Millî Görüş* (National Outlook) movement to establish the *Adalet ve Kalkınma Partisi* (Justice and Development Party, AKP) on 14 August 2001, in order to contest the general elections scheduled for 3 November 2002 (Birand and Yıldız 2012, 340–44). Once again, the country witnessed the fracture of a major political party under the weight of the authoritarianism of its leader.

The new party selected Recep Tayyip Erdoğan as its leader, and, along with Gül, Şener and Arınç, forty-nine of the hundred *Fazilet* parliamentarians crossed to form the AKP. Distancing themselves from Erbakan, the AKP declared itself to be conservative democrats, with a commitment to free market economy principles, stability and political reforms (Birand and Yıldız 2012, 344, 354–55).

The electorate rewarded the AKP with an overwhelming victory at the ballot box, winning an absolute majority of parliamentary seats with 34.3 percent of the vote (see Table 6.1). The electoral system, a remnant of the 1980 military junta and further amended under Turgut Özal (see Chapter 4), ensured that Erdoğan's AKP picked up most of the Assembly seats which the *Doğru Yol Partisi* (DYP) and the *Anavatan* (ANAP) would have received, had they not fallen short of the ten-percent threshold (Çağaptay 2017, 88). What was unforeseen was Erdoğan securing votes from Bülent Ecevit's *Demokratik Sol Parti* (DSP) when it failed to meet the ten-percent threshold. The overall outcome further demonstrated the disenchantment of the electorate with the leadership of the 1990s (Waldman and Calışkan 2017, 62). This ensured that the AKP, despite only enjoying one-third of the popular vote, gained two-thirds of the seats in the legislature. This quirk in the system enabled Erdoğan and his colleagues to emerge from the political margins with full control of the Assembly (Çağaptay 2017, 88–89).

Table 6.1 2002 Election Results

Political Party	Percentage of Votes	Parliamentary Seats (Total 550)
AKP	34.3	363
CHP	19.4	178
Independents	1	9
DYP	9.5	0
Genç Parti (GP)	7.2	0
Demokratik Halk Partisi (HADEP)	6.2	0
ANAP	5.1	0
SP	2.5	0
DSP	1.2	0

Source: http://www.turkstat.gov.tr/UstMenu.do?metod=temelist

However, Erdoğan would have to wait five months before becoming Prime Minister: in that time, the parliament negotiated a constitutional amendment to the political ban that he had received after serving a prison sentence for reciting a poem judged to be against the secular order in 1999. Gül, who had taken office as Prime Minister in November, gave up the position for Erdoğan and moved to the Foreign Ministry. This episode would set the tone of the relationship between the two, wherein Erdoğan would always be the dominant and Gül the compliant.

2002–7: Democracy's Golden Era

Building on the democratisation packages enacted by the previous Ecevit government to meet EU candidate status,[1] the first term of Erdoğan's rule came to be known as the 'golden years' for democracy in Turkey (Lagendijk 2012, 167–68). The AKP looked committed to joining the EU and kept pace with the accession program, spearheaded largely by Gül as Foreign Minister (Sever 2015). The era witnessed many liberalising amendments (Özbudun 2014, 2011a, 103–7), the improvement of civilian-military relations, increased civilian oversight of the military (Heper 2005, 23–24; Waldman and Calışkan 2017),[2] major economic growth and much needed political stability (Turan 2007).

Erdoğan over the AKP

Between 2002 and 2007, democratic freedoms appeared to be improving across a range of areas. This correlated with Erdoğan's display of an inclusive style of intra-party governance, as Suat Kınıklıoğlu, who served as a parliamentarian for the AKP from 2007 to 2012, recalled:

> While I was in parliament and on the AKP's Executive Board from 2009 to 2012, Erdoğan was not the Erdoğan we see now. He listened, and he accepted advice. Contrary to our Turkish political culture, he allowed people on the board to speak, to raise questions. But not everyone was critical. This is because in our politics you cannot be openly critical of the leader. You sort of hint at it, or you come up with constructive suggestions. It is different from Anglo-Saxon political culture [. . .] Yet, Erdoğan, to his credit, allowed everyone to speak and raise anything with him. If you had an issue, you could write it on a piece of paper, put it in front of him, and he would read it and take notes. Throughout this period, I travelled with him extensively abroad, especially on foreign travel, and I got to see that there are two sides to the man. One is private where he is rather quiet, a particularly good listener and very engaged. And there is the public side to him, which is yelling and angry [. . .] He certainly is a man who has strong views, he has extraordinarily strong self-confidence, and part of his success, especially during his first term, was willingness to listen to advice [. . .] he understood his weaknesses and accepted them. When you look at the first seven to eight years, you see Recep Tayyip Erdoğan and the AKP step-by-step building up its legitimacy in Turkey. The EU process, for instance, was a huge element of achieving that. (Interview, May 2016)

This conciliatory approach had much to do with the fact that Erdoğan had not fully consolidated his power. Other prominent politicians and co-founders such as Gül, Arınç and Şener were held in high regard by their peers and offered informal checks on Erdoğan's power inside the central party apparatus, which placed certain constraints on the leader. Throughout this period Erdoğan was careful to avoid antagonising them, particularly Gül and Arınç, both of whom had a strong following within the party (Jenkins 2009b). Experienced politicians from the ANAP and the DYP joined the AKP's ranks, giving the AKP the semblance of an inclusive political organisation – a mosaic of conservative-religious and centrist ideologies.

However, this did not halt regulatory changes to the party by-laws, which would increase Erdoğan's power and repeal the founding democratic processes inside the AKP. The party regulations, originally shaped by a commitment to internal party democracy, after the experience of working under Erbakan's leadership (Tepe 2005, 74) were amended in February of 2003, two months after Erdoğan's political ban had been lifted (Arda Can Kumbaracıbaşı 2016, 12). In particular, the process of electing the fifty members of the *Merkez Karar ve Yönetim Kurulu* (Central Decision Making and Executive Committee, MKYK), the second-highest authority of the party, was altered to a closed system in order to allow Erdoğan's list of candidates to dominate selection processes (Tepe 2005, 74).[3] He was also given sole authority to select the most powerful body in the AKP, the twelve-member *Merkez Yürütme Kurulu* (Central Executive Committee, MYK) (Tepe 2005, 74). Most importantly, the candidate primaries selection process was transferred to the central party authority dominated by Erdoğan (Arda Can Kumbaracıbaşı 2016, 12).

This increased hegemony of the leader resulted in the resignation of eleven parliamentarians from the party (Birgün 2006). One of the eleven, Minister for Tourism and Culture Erkan Mumcu, cited as reason his inability to influence Erdoğan on government policy and refusal to comply with his leader's autocratic character (*Milliyet* 2005).

These changes allowed Erdoğan to steadily centralise political power from 2007 onwards (Arda Can Kumbaracıbaşı 2016, 12). He removed those who challenged his authority during the first term, by leaving them off the candidate lists in the following election (Jenkins 2009b). The close reign over appointments also allowed Erdoğan to remove and fill positions inside the government more freely. For example, in March 2009 Erdoğan expelled eight ministers from the cabinet for failing to win key municipalities in the local elections (Bayraktar and Altan 2013, 17). Around the same years, the three main counterweights to his power were also sidelined or removed. Gül was transitioned out of the party to the presidency; Şener resigned from the AKP; and Arınç remained as the only potential challenge to Erdoğan's single-handed rule; however, isolated, he could not offer a robust check on Erdoğan's leadership.

Kınıklıoğlu argued that it was Gül's rise to the presidential office that left Erdoğan's ambitions mostly unchecked:

What needs to be understood is that the [AKP] project started out with four people, Abdüllatif Şener, Bülent Arınç, Abdullah Gül and Tayyip Erdoğan. These were the four pillars of the party. In 2007 Abdüllatif Şener leaves the party, then in August 2007 Gül is elected as the President. So, by 2007, you have two of those key pillars gone. And over time Bülent Arınç was slowly marginalised. Gül's departure to the presidency was a key turning point because he was the internal balance in the Council of Ministers. He would provide counsel to Erdoğan. When Erdoğan would say something or do something that would look irrational, he would balance him, he would speak to him. Gül had a way within the party to limit Erdoğan's excesses. Unfortunately, these constraints on Erdoğan were lost by 2007, particularly when these key figures left the AKP. (Interview, May 2016)

As Kınıklıoğlu has noted, Gül and Şener's departure meant that the informal checks on Erdoğan were largely lost. Journalist Cengiz Çandar, who had close ties to the AKP, stated that, despite the other influential party figures and co-founders, Erdoğan's authoritarian personality was always going to see him remove his rivals:

In political parties, there are always *primus inter pares*, the first-among-equals. In the AKP, Erdoğan was that. As the power struggle in political science teaches us, the *primus inter pares* gets rid of the rest at a certain point. One good example is Stalin. He removed all threats to his power, one by one. He never kept a second man. In the AKP, the repetition of this case is nothing surprising – even if the other key members wanted, they simply couldn't match Erdoğan. He was always going to come out on top and rule over the party single-handedly. (Interview, October 2016b)

Importantly, Erdoğan's monopolisation of power and denial of intra-party democracy is in keeping with the Turkish model of political leadership. Former Speaker of Parliament (2007–9) and AKP representative Köksal Toptan furthered this:

During my time in the AKP, Erdoğan didn't get too involved in the day-to-day running of the party. He let others do that. Nonetheless, it was his decisions and views that held overwhelming weight. But this is not exclusive to Erdoğan either. We can't speak of real intra-party democracy in the Turkish experience. There is no room to challenge the party leader. The local branches don't have much influence. Leaders decide on the candidates. The local branches can merely suggest. Leaders are also suspicious of being overthrown, and so no one is allowed close enough for fear of challenge. This *tek adam* culture has been the pattern for leaders all the way back to Atatürk. This is something that can be taken away when trying to understand the AKP under Erdoğan. (Interview, March 2016)

As Toptan diplomatically pointed out, under Erdoğan the AKP operated as another leader-dominated party: maintaining the centralised character of rule was the norm and not an exception. Yet, as previously discussed, this pattern stood opposed to the concept of party institutionalisation, which is a key component for democratic consolidation (Garretón Merino 2003; Kalaycıoğlu 2013). Deinstitutionalisation leads to parties becoming the personal instruments of its leader, according to Mainwaring and Torcal (2005). Hence, by the 2011 elections Erdoğan was directing the party largely unopposed, purging the remaining liberal and centrist elements in the AKP's parliamentary rank and file, by leaving them off the 2011 electoral list:

> By this stage, the party leader and a small clique within the party prepared the candidate lists, but Erdoğan had the last call. For instance, myself and many other centrists were excluded from the candidate lists of the 2011 elections [. . .] After looking over the individuals that were left off the lists, one noticed that it was largely the centrists, those who could speak different languages and who had outside networks, who were ousted from the party. However, when you looked over the people that were replacing them, they were all more provincial, more devout, more conservative, but most importantly totally loyal to Erdoğan.
>
> I saw what was going on because it was clear that by 2011 Erdoğan had decided that he was going to take complete control over the AKP. Why 2011? After winning the constitutional referendum in 2010, Erdoğan realised that he had the power to dominate the judiciary. The referendum was the final step to beat the established order. However, at the time, we thought that Turkey was continuing on its path of democratisation with these constitutional amendments. Accordingly, the judiciary was no longer going to be dominated by the old state elites that we viewed as static and authoritarian. Regrettably, it is now clear that Erdoğan had something else in mind, and this was complimented by the way in which he structured the party in 2011. (Interview with Suat Kınıklıoğlu, May 2016)

The 2010 constitutional amendments (to be discussed below) gave the government influence over critical institutions. As Kınıklıoğlu noted, Erdoğan engineered changes in the AKP to act on his personal ambitions, blurring the distinction between his interests and those of the government. From this point onwards, he exploited his unrestrained power inside the AKP, making decisions with a small circle of loyal advisors, without consulting others in the parliamentary group:

> In the post-2011 period, Erdoğan decided that he knew best, that he understood all of the country's issues, and that he had a personal project in mind, which he alone was going to achieve [. . .] By 2011, his patience had shortened. He was no longer seeing as many people as he used to. He became almost hostage to a small group of advisors. Even some of his ministers had difficulty seeing him, let alone the average AKP members of parliament. (Interview with Suat Kınıklıoğlu, May 2016)

What we draw from this is that Erdoğan's rule became confined to an inner circle of trusted advisors, whereas he rarely communicated – much less consulted – with other members of the party, a practice reminiscent of Turgut Özal and Tansu Çiller. This allowed him to take greater control of policy direction within the government, with ministers relegated to implementing his wishes or face dismissal from the cabinet (Waldman and Calışkan 2017, 96–97). This included using the September 2012 party congress to continue the purge of potential intra-party opposition: members with perceived sympathy towards Gül were removed from the party's Executive Body (Waldman and Calışkan 2017, 75). Former Deputy Prime Minister Ali Babacan detailed the centralisation of Erdoğan's power inside the AKP in this period and its detriment to Turkey:[4]

> From 2012, the AKP experienced a dramatic decline in the quality of politicians because individuals were brought into the party who didn't necessarily have the public good at heart, but more to accommodate Erdoğan's rule. This is an important point. The other point is that party decisions began to be taken without consultation. In fact, a very small circle of people began making decisions for the party and a country of 83 million citizens. (Özdemir 2020)

The AKP's overwhelming legislative majority, together with Erdoğan's power over the party, allowed him to monopolise politics, with the authoritarianism inside the AKP mirroring the practices of the government. Turkey began experiencing a democratic backslide from 2007 onwards, once the AKP was consolidated under Erdoğan's rule (Arda Can Kumbaracıbaşı 2016, 12–14). After a promising first term in office, Erdoğan became outwardly aggressive towards his opponents in the broader political milieu (Görener and Ucal 2011, 371), and by the end of 2008 his language had shifted from a rights-based and inclusive discourse (Turam 2007, 138–39) to an authoritarian tone (White 2013, 52–53). Gareth Jenkins also noted (2009b):

> Through late 2008 and early 2009, Erdoğan became not only more outspoken but increasingly aggressive; mixing threats and insults in an unprecedented barrage of attacks against everyone from advocates of Kurdish cultural rights to the IMF, the EU, the oppositional media, Israel, the Palestine Liberation Organization (PLO) and the World Economic Forum. (WEF)

This observation further demonstrates that, once Erdoğan's hold over the AKP had increased, he began to display similar autocratic tendencies and disdain for those who opposed him within the inter-party and the policy arena. As a result, the political developments and changed practices following Erdoğan's first term are inextricably tied to the AKP succumbing to his personalised rule. However, two major hurdles remained: both the military and the courts continued to provide substantive oversight.

Dismantling the Military Tutelage: Ergenekon and Beyond

As seen in the events of 1960, 1971 and 1980, Turkey's military had frequently played the role of grand arbiter of politics. Erdoğan and his AKP co-founders had been, over the years, subjected to numerous interventions by the courts and the military during their time in Erbakan's parties. Given this organic link back to Erbakan and Turkey's leading political Islamist movement, *Milli Görüş*, certain high-ranking members of the Turkish military were deeply disturbed by the victory of the AKP in the November 2002 general election (Jenkins 2010). However, the democratising reforms aimed at meeting the EU's candidature criteria gradually weakened the hold of the military over civilian politics, by either diluting or removing their role entirely from key government bodies.

If Erdoğan and his party were to avoid the spectre of military tutelage that had routinely befallen Erbakan, their next step would be to eliminate the military's role in politics. In fact, the military's ongoing contempt towards the AKP was revealed in 2007: in opposition to Gül's nomination for the presidency, the military on 27 April released a memorandum which was a veiled threat towards the AKP's decision to nominate Gül for the office. Caught in a politically intractable position, the government called an early election in an attempt to resolve the crisis. The resounding 46.6 percent that the AKP received secured Erdoğan's second term (see Table 6.2).[5] With the substantive increase in public support, Erdoğan was able to confidently defy the military's overtures to elect Gül to the presidential office through the parliamentary vote on 28 August 2007.[6]

Table 6.2 2007 Election Results

Political Party	Percentage of Votes	Parliamentary Seats (Total 550)
AKP	46.6	341
CHP	20.9	112
MHP	14.3	71
Independents	5.2	26

Source: http://www.turkstat.gov.tr/UstMenu.do?metod=temelist

Despite successfully resisting the military, the AKP faced another critical test in March 2008, when the state's chief prosecutor, Abdurrahman Yalçınkaya, brought a case against the government to the Constitutional Court (Traynor 2008). Yalçınkaya requested the closure of the AKP and a ban on seventy-one members, including Erdoğan and Gül, for five years, on the grounds that the party was acting against the secular order of the republic (Çağaptay, Ünver and Arifağaoğlu 2008).[7] With a one-vote majority, the Constitutional Court ruled against the AKP's closure, but removed 50 percent of the AKP's state funding and issued a warning to the party (Waldman and Calışkan 2017, 30–31). By not yielding to the military establishment,

Erdoğan was able to demonstrate that the once-feared military power was now largely obsolete.

The Launch of the Ergenekon and Balyoz (Sledgehammer) Investigations

Erdoğan's second term was focused on eradicating any future threats remaining within the military. The Ergenekon investigations began in early 2008, when thirty-one retired military officials, including retired Chief of General Staff İlker Başbuğ, were detained for plans to undertake a coup. The number of arrests increased to 275, including journalists, bureaucrats, academics, civil society figures, opposition lawmakers and figures involved in organised crime. The suspects were charged with being members of a centralised clandestine organisation that allegedly controlled every terrorist group and was responsible for all acts of political violence in Turkey over the previous twenty years (Jenkins 2009a). The defendants, sixty-six of whom were in prison at the time of the verdict, were found guilty of aiding and abetting, or being members in a 'terrorist organisation'; they received a range of sentences, including life imprisonment for Başbuğ and a number of other defendants.[8]

The Balyoz investigation that followed saw further arrests, with the focus squarely on the military. In September 2012, a total of 331 serving and retired military personnel were convicted of plotting a coup code-named *Balyoz* (sledgehammer). The number of high-ranking officials arrested constituted close to 20 percent of Turkey's serving generals and admirals (Dombey 2014), with the prosecution claiming that the defendants had discussed staging a coup against the AKP at a military seminar in Istanbul between 5 and 7 March 2003 (Jenkins 2010).

However, early into the investigation, suspicious irregularities in the evidence began to surface. It was exposed that the so-called coup plot, which allegedly dated back to 2003, was written with Microsoft Office 2007 software, which had not yet been created at that point (Jenkins 2014a; Rodrik 2014). In addition, key testimony against defendants came from 'secret witnesses' (*Hürriyet* 2013a). Further fuelling questions around the legitimacy of the trials was the fact that, beyond these two cases, there had been no other attempts to investigate abuses or criminal activity by the Turkish military (Sinclair-Webb 2013). Finally, there was a lack of credible evidence tying the individuals to one another: the connection between the defendants – many from opposing ideological camps, criminal organisations and professional backgrounds – could not be legally rationalised (Waldman and Calışkan 2017, 32–36).

The investigations were made possible, in part, by Erdoğan's alliance with the religious network, the Gülen Movement (GM), which enabled the government to employ GM-affiliated individuals inside the judiciary and police force against the military (to be discussed below). In 2013, the bitter falling-out between the GM and the AKP resulted in the high court overturning the Ergenekon and Balyoz convictions (Dombey 2014; *Hürriyet* 2016, 2015a).[9] By this point, however, the armed forces had suffered immeasurable damage, with hundreds of military members incarcerated, or held without trial for lengthy periods, often in inhumane conditions. A certain number died from illness, and others took their own lives (*Milliyet* 2013). In addition, leading members of the military resigned *en masse* in protest of the trials before the verdicts were overturned, the most notable being the resignation of the entire high command, including Acting Chief of General Staff Işık Koşaner (Righter 2011). The Ergenekon-Balyoz investigations eliminated any vestige of the old establishment and removed potential anti-Erdoğan elements from the military's upper echelons; instead, it solidified pro-Erdoğan elements thanks to the legal amendments passed by the AKP government, which enabled Erdoğan (with Gül as President) to appoint to the vacant posts officers favourable to the government and its allies (Righter 2011).[10]

These cases inevitably became a battleground for those who wished to establish power and ultimately control Turkish politics; Erdoğan proved to be the clear winner (Cizre and Walker 2010). He effectively dismantled the strongest and most effective check against the government, the one body that historically had stepped in to curb the authoritarian abuses of Turkey's political class. Without the military, other organisations that could have offered a tough opposition to the government, such as the courts, the media, business communities and civil societal organisations, were left powerless (Çağaptay 2017, 118).

The Erdoğan–Gülen Alliance: Breaking the State's Tutelage

Subsequent evidence has indicated that the cases against the military and the secular establishment were driven by Erdoğan's alliance with the GM and its elements inside the police force and judiciary (see Yavuz and Balcı 2018). As a religious and social movement, led by the teachings of the self-exiled preacher Fethullah Gülen,[11] the GM has traditionally had hostile relations with the secular and military-bureaucratic establishment, similar to the experiences of the *Millî Görüş* movement, whence Erdoğan comes (see Tittensor 2014; Yavuz 2013).[12]

In the early years of Erdoğan's rule, the GM not only backed the AKP's policies, via their vast media outlets, but they also took advantage of government contracts and concessions (Waldman and Calışkan 2017, 65). With Erdoğan's patronage, Gülenists entered the ranks of the bureaucracy, the judiciary and the police *en masse*, in order to eradicate the dominance of the secular regime over the state and its institutions (Waldman and Calışkan 2017, 65).

Gülen sympathisers in the judiciary and media outlets served as the driving force behind highly politicised judicial investigations, most notoriously the Ergenekon and Balyoz trials (see Yavuz and Balcı 2018). The AKP government threw its support behind the investigations, which were viewed as retaliation against the military (see Sözcü 2016). For example, then Deputy Prime Minister Bülent Arınç announced that the case was 'Turkey cleaning out its bowels', while Erdoğan underlined his support by proclaiming in July 2008: 'I am the prosecutor of this case' (Sözcü 2016). The Gülenist media, spearheaded by the newspaper *Zaman*, focused its reporting on supporting the ongoing trials and broadcasting the growing number of arrests.[13] The GM media was also undertaking a systematic campaign to intimidate vocal critics of the court cases and of Prime Minister Erdoğan (Çağaptay 2017, 116; Jenkins 2013). With the government's support, pro-Gülen elements were also emboldened to undertake retributive operations against traditional critics of the GM itself (see Sever 2015, 99–103; Jenkins 2014b).[14]

The vigour with which the cases were pursued by the AKP-Gülen coalition raised serious concerns about the Turkish judicial system and its ability to make decisions autonomously. The cases seemed to illustrate that the fate of those hauled in front of the courts was not governed by the principles of law, but rather by political power. According to a former Minister of Justice, one judge was known to have telephoned Fethullah Gülen for instructions before delivering a verdict (Waldman and Calışkan 2017, 98). Similarly,

Ahmet Davutoğlu (while Prime Minister) later corroborated this by claiming that there existed recordings of judicial officers taking orders from Gülen to release seventy-five defendants accused of plotting against the government (*Hürriyet* 2015g).

These developments illustrate that court cases such as Ergenekon and Balyoz were primarily shaped by the desire to overtake the state and use its power against those regarded as opponents. The coalition between the AKP and the GM, by now allies of convenience, gradually purged the state by using the judiciary and police force as a political weapon (Jenkins 2014a). Once the power of the military and the remaining pockets of opposition were removed from state institutions, the void was replaced by Erdoğan and GM loyalists (Kaya and Cornell 2012, 65–66; Waldman and Calışkan 2017). And, similar to the experiences under Demirel, Ecevit and Özal (see Chapters 3 and 4), their efforts to control critical institutions were troubling and would ultimately worsen.

The 2010 Constitutional Amendments: Erdoğan Emboldened

Having subdued the military and filled critical posts within the state with allies and loyalists, Erdoğan set out to remove the remaining substantive check on his power: that of the judiciary. The most significant marker of this consisted of the twenty-six proposed amendments to the military-drafted constitution.[15] The changes, so argued the Prime Minister, were aimed at bringing the document in line with the EU member states, therefore facilitating Turkey's accession to the EU (Tisdall and Tait 2010). The proposed amendments, taken to a referendum on 12 September 2010, resulted in a victory for Erdoğan, after the in-favour vote received 58 percent, leading the Prime Minister to declare: 'Our democracy is the winner [. . .] The mentality that opposes change has lost' (Çağaptay 2017, 119).

The constitutional reforms were not, however, the outcome of an inclusive and deliberative process undertaken with the involvement of opposition parties and civil society: the amendments were tabled under the AKP's exclusive authority (Öztürk and Gözaydın 2017). In response, the two opposition parties, the *Cumhuriyet Halk Partisi* (Republican People's Party, CHP) and the *Barış ve Demokrasi Partisi* (Peace and Democracy Party, BDP) boycotted the parliamentary vote, whilst the *Milliyetçi Hareket Partisi* (Nationalist Movement

Party, MHP) voted against them. The amendments, backed by President Gül, were presented to a popular vote after the AKP parliamentary members had voted in favour.

This is a critical example of the government's abandonment of institutional forbearance in order to exploit its prerogatives, despite large-scale opposition. These actions raised further doubts about the sincerity of the government's democratising initiatives, which pertained to structures and procedures rather than the expansion of individual liberties and civil rights (Turam 2012). Although the reforms to civil rights appeared to be bolstered by the changes, critics deemed these to be merely cosmetic.[16] For instance, the amendments ignored the critical impediments to liberalising the regime, such as the abolition of the ten-percent threshold for parliamentary representation established in the Election Act of 1983, nor did they address the demands of the Kurdish minority for greater political and cultural autonomy. Had the amendments been more liberal, representative and accessible, they would have strengthened both horizontal and vertical mechanisms of accountability.

The changes to the *Hâkimler ve Savcılar Yüksek Kurulu* (Supreme Board of Judges and Prosecutors, HSYK) and the Constitutional Court generated the most intense controversy, as they were viewed as a means to bring them under the influence of the executive branch (Yeğen 2017, 79; Özbudun 2014, 156; Turam 2012, 110–11; Waldman and Calışkan 2017, 97–98). Prior to the 2010 amendments, both the HSYK and the Constitutional Court displayed markedly secularist tendencies (Özbudun 2014, 156), with judicial appointments largely conducted as an internal process. After the amendments, the power to select the country's prosecutors and judges shifted to the (AKP-dominated) government (Özbudun 2012, 162). The most troubling change pertained to President Gül, who was tasked with the power to elect fourteen out of the seventeen new judges to the Constitutional Court, without the oversight of the Assembly (Turam 2012).[17] With a large majority in parliament and Gül as President, Erdoğan's administration was free to appoint the judiciary with little interference. Gül stated that, by the end of his presidential term in August 2014, he had personally appointed the majority of the judges who presided over the Constitutional Court (Waldman and Calışkan 2017, 97). Similarly, the HSYK, the central body that provides oversight over the country's judges and prosecutors, had its membership raised from seven to twenty-two, with the newly created posts filled by AKP- or Gülen-aligned judges and prosecutors (Yeğen 2017, 78; Kalaycıoğlu 2012, 6).

On the surface, the constitutional amendments were a critical development providing the judiciary with greater plurality (Özbudun 2012). However, once the government became the main appointer of judicial officers, the institution's capacity to remain independent became heavily questionable. To illustrate the power that the government held over judicial appointments, the winners of the 12 October 2014 elections to the HSYK were drawn entirely from a list prepared by the Minister of Justice (Akyol 2014a; Tekdal 2015). This was mainly because promotions to higher courts were dependant on the ministry. Local judges, wanting to ensure their career progression, rarely voted differently from the wishes of the office (Akyol 2014b). As such, government loyalists slowly filled the judicial ranks.

The high courts had never been harbingers of liberal democracy in Turkey; for most of the multi-party history, they had been under the direction of a judicial cadre, influenced by a statist and tutelary philosophy towards civilian politics (Özbudun 2011b). Thus, the judiciary was used by the military to limit the power of elected governments and as a means with which to maintain the institution's political tutelage. Nevertheless, the capitulation of the judiciary signified the end of another key democratic mechanism of oversight on political power, which allowed Erdoğan to instrumentalise the institution for political purposes. Outside of Menderes and Bayar, capturing the judiciary was not a measure that his predecessors had achieved or even attempted (see Chapter 1). Erdoğan, as the above discussion illustrates, was the first in the history of multi-party politics to truly succeed in his attempt.

The Removal of the Media as a Check on Power

Measures to silence the media became a common practice of the Erdoğan government, which usually charged media owners for improper business practices or put them under state receivership, before selling the media assets to Erdoğan associates. Over time, these methods saw large independent or critical print media such as *Milliyet*, *Sabah*, *Star* and *Akşam* and television networks transformed into pro-Erdoğan outlets (Çağaptay 2017, 122–23).

The media landscape has undergone an astonishing transformation since the rise of the AKP: in 2002, pro-government business owned less than a quarter of the Turkish media, but by late 2018 twenty-one out of twenty-seven daily newspapers were under the control of companies loyal to Erdoğan, with 90 percent of the entire newspaper circulation being pro-government (Coşkun 2018) and 85 percent of Turkey's news channels under government control or influence (Şanlı 2016). This power has enabled Erdoğan to shape the political narrative, thereby giving him unprecedented hold over the electorate:

> Erdoğan has full control of the Turkish media right now, full control. This allows him to dictate the discourse. The AKP can spin anything, and there are no ethical standards in the media to prevent them from doing so. We never had ethical media, but we have never seen it this bad. I mean they now can write anything that furthers their interests and curb the influence of their opponents [. . .] Unfortunately, 80 percent of Turks get their news from television. Whoever controls television in this country controls the discourse. It's not so much anymore about newspapers or social media because it is only the elite that follows these platforms. It's really the television where Turks get all their news from, so control of television is very important in Turkish politics. (Interview with Suat Kınıklıoğlu, May 2016)

Erdoğan's influence over the media enabled him to manipulate the political narrative, eroding the plurality of the press. It has allowed Erdoğan to regularly intervene and stop broadcasts critical of him or his government. Leaked recordings reveal that he ordered the owner of *Habertürk TV*, Mehmet Fatih Saraç, to immediately suspend a live broadcast by MHP leader Devlet Bahçeli who was criticising the AKP government (Waldman and Calışkan 2017, 129). Another recording, from the same news channel, reveals that Erdoğan ordered the station to stop showing the Gezi Park protests in 2013 (Cengiz 2014).[18] Similarly, following a telephone call voicing his disapproval of an editorial in the newspaper *Habertürk*, which was critical of Turkey's health services, the three journalists involved in writing and editing the report were fired (Cengiz 2014). The plight of the media in Turkey became so dire that Erdoğan has been dubbed 'Turkey's biggest media boss' (Şanlı 2016), a situation that led Turkey analyst Soner Çağaptay to later declare: 'Erdoğan can successfully edit out reality' (quoted in Gall 2018).

The government also exploited vaguely defined anti-terror laws to target journalists who held a critical view of the government (Committee to Protect Journalists 2013). This first became apparent during the Ergenekon and Balyoz trials, when journalists covering the affair became suspects themselves. Investigative reporters such as Ahmet Şık, Nedim Şener, Soner Yalçın and editor-in-chief of *Cumhuriyet*, İlhan Selçuk, were arrested and charged with being part of a 'terrorist' organisation (Genç 2016, 14–16). Erdoğan defended the arrests by saying: 'There are some books that are more effective than bombs' (Genç 2016). These initial arrests sent the clear message that journalists reporting on government malpractice or painting it in a negative light would be targeted.[19]

In acts reminiscent of the later Menderes years (see Chapter 1), these crackdowns were extended to include reporting deemed critical of Turkey's economy. An indictment against two Bloomberg reporters, Kerim Karakaya and Fercan Yalınkılıç, who had written a story on the 2018 currency crash, were charged with trying to undermine Turkey's economic stability. Another thirty-six defendants, including journalists Mustafa Sönmez, Merdan Yanardağ and Sedef Kabataş, were also named in the indictment for sharing the article on social media and making comments considered critical of Turkey's economy (Reporters Sans Frontières 2019a).

In 2008, Turkey had only one journalist behind bars. By December 2012, the number had risen to forty-nine, near doubling to eighty-six in 2016. These incarcerations made Turkey one of the leading jailers of the press in the world (Committee to Protect Journalists 2013, 2017, 2018). As a result, Turkey's media has been labelled as 'Not Free' by Freedom House since 2013 (2014, 2015, 2016, 2017, 2018a),[20] and Reporters Sans Frontières has ranked Turkey below 150 out of 180 countries when it comes to freedom of the media (2017, 2016, 2015, 2014, 2013, 2019b), labelling the country as the 'world's biggest prison for professional journalists' (2019b).

However, Erdoğan is not alone in his attempt to dominate the media: the desire to control the media has been central to the Turkish political culture over the course of many decades. Turkey's leaders, especially Menderes and to a lesser extent Özal, frequently targeted the critical press (see Chapters 1 and 4). The parallels with the Menderes era are also evident in the AKP's current monopoly over the state broadcaster, TRT, which now effectively acts as another arm of the government.[21] As a result, the media is curtailed in its capacity to function as a mechanism of accountability, and its role of introducing a plurality of views to the public sphere has also been stymied. Thus, by silencing the media, Erdoğan removed a key foundation of democracy: that of vertical mechanism of accountability (see Keane 1992), hallmark of a consolidated system.

2011–15: The Assembly becomes Erdoğan's Rubber Stamp

Erdoğan was emboldened by his third general election win on 12 June 2011, which increased his support to its highest level, at 49.8 percent. Not only did he seek to cow the military and the media, but he also set out to further weaken institutional checks and balances on the government.

Table 6.3 2011 Election Results

Political Party	Percentage of Votes	Parliamentary Seats (Total 550)
AKP	49.8	327
CHP	26	135
MHP	13	53
Independents	6.6	35

Source: http://www.turkstat.gov.tr/UstMenu.do?metod=temelist

Utilising his absolute majority, Erdoğan passed new laws without broad public consultation and with little input from opposition parties, denying the parliament of its representative role.[22] Former AKP General Secretary Ertuğrul Yalçınbayır captured Erdoğan's dominance over the Assembly during the 2011–15 legislative terms:

> Ninety-eight percent of the laws adopted were prepared entirely by the government. Only two percent of the legislative proposals were discussed by the opposition beforehand, but these were also brought to the parliament under the initiative of the AKP government [. . .] In fact, the influence of the executive on the legislative body turned into a tutelage. Parliament turned into a factory producing laws. But the quality of laws went down. Defective laws that disregard the rule of law were passed. (quoted in Kılıç 2015)

This spotlights the level of control that Erdoğan has wielded over the legislature and the means by which it was exploited to erode its democratic capacity. The legislation proposed by opposition parties was not considered seriously and routinely voted down by the AKP majority (Waldman and Calışkan 2017, 91). Erdoğan's power over the AKP ensured that he enjoyed almost complete control of the legislative process, which in 2011 enabled his government to introduce thirty-five decrees to bypass parliamentary oversight (Erem 2017).

This disregard for democratic precedence was further highlighted with the use of the *torba yasası* (omnibus laws) – a package of unrelated laws that fast-tracks legislative changes and is only intended for rare cases when there is a suite of issues that need to be rectified urgently – in order to pass legislation which side-stepped the scrutiny of the Assembly. Nonetheless, the AKP-majority under Erdoğan employed the *torba yasası* to regularly rush through rafts of oppressive and authoritarian measures. In fact, the application of omnibus laws reveals Erdoğan's changing nature: during his first term (2002–7) there were only two, whereas in his second term (2007–11) the AKP's use of omnibus laws experienced a 450-percent jump to a total of eleven, which then nearly doubled to twenty-one during this third legislative period and equalled 15.3 percent of the legislation passed in this period (Erem 2017). Amendments providing the government with greater control over the judiciary and tighter control over the internet were passed using this practice (Zeldin 2014b, 2014a). Continuing this upward trajectory, between 2015 and 2017 omnibus laws accounted for 43.4 percent of all legislation (Erem 2017).

Indicative of the growing unease towards the illiberal direction of government, from May to June 2013 large anti-government protests erupted. The protests were sparked by the arbitrary decision to erase one of the last remaining green spaces in the heart of Istanbul, Gezi Park, and quickly transformed into a nation-wide protest against the increasingly authoritarian character of Erdoğan's rule. The Prime Minister's remarks about 'looters', 'extremists' and 'terrorists' highlighted his intolerance of the protests (Çağaptay 2010; Genç 2016; Özbudun 2014). These public statements against the demonstrations were strikingly similar to those of Menderes and Bayar concerning public discontent. Similarly, the words were matched by heavy-handed violent responses against the protestors. Despite the deaths and injuries suffered by demonstrators at the hands of the police, Erdoğan publicly declared that the police had acted under his orders (*Radikal* 2013) and had written their own hero-legend in their acts against the protestors (NTV 2013). The crackdown witnessed thousands being detained and forced to stand trial for joining 'unauthorised demonstrations', 'resisting police' and 'damaging public property', while large numbers also faced the charge of 'terrorism' and attempting to 'overthrow the government' (Traynor and Letsch 2013), displaying the instrumentalisation of the judiciary against critics and opponents.[23] The government also passed a number of legal measures to increase police powers and broaden the circumstances under which lethal force may be used against demonstrators. This regulated a culture of impunity for abuses by state officials against civilians and, at the same time, closed the streets to public demonstrations (Human Rights Watch 2015).

Gül's presidency, in effect, accommodated these growing authoritarian practices. Although having veto powers, the President refused to ratify only two laws, which he then sent back to parliament to be amended.[24] Both bills were later passed by Gül, even though he did not believe that the changes were adequate (Sever 2015, 149–54; *Cumhuriyet* 2014). It is this complicity which enabled the AKP to pass a highly controversial bill restricting alcohol consumption and sales. Despite public pressure, Gül signed the bill into law, a development which has been identified as one of the principal antecedents to the country-wide Gezi Park protests in 2013 (*Hürriyet* 2013c).

Gül's compliance with his former party raised serious questions about his supposed neutrality as President. Timur Kuran, a Turkish-American academic, argued that his unwillingness to oppose Erdoğan ensured that 'Abdullah Gül will probably be remembered as the Neville Chamberlain of Turkish politics. He spent the past decade appeasing Erdoğan, missing every chance to stop the destruction of Turkey's democracy' (quoted in Çandar 2018). Therefore, much like President Bayar with Menderes's government (see Chapter 1), Gül, through his partisanship, failed to provide an important horizontal accountability mechanism and enabled Erdoğan to impose legislation that fundamentally undermined the democratic order.

Evidence of this was Gül rubber-stamping the anti-democratic laws that removed checks on government spending and the allocation of public resources. Esra Gürakar (2016) found that more than 150 amendments to the Public Procurement Law (Law Nr 4734)[25] have been made under Erdoğan's administration, which gave his personal networks and supporters unfettered access to public contracts and state resources. Corruption had not been unusual amongst the political class prior to 2002; Özal, Çiller and Yılmaz were known to have bent the law for personal gain, but such corruption was an *ad hoc* affair and largely undertaken on an individual basis. In contrast, the changes instituted by Erdoğan put in place a regulated system of corruption by the government – a first in Turkey's political history (Gürakar 2016).

Indicative of the systemic nature of the corruption, the AKP between 2012 and 2015 passed a series of laws that paralysed the authority of the judicial department, the *Sayıştay* (Court of Accounts), charged with monitoring and reporting to parliament on government spending (Soyaltın 2013; *Hürriyet* 2013b).[26] As such, Erdoğan was able to solidify his control over an extensive patronage network, in a regime that was openly able to exploit state and public resources (Gürakar 2016; Hansen 2017).

The extent of state-business interactions came to light in the midst of Turkey morphing into a clientelist state. On 17 December 2013, the country awoke to a wave of corruption allegations, culminating in the arrest of fifty-two people connected to the core of Erdoğan's administration (Gürsel 2013).[27] The allegations concerned bribery around state construction tenders, money-laundering, gold-smuggling and circumventing sanctions against Iran. Four AKP cabinet members resigned due to their involvement. Three of the four ministers also had their sons implicated and brought into custody (Letsch 2013). A second wave of allegations targeted Erdoğan and his son Bilal, but neither police nor prosecutors could follow through to press charges (Jenkins 2014d). Instead, incriminating telephone recordings were leaked to the press and online, featuring the Prime Minister ordering Bilal to urgently dispose of tens of millions of dollars before the police would arrive.

The investigations reflected the growing power struggle between the GM and Erdoğan (Jenkins 2014c). Having already disposed of key institutions which had offered checks and balances on their activities, the former allies came into open conflict over the direction of political developments in the country (see Yavuz and Balcı 2018). The government's backing of the GM enabled it to strategically place its members in the various departments of the state, which weakened state institutions, left them open to manipulation and ultimately allowed the GM to act against its former supporter (Waldman and Calışkan 2017, 9–10; Yavuz and Koç 2018, 79).

The damage was quickly contained, as the AKP-dominated Assembly protected the government from judicial scrutiny. The government's numbers blocked a motion introduced by the opposition to try the cabinet members accused of corruption by the *Yargıtay* (Supreme Court) (Human Rights Watch 2014, 2015)[28] – a move which MHP Deputy Chairman Mehmet Şandır denounced as a government effectively exploiting its 'parliamentary majority in favour of corruption' (quoted in Kılıç 2015). This once again underlined the systematic abandonment of forbearance in order to protect Erdoğan's rule from any challenge.

Erdoğan was untroubled, dismissing the whole investigation as a 'coup plot' by the GM against the government and initiated a number of authoritarian counter-measures (Oruçoğlu 2015). In the name of fighting the Gülenist 'parallel structure', the government continued to instrumentalise its legislative majority by enacting a series of laws to extend its control over the state, thereby further eroding the democratic capacity of the parliament. The amendments provided the government with power to purge the judiciary of members who failed to pass rulings in line with its interests (Özbudun 2015). The Minister of Justice was given control over HSYK meetings and the authority to reorganise the judicial body (Özbudun 2015, 47; *Hürriyet* 2014a). This allowed the government to remove the judge, four state prosecutors and police officers working on the corruption investigation (*Hürriyet* 2015e).[29] Within two months, the case was closed by the new government-appointed prosecutors, who cited improper collection of evidence. A court ruling subsequently placed a ban on media reporting on the cases. The four cabinet members who had been forced to resign were acquitted of their charges through a parliamentary vote (Peer 2017, 111–12; *Hürriyet* 2015e; Solaker 2014). Later, the AKP voted to destroy the incriminating audio clips that featured the accused ex-ministers and their sons (Oruçoğlu 2015).

To remove the possibility of additional corruption investigations against the government, a total of 2,000 judges and prosecutors were arbitrarily reassigned (Tekdal 2015), twenty-nine police chiefs were removed from their positions in Ankara and Istanbul, and 500 police officers were purged (Gürsel 2013; Jenkins 2016a). The judge and the state prosecutors who had conducted the operation were also put under criminal investigation (Tekdal 2015).

Ultimately, the legislative period (2011–15) saw the gravest and most pervasive decline in Turkey's democracy up to that point. Erdoğan abandoned virtually all practice of restraint, exploiting his majority in parliament so as to avoid judicial, political and societal oversight to protect his position. Included in the swathe of measures to exert executive control and to repeal rights were regular applications of the Press Law's gagging orders, which banned reporting on 'sensitive' information (Amnesty International 2015). An unprecedented number of citizens, including school-aged children, were hauled before courts to face criminal charges of 'insulting' Erdoğan (*Reuters* 2016). In a striking assessment of the developments, Amnesty International (2015) noted that Turkey's human rights were worse than in the decade preceding Erdoğan's coming to power, while Human Rights Watch underscored the 'roll back of human rights and the rule of law' and the 'authoritarian drift' of Turkey during these years (2014, 2015). Others, such as Kalaycıoğlu, went even further, declaring that Turkey had fallen into the category of an authoritarian regime (Muhsin 2014). This was highlighted by CHP parliamentarian Engin Altay, when he said that 'the 24th term [2011–15] went down in history as one when democracy regressed in order to establish single-man rule' (quoted in Kılıç 2015). From this point on, we see Erdoğan take greater strides to dismantle any remaining democratic checks.

Conclusion

Reflecting on Erdoğan's character as a ruler allows us to see that it firmly sits within the culture of authoritarian leadership discussed in the preceding chapters. This was first made evident as his intra-party leadership came to mirror the same authoritarian style of Erbakan that had sparked the AKP's creation. From 2007 onwards, the slow purge of rivals and dissenters ensured that the interests of the governing party were dominated by its leader's wishes.

We also observe that the transition to authoritarian rule reflected the changing nature of Erdoğan's government over the same period. Erdoğan showed that, after his first term in office, he was uninterested in further democratisation. Much like with the experiences under previous leaders, once his majority increased in his second electoral victory in 2007, he used his tutelage over the governing party to act against institutions that could check his decisions. Through his mutually beneficial alliance with the GM, Erdoğan was able to undertake these measures, mirroring the practice of past leaders who had routinely filled state institutions with loyalists and allies to attain control over them. Furthermore, attacks on the military and on critics of the AKP and the GM became a symbol of this anti-democratic alliance. Constitutional changes in 2010 allowed Erdoğan's government to influence key state institutions, including the judiciary. The whitewashing of the 17 December 2013 corruption investigations highlighted the AKP's power over the judiciary, which was exploited to protect the government from any legal challenge. This period also witnessed a government abuse its powers in order to severely curtail the voice of independent media outlets and journalists, ultimately denying media institutions the opportunity to act as a key mechanism of democratic accountability and enabling Erdoğan to monopolise the political narrative.

In the shadow of a compromised democratic system, a subservient Assembly group and a compliant President Gül, Erdoğan hastened his authoritarian descent, hollowing out the capacity of democratic institutions and increasing his power over the political landscape. As Kalaycıoğlu noted in the opening of this chapter, 'under these circumstances he was able to ravage the state'. This was most significant in the third legislative period (2011–15), when the key pillar of democracy, the parliament, was transformed into a rubber-stamp institution used to further Erdoğan's political and materialistic ambitions. By the end of this period, the country had slowly transitioned to a *de facto* authoritarian regime.

The next chapter will discuss Erdoğan's move to the presidency and illustrate how his appetite for authoritarianism was not curbed by constitutional restrictions of the presidential office, but rather accelerated the institutionalisation of his single-man rule.

Notes

1. The Ecevit coalition had already introduced three EU harmonisation packages in 2002, before the elections, and the AKP tabled another six in 2003 and

2004. All these packages were aimed at harmonising Turkish legislation and the Turkish constitution in keeping with EU rules and regulations.

2. The AKP's reforms demoted the *Millî Güvenlik Kurulu* (National Security Council, MGK) to an advisory council without real executive power and increased the number of civilians in the institution. Thus, it took away the military's veto power over the civilian governments (Waldman and Calışkan 2017, 22–24). In addition, the freedom of the press and the freedom of expression were partially improved. The use of local languages other than Turkish in radio and television broadcasting was also permitted (Lagendijk 2012).

3. For a good discussion of the AKP party structure, see Hale and Özbudun (2010, 45–47).

4. Under the AKP government, Babacan served as Deputy Prime Minister from 2009 to 2015, as Minister of Foreign Affairs from 2007 to 2009 and as Minister of Economic Affairs from 2002 to 2007. He resigned from the AKP in 2019.

5. Although the AKP vote increased, its parliamentary numbers were reduced from the 2002 elections. This was largely due to an increase in the number of parties passing the ten-percent electoral threshold and entering parliament.

6. After three rounds of parliamentary voting, Gül was elected as President on 28 August 2007 (Tran 2007).

7. The charge sheet by the prosecutor stated: 'The AKP is founded by a group that drew lessons from the closure of earlier Islamic parties and uses democracy to reach its goal, which is installing sharia law in Turkey [. . .] There is an attempt to expunge the secular principles of the constitution' (Traynor 2008).

8. Along with İlker Başbuğ, other high-profile military and civilian suspects such as the retired generals Hurşit Tolon, Veli Küçük and Şener Eruygur, as well as the journalists Tuncay Özkan and Mustafa Balbay also received long prison sentences.

9. The Constitutional Court in June 2014 ruled that the rights of the Balyoz defendants had been violated, ordering a retrial (Dombey 2014), and by March 2015 all had been acquitted of their charges. Additionally, by April 2016, the *Yargıtay* (Supreme Court of Appeals) annulled the convictions of the 275 alleged Ergenekon members (*Hürriyet* 2016). The most critical information underlying the verdict was expert testimony that the key evidence had been fabricated (*Hürriyet* 2015a).

10. On 30 November 2018, prosecutors in their final report declared that they had not found any evidence to show that an organisation such as Ergenekon had ever existed (*Hürriyet* 2018c). After this report, a Turkish court on 1 July 2019 formally acquitted the 235 suspects from 'forming and managing, membership

of, or aiding and abetting an armed organisation' (Ahval 2019). This further adds support that these investigations were politically motivated and that the judiciary was being instrumentalised against critics and opponents of government from an early period onwards.

11. On 19 June 1999, the national television channel ATV broadcast two video clips apparently showing Gülen instructing his followers to infiltrate the Turkish bureaucracy and bide their time until they were numerous enough to be able to implement their agenda. Following the broadcasting of the tapes, Gülen fled to the United States before the Turkish authorities could charge him with undermining the principle of secularism (Jenkins 2007).

12. For example, the Gülenist network was always held under suspicion by the state, and this was largely to do with the belief that the motive behind the group was to replace the secular nature of the state with an Islamic identity. In fact, most of the officers regularly expelled from the Turkish military for suspected Islamist activism were believed to be Gülen sympathisers (Jenkins 2007).

13. For a good outline of the GM's media arms, see Yavuz (2013).

14. In other high-profile investigations, the Gülenist arm of the judiciary targeted thousands of individuals on charges of membership of the Group of Communities in Kurdistan (KCK), an umbrella organisation dominated by the PKK. Some actors were merely critics of the GM or worked in charities that were rivals of the pro-Gülen NGOs and active in the predominantly Kurdish Southeast of Turkey (Jenkins 2009a).

15. It should also be noted that in the process Fethullah Gülen personally urged his followers to support the amendments and to vote 'yes' (Öztürk and Gözaydın 2017, 214).

16. For example, these included removal of the temporary articles of the 1982 Constitution that protected the coup leaders and their associates from litigation. One amendment extended the right of collective bargaining to the unions of state employees, but banned their right to strike. The amendment concerning positive discrimination for women was criticised by feminist organisations as a hollow gesture. Protection of minors had already been covered by various laws, and the amendment hardly made a new contribution. An amendment concerning the right to privacy was also heavily criticised by the opposition, for it had become clear that almost all citizens of Turkey could be placed under electronic surveillance by the executive branch since 2005.

17. The changes to the Constitutional Court increased its number of judges from eleven to seventeen.

18. Due to the climate of fear, the vast majority of outlets chose to screen wildlife documentaries or speeches by Erdoğan during the country-wide Gezi protests. Those who did show the protests suffered according to the figures of the *Türkiye Gazeteciler Sendikası* (Turkish Union of Journalists); these found that fifty-nine journalists lost their jobs due to their coverage of Gezi (Altıparmak and Akdeniz 2015, 170).

19. In the period following these initial arrests such tactics against the media became common practice. For example, once *Milliyet* was sold to the Demirören group, the newspaper began to dismiss many of its critical journalists. This included Ece Temelkuran who was fired from the daily (and also from the television channel Habertürk), after she had published a column implicating the government in the bombing raid of Uludere, which resulted in the death of thirty-four persons mistaken for terrorists (Temelkuran 2015, 175). Nuray Mert was dismissed from her role on NTV and *Milliyet* after Erdoğan publicly labelled her as 'despicable' for her writings questioning government policy towards the Kurdish ethnic population (Corke et al. 2014, 8–9). In 2013, the newspaper fired two renowned and experienced columnists, Hasan Cemal and Can Dündar, who had filed separate reports about the government, and later also Kadri Gürsel for a tweet criticising Erdoğan (Greenslade 2015; Preston 2013). Many of these dismissals, according to Abdullattif Şener, were due to Erdoğan who would regularly order the dismissal of journalists because of their critical stance against the government (Waldman and Calışkan 2017, 133). This view is also shared by Ahmet Sever who served as Gül's advisor for twelve years (Sever 2015, 113).

20. During fieldwork, the author encountered the story of an economic expert who had his scheduled television interview cut because he was offering a view critical of the economic forecast. On another occasion, a well-known political expert personally relayed to the author that they had been permanently black-listed from appearing on television panels due to their known opposition to the government.

21. The outlet follows the government narrative and dedicates ten times more air-time to Erdoğan and his party than to any of the opposition (Waldman and Calışkan 2017, 130). Therefore, the freedom and fairness of elections is questionable. For instance, in the run-up to the 10 August 2014 presidential election campaign, TRT denied the opposition airtime while it visibly promoted and covered Erdoğan's campaign (İdiz 2014). According to figures provided by the *Radyo ve Televizyon Üst Kurulu* (Radio and Television Supreme Council, RTÜK), in the first days of campaigning, between 29 June and 10 July, Erdoğan

appeared on the public broadcaster's news channel TRT Haber for 559 minutes, while, of the other two candidates, Ekmeleddin İhsanoğlu was only covered for 137 minutes and Selahattin Demirtaş for merely eighteen minutes (*Hürriyet* 2014c). In the campaign period for the general elections on 7 June 2015, the AKP was given 54.4 hours of airtime by the TRT, while the main opposition CHP received only fourteen hours. Furthermore, the state broadcaster banned the CHP's campaign advert on the grounds that it was critical of the government (*Hürriyet* 2015c; BBC 2015). A CHP member of RTÜK, Ali Öztunç, later stated that the ad had not broken any laws and that the government had ordered the censorship (Post-Medya.com 2015). The minor opposition party MHP also received fourteen hours of airtime, followed by the Kurdish-rights-focused *Halkların Demokratik Partisi* (Peoples' Democratic Party, HDP) which was given 7.5 hours. This pattern continued in the last twenty-five days of the campaign for the general elections on 1 November 2015. RTÜK member Ersin Öngel tweeted that TRT TV had covered President Erdoğan and the AKP twenty-nine and thirty hours, respectively. By contrast, the CHP was given five hours of airtime, while the MHP had one hour and ten minutes in total, and the HDP was covered a mere eighteen minutes over twenty-five days of campaigning (*Milliyet* 2015).

22. The process to introduce a law, or to abrogate existing laws, is normally undertaken through the proposition of a legislative bill by an individual deputy or the Council of Ministers. The bill is then debated and adopted in the Assembly during plenary session, before being submitted to the President to ratify the legislation in the second pass. Since there is no senate, the President holds the only veto power against the wishes of the parliamentary majority.

23. Nine years after the protests, on 25 April 2022, philanthropist and activist Osman Kavala was sentenced to life in prison without parole for 'orchestrating' and 'financing' the nationwide Gezi Park protests in an 'attept to overthrow' the government, by the Istanbul 13th Assize Court. Along with Kavala, seven other activists – Mücella Yapıcı, Çiğdem Mater, Hakan Altınay, Mine Özerden, Can Atalay, Tayfun Kahraman and Yiğit Ali Ekmekçi – were sentenced to eighteen years in prison on similar charges. The convictions were politically motivated, resulting in a tragic miscarriage of justice by the 'sham trial' (Human Rights Watch 2022).

24. The law was incorporated into omnibus laws. After being split into two, yet still containing its illiberal character, it was sent back to the President and then ratified. Yet, Gül later noted that he should have opposed the bill again instead of

ratifying it (Sever 2015, 149–54). The other bill related to changes to the HSYK to bring it under tighter control of the Minister of Justice. The President sent it back to the government, with required changes to the fifteen articles that he saw as posing a direct violation of the constitution. Once these were changed, Gül ratified the bill into law, although he remarked that some of the bill's articles could still be deemed unconstitutional (*Cumhuriyet* 2014). Therefore, given his suspicions, these were puzzling decisions. We can only assume that one reason might have been that he did not want to cause conflict with the government; hence, Gül chose appeasement instead.

25. Public Procurement is a term used to refer to the government's purchasing activities of goods, services and construction of public works. As one of the most important areas where the state and the private sector interact extensively, public procurement processes are open to the use of public resources for interests other than the public good (see Gürakar 2016).

26. A law passed in June 2012 limited the court's autonomy to pursue audits. The Constitutional Court overturned this in December 2012, yet the government passed an amendment that exempted state institutions from providing account details to the Court of Accounts. This meant that the public losses of state institutions went unrecorded. Through another series of legislative changes during the years 2013, 2014 and 2015, the Finance Ministry was authorised to forward only brief and consolidated reports on the spending of government institutions to the Court of Accounts. This was also an impediment to the inspection of government spending. Also, audit reports for the periods before 2012 have been removed from the Court of Accounts' website (Soyaltın 2013; *Hürriyet* 2013b).

27. Police officers raided several homes, including two belonging to the families of the ruling elite. In the course of the investigation, the police confiscated some USD 17.5 million in cash, money allegedly used for bribery: USD 4.5 million was found in the residence of Süleyman Aslan, the director of the state-owned Halkbank, and USD 750,000 in the home of Barış Güler, son of the former Minister of the Interior. At the heart of the probe was businessman Reza Zarrab, who was reportedly involved in a money-laundering scheme as part of a strategy to bypass US-led sanctions on Iran. All of the fifty-two people detained that day were in various ways connected with the AKP. Prosecutors accused fourteen persons—including Aslan, Zarrab and several family members of cabinet ministers—of bribery, corruption, fraud, money-laundering and gold-smuggling (Gürsel 2013).

28. On 5 January 2014, the parliamentary Corruption Investigation Commission decided to vote down the parliamentary motion to refer the cases against the ex-ministers to the *Yargıtay*.

29. The four prosecutors were Zekeriya Öz, Muammer Akkaş, Celal Kara and Mehmet Yüzgeç, as well as judge Süleyman Karaçöl (*Hürriyet* 2015e).

7

2015–21: PRESIDENT ERDOĞAN AND THE INSTITUTIONALISATION OF SINGLE-MAN RULE

Introduction

This chapter follows Erdoğan's rise from Prime Minister to President in 2015. It illustrates how a severely compromised democratic system enabled Erdoğan's arbitrary rule to remain unchecked and brought Turkey's dalliance with democracy to an end. Erdoğan as the President maintained his authority over the AKP, despite the constitutional limits placed on his role, which allowed him to remove the remaining divisions of powers between the two arms of the executive – the parliament and the presidential office – in order to increase his dominance over the political landscape. The failed putsch on 15 July 2016 and the subsequent state of emergency imposed on the country led to a *de facto* one-man regime, which granted Erdoğan key controls over the state. The sweeping powers were used to continue the authoritarian transformation of state institutions. With these events as a backdrop, Turkey was thrust into a referendum on 15 April 2017, handing his office largely unchecked power of the state. These developments reveal that Turkey's descent into an authoritarian system were largely due to Erdoğan's quest to put in place a system serving his autocratic impulses.

Re-shaping the Presidency

In 2014, Erdoğan made the decision to nominate himself for the presidency, although Gül occupied the office and was free to be nominated for a second term. Gül, who was subjected to a campaign of harassment from the AKP, which he lamented as 'great disrespect from within his own camp' (Zeyrek 2014),[1] decided not to seek a second term, thus once more stepping aside for Erdoğan (see Sever 2015, 123–29). Until that point, the election of the head of state had rested with the parliament. However, a legal amendment was made whereby the presidential election would now happen by popular vote. The resulting elections on 10 August saw Erdoğan elected as President of Turkey, with 51.8 percent of the vote.

In a telling demonstration of his desire to control the parliamentary government, Erdoğan blocked Gül from returning to the AKP in order to prevent him from taking up the vacated prime ministership. For Erdoğan, Gül constituted a critical threat to his rule due to his popularity both within the party and electorally (Çandar 2018). By blocking Gül's return to the AKP, Erdoğan was able to do away with the one person who could have derailed his efforts to run the government from the presidency (Lancaster 2014).

Importantly, the constitutional limits imposed on the presidency seemed to matter little, as Erdoğan's behaviour was no different from his authoritarian conduct as Prime Minister: unconstitutional and tutelary (Sever 2015, 163). Public and political criticism did not discourage Erdoğan from driving the day-to-day policies of the government. Like his predecessor Özal, Erdoğan hand-picked Ahmet Davutoğlu, whom he assumed to be a safe choice because he had been a long-time subservient ally (Lancaster 2014; Arango and Yeğinsu 2016), as his successor to head the party and as Prime Minister. This allowed Erdoğan to freely summon and chair cabinet meetings from his Presidential Palace (Gürsel 2015, *Hürriyet* 2014b).[2] Although doing so was not beyond constitutional limits, it contradicted traditional bounds and broke away from established norms of government-president relations, reflecting his rejection of institutional forbearance. Erdoğan's actions further emphasised that he would not abide by constitutional barriers to his ambitions. This was evident when he signed a secret decree that transformed the institutional structure of the presidential office to create a shadow cabinet to work under him and monitor the work of the parliamentary government (*Hürriyet* 2014b).[3] Again, this had parallels with Özal's presidency, although Özal's shadow cabinet had operated in a *de facto* manner, whereas Erdoğan had it enacted into law.

The AKP government passed legislation (in an omnibus law) to create a 'secret' presidential fund: this law removed administrative oversight and interference with Erdoğan's expenditures, leaving the use of state finances at his discretion alone (Yılmaz 2015). The unfettered access to state funds was used to run campaigns in support of the AKP's re-election in both 2015 elections,[4] where the President regularly partnered with Davutoğlu at AKP rallies to denounce opposition parties and leaders (*Hürriyet* 2015f; Doğan 2015).

The AKP's candidate lists for the two 2015 general elections continued to reflect the President's influence:185 (two-thirds) of the 326 incumbent AKP deputies were struck off candidature lists at the June 2015 general elections (Kaya 2015a).[5] Many of the new candidates were drawn from the President's inner circle, such as his son-in-law Berat Albayrak and his staff, including his lawyer, advisor, speech-writer and former chauffeur (Demirtaş 2015; Kaya 2015a). Journalist Levent Gültekin observed that the only requirement to be a candidate was absolute loyalty to Erdoğan, thus transforming the AKP into a *devşirme* system (2015).[6] Academic Çağlar Ezikoğlu argued that the events represented a purge of the same reformist cohort who had challenged and broken away from Erbakan's questionable leadership of Turkey's Islamist movement to form the AKP. Erdoğan, in fact, became another Erbakan and was similarly seen by his followers as 'the commander of the faithful' (Ezikoğlu 2015).

Table 7.1 June 2015 Election Results

Political Party	Percentage of Votes	Parliamentary Seats (Total 550)
AKP	40.9	258
CHP	25	132
MHP	16.3	80
Halkların Demokratik Partisi (HDP)	13.1	80

Source: http://www.turkstat.gov.tr/UstMenu.do?metod=temelist

Table 7.2 November 2015 Election Results

Political Party	Percentage of Votes	Parliamentary Seats (Total 550)
AKP	49.5	317
CHP	25.3	134
HDP	10.8	59
MHP	11.9	40

Source: http://www.turkstat.gov.tr/UstMenu.do?metod=temelist

When Prime Minister Davutoğlu attempted to exercise a degree of autonomy by altering the composition of the AKP's fifty-member Executive Body, Erdoğan blocked the move, imposing his own candidate choices to sit on the board, including his son-in-law Albayrak and other loyalists (Kaya 2015b). Erdoğan also used the opportunity to remove influential individuals from the body, such as AKP veterans Bülent Arınç, Ali Babacan and Mehmet Şimşek, all of whom had a strong standing inside the party and demonstrated a level of autonomy (*Hürriyet* 2015d). Arınç expressed frustration with Erdoğan, complaining: 'We were the party of "us", but now we have turned into a party of "me"'(Çandar 2015). This mirrored Kalaycıoğlu's observations that 'any counter power within the party had gone. Anybody who had a say in the party was sidelined. Erdoğan's power over the party has no limitations' (Interview, April 2016).

This was exemplified on 5 May 2016, when Erdoğan, dissatisfied with Davutoğlu's loyalty, unceremoniously forced the Prime Minister to resign (Jenkins 2016b). Erdoğan's move was widely criticised as '*saray darbesi*' (palace coup) (*Cumhuriyet* 2016), an act comparable to Demirel's interference in the Erbakan-Çiller coalition. In an interview with the author on the following day, Kınıklıoğlu stressed that the event illustrated Erdoğan's ambition to institute a one-man rule (2016):

Davutoğlu, as someone who really did not divert from Erdoğan publicly, was even seen as not loyal enough by Erdoğan [. . .] Ultimately, the reason why Erdoğan got rid of Davutoğlu was that Davutoğlu was not overly enthusiastic about the idea to move from a parliamentary system to an executive presidency. Erdoğan only wants someone who is obedient, who doesn't go up and meet [Angela] Merkel, who just sits there and allows his plan to *de jure* become executive. Not to hinder his wishes.

Davutoğlu's removal solidified and confirmed what many feared was going to happen. There were some who thought Davutoğlu might in the future gain some independence [from Erdoğan] and that there would be some [political] normalisation. But now people understand that's over. Davutoğlu is out. There will be some compliant Prime Minister on paper, but he will really act like a Vice President. He will do whatever Erdoğan tells him to do. He will appoint everyone who Erdoğan wants him to appoint. Not a *de jure*, but a *de facto* Presidency.

As Kınıklıoğlu predicted, Davutoğlu's replacement was the staunch loyalist Binali Yıldırım.[7] The selection was designed to place the powers of both the parliament and the presidency in Erdoğan's hands, prompting former AKP co-founder and Deputy Prime Minister Abdullattif Şener to reflect on a television programme (2017):

During my five years as Deputy Prime Minister (2002–07), there were strong disputes between us. At times, these disputes were reported in the media, but Erdoğan did not act in an aggressive manner towards me. Why? The balance of power inside the party during that period wouldn't allow him to act that way. Even though he was the party leader he wasn't able to fight with me [. . .] This was the AKP back ten years ago [2007]. Since I resigned from the party [in 2007], much has changed. Today, the AKP parliamentarians do not dare talk to journalists, for fear they might utter something that will have them removed by Erdoğan from the next election's candidature lists. This is the point where the governing party [AKP] is at currently. Now we are talking about someone who is both the President and at the same time sits as a party leader. This gives him complete authority over the governing party. It is absolute power, and he can do everything he wants. When he orders the party not to pass a law, the party cannot disobey and pass the law. If he says, 'I don't like that parliamentarian, and I will leave him off the candidature list', there is no one in the party who can argue otherwise. This is the situation we have arrived at today. We are at such a point that the parliament no longer has the power of oversight.

Şener's statement provides a comparative assessment between the AKP's early years and the current state of affairs: the shift from internal party pluralism to the personalisation of power under Erdoğan, which enabled him to exercise direct rule over the legislature, ended the separation between the government and the presidential office and severely impeded the parliament's role as representative body.

In many ways, Erdoğan displayed patterns of behaviour similar to Menderes and Bayar, and later Özal. However, Menderes and Bayar both failed to quash the military in their efforts to control the state and silence opposition. Özal pushed the limits of his presidency, but while he was obstructed by a strong parliamentary opposition and his loss of control over the ANAP, Erdoğan, who had control of the AKP, succeeded in bringing the state under his authority. Parallels can also be drawn between Erdoğan and Atatürk, in the way in which Erdoğan incrementally took measures to capture the state:

> Erdoğan is the best political animal Turkey has produced since Mustafa Kemal Atatürk. When his instincts command him to be ruthless, he becomes ruthless. When they tell him to be very flexible and pragmatic, he can go for it. These all bring him political success and victories. It is why he has been successful politically. (Interview with Cengiz Çandar, October 2016b)

Sabri Sayarı has noted that Erdoğan gradually took over the state, undermining the traditional characteristics of the republic formed under Atatürk, in order to grow the scope of his political power:

> Initially Erdoğan gave the impression that he was a true democrat, that he was for EU membership, and this gained him lots of support from people in society who were not necessarily AKP voters. Then, slowly and unmistakably, he showed his true character. But this [current] situation is quite unusual. He has cleared the decks and become an omnipotent person [. . .] He is restructuring Turkey. This is a counter-revolution. He is trying to dismantle many things that are associated with the foundations of the republic, and he is succeeding [. . .] People ask if he is going to get softer? No, he is going to get harder, that is his style and character. (Interview, July 2016)

Given that the interview with Sayarı took place four days after the attempted coup on 15 July 2016, his comments accurately forecast the changes to come.

The Failed Putsch: Legitimising the Institutionalisation of Single-man Rule

Erdoğan made his most direct attempt at consolidating his power after the failed coup on 15 July 2016. Labelling it as a 'blessing from God', the President accused his one-time ally, the Gülen Movement, as the perpetrators (Şık 2016). Investigations indicate that Gülen supporters inside the armed forces were part of the coalition that was engaged in the coup (Jenkins 2016a); however, it is hard to discern who else was involved, how broad the coalition was and what the organisers' objectives were (Jenkins 2016a; Cornell 2016). What became clear is that the coup marked an attempt by elements within the armed forces to reverse Turkey's trajectory under Erdoğan. In this regard, the attempted coup was not dissimilar to the military intervention faced by Menderes and Bayar, Demirel, Ecevit, Çiller and Erbakan, in response to their leadership.

In the coup's immediate aftermath, an *Olağanüstü Hâl* (state of emergency, OHAL) was declared, lasting two years until July 2018. This period gave Erdoğan expansive discretionary powers, including the authority to administer the country through emergency decrees, which he declared as necessary to stabilise the country and protect democracy. Yet, in stark contradiction to the principles of democracy, he exploited the decree's function by swiftly passing laws without going through the Assembly, in order to avoid the prevailing checks and balances and to suspend the rule of law.

The breadth and arbitrariness of purges and incarcerations were evidence that Erdoğan's actions were lacking restraint and forbearance – key norms that leaders and elites must demonstrate in order for democracy to be sustained (see Levitsky and Ziblatt 2018b, 2018a). Instead of protecting and strengthening institutions and practices, Erdoğan attacked opponents and institutions which he believed were problematic for his rule. This was a fact not lost on the Europe and Central Asia director at Human Rights Watch, Hugh Williamson, who noted that the government had exploited the coup attempt in order to justify a 'ruthless crackdown on critics and opponents' (Human Rights Watch 2017a). As Sayarı had predicted, Erdoğan's autocratic character would worsen as his power grew, creating a 'climate of fear' across the country (Shaheen 2018).

During the country's two years under OHAL, a total of thirty-six decrees were issued, constraining civil and political rights, expanding the powers of authorities, as well as purging and jailing citizens viewed by the government as perpetrators of the attempted coup (İnsan Hakları Ortak Platformu 2018, 5). Almost 78,000 citizens were arrested, 150,000 detained and more than 152,000 dismissed from their positions (European Commission 2019). The wide-ranging purges targeted the military, the judiciary, the police force, academia, doctors, teachers and low-skilled workers. Close to 6,000 of Turkey's 150,000 academics were dismissed (Hansen 2019), with the worst affected university faculties left on the verge of collapse (Hürtaş 2017a). Critics went so far as to say that the regime was aiming to fill vacant academic posts with a cadre of political and ideological sympathisers (Kirişci 2018; Hansen 2019).

Human rights workers and lawyers were detained, accused of being part of a terrorist group (Zaman 2017d). The media was greatly affected. The harsh government clamp-down led to Turkey's number-one ranking as the foremost jailer of journalists in the world (Hong 2018), with over 310 journalists arrested, while fifty newspapers, six news agencies, eighteen television channels, twenty-two radio stations, twenty magazines and twenty-nine publishers were arbitrarily shut or taken over by government-appointed administrators for alleged links to the GM (Ahval 2018). Altogether, more than 1,000 organisations were shut down, and the total value of assets seized by the government totalled around USD 11 billion (Srivastava 2017).

The military continued to suffer: nearly 4,200 officers were purged, including half of the acting generals and admirals. All military academies were abolished, and detained officers were denied access to legal representation and fair trials.[8] The decrees, under Erdoğan's direction, were also used to reshape and restructure the Turkish military (Yayla 2017; Haugom 2017; Zaman 2017a). Later decrees provided the President full discretion over the defence industry and defence contracts (Gürcan 2018).

The government initiated a systematic purge of judicial officers, suspending nearly 3000 judges and prosecutors, with over 1000 more removed later. The expeditious government response indicates the purges may have been calculated, throwing suspicion on the credibility of the government's claims (Eissenstat 2017, 13). To fill the vacant positions, 900 lawyers were promoted by the government to the position of judge, and 800 of these appointments had direct links to the AKP (Ayasun 2017).[9] The selection process, or lack thereof, gave further weight to the speculation that the decrees targeted the last vestiges of an independent judiciary and replaced it with AKP loyalists who would rubber-stamp the government's political agenda (*Cumhuriyet* 2017a).[10] This created an important void: the country's 14,000 judges now had on average of two-and-a-half years experience in practising law (Gall 2019).

Civil society was targeted, with the government closing down non-government judicial bodies in order to underscore Erdoğan's campaign to eliminate judicial scrutiny and criticism. For example, the *Yargıçlar ve Savcılar Birliği* (Association of Judges and Prosecutors, YARSAV), a secular group of 500 lawyers who regularly criticised attacks on judicial independence, was dissolved in the first round of decrees (Hürtaş 2016; DW 2016).[11] Numerous lawyers from the association, who represented individuals charged under terrorism laws, were incarcerated on the same charges as their clients (Hürtaş 2017b). These punitive measures enabled Erdoğan to supress organised resistance by lawyers and to strip the judiciary of its remaining independence and authority.

In the post-coup environment, Erdoğan's image was elevated to that of the heroic saviour of the Turkish nation. Turkey's public squares, buildings and roads were adorned with large placards of the President as both the target of the coup and the protector of his country. The government portrayed 15 July 2016 as the 'second independence war', with Erdoğan referred to as *başkomutan* (supreme commander) and likened to the defender of the nation in the public school curriculum (*Cumhuriyet* 2017b). Soon, Erdoğan came to be the personification of the Turkish state: an attack on the leader was characterised as an attack on Turkey. Hence, traitors and non-patriots were construed as an existential threat to the Turkish state, leading to the normalisation of the violation of the rights of opponents or of those critical of the President and the government. This was similar to Demirel's portrayal of his opponents during the 1960s and 1970s (see Chapters 2 and 3).

A Democracy without Opposition

Reminiscent of the leaders that came before him, Erdoğan used the post-coup climate of chaos and fear to justify steps that removed his political opponents from office. This was particularly evident in the treatment of the *Halkların Demokratik Partisi* (Peoples' Democratic Party, HDP), a left-leaning party whose focus is on attaining greater Kurdish rights. Beginning in late 2014, the Kurdish peace process stalled, and fighting increased between Turkish security forces and the PKK in the Southeast of Turkey. In the highly securitised atmosphere of the post-coup period, the country saw the resumption of PKK terror attacks in urban and rural areas. The government undertook a systematic campaign to portray Turkey's third-largest party, the HDP, as supporters of Kurdish terrorism. A parliamentary vote stripped the immunities of the 154 opposition party parliamentarians who had pending criminal investigations.[12] Yet, it was the fifty-five HDP politicians which were singled out by prosecutors.

This had immediate implications: party co-leaders Selahattin Demirtaş and Figen Yüksekdağ were jailed, along with eleven other HDP deputies (Zaman 2017b), reminiscent of the 1994 events that saw a similar operation against the Kurdish-focused DEP during Çiller's leadership (see Chapter 5).[13] In addition, 5,471 HDP officials, including heads of provincial and district branches, were detained, with 1,482 sent to pretrial detention (Human Rights Watch 2017b). A second decree gave the government the power to purge eighty-five of 103 municipalities in the Southeast, held by HDP's regional arm *Demokratik Bölgeler Partisi* (Democratic Regions Party, DBP). All suspended mayors were replaced with government-appointed administrators (Human Rights Watch 2017b; Zaman 2017c).

This was yet another example of Erdoğan exploiting his powers under the OHAL in order to undermine the ability of both parties to effectively organise strong opposition, particularly in the eastern and southeastern regions of the country. These punitive measures helped Erdoğan extend his rule over areas he otherwise would have had trouble winning at the ballot box. This further alienated the ethnic Kurdish population from the political process and undermined the electoral will.

Such actions became symbolic of a government that showed little regard for upholding the political and civil rights of its citizens, and they contributed to the weaking of the opposition's power, as Kalaycıoğlu highlighted:

Number one is that Erdoğan has done everything in his power, so the opposition cannot get organised and challenge his position. Number two, to undermine the opposition, he has silenced the media and even social media. This also includes any type of organisation that is not under his control. For the rest, it is only a matter of time until they are prosecuted. This is huge pressure on any kind of opposition. The opposition itself is intimidated. Because Erdoğan turns around and accuses them of being conspirators and undermining the state, and that rallies the masses around him. (Interview, April 2016)

Civilians had to be careful when publicly discussing politics or criticising the government or Erdoğan, for fear of arbitrary incarceration by authorities, potential loss of employment, or physical intimidation and violence by government supporters. Self-censorship became widespread and left the non-Erdoğan supporter base – over half of the voting population – to live in a tense and repressive environment. As a result, the two halves of Turkish society, split along pro- and anti-Erdoğan lines, particularly under the OHAL, experienced contrasting political environments within the same country, which further added to the polarisation.

Instituting Single-man Rule

With a weakened opposition and the OHAL still in place, the AKP introduced eighteen proposed constitutional changes to parliament on 10 December 2016. Numbers from the nationalist MHP, which had now closely aligned itself with the AKP, secured Erdoğan the minimum 330 parliamentary votes required for a public referendum on the transition from parliamentary democracy to a presidential system with vastly expanded and unchecked executive powers. Ergun Özbudun remarked that the system change was aimed to merely formalise the *de facto* style of authoritarian rule that Turkey had been living under in recent years:

> At this point, I characterise the current system as *competitive authoritarianism*. It fits the present Turkish case perfectly. When you talk about electoral democracy or semi-democracy you still term it a sub-type of democracy. I'm afraid Turkey is no longer a sub-type of democracy. The country is a sub-type of the authoritarian system. It is getting increasingly less competitive and more authoritarian. I see no easy way out. This is why I am pessimistic [. . .] the authoritarian drift

started after 2011, when the AKP had their third consecutive victory with nearly 50 percent of the vote, which allowed them to feel more secure in their ambitions. Up to that point, they were mindful of the military, and the judiciary was not on their side. But now there are no checks and balances. The government's mentality completely ignores the notion of checks and balances. Currently, a kind of presidential system exists in *de facto* terms. They just want to institutionalise it with a system change. (Interview, April 2016)

On 15 April 2017, Erdoğan won the referendum by a slim 51 percent of the vote (*Hürriyet* 2015b). However, the win was tainted by claims of voter manipulation. Observers from the Organization for Security and Co-operation in Europe (OSCE) and the Council of Europe urged Turkey to launch 'transparent investigations' into alleged voting irregularities, 'marred by late procedural changes that removed key safeguards' (OSCE 2017). Despite complaints from both domestic opponents and international observers, Turkey's *Yüksek Seçim Kurulu* (Supreme Electoral Board, YSK) refused to investigate (*Hürriyet* 2017). The OSCE further noted that holding elections under OHAL created an 'unlevel playing field' due to the repressive conditions for the 'No' campaign and due to the fact that state resources were diverted to heavily advantage Erdoğan's 'Yes' campaign (OSCE 2017).[14]

The Council of Europe's forty-nine-member Group of States against Corruption (GRECO) found that the constitutional changes formalised the end of judicial independence, with the HSYK being placed under the tutelage of the government and the president (GRECO 2018). Indeed, the judiciary was seemingly transformed into a political weapon to harass and silence prominent critics. In one key example, on 11 January 2018, journalist Mehmet Altan and academic Şahin Alpay, who had been held under 'terrorism' charges, were released by the Constitutional Court (T24 2018). Government ministers were quick to condemn the court, with Deputy Prime Minister Bekir Bozdağ warning that it had 'overstepped its limit', while Prime Minister Binali Yıldırım stated that it was up to the lower court to decide on how to proceed (Pitel 2018). Following these comments, the lower courts handling the cases made the unprecedented decision to disobey the higher court's decision (*Hürriyet* 2018b).[15] Altan, along with five other co-defendants, received aggravated life sentences from the same lower courts (DW 2018).[16]

Freedom House President Mike Abramowitz commented on the growing irregularity of verdicts and the use of the judiciary for political purposes by the government: 'When a lower court feels empowered to interpret the Constitution in direct contradiction to a ruling of the highest court in the land, government officials are acting outside the law and with complete impunity' (2018b).[17] Reflective of this, the World Justice Project, in its annual 2017–18 *Rule of Law Index* ranked Turkey's authoritarian trajectory 101 out of 113 countries.[18] At the same time, the Constitutional Court in February 2018 released a report that found the majority of its decisions related to violations against the right to fair trial by the state (*Hürriyet* 2018a), illustrating the arbitrary manner with which the judiciary treats defendants targeted by the government.[19]

With emergency rule still in place, the country went to the polls on 24 June 2018. The general election marked the formal transition to the presidential system, with both the parliament and the presidency contested simultaneously. The new system, with its increased Assembly representatives – from 550 to 600 – witnessed political parties enter alliance blocs to contest the elections.[20] The ensuing outcome handed the parliamentary majority to the AKP-MHP[21] alliance of the *Cumhur İttifakı* (People's Alliance) with a combined 53.7 percent of the vote (see Table 7.3);[22] Erdoğan, with a decisive vote, was re-elected President (see Table 7.4). From this point forward, Erdoğan was legally permitted to head the AKP and sit as the President of the country, doing away with any legal pretense of neutrality or division between parliament and presidential office.

Table 7.3 June 2018 Parliamentary Election Results

Political Party	Percentage of Votes	Parliamentary Seats (Total 600)
AKP	42.6	295
CHP	22.6	146
HDP[23]	11.7	67
MHP	11.1	49
İYİ Parti (Good Party)	10	43

Source: https://secim.haberler.com/2018/

Table 7.4 June 2018 Presidential Election Results

Candidate	Party	Percentage of Votes
Recep Tayyip Erdoğan	AKP	52.6
Muharrem Ince	CHP	30.6
Selahattin Demirtaş	HDP	8.4
Meral Akşener	İYİ	7.3

Source: https://secim.haberler.com/2018/cumhurbaskanligi-secim-sonuclari/

Under the presidential system, and unable to provide a check on the President and his decisions, parliament effectively ceased to function as a democratic body (European Commission 2019). From July 2018 to July 2019, the President issued thirty-nine decrees that introduced 1,892 articles of legislation, accounting for 77 percent of all of the period's legislation. This is in comparison to parliament enacting thirty-five bills representing 555 legislative articles; thirteen of these, making up 404 pieces of legislation, were passed as omnibus laws (Solaker 2019). The laws enacted by the Assembly are also under the direction of the President: the presidency formulates legislative amendments, which are passed as omnibus laws to the AKP parliamentary group to introduce, who use their majority numbers with the MHP to vote them into law (Kaboğlu 2018). During this period, parliamentarians posed 18,895 questions, in writing, to government ministers; yet, only 7 percent of these questions received a response within the constitutionally mandated two-week period (FOX Türk 2019).[24] This further reveals that the Grand National Assembly, under the new system, operates with no legislative independence or authority. This reality has left AKP representatives frustrated. Yunus Kılıç, AKP parliamentarian for Kars, lamented in an intra-party meeting:

> We [parliamentarians] are like village-heads that have had their villages taken away from them. The people are waiting for something from their parliamentarian. But we have no authority. The ministers don't answer our calls. When we cannot reach ministers, we cannot get them to do anything about our concerns. Parliamentarians don't hold any weight [in the new system]. (HaberTürk 2019)

When the government lifted the OHAL on 18 July 2018, some of the practices that had undermined democracy and fundamental rights, were made into law, which normalised the state of emergency and consolidated its anti-democratic conditions (Human Rights Watch 2018).

With his firm hold on power, Erdoğan's autocracy grew bolder. A critical example was the municipal elections held on 31 March 2019.[25] When faced with the loss of the country's largest city, Istanbul, to the opposition candidate Ekrem İmamoğlu, Erdoğan cancelled the outcome and announced a re-run for the municipality without providing a credible legal justification.[26] Having lost Istanbul and other major cities, whose economies account for almost two-thirds of the country's GDP, the government amended laws targeting the powers of opposition mayors in order to safeguard its patronage networks (Zaman 2019).[27]

The election outcomes fuelled the President's intent to further undermine the HDP's capacity to function as a meaningful opposition party. The HDP won sixty-five municipalities in the March elections,[28] and within five months all three HDP mayors who had won metropolitan cities (Diyarbakır, Mardin and Van) were dismissed under terrorism-related charges and replaced by government-appointed trustees. The charges and subsequent penalty to remove the elected officials failed to follow proper legal processes and were publicly supported by Erdoğan:[29]

> By replacing the mayors of Diyarbakır, Mardin and Van with government-appointed trustees, we are undertaking our responsibility to the nation. Everyone who uses municipalities for [anything] other than providing services will be subject to the same fate. [For this reason] there was no serious reaction against the steps taken [to remove HDP mayors]. (quoted in T24 2019)

By 2021, forty-eight out of the sixty-five HDP municipalities had been taken over by government-appointed trustees,[30] many of whom suspended municipal councils, the democratic decision-making body at the local level (Bianet 2021). In addition, a number of investigations have been levelled against the HDP, using Turkey's broad anti-terror laws.

Parliamentarians jailed in 2016 remain incarcerated, including the former party co-chairs Demirtaş and Yüksekdağ.[31] On 17 March 2021, State

Prosecutor Bekir Şahin applied to the Constitutional Court to ban 687 HDP politicians and officials from politics for five years and to close down the party, which would ultimately nullify nearly six million ballots cast in the 2018 general elections.

In order to broaden and secure the President's monopoly over electoral districts, including Kurdish-majority regions, authorities persisted in their arbitrary approach to legal proceedings against the HDP. Their aim was to intimidate the HDP and restrict the party's capacity to effectively act as the opposition in the HDP's electoral strongholds. This political manoeuvring is reminiscent of Menderes, whose approach it was to use the DP's legislative hegemony to dismantle his main opposition, the CHP. Çiller also used this strategy by subjecting the pro-Kurdish-rights HEP to repressive and anti-democratic measures.

Erdoğan, in a bid to strengthen and consolidate his authority, persisted in appointing AKP loyalists and political allies to positions within the bureaucracy, thus ensuring its subservience and compliance. It also set in place a structure which is highly resistant to potential transitions of power and hostile to any political opponents, as Selim Koru has argued (2021). This has given rise to clientelistic political pockets, which pose a real threat to stability, should a falling-out transpire, similar to that between the AKP and the GM.

O'Donnell, Garretón Merino, Shedler and Keane have argued for the necessity of mechanisms of accountability to check the power of leaders (see Introduction). In the absence of such structures, political consolidation cannot take place, and democracy soon becomes an illusion. By stripping institutions of their powers, Erdoğan ensured that his authoritarian ambitions were unhindered by any democratic safeguards or internal opposition.

Jenny White has lamented that this means that the future of Turkey is unclear, now that it is entirely beholden to one person:

> Who knows what will happen in the future? You used to be able to make some sort of predictions based on social and political trends, but I don't think they are useful anymore because we are talking about the country now at the whim of one man. Therefore, you can't predict what will happen in Turkey anymore. (Interview, September 2016)

This is an outcome consistent with Diamond's observations, who found that safeguards against democratic failure are ineffective when leaders fail to respect political rights and constraints and civil liberties, as has been the case throughout Erdoğan's leadership. His repeated abuse of institutional privileges, used to modify and amend the constitution, is reflective of a one-man political apparatus.

Erdoğan has unabashedly expressed his displeasure for returning to a democratic system, stating in an interview: 'Parliamentary democracy has become a thing of the past for our nation. Because Turkey cannot find peace from the multi-party system' (Sayın 2021). Turkey's trajectory, it seems, has been largely directed by Erdoğan's personal and political pursuits. Yet, as underscored in this book, Turkey has been overwhelmingly ruled by authoritarian leaders, and Erdoğan is no exception:

> The current era is very troubling, yet Erdoğan's personality and vision also correspond to Turkey's long sustained political culture, which has seen sultans, Atatürk, İnönü, Menderes, Demirel and so on. Erdoğan wants to be listed in the chain of Menderes, Demirel and Özal [. . .] he wants to present himself, by all means, as the founder of the new Turkey, the second republic, a better version than Mustafa Kemal Atatürk's state. Therefore, he exhibits all the monopolistic, authoritarian leadership traits that come with all these ambitions, which is why he is now the new Republican Sultan. (Interview with Cengiz Çandar, October, 2016b)

The precarious nature of democracy in Turkey is linked to the ongoing pattern of authoritarian leadership. As Sayarı has noted, this has manifested in leaders who have not shown strong preferences for democratic norms or attempts to strengthen democracy (Interview, July 2016):

> It is difficult to know how strongly leaders in Turkey have believed in democracy. They will say they are for democracy, but have they really been for democracy? There is a large gap between their discourse and their behaviours and practices. I think almost all of these leaders we talk about, say Demirel, Özal, Menderes and so forth, had a majoritarian tendency. Almost all of them, whether they are from the Right, Left, Socialist and Islamist spectrum, are basically populists. They will say things in the hope that it will make them popular with the masses.

When it comes to setting up strong institutions, they don't seem to be interested. For example, look at the electoral system, the ten-percent threshold, it has been discussed over and over again for over thirty years, but since it works to the advantage of the first and in some ways the second party, they don't change it [. . .] the lesson to be drawn from this is that, unless leaders work to strengthen institutions, you don't get anywhere. Just writing constitutions doesn't get you anywhere.

The quote highlights that Turkey's leaders, although having embraced a democratic narrative to reach their electorate and having benefitted from opportunities afforded by democratic institutions, have been unwilling to incorporate meaningful democratic practices within their leadership. As noted in the Introduction, the consolidation of democracy is made possible by the leadership adopting those values and implementing those standards of practice that are conducive to deepening and strengthening democratic processes. Turkish leadership has overwhelmingly failed at strengthening or putting into place such systems and structures.

Conclusion

The final chapter has revealed how Erdoğan's lack of respect for democratic norms and institutions has continued to shape his rule while on his journey to the presidential office: he has disregarded the constitutional bounds of the presidency, maintained partisan support for the AKP and aggressively pursued control of the party by engineering the removal of an elected Prime Minister, to be replaced by one who provided him with unquestioned loyalty. In doing so, the practical separation between Assembly and President ceased to exist and resembled *de facto* one-man rule, thus successfully removing one of the most fundamental institutions of oversight and accountability in a democracy: the parliament.

Erdoğan, over the course of his leadership, exploited his privileges in order to advance his political and personal agenda. This led to the further weakening of an already fragile democracy and stripped institutions of their political plurality. This was best exemplified by the measures put into place after the failed coup, which granted Erdoğan unfettered authority and the power to issue arbitrary decrees. During this period, the country experienced mass purges, extensive incarcerations and the systemic violation of basic rights for both citizens and politicians critical of Erdoğan. These tactics of intimidation and coercion strengthened his hold and power over the judiciary, the parliament, civil society and media – all of which are critical to upholding democracy.

In spite of this climate of fear and repression, Erdoğan called a referendum in 2017, which would result in the end of Turkey's parliamentary democracy in favour of a presidential system. This win provided him with largely unrestricted powers. Erdoğan's authoritarianism and unwillingness to lead in a way that respects and adheres to democratic systems and principles strongly echoes the approach of past leaders, but at a larger scale and to a greater extreme. Ultimately, Erdoğan's sweeping assault on democratic institutions has led to the dismantling of the Turkish democracy, with a 'Republican Sultan' at its helm.

Notes

1. Erdoğan engineered legislative amendments to restrict his former colleague to a single term; yet, after the CHP brought the case to the Constitutional Court, it was annulled on the grounds of it being unconstitutional (Sever 2015, 122–23).
2. Erdoğan was only the sixth Turkish president to chair a cabinet meeting in the history of the modern republic (*Guardian* 2015).
3. The number of Directorate-Generals in the presidential office was increased from four to thirteen. The new departments were created to be in charge of a wide range of government policy, including homeland security, external relations, economy, defence, investment monitoring, energy and social affairs (*Hürriyet* 2014b). Indeed, doing so was not unconstitutional, but it was beyond the bounds of practice and norms between the parliamentary government and the President, and thus viewed as another measure to coalesce greater powers in his office.
4. Turkey went to the polls twice in 2015, on 7 June and on 1 November. The June elections resulted in a hung parliament due to the AKP dropping its vote share by 9 percent, yet negotiations failed to produce a coalition government. President Erdoğan called a snap election in November to break the impasse, which resulted in the AKP regaining its majority (see Tables 9.1 and 9.2).
5. Due to the internal statutes of the AKP rule against re-election for more than three consecutive terms, seventy parliamentarians were ineligible to run for a fourth re-election, as they had served three consecutive terms in parliament.

6. This was a system practised in the Ottoman Empire, whereby Christian boys were taken from their families, mainly on the Balkans, converted to Islam and made into the property of the sultan in order to become part of the Janissaries or the administration. Although members of the *devşirme* class were technically slaves, they were of great importance to the sultan because they became vital to his power.

7. For a concise outline of Binali Yıldırım's close relationship with Erdoğan and political background, see Cengiz Çandar (2016a).

8. The author was personally aware of the case of a high-ranked officer who had been jailed immediately after the coup attempt. His legal representation was continually denied access to the prosecutor's files against him or the supposed evidence that he was part of the coup. In addition, he was arbitrarily purged from the armed forces without right to recourse. This meant that he was also denied his financial benefits that had accrued after he had spent the majority of his life serving as an officer.

9. For example, Kadir Nozoğlu had served as AKP provincial bureau chief in the eastern province of Elazığ before being appointed as a judge. Behice Cavuşoğlu, the head of the AKP women's body in the province of Giresun, Ceyda Bozdağ, a leading party official in the western province of Edirne, and Hacer Alan, a lawyer who represented the former Ankara Mayor Melih Gökçek were also promoted to the position of judge (Ayasun 2017).

10. Traditionally, Turkey's aspirant judicial officials, whether prosecutors or lawyers, take judgeship exams after a grueling preparation period. Then, they undergo in-depth committee-like hearings by a bi-partisan jury of high justices, to measure their fitness for the prestigious job. However, according to the press statement of CHP deputy Barış Yarkadaş, research has uncovered that the promotions were given after a very brief interview and that many AKP-linked promotions had much lower exam scores than those overlooked (Ayasun 2017).

11. Another two prominent lawyers' associations, the *Çağdaş Hukukçular Derneği* (Progressive Lawyers Association, CHD) and the *Özgürlükçü Hukukçular Derneği* (Liberal Lawyers Association, OHD), were also closed by decree, for being a 'threat to national security'. However, instead of charges of links to the GM, these organisations specialised in defending Kurdish rights and, thus, were charged for having ties to the PKK (Hürtaş 2017b).

12. The amendment lifted the immunity of fifty-five of the fifty-nine HDP members, fifty-nine of the 134 members from the main opposition CHP, twenty-nine of the 316 from the ruling AKP, ten of the forty from the opposition MHP,

and one independent. However, HDP parliamentarians have been the only ones to face criminal investigation and detention.

13. The DEP parliamentarians were Leyla Zana, Orhan Doğan, Hatip Dicle and Selim Sadak

14. The commission noted: 'Democratic process were curtailed under the state of emergency, and the two sides did not have equal opportunities to make their case to the voters [. . .] along with restrictions on the media, the arrests of journalists and the closure of media outlets, reduced voters' access to a plurality of views [. . .] We observed the misuse of state resources, as well as the obstruction of No campaign events [. . .] some senior officials equating No supporters with terrorist sympathisers, and in numerous cases No supporters faced police interventions' (GRECO 2018).

15. For example, the constitution states that the Constitutional Court is the most superior court and that its rulings are binding.

16. Along with Mehmet Altan, five others received the same sentence, including his brother Ahmet Altan, former parliamentarian Nazlı Ilıcak, Fevzi Yazıcı, Yakup Şimşek and Şükrü Tuğrul Özşengül (DW 2018). In later developments, Mehmet Altan was released on 27 June 2018, Ilıcak on 5 November 2019, and Ahmet Altan on 15 April 2021.

17. In a similar example, Taner Kılıç, the chairman of Amnesty International Turkey, in pre-trial detention on charge of being part of the GM, was released from his pre-trial detention by a court. After a prosecutor appealed, a second court accepted it; then, the same Istanbul trial court that had ordered his release reversed its decision the following day and agreed to the continued detention of Kılıç (BBC 2018).

18. The Rule of Law Index measures countries' rule of law performance across the following crtiteria: Constraints on Government Power; Absence of Corruption; Open Government; Fundamental Rights, Order and Security; Regulatory Enforcement; Civil Justice and Criminal Justice.

19. The Constitutional Court was authorised to take on individual applications as of 2012. Since then, it found that in 2,536 cases 'a right was breached'. Out of the 2,071 violations in the 'right to a fair trial' made by the court of 1,783 rulings (81 percent) stemmed from a breach of the right to trial within a reasonable time; 154 rulings (7 percent) stemmed from a breach of the right to access to court; and 105 rulings (5 percent) stemmed from a breach of the applicant's right to receive a justified decision regarding their case from a local court (*Hürriyet* 2018a).

20. A legislative change before the elections permitted the formation of electoral alliances, which allow smaller parties to win some seats in the legislature if their alliance as a whole cross the ten-percent threshold.

21. The alliance was rounded out by the *Büyük Birlik Partisi* (Grand Unity Party).

22. The opposing alliance was the *Millet İttifakı* (Nation Alliance) between the CHP, the *İYİ Parti* (Good Party), a newly formed centre-Right party whose most prominent members had broken away from the MHP, the Islamist *Saadet Partisi* (Felicity Party) and the centre-Right *Demokrat Parti* (Democrat Party). This alliance attained 34 percent of the vote, with a combined 189 seats in the Assembly.

23. The HDP did not join a coalition, competing as a stand-alone party.

24. With the system change, the President was given the power to appoint cabinet ministers and high-level bureaucrats without a vetting process by the parliament. Cabinet members no longer need to sit in parliament and are entirely under the tutelage of the presidency.

25. Other prominent examples of Erdoğan's decisions involve sacking the Central Bank Governor Murat Çetinkaya for purportedly not meeting the President's demands to cut interest rates. Later, nine high-ranking officials from the Central Bank were also removed from their posts (Ant 2019).

26. The original winner, Ekrem İmamoğlu from the CHP, was re-elected with a margin increasing from 48.7 percent on 31 March to 54.2 percent in the 23 June re-run.

27. In May, the Ministry of Commerce took away the authority of mayors to appoint the heads of municipality-run business enterprises and handed it over to district councils. According to Istanbul municipality figures, these enterprises in the city have an annual turnover of USD 4 billion (Zaman 2019).

28. This figure incorporates three metropolitan cities, five provinces, forty-five districts and twelve town municipalities.

29. Following the dismissals, twenty-nine municipal officers and eight municipal workers were also dismissed, and the Mardin Governorship announced a one-month ban on all protests, press reports, rallies and sit-ins after the sacking of the mayors.

30. Three metropolitan municipalities, five provincial municipalities and thirty-three district municipalities.

31. On 23 December 2020, the European Court of Human Rights judged that the incarceration of Demirtaş went against 'the very core of the concept of a democratic society' and ordered Turkish courts to release him; however, Turkey has not complied. This is similar to the situation that the prominent civil society activist Osman Kavala has endured in pre-trail detention since 2017. While the European Court has called his detention unlawful and ordered his release, Turkish courts have not complied.

CONCLUSION

The book has demonstrated how political leaders have played a key role in the failings of the country's democratic system over seventy years of multi-party politics. Understanding their overwhelming drive for power is critical, if we are to understand the nature of political developments in Turkey: the outcomes of their beliefs, values and choices have largely shaped the path that Turkish democracy has followed. Although Turkey has had institutional provisions which are required for democratic consolidation, the elites have not harmonised these formal rules, mechanisms and processes with the required beliefs, values and practices. O'Donnell suggests that consolidation is achieved when there is a close match between the practices of the elites and the formal democratic institutions and processes. Yet, throughout Turkey's political history, the elites have overwhelmingly failed to fulfill these requirements.

Indeed, some leaders did make contributions that supported democracy. As Chapter 1 shows, Menderes and Bayar played a significant role in Turkey's democratisation – they broke the CHP's monopoly on power and helped open the door to a multi-party system. Their efforts introduced the rural masses to their political importance and stake in the democratic processes. Demirel's humble origins made him sensitive to the needs of the rural population. He often chose to accommodate the military to maintain the parameters of civilian politics. This was reflected in the immediate aftermath of the post-1960 coup, when he played a crucial role in navigating the democratic regime through a highly turbulent period between the military and civilian politics, as noted in Chapter 2. With Ecevit, mainstream politics was introduced to *merkez-sol* (centre-Left) ideals and policies. A minister under İnönü's coalition governments of the early 1960s, he championed policies to address the needs of workers, peasants and farmers, who remained at the forefront of his politics of social equality throughout the 1970s (see Chapter 3). And Özal did away with many taboo subjects and encouraged others to debate them freely, such as the Kurdish question, proposing a political solution to an issue that until that point had been seen through a strictly securitised lens. At the same time, his economic liberalisation created spaces for democratic growth in certain areas, touched upon in Chapter 4.

Their authoritarian and undemocratic traits, nonetheless, far eclipsed the accomplishments that benefitted democracy, owing to a culture of authoritarianism that runs throughout Turkey's multi-party era. Leaders have repeatedly displayed a penchant for single-handed, personalised governing style, which sits as an antithesis to the democratic principles of leadership renewal, mutual tolerance, pluralism, compromise, consensus-driven politics, political self-restraint and respect for a rules-based system.

The political realities of each leader, their socio-economic and ideological backgrounds, and their political outcomes and legacies differ greatly. I have not set out to demonstrate a uniform strategy; rather, the aim has been to underline the consistent failure of the elite political class to show democratic leadership and forsake authoritarianism.

Prominent political leaders, within Turkey's multi-party period, have consistently displayed a desire to sustain their rule through authoritarian measures, best observed in their party leadership style. Turkish political parties overwhelmingly have weak intra-party democratic structures and practices: this book demonstrates how party behaviour is reflective of the way in which the party is ruled – that is, there exists a symbiotic relationship between the intra- and inter-party sphere. 'A party that is not internally democratic cannot really be externally democratic', as Mersel has noted (2006, 97). As such, intra-party democracy, a key component for consolidation, has been inadequate among the major parties within this period, resulting in the inability of parties to reign in their leaders' authoritarian impulses and the personalisation of power.

These leadership patterns signify that Turkey suffers from a culture of office dependency: within a consolidated democratic system, leadership renewal is an established norm, whereas office dependency, according to Keane (see Introduction), is a potent obstacle to the attainment of a consolidated system. Despite coups, party closures, electoral losses and debilitating crises during their reigns, leaders have consistently refused to resign as the heads of their political parties or leave politics altogether. The unwillingness of leaders to accept legitimate challenges or concede the seats of power has been the norm, and not the exception, as exemplified by the protracted tenures of Demirel, Ecevit, Erbakan and Türkeş.

If the distinction between owning and leaving office is a critical indicator of whether a particular leadership can be considered democratic, then the leaders within this book clearly fall into the former category. The outcome has been ongoing party schisms (see Table 8.1), with some of these ruptures having far-reaching consequences for the political party and the country's political landscape.

The ascension of authoritarian leaders was made easier once the *Siyasi Partiler Kanunu* (Political Parties Law, SPK) was amended during the military junta of 1980, which formalised the intra-party authoritarian structure. No Turkish leader since then has made a concerted effort to amend these laws and implement more democratic structures within political parties. Rather, the preference to retain the SPK in its present form provides yet another example of the unwillingness of Turkey's leaders to decentralise power and expand the parameters of democratic checks and balances on their rule.

As noted by Levitsky and Ziblatt (see Introduction), democratic norms founded on mutual tolerance and forbearance is key to maintaining institutions: Turkey, however, has regularly failed to meet this specification, with the ballot box, or majoritarian interpretation, valued as the foremost democratic yardstick throughout the multi-party era. This has enabled the ruling leadership to dismiss the opposition as illegitimate or to openly exploit their institutional prerogatives in order to promote their own interests, all in the name of the *milli irade* (national will).

Table 8.1 Party Fragmentation and Formation of New Parties in Turkey

Original Party	Leader	Splinter Party	Date
Cumhuriyet Halk Partisi (Republican Peoples' Party, CHP)	İsmet İnönü	*Demokrat Parti* (Democrat Party, DP)	1946
DP	Adnan Menderes	*Millet Partisi* (Nation Party)	1948
		Türkiye Köylü Partisi (Peasants' Party of Turkey)	1952
		Hürriyet Partisi (Freedom Party)	1955
CHP	İsmet İnönü	*Güven Partisi* (Reliance Party)	1967
Adalet Partisi (Justice Party)	Süleyman Demirel	*Demokratik Parti* (Democratic Party)	1970
CHP	Bülent Ecevit	*Cumhuriyetçi Parti* (Republican Party)	1972
Post-1980			
Anavatan Partisi (Motherland)	Mesut Yılmaz	*Yeni Parti* (New Party)	1993
Milliyetçi Hareket Parti (Nationalist Action Party, MHP)	Alparsan Türkeş	*Büyük Birlik Partisi* (Great Unity Party)	1993
Doğru Yol Partisi (True Path Party)	Tansu Çiller	*Demokrat Türkiye Partisi* (Democrat Turkey Party)	1997
Demokratik Sol Partisi (Democrat Left Party, DSP)	Bülent Ecevit	*Değişen Türkiye Partisi* (Changing Turkey Party)	1998
Fazilet Partisi (Virtue Party)	Necmettin Erbakan	*Adalet ve Kalkınma Partisi* (Justice and Development Party, AKP)	2001
DSP	Bülent Ecevit	*Yeni Türkiye Partisi* (New Turkey Party)	2002
MHP	Devlet Bahçeli	*İyi Parti* (Good Party)	2018
AKP	Recep Tayyip Erdoğan	*Gelecek Partisi* (Future Party)	2019
AKP	Recep Tayyip Erdoğan	*Demokrasi ve Atılım Partisi* (Democracy and Progress Party, DEVA)	2020

Conversely, Turkey's leaders have not used their legislative power to take substansive steps to strengthen democracy: the commitment to deepening and strengthening democratic institutions and processes, a requirement of democratic consolidation, has been questionable or missing entirely. Leaders have predominantly refrained from trying to create more liberal, account-able, representative and accessible systems and structures, as consistent with Diamond's requirement for a consolidated system. Elites must establish vari-ous sites for maintaining accountability, popular expression, collective action and non-violation of a wide range of political and civil freedoms. These are mechanisms to keep leaders accountable, which exist in both horizontal and vertical forms, as discussed by authors such as O'Donnell, Keane and Garretón Merino (see Introduction).

Yet, as I have shown, leaders have failed to make any genuine effort to strengthen institutions, beyond rhetoric. Strong autonomous legislative, judiciary and bureaucratic branches of government are necessary for dem-ocratic governance; however, Turkish leaders have consistently abused the power afforded to them, through concerted efforts to diminish the capacity of institutions to act as robust checks on leadership and erode their auton-omy, as was made immediately apparent under Menderes and Bayar's rule (see Chapter 1). Historically, this is largely due to a lack of tolerance and without institutional forbearance, resulting in institutions weakened and robbed of their representative and pluralist essence. This is consistent with Sayarı's statement that, '[u]nless you work to strengthen institutions, you don't get anywhere. Just writing constitutions doesn't get you anywhere'.

The penchant for authoritarianism amongst Turkey's leaders has also led to a disregard for political opposition: reconciling differences and making compromises is not the norm, even when faced with a possible collapse of the democratic system. Şerif Mardin, drawing on the nature of political com-petition, declared that 'we can deduce there is an element in Tukish political culture to which the notion of opposition is deeply repugnant' (1966, 380). Mardin's observation, published in the late 1960s, remains accurate to this day, due mostly to the zero-sum view of politics held by leaders: when faced with major political problems, leaders have been reluctant or altogether unwilling to adapt their leadership to steer the country out of trouble. Rather, they forged ahead, with their own interests at the forefront of decisions, and when faced with opposition or push-back, they retaliated with more severe measures. Their main pregorative was to hold on to office, despite the consequences, which often included the breakdown of political order.

There are indeed extreme and uncompromising elements in all systems, but consolidated democracies are much better equipped to deal with these kinds of developments. Turkey has regularly experienced polarisation, which has led to crises in democracy, due to the absence of practices aligning with these key democratic norms. In fact, at certain periods, polarisation was so extreme that competing elites saw their rivals as existential threats, such as Demirel's portrayal of the Left throughout the 1960s and 1970s (see Chapters 2 and 3).

The encouragement of violence and repression against any form of opposition exemplifies the pervading culture. Throughout the multi-party history, leaders have often personally directed authorities to repress opposition with physical force, as was observed under Çiller's leadership (see Chapter 5), whereby systematic violence was meted out against rights activists. Journalists and media outlets have also regularly been the target of troubling repression, aimed at curbing their rights, as was the case under Menderes and Özal's tenures (see Chapters 1 and 4). As noted in the Introduction, uncompromising positions held by the elites set an example for society. The leadership's intolerance for opponents trapped the country in a cycle of ever-increasing violence and polarisation, leading to protracted crises, as was the case during the 1970s with the clash between Ecevit and Demirel (see Chapter 3).

A Note on Military Coups and Leaders

Undeniably, the armed forces have played a central role in bringing to an end civilian rule in 1960, 1971 and 1980, and partially in 1997. There is a general consensus that the military has thus hindered the chances for democratisation, due to its role as grand arbiter of political developments. I do not refute the military's presence in politics; however, in each of these cases, the military did not act in a vacuum or without reason: when faced with debilitating political crises, the inability of leaders to negotiate, accommodate and compromise created conditions that made military interventions seemingly unavoidable, for an institution already predisposed to interventions. Rather than act with responsibility and foresight to salvage the civilian regime, leaders held steadfast to their autocratic style of rule, further debilitating the chances at a resolution through the political process. The military, in this regard, has intervened when leaders have pushed parameters to breaking point.

However, the elites did not act in a manner or make decisions that would have minimised the role of the armed forces in politics. In fact, some leaders even invited the military to play a role in the political sphere in order to fulfill their personal and political ambitions, as did Demirel and Çiller. Had they conducted themselves differently, the military intervention would have been unnecessary, as stated by the leading officers of the coups. Even in hindsight, many leaders refused to acknowledge their role in these interventions.

In analysing the attempted coup of 15 July 2016, this is critical for understanding the officer's rationale behind their act. The armed forces faction which initiated the putsch against Erdoğan's rule was most likely part of a pro-Gülen network and anti-Erdoğan officers, reacting to the power struggle between the two former allies. In essence, this attempted intervention was the causal outcome of Erdoğan's action to unlawfully wrest control from the military, for his own political purposes.

Final Remarks

The history of democracy in Turkey is a testament to the fact that democratic consolidation is not just a matter of creating rules and institutions: the political elite themselves must reflect a democratic character, which Turkish leaders have repeatedly failed to embody. For instance, although Turkey has had numerous constitutions, all differing in nature, these have had little impact on curbing democratic crises or diminishing the leaders' appetite for authoritarian rule. Rather, they have openly challenged and violated constitutional articles that hindered their political aims or pursuit of power, thus failing to act with self-restraint – forbearance – when their rule or the security of their position was challenged. Thus, they are largely responsible for undermining democratic mechanisms and processes. None have accepted responsibility for the crises that their leaderships created. As noted by Kalaycıoğlu, Turkey's problems with democracy 'is a matter of elite political culture. Not simply a matter of changing characters and constitutions'.

Given the continuity of the party leaders' undemocratic behaviour from the very beginning of the multi-party era, this could be regarded as a logical endpoint. The multi-party era has not benefitted from a counter-leadership culture: had there been one, liberalisation and democratic consolidation might have been achieved. Aside from İsmet İnönü and his son Erdal İnönü, both examples of leaders who embodied democratic values, the remaining actors behaved in ways which ran counter to democratic values.

Thus, institutions have indeed existed, but their strength has remained limited, and their autonomy eroded because the required norms to maintain or strengthen them have sat opposed to leaders' values and practices. Rather, authoritarianism has been the normative preference of these leaders' rule. Democracy has remained tenuous and even untenable throughout its history, as a result. Looking at this period in Turkish politics through a longitudinal lens reveals that the country's current nature of politics was not unforeseeable: Erdoğan's authoritarianism has been extensive, protracted and most detrimental, forcing the transition from a multi-party democracy to a one-man system of government, so that now any semblance of democratic processes and institutions is in name only.

Erdoğan is simply the most extreme manifestation of what is symptomatic of an ongoing political cultural crisis in Turkey, an unending cycle of authoritarian leadership. As the biographical vignettes have demonstrated, he did not emerge from a vacuum and is far from being unique in Turkish political history. For example, Erdoğan's leadership presents similarities to that of Menderes and Bayar, Demirel, Ecevit and Erbakan, in both inter- and intra-party spheres. Actions taken by Özal and Çiller are precedents to Erdoğan's behaviour: Özal flouting the parameters of presidential rule and Çiller removing the immunities of pro-Kurdish parliamentarians from HEP were precursors to what was to come eventually. Erdoğan is the by-product of a political culture that has normalised the authoritarian behaviour of its leaders. The key difference is that Erdoğan has completely broken the system. While Erbakan expressed similar anti-system impulses, Erdoğan stands apart, owing to a conscious, outward and systematic assault on the entire democratic system. He is, in effect, an unashamed enemy of democracy. Erdoğan's efforts and its outcomes are obvious and observable; yet, as the chapters illustrate, undermining institutions and backsliding takes a variety of forms, which become evident under closer examination.

It is one thing to establish a democracy, but its sustenance and consolidation is largely incumbent on the elite's adoption and internalisation of values conducive to deepening democracy. Without this, as the Turkish experience offers us a critical example, democracy's existence is tenuous, oscillating between enduring and ephemeral, clearly implicating the critical role that leaders play in a country's inability to consolidate democracy.

EPILOGUE

Today, Turkey's political climate, under Erdoğan's iron-fisted authoritarian rule, continues to head down a perilous and uncertain path. Laws which have taken on conservative religious undertones are haphazardly introduced or amended, in order to maintain the power of the President, and appeals or legal challenges are proscribed. The electoral law has been changed to further disadvantage the opposition parties. Steps to remove more opposition parliamentarians' immunity have been flagged. Public spaces are closed off to gatherings of a political nature, and police act with impunity, violently shutting them down. After losing key municipalities in the 2019 local elections, the government is taking steps to curtail the legislative powers of opposition mayors, and these steps will continue to suffocate areas that are not under the direct control of Erdoğan and the AKP. The President and his allies' verbal attacks against individuals and groups are more aggressive and mean-spirited than ever. Supporters of the government seem ever-more emboldened, resulting in an increase of violent assaults on opposition figures and journalists, with the offenders either let off with minimal punishment or authorities displaying little interest in investigating crimes further. There exist serious accusations and evidence of systematic government malpractice, corruption and government-mafia relations across all levels; yet, the judiciary does not act, and the media landscape, monopolised by the AKP, turns a blind eye to these stories. The government and its networks act with impunity, as a law unto themselves. Democratic institutions merely exist in name. The arbitrary, top-down approach to fiscal decisions has been the cause of the rapid decline of the economy, resulting in high unemployment rates and an ever-increasing cost of living for the average citizen. The political opposition has made small gains, reflected by its municipal victories, and has remained steadfast in spite of the authoritarian system, offering hope for the re-democratising of the country in a post-Erdoğan era. That said, Erdoğan's and the AKP's electoral ratings, albeit in slow decline, remain ahead of the opposition.

Considering the subject studied in this book, authoritarianism and leadership culture, two inter-related questions remain: why do Turks prefer to elect leaders with authoritarian traits, and why has authoritarianism remained a salient feature of Turkish politics?

A rigorous answer lies beyond the scope of this book; however, there are a number of studies that could provide a starting point. Research indicates that attitudes and values held by Turkish citizens show a democratic deficiency, in line with the that of the leaders. Since politicians in Turkey are drawn from society, owing to the healthy levels of social mobility in the country, this offers critical insight. For example, Tessler and Altınoğlu's article 'Political Culture in Turkey' (2004) found that only 31.2 percent of citizens could be classified as 'true democrats'. In other words, attitudes conducive to democracy and democratisation are held by a relatively limited number of citizens. Yılmaz Esmer's regular studies expose a similar trend. Survey outcomes published in Esmer's (2012) *Türkiye Değerler Atlası 2012* (2012 Atlas of Turkey's Values) demonstrate that the majority of Turks oppose participating in democratic activities such as 'peaceful demonstrations' (66 percent), 'boycotting' (70 percent) and 'strikes' (72 percent). Even more striking is that most citizens prefer to be governed by a 'strong leader who does not have to deal with parliament and elections'. Correlating with these findings is research published by Paşa, Kabasakal and Bodur in their article 'Society, Organisations, and Leadership in Turkey' (2001), which reveals that workers in Turkey consider autocratic qualities in their leaders as a desired attribute. They want leaders to demonstrate assertive and aggressive qualities.

Indeed, this is not exhaustive or rigorous research, but my hope is that it gives readers and researchers food for thought when we seek an answer as to 'why' Turkey has experienced a pattern of authoritarian leadership; the answers might lie in values held in society.

REFERENCES

Acar, Feride. 2002. 'Turgut Özal: Pious Agent of Liberal Transformation'. In *Political Leaders and Democracy in Turkey*, edited by Metin Heper and Sabri Sayarı, 163–80. Lanham: Lexington Books.

Ahmad, Feroz. 1977. *The Turkish Experiment in Democracy, 1950–1975*. London: C. Hurst for the Royal Institute of International Affairs.

Ahmad, Feroz. 1981. 'Military Intervention and the Crisis in Turkey'. *Merip Reports* 11(1):5–32.

Ahmad, Feroz. 1993. *The Making of Modern Turkey*. London: Routledge.

Ahmad, Feroz. 2016. 'Personal Interview with Author'. 11 October.

Ahval. 2018. '116 Media Outlets Closed under Turkish State of Emergency'. *Ahval*, 10 May. Accessed 11 May 2018. https://ahvalnews.com/media/116-media-outlets-closed-under-turkish-state-emergency

Ahval. 2019. 'Turkish Court Acquits All Suspects in Ergenekon Trial'. *Ahval*, 1 July. Accessed 06 July 2019. https://ahvalnews.com/ergenekon/turkish-court-acquits-all-suspects-ergenekon-trial

Akar, Rıdvan, and Can Dündar. 2008. *Ecevit ve Gizli Arşivi*. 2nd ed. Ankara: Imge Kitabevi.

Akar, Rıdvan, Can Dündar and Murat Özcan. 2004. *Karaoğlan*. CNN Türk.

Akyol, Taha. 2014a. 'Cumhurbaşkanı ve Hukuk'. *Hürriyet*, 27 June. Accessed 20 December 2017. http://www.hurriyet.com.tr/yazarlar/taha–akyol/cumhurbaskani–ve–hukuk–26692893.

Akyol, Taha. 2014b. 'Playing with Justice like a Jigsaw Puzzle'. *Hürriyet Daily News*, 27 November. Accessed 19 December 2017. http://www.hurriyetdailynews.com/opinion/taha-akyol/playing-with-justice-like-a-jigsaw-puzzle--74854.

Albayrak, Mustafa. 2004. 'Demokrat Parti Döneminde İktidar-Muhalefet İlişkileri (1950–1960)'. Accessed 16 April 2017. https://www.mustafaalbayrak06.com/tr/?p=80

Albright, Madeleine. 2019. *Fascism: A Warning*. London: HarperCollins.

Alonso, Sonia, John Keane and Wolfgang Merkel. 2011. *The Future of Representative Democracy*. Cambridge: Cambridge University Press.

Altıparmak, Kerem, and Yaman Akdeniz. 2015. 'The Silencing Effect on Dissent and Freedom of Expression in Turkey'. In *Journalism at Risk: Threats, Challenges and Perspectives*, edited by Council of Europe, 145–72. Paris: Council of Europe Publishing.

Amnesty International. 2015. *Amnesty International Report 2014/15 – Turkey*. London: Amnesty International.

Anderson, Ivy. 1994. 'Mafia and Mrs [Tansu] Ciller: The Turkish Mafia is in Cahoots with the Government . . . and the Peasants are First in the Firing Line'. *New Internationalist* 256:24. Accessed 14 September 2017. https://newint.org/features/1994/06/05/mafia

Ant, Onur. 2019. 'Turkey Central Bank Removes Chief Economist, Key Officials'. *Bloomberg*. 9 August. Accessed 20 August 2019. https://www.bloomberg.com/news/articles/2019-08-08/turkey-central-bank-removes-chief-economist-other-officials-jz34v7c6

Arango, Tim, and Ceylan Yeğinsu. 2016. 'How Erdoğan Moved to Solidify Power by Ousting a Pivotal Ally'. *The New York Times*, 5 March. Accessed 12 July 2018. https://www.nytimes.com/2016/05/06/world/europe/ahmet-davutoglu-turkey-prime-minister.html.

Arat, Yeşim. 1998. 'A Woman Prime Minister in Turkey: Did It Matter?' *Women & Politics* 19(4):1–22.

Arat, Yeşim. 2002. 'Süleyman Demirel: National Will and Beyond'. In *Political Leaders and Democracy in Turkey*, edited by Metin Heper and Sabri Sayarı, 88–105. Lanham: Lexington Books.

Aslan, Emel. 2014. 'Türkiye'nin İç Siyasetinde Demokrat Parti (1950–1960)'. Unpubl. Master's Thesis, Sosyal Bilimler Enstitüsü, Ahi Evran Üniversitesi.

Atacan, Fulya. 2005. 'Explaining Religious Politics at the Crossroad: AKP-SP'. *Turkish Studies* 6(2):187–99.

Ateş, Gülbin Ayşı. 2012. 'Representing Centre-Right or Conservative Right? The Case of the Democratic Party in Turkey, 1970–1980'. Unpubl. Master's Thesis, Political Science and Public Administration, Middle East Technical University.

Ayan, Pelin. 2010. 'Authoritarian Party Structures in Turkey: A Comparison of the Republican People's Party and the Justice and Development Party'. *Turkish Studies* 11(2):197–215.

Ayasun, Abdullah 2017. 'In Turkey, Road to Judicial Posts Passes through Party Membership'. *The Globe Post*, 28 April. Accessed 21 January 2018. http://www.theglobepost.com/2017/04/28/road-to-judicial-posts-in-turkey-passes-through-party-membership/.

Bal, İhsan, and Sedat Laçiner. 2001. 'The Challenge of Revolutionary Terrorism to Turkish Democracy 1960–80'. *Terrorism and Political Violence* 13(4):90–115.

Basın Konseyi Dergisi. 1989. *Basın Konseyi Dergisi* 1:4.

Bayraktar, Ulaş S, and Cemal Altan. 2013. 'Explaining Turkish Party Centralism: Traditions and Trends in the Exclusion of Local Party Offices in Mersin and Beyond'. In *Negotiating Political Power in Turkey: Breaking Up the Party*, edited by Elise Massicard and Nicole Watts, 17–36. London and New York: Routledge. https://www.bbc.com/turkce/haberler-turkiye-43592512

BBC. 2015. 'Turkish State TV Bans Opposition Advert'. *BBC*, 11 April. Accessed 15 July 2018. http://www.bbc.com/news/world-europe-32266195.

BBC. 2018a. '1989'da Türkiye: Özal, İnönü ve Perinçek Türkiye'nin Sorunlarını Yorumluyor'. *BBC News Türkçe*, 30 March. Accessed 3 April 2018.

BBC. 2018b. 'Turkey Court "Reverses Release" of Amnesty Head Taner Kilic'. *BBC.com*. 1 February. Accessed 1 February 2018. https://www.bbc.com/news/world-europe-42892643

Bektaş, Arsev. 1993. *Demokratikleşme Sürecinde Liderler Oligarşisi, CHP ve AP (1961–1980)*. Istanbul: Bağlam Yayıncılık.

Bermeo, Nancy, and Deborah J. Yashar. 2016. *Parties, Movements, and Democracy in the Developing World*. New York: Cambridge University Press.

Best, Heinrich, and John Higley. 2010. 'Introduction: Democratic Elitism Reappraised'. In *Democratic Elitism: New Theoretical and Comparative Perspectives*, edited by Heinrich Best and John Higley, 1–22. Leiden: Brill.

Bianet. 2021. HDP Report on Trustees: 'Trustees Appointed to 48 HDP Municipalities since 2019'. *Bianet English*, 24 February. Accessed 19 May 2021. https://m.bianet.org/english/politics/239885-trustees-appointed-to-48-hdp-municipalities-since-2019

Birand, Mehmet Ali. 1987. *The Generals' Coup in Turkey: An Inside Story of 12 September, 1980*. London: Brassey's Defence Publishers.

Birand, Mehmet Ali. 2012. *Son Darbe: 28 Şubat*. Kanal D.

Birand, Mehmet Ali, Hikmet Bila and Rıdvan Akar. 1999. *12 Eylül: Türkiye'nin Miladı*. 2nd ed. Istanbul: Doğan Kitapçılık.

Birand, Mehmet Ali, Can Dündar and Bülent Çaplı. 1991. *Demirkırat: Bir Demokrasinin Doğuşu*. TRT.

Birand, Mehmet Ali, Can Dündar and Bülent Çaplı. 1994. *12 Mart: İhtilalin Pençesinde Demokrasi*. Show TV.

Birand, Mehmet Ali, Can Dündar and Bülent Çaplı. 2016a. *12 Mart: İhtilalin Pençesinde Demokrasi*. 11th ed. Istanbul: Can Sanat Yayınları.

Birand, Mehmet Ali, Can Dündar and Bülent Çaplı. 2016b. *Demirkırat: Bir Demokrasinin Doğuşu*. 17th ed. Istanbul: Can Sanat Yayınları.

Birand, Mehmet Ali, and Soner Yalçın. 2000. *Özal'lı Yıllar*. CNN Türk.

Birand, Mehmet Ali, and Soner Yalçın. 2001. *Özal: Bir Davanın Öyküsü*. 14th ed. Istanbul: Doğan Kitap.

Birand, Mehmet Ali, and Reyhan Yıldız. 2012. *Son Darbe: 28 Şubat*. Istanbul: Doğan Kitap.

Birgün. 2006. '2005'e İstifalar Damga Vurdu'. *Birgün*, 1 January. Accessed 21 December 2017. https://www.birgun.net/haber-detay/2005-e-istifalar-damga-vurdu-25546.html.

Bodgener, Jim. 1993. 'Ciller Raises Great Expectations'. *Middle East Economic Digest* 37(28):35.

Bodgener, Jim. 1997. 'Soft Coup Imposes a New Agenda'. *Middle East Economic Digest* 41(31):7.

Brown, John Murray. 1994. 'Tansu Ciller and the Question of Turkish Identity'. *World Policy Journal* 11(3):55.

Bryman, Alan, Michael Bresnen, Alan Beardsworth and Teresa Keil. 1988. 'Qualitative Research and the Study of Leadership'. *Human Relations* 41(1):13–29.

Buğra, Ayşe. 1994. *State and Business in Turkey*. Albany: State University of New York Press.

Çağaptay, Soner. 2010. 'Turkey under the AKP-II: The Rise of Authoritarian Democracy and Orthopraxy'. *Hürriyet Daily News*, 11 April. Accessed 7 March 2015. http://www.hurriyetdailynews.com/default.aspx?pageid=438&n=turkey8217s-transformation-under-akp-ii-rise-of-authoritarian-democracy-and-orthopraxy-2010-04-11.

Çağaptay, Soner. 2017. *The New Sultan: Erdogan and the Crisis of Modern Turkey*. London: I. B. Tauris.

Çağaptay, Soner, H. Akin Ünver and Hale Arifağaoğlu. 2008. 'Will the Turkish Constitutional Court Ban the AKP?' *The Washington Institute*, 19 March. Accessed 29 January 2018. https://ciaotest.cc.columbia.edu/pbei/winep/0002090/f_0002090_1143.pdf

Çağlayangil, İhsan Sabri 1990. *Anılarım*. Istanbul: Yılmaz Yayınları.

Çandar, Cengiz. 2015. 'Is AKP Heading for a Split?' *Al-Monitor: Turkey Pulse*, 18 September. Accessed 9 December 2017. https://www.al-monitor.com/originals/2015/09/turkey-erdogan-strong-grip-may-cause-possible-split-akp.html

Çandar, Cengiz. 2016a. 'New Turkish PM Helps Erdogan Revive "Ottoman Glory"'. *Al-Monitor: Turkey Pulse*, 20 May. Accessed 8 September 2018. http://www.al-monitor.com/pulse/originals/2016/05/turkey-new-prime-minister-binali-yildirim-erdogan.html#ixzz53YzDVOTF.

Çandar, Cengiz. 2016b. 'Personal Interview with Author'. 13 October.

Çandar, Cengiz. 2018. 'Turkey in 2018: The War of the Presidents'. *Al-Monitor: Turkey Pulse*, 5 January. Accessed 12 January 2018. http://www.al-monitor.com/pulse/originals/2018/01/turkey-the-war-between-erdogan-and-gul-began.html#ixzz54m4WBI4Q.

Capoccia, Giovanni, and Daniel Ziblatt. 2010. 'The Historical Turn in Democratization Studies: A New Research Agenda for Europe and Beyond'. *Comparative Political Studies* 43(8/9):931–68.

Celasun, Oya. 1998. *The 1994 Currency Crisis in Turkey*. Washington, DC: The World Bank.

Çelep, Ödül. 2014. 'Intra-Party Autocracy of Turkey's Party System'. *In the 4th International Conference on European Studies*.

Cemal, Hasan. 1989a. 'Korkut Özal Ne Diyor?' *Nokta*, 24 April: 15.

Cemal, Hasan. 1989b. *Özal Hikâyesi*. 3rd ed. Ankara: Bilgi Yayınevi.

Cengiz, Orhan Kemal. 2014. 'Opposition Claims Erdogan May be Media Owner'. *Al-Monitor: Turkey Pulse*, 12 February. Accessed 20 December 2017. https://www.al-monitor.com/pulse/originals/2014/02/turkish-opposition-claims-erdogan-owns-media.html.

Çetin, Bilal. 1999. 'Eski DYP'lilerin Yuvaya Dönüş Hazırlığı'. *Milliyet*, 23 June. Accessed 30 November 2017. http://gazetearsivi.milliyet.com.tr/GununYayinlari/FG7DBCf_x2F_nJtktdBI1gErSA_x3D__x3D_

Chou, Mark. 2012. 'Sowing the Seeds of Its Own Destruction: Democracy and Democide in the Weimar Republic and Beyond'. *Theoria* 59(133):21–49.

Chou, Mark. 2014. *Democracy Against Itself: Sustaining an Unsustainable Idea*. Edinburgh: Edinburgh University Press.

Çınar, Alev, and Ergun Özbudun. 2002. 'Mesut Yılmaz: From Özal's Shadow to Mediator'. In *Political Leaders and Democracy in Turkey*, edited by Metin Heper and Sabri Sayarı, 181–98. Lanham: Lexington Books.

Cizre-Sakallıoğlu, Ümit. 1992. 'Labour and State in Turkey: 1960–80'. *Middle Eastern Studies* 28(4):712–28.

Cizre, Ümit 1993. *AP-Ordu İlişkileri: Bir İkilemin Anatomisi*. Istanbul: İletişim.

Cizre, Ümit. 2002a. 'From Ruler to Pariah: The Life and Times of the True Path Party'. *Turkish Studies* 3(1):82–101.

Cizre, Ümit. 2002b. 'Tansu Çiller: Lusting for Power and Undermining Democracy'. In *Political Leaders and Democracy in Turkey*, edited by Metin Heper and Sabri Sayarı, 199–216. Lanham: Lexington Books.

Cizre, Ümit, and Joshua Walker. 2010. 'Conceiving the New Turkey after Ergenekon'. *The International Spectator* 45(1):89–98.

Çölaşan, Emin. 1987. *Yalçın Nereye Koşuyor?* Istanbul: Milliyet Yayınları.

Çölaşan, Emin. 1988. 'Emin Çölaşan'ın Pazar Sohbeti'. *Hürriyet*, 13 March.

Committee to Protect Journalists. 2013. '2013 Prison Census: 211 Journalists Jailed in the World'. *Committee to Protect Journalists*, 1 December. Accessed 20 December 2017. https://cpj.org/reports/2013/12/2013-2/

Committee to Protect Journalists. 2017. 'Record Number of Journalists Jailed as Turkey, China, Egypt Pay Scan Price for Repression'. *Committee to Protect Journalists*, 13 December. Accessed 2 September 2017. https://cpj.org/reports/2017/12/journalists-prison-jail-record-number-turkey-china-egypt/

Committee to Protect Journalists. 2018. 'Hundreds of Journalists Jailed Globally Becomes the New Normal'. *Committee to Protect Journalists*, 13 December. Accessed 20 January 2021. https://cpj.org/reports/2018/12/journalists-jailed-imprisoned-turkey-china-egypt-saudi-arabia/

Conger, Jay A. 1998. 'Qualitative Research as the Cornerstone Methodology for Understanding Leadership'. *Leadership Quarterly* 9(1):107–22.

Corke, Susan, Andrew Finkel, David J. Kramer, Carla Anne Robbins and Nate Schenkkan. 2014. *Democracy in Crisis: Corruption, Media, and Power in Turkey*. Washington, DC: Freedom House.

Cornell, Svante E. 2016. 'Is Turkey Becoming a Banana Republic?' *Turkey Analyst*, 20 July. Date Accessed 12 December 2017. http://turkeyanalyst.org/publications/turkey-analyst-articles/item/561-is-turkey-becoming-a-banana-republic?.html

Coşkun, Orhan. 2018. 'Pro-Erdogan Group Agrees to Buy Owner of Hurriyet Newspaper, CNN Turk'. *Reuters*, 22 March. Accessed 2 May 2018. https://www.reuters.com/article/us-dogan-holding-m-a-demiroren/pro-erdogan-group-agrees-to-buy-owner-of-hurriyet-newspaper-cnn-turk-idUSKBN1GX23R.

Cross, William P., and Richard S. Katz. 2013. *The Challenges of Intra-Party Democracy*. Oxford: Oxford University Press.

Cumhuriyet. 2009. '1 Mayıs 1977'de Ne Oldu?' *Cumhuriyet*, 1 May. Accessed 6 July 2018. http://www.cumhuriyet.com.tr/haber/diger/59068/1_Mayis_1977_de_ne_oldu_.html#.

Cumhuriyet. 2014. 'Gül'den Tuhaf Onay'. *Cumhuriyet*, 26 February. Accessed 4 September 2018. http://www.cumhuriyet.com.tr/haber/turkiye/45399/Gul_den_tuhaf_onay.html#.

Cumhuriyet. 2016. '#4 Mayıs Saray Darbesi'. *Cumhuriyet*, 4 May. Accessed 4 May 2016. https://www.cumhuriyet.com.tr/haber/4-mayis-saray-darbesi-527169.

Cumhuriyet. 2017a. 'CHP'li Vekilden Çarpıcı İddia: AKP'li 800 Avukat Hakim Yapıldı'. *Cumhuriyet*, 26 April. Accessed 21 January 2018. http://www.cumhuriyet.com.tr/ haber/siyaset/728580/CHP_li_vekilden_carpici_iddia__AKP_li_800_avukat_ hakim_yapildi.html.

Cumhuriyet. 2017b. 'Yeni Müfredata Göre Hazırlanan Ders Kitapları AKP Broşürünü Aratmadı'. *Cumhuriyet*, 5 September. Accessed 5 August 2017. http://www. cumhuriyet.com.tr/haber/egitim/817296/Yeni_mufredata_gore_hazirlanan_ ders_kitaplari_AKP_brosurunu_aratmadi.html.

Dahl, Robert. 1982. *Dilemma of Pluralist Democracy: Autonomy versus Control*. New Haven: Yale University Press.

Davison, Roderic H. 1968. *Turkey*. Englewood Cliffs: Prentice-Hall/Spectrum Books.

Demirel, Tanel. 2003. 'The Turkish Military's Decision to Intervene: 12 September 1980'. *Armed Forces & Society* 29(2):253–80.

Demirtaş, Serkan. 2015. 'Erdoğan's Turkey No Longer Has Rule of Law'. *Hürriyet Daily News*, 9 May. Accessed 22 May 2015. http://www.hurriyetdailynews.com/ erdogans-turkey-no-longer-has-rule-of-law-.aspx?pageID=449&nID=82161& NewsCatID=429.

Denzin, Norman K., and Yvonna S. Lincoln. 2011. *The SAGE Handbook of Qualitative Research*. 3rd ed. Thousand Oaks: Sage Publications.

Diamond, Larry. 1997. 'Civil Society and the Development of Democracy'. *Working Paper, Instituto Juan March de Estudios e Investigaciones*.

Diamond, Larry. 1999. *Developing Democracy: Toward Consolidation*. Baltimore: Johns Hopkins University Press.

Diamond, Larry. 2008. *The Spirit of Democracy: The Struggle to Build Free Societies Throughout the World*. New York: Holt Paperbacks.

Diamond, Larry. 2018. 'The Liberal Democratic Order in Crisis'. *The American Interest*, 16 February. Accessed 16 February 2018. https://www.the-american-interest.com/2018/02/16/liberal-democratic-order-crisis/.

Diamond, Larry, Jonathan Hartlyn and Juan José Linz. 1990. 'Introduction: Politics Society and Democracy in Latin America'. In *Democracy in Developing Countries: Latin America*, edited by Larry Diamond, Jonathan Hartlyn, Juan José Linz and Semour Martin Lipset, 3–27. Boulder: Lynne Rienner.

Diamond, Larry, Juan J. Linz and Seymour Martin Lipset, eds. 1990. *Democracy in Developing Countries*. Boulder: Lynne Rienner.

Dodd, Clement Henry. 1969. *Politics and Government in Turkey*. Manchester: Manchester University Press.

Doğan, Yalçın. 2015. 'The Last Example of a Party-State'. *Hürriyet Daily News*, 29 May. Accessed 29 May 2015. https://www.hurriyetdailynews.com/opinion/ yalcin-dogan/the-last-example-of-a-party-state--83122

Doğan, Zülfikar. 1994. 'Gültekin'den Şikayet'. *Milliyet*, 2 February: 17. Accessed 22 October 2017. http://gazetearsivi.milliyet.com.tr/GununYayinlari/8sS4EKl onFtny7r3_x2F_ty2jw_x3D__x3D_

Dombey, Daniel. 2014. 'Court in Turkey Orders Release of Army Officers'. *Financial Times*, 20 June. Accessed 8 January 2018. https://www.ft.com/content/6a1d00e2-f7d1-11e3-baf5-00144feabdc0.

Donat, Yavuz. 1992. 'Yılmaz'a Göre "Çankaya'ya by-pass" Gerginlik Yaratır: "Özal'ı İndirmek Hayaldır"'. *Milliyet*, 2 January: 1. Accessed 2 November 2017. http://gazetearsivi.milliyet.com.tr/GununYayinlari/_x2B_G2aKNoTa_x2F_rGAIBoj_ x2B_oM_x2B_w_x3D__x3D_

Donat, Yavuz. 1997. *Özalizmin Son Yılları*. 1st ed. Ankara: Ümit Yayıncılık.

Dündar, Can, and Rıdvan Akar. 2015. *Karaoğlan*. 2nd ed. Istanbul: Can Sanat Yayınları.

Dunleavy, Patrick, and Brendan O'Leary. 1987. *Theories of the State: The Politics of Liberal Democracy*. Basingstoke: Macmillan Education.

DW. 2016. 'Turkey Closes Lawyers' Groups as Thousands Languish in Jail in Post-Coup Crackdown'. *Deutsche Welle*, 12 November. Accessed 18 January 2018. https://www.dw.com/en/turkey-closes-lawyers-groups-as-thousands-languish-in-jail-in-post-coup-crackdown/a-36366872

DW. 2018. 'Altan Kardeşler ve Ilıcak'a Müebbet'. *Deutsche Welle*, 16 February. Accessed 16 February 2018. https://www.dw.com/tr/altan-karde%C5%9Fler-ve-il%C4%B1caka-m%C3%BCebbet/a-42616633

Eissenstat, Howard. 2017. *Erdoğan as Autocrat: A Very Turkish Tragedy*. Washington, DC: Project on Middle East Democracy.

El-Khider, Ali Musa. 2000. 'Ten State-Owned Enterprises and Privatization in Turkey: Policy, Performance and Reform Experience, 1985–95'. In *State-Owned Enterprises in the Middle East and North Africa: Privatization, Performance and Reform*, edited by Merih Celâsun, 224–52. New York: Routledge.

Erem, Onur. 2017. 'Son 2 Yılda Torba Yasalardaki Rekor Artışın Arkasında Ne Var?' *BBC Türkçe*, 20 December. Accessed 9 July 2019. https://www.bbc.com/turkce/haberler-turkiye-42280958

Ergüder, Üstün. 1991. 'The Motherland Party, 1983–1989'. In *Political Parties and Democracy in Turkey*, edited by Metin Heper and Jacob M. Landau, 152–96. London and New York: I. B. Tauris.

Erim, Nihat. 1972. 'The Turkish Experience in the Light of Recent Developments'. *Middle East Journal* 26(3):245–52.

Erişen, Cengiz, and Paul Kubicek. 2016. 'Democratic Consolidation in Turkey'. In *Democratic Consolidation in Turkey: Micro and Macro Challenges*, edited by Cengiz Erişen and Paul Kubicek, 1–17. New York: Routledge.

Esen, Berk. 2015. 'Ergun Özbudun, Party Politics and Social Cleavages in Turkey'. *International Journal of Middle East Studies* 47(1):207–10.

Esen, Berk, and Şebnem Gümüşcü. 2016. 'Rising Competitive Authoritarianism in Turkey'. *Third World Quarterly* 37(9):1581–1606. doi: 10.1080/01436597. 2015.1135732.

Esmer, Yılmaz. 2010. 'Elite and Mass Values: Religion as an Intervening Factor'. In *Democracy under Scrutiny: Elites, Citizens, Cultures*, edited by Ursula J. Van Beek, 221–40. Opladen and Farming Hill, MI: Barbara Budrich Publishers.

Esmer, Yılmaz. 2012. *Türkiye Değerler Atlası 2012*. Istanbul: Bahçeşehir Üniversitesi Yayınları.

Esmer, Yılmaz. 2015. 'Economic Crisis and Political Polarization: A Challenge to Civic Culture?' *Taiwan Journal of Democracy: An International Journal of Politics* 11(1):129–46.

European Commission. 2019. *Turkey Report: Communication on EU Enlargement Policy*. Brussels: European Commission.

Ezikoğlu, Çağlar. 2015. 'Tasfiyenin Şifresi Mi Tarihin Tekerrürü Mü?' *Diken*, 9 April. Accessed 25 January 2018. http://www.diken.com.tr/tasfiyenin–sifresi–mi–tarihin–tekerruru–mu/.

FOX Türk. 2019. *Fatih Portakal ile FOX Ana Haber*, 3 October. Accessed 3 October 2019. https://www.youtube.com/watch?v=nCz96TMYB70

Frankel, Norman. 1991. 'Conversations in Istanbul: An Interview with Bulent Ecevit'. *Political Communication* 8:63–78.

Freedom House. 2014. *Freedom of the Press 2014: Turkey*. Washington, DC: Freedom House.

Freedom House. 2015. *Freedom of the Press 2015: Turkey*. Washington, DC: Freedom House.

Freedom House. 2016. *Freedom of the Press 2016: Turkey*. Washington, DC: Freedom House.

Freedom House. 2017. *Freedom of the Press 2017: Turkey*. Washington, DC: Freedom House.

Freedom House. 2018a. *Freedom in the World: Turkey*. Washington, DC: Freedom House.

Freedom House. 2018b. 'Turkey: Obey Constitutional Court Ruling to Release Imprisoned Journalists'. *Freedom House*, 12 January. Accessed 18 January 2018. https://freedomhouse.org/article/turkey-obey-constitutional-court-ruling-release-imprisoned-journalists.

Frey, Frederick W. 1975. 'Patterns of Elite Politics in Turkey'. In *Political Elites in the Middle East*, edited by George Lenczowski, 41–82. Washington, DC: American Enterprise Institute for Public Policy Research.

Gage, Nicholas. 1979. 'Roughhouse Politics Help Keep Turkey on its Knees'. *New York Times*, 27 May, E2. Accessed 10 September 2016. https://www.nytimes.com/1979/05/27/archives/roughhouse-politics-help-keep-turkey-on-its-knees.html

Gall, Carlotta. 2018. 'Erdoğan's Next Target as He Restricts Turkey's Democracy: The Internet'. *New York Time*, 4 March. Accessed 14 September 2018. https://www.nytimes.com/2018/03/04/world/europe/turkey-erdogan-internet-law-restrictions.html

Gall, Carlotta. 2019. 'Erdoğan's Purges Leave Turkey's Justice System Reeling'. *The New York Times*, 21 June. Accessed 23 June 2019. https://www.nytimes.com/2019/06/21/world/asia/erdogan-turkey-courts-judiciary-justice.html.

Garretón Merino, Manuel A. 2003. *Incomplete Democracy: Political Democratization in Chile and Latin America*, translated by R. Kelly Washbourne and Gregory Horvath. Chapel Hill: University of North Carolina Press.

Gaytancıoğlu, Kaan. 2014. *Politik Liderlik ve Bülent Ecevit*. Ankara: Paradigma Kitabevi Yayınları.

Genç, Kaya. 2016. *Under the Shadow: Rage and Revolution in Modern Turkey*. London and New York: I. B. Tauris.

Geyikçi, Şebnem Y. 2011. 'The Impact of Parties and Party Systems on Democratic Consolidation: The Case of Turkey'. Working Paper. University of Essex.

Gönenç, Levent. 2008. 'Presidential Elements in Government: Turkey'. *European Constitutional Law Review* 4(3):488–523. doi: 10.1017/S1574019608004884.

Görener, Aylin Ş , and Meltem Ş Ucal. 2011. 'The Personality and Leadership Style of Recep Tayyip Erdoğan: Implications for Turkish Foreign Policy'. *Turkish Studies* 12(3):357–81.

Gourisse, Benjamin. 2013. 'Party Penetration of the State: The Nationalist Action Party in the Late 1970s'. In *Negotiating Political Power in Turkey: Breaking Up the Party*, edited by Elise Massicard and Nicole Watts, 118–39. London and New York: Routledge.

Göymen, Korel. 2016. 'Personal Interview with Author'. 12 April.

GRECO. 2018. *Corruption Prevention in Respect of Members of Parliament, Judges and Prosecutors: Compliance Report Turkey*. Strasburg: The Council of Europe, Group of States against Corruption.

Greenslade, Roy. 2015. 'Turkish Newspaper Columnist Fired over Tweet Critical of Erdoğan'. *The Guardian*, 27 July. Accessed 20 December 2017. https://www.theguardian.com/media/greenslade/2015/jul/27/turkish-newspaper-columnist-fired-over-tweet-critical-of-erdogan.

GSNSC, General Secretariat of the National Security Council. 1982. *12 September in Turkey: Before and After*. Ankara: Ongün Kardeşler Printing House.

Guardian. 2015. 'Erdoğan Holds First Cabinet Meeting as Turkish President'. *The Guardian*, 19 January. Accessed 12 August 2018. https://www.theguardian. com/world/2015/jan/19/erdogan-first-cabinet-meeting-turkish-president

Gülsevin, Filiz. 2009. 'Demokrat Parti Döneminde Nadir Nadi Gazeteciliği'. Unpubl. Master's Thesis, Atatürk İlkeleri ve İnkılap Tarihi Enstitüsü, Dokuz Eylül Üniversitesi.

Gültekin, Levent. 2015. 'AK Parti'deki Tasfiyenin Şifresi'. *Diken*, 8 April. Accessed 25 January 2018. http://www.diken.com.tr/ak–partideki–tasfiyenin–sifresi/.

Güneş-Ayata, Ayşe. 2002. 'The Republican People's Party'. In *Political Parties in Turkey*, edited by Barry M. Rubin and Metin Heper. London: Routledge.

Gunter, Michael M. 1989. 'Political Instability in Turkey during the 1970s'. *Journal of Conflict Studies* 9(1):63–77.

Gürakar, Esra Çeviker. 2016. *Politics of Favoritism in Public Procurement in Turkey*. New York: Palgrave Macmillan.

Gürcan, Metin. 2018. 'Erdogan Takes Total Control of Turkish Defense Industry'. *Al-Monitor: Turkey Pulse*, 5 January. Accessed 8 January 2018. https://www. al-monitor.com/pulse/originals/2018/01/turkey-erdogan-assumes-turkish-defense-industry.print.html.

Gürsel, Kadri. 2013. 'Crackdown Shatters AKP "Anti-Corruption" taboo'. *Al-Monitor: Turkey Pulse*, 19 December. Accessed 2 January 2018. https://www.al-monitor. com/pulse/originals/2013/12/corruption-crackdown-damages-akp.html.

Gürsel, Kadri. 2015. 'Davutoğlu'nun Trajedisi'. *Al-Monitor: Turkey Pulse*, 12 February. Accessed 21 January 2018. https://www.al-monitor.com/pulse/tr/ originals/2015/02/turkey-davutoglu-tragedy-erdogan-elections.html.

HaberTürk. 2019. 'Milletvekilleriyle Buluşmada Züğürt Ağa Diyaloğu!' *HaberTürk*, 11 July. Accessed 11 July 2019. https://www.haberturk.com/milletvekilleriyle-bulusmada-zugurt-aga-diyalogu-2503326

Hale, William. 1994. *Turkish Military and Politics*. London: Routledge.

Hale, William M. 2013. *Turkish Foreign Policy since 1774*. 3rd ed. New York: Routledge.

Hale, William, and Ergun Özbudun. 2010. *Islamism, Democracy and Liberalism in Turkey: The Case of the AKP*. New York: Routledge.

Hansen, Suzy. 2017. 'State of Sleaze: Erdoğan's Authoritarian Hustle'. *The Baffler*, 37. December: 112–19.

Hansen, Suzy. 2019. 'The Era of People Like You is Over: How Turkey Purged Its Intellectuals'. *The New York Times*, 24 July. Accessed 25 July 2019. https://www. nytimes.com/2019/07/24/magazine/the-era-of-people-like-you-is-over-how-turkey-purged-its-intellectuals.html.

Haque, Mohammad Zahirul. 1996. 'Turkey's New Government'. *Economic Review*, August: 42.

Harris, George. 2002. 'Celal Bayar: Conspiratorial Democrat'. In *Political Leaders and Democracy in Turkey*, edited by Metin Heper and Sabri Sayarı, 45–63. Lanham: Lexington Books.

Haugom, Lars. 2017. 'An Uncertain Future for the Turkish Armed Forces'. *Turkey Analyst*, 26 September. Accessed 27 September 2017. http://www.turkeyanalyst. org/publications/turkey-analyst-articles/item/588-an-uncertain-future-for-the-turkish-armed-forces.html

Heper, Metin. 1989. 'Motherland Party Governments and Bureaucracy in Turkey, 1983–1988'. *Governance* 2(4):460–71.

Heper, Metin. 1990a. 'The State and Debureaucratization: The Case of Turkey'. *International Social Science Journal* 42(4):605–15.

Heper, Metin. 1990b. 'The State, Political Party and Society in Post-1983 Turkey'. *Government and Opposition* 25(3):321–33.

Heper, Metin. 1992a. 'Consolidating Turkish Democracy'. *Journal of Democracy* 3(2):105–17.

Heper, Metin. 1992b. 'The Strong State as a Problem for the Consolidation of Democracy Turkey and Germany Compared'. *Comparative Political Studies* 25(2):169–94.

Heper, Metin. 1998. *İsmet İnönü: The Making of a Turkish Statesman*. Leiden: Brill.

Heper, Metin. 2000. 'The Ottoman Legacy and Turkish Politics'. *Journal of International Affairs* 54(1):63–82.

Heper, Metin. 2001. 'Turkey: Yesterday, Today and Tomorrow'. *Southeast European and Black Sea Studies* 1(3):1–19.

Heper, Metin. 2002a. 'Conclusion'. In *Political Leaders and Democracy in Turkey*, edited by Metin Heper and Sabri Sayarı, 217–38. Lanham: Lexington Books.

Heper, Metin. 2002b. 'Conclusion: The Consolidation of Democracy versus Democratization in Turkey'. *Turkish Studies* 3(1):138–46.

Heper, Metin. 2005. 'The Justice and Development Party Government and the Military in Turkey'. *Turkish Studies* 6(2):215–31.

Heper, Metin. 2007. *The State and Kurds in Turkey: The Question of Assimilation*. New York: Palgrave Macmillan.

Heper, Metin. 2013. 'Islam, Conservatism, and Democracy in Turkey: Comparing Turgut Özal and Recep Tayyip Erdoğan'. *Insight Turkey* 15(2):141–56.

Heper, Metin, and E. Fuat Keyman. 1998. 'Double-Faced State: Political Patronage and the Consolidation of Democracy in Turkey'. *Middle Eastern Studies* 34(4):259–77.

Heper, Metin, and Sabri Sayarı. 2002. *Political Leaders and Democracy in Turkey*. Lanham: Lexington Books.

Higley, John, and Michael G. Burton. 2006. *Elite Foundations of Liberal Democracy*. Lanham: Rowman & Littlefield.

Higley, John, and Michael G. Burton. 2012. 'The Elite Variable in Democratic Transitions and Breakdowns [1989]'. *Historical Social Research/Historische Sozialforschung* 37(1):245–68.

Higley, John, and Richard Gunther. 1992. *Elites and Democratic Consolidation in Latin America and Southern Europe*: Cambridge and New York: Cambridge University Press.

Hong, Joanna. 2018. 'Erdogan's Turkey: The World's Biggest Prison for Journalists | Opinion'. *Newsweek*, 18 September. Accessed 18 September 2018. https://www.newsweek.com/erdogans-turkey-worlds-biggest-prison-journalists-opinion-1125718

Human Rights Watch. 1997. *Turkey: Torture and Mistreatment in Pre-Trial Detention by Anti-Terror Police* 9(4). New York: Human Rights Watch.

Human Rights Watch. 2014. 'Turkey: Authoritarian Drift Threatens Rights'. *Human Rights Watch*, 29 September. Accessed 5 April 2015. https://www.hrw.org/news/2014/09/29/turkey-authoritarian-drift-threatens-rights

Human Rights Watch. 2015. 'Turkey: Authoritarian Drift Undermines Rights'. *Human Rights Watch*, 29 January. Accessed 5 April 2015. https://www.hrw.org/news/2015/01/29/turkey-authoritarian-drift-undermines-rights

Human Rights Watch. 2017a. 'Turkey: Alarming Deterioration of Rights'. *Human Rights Watch*, 12 January. Accessed 21 January 2018. https://www.hrw.org/news/2017/01/12/turkey-alarming-deterioration-rights

Human Rights Watch. 2017b. 'Turkey: Crackdown on Kurdish Ahead of Referendum'. *Human Rights Watch*, 20 March. 11 January 2018. https://www.hrw.org/news/2017/03/20/turkey-crackdown-kurdish-opposition

Human Rights Watch. 2018. 'Turkey: Normalizing the State of Emergency'. *Human Rights Watch*, 20 July. Accessed 17 August 2018. https://www.hrw.org/news/2018/07/20/turkey-normalizing-state-emergency

Human Rights Watch. 2022. 'Turkey: Life Sentence for Rights Defender Osman Kavala'. *Human Rights Watch*, 26 April. Accesssed 26 April 2022. https://www.hrw.org/news/2022/04/26/turkey-life-sentence-rights-defender-osman-kavala

Huntington, Samuel P. 1968. *Political Order in Changing Societies*. New Haven: Yale University.

Hürriyet. 2001. 'Fazilet Partisi Kapatıldı'. *Hürriyet*, 22 June. Accessed 23 September 2018. https://www.hurriyet.com.tr/gundem/fazilet-partisi-kapatildi-39250176

Hürriyet. 2013a. 'Turkey Looks to Germany in Improving Controversial Secret Witness System'. *Hürriyet Daily News*, 3 October. Accessed 12 July 2019. https://www.hurriyetdailynews.com/turkey-looks-to-germany-in-improving-controversial-secret-witness-system--55645

Hürriyet. 2013b. 'Turkish Court of Accounts Won't Audit Public Spending for Another Three Years: Report'. *Hürriyet Daily News*, 13 December. Accessed 18 January 2018. http://www.hurriyetdailynews.com/turkish-court-of-accounts-wont-audit-public-spending-for-another-three-years-report-59489.

Hürriyet. 2013c. 'Turkish President Gül Approves Controversial Bill Restricting Alcohol'. *Hürriyet Daily News*, 10 June. Accessed 1 February 2018. http://www.hurriyetdailynews.com/turkish-president-gul-approves-controversial-bill-restricting-alcohol-48573.

Hürriyet. 2014a. 'Key Regulations Become Battleground as Gov't Moves to Control Judiciary'. *Hürriyet Daily News*, 13 December. Accessed 14 December 2014. http://www.hurriyetdailynews.com/key-regulations-become-battleground-as-govt-moves-to-control-judiciary-75586.

Hürriyet. 2014b. 'President Erdoğan to Chair Cabinet in 2015'. *Hürriyet Daily News*, 11 December. Accessed 19 January 2018. http://www.hurriyetdailynews.com/president-erdogan-to-chair-cabinet-in-2015-75519.

Hürriyet. 2014c. 'Public Broadcaster TRT at Center of Contention during Campaign'. *Hürriyet Daily News*, 10 August. Accessed 20 December 2017. http://www.hurriyetdailynews.com/public-broadcaster-trt-at-center-of-contention-during-campaign-70204.

Hürriyet. 2015a. '236 Acquitted in Balyoz Coup Case'. *Hürriyet Daily News*, 31 March. Accessed 6 January 2018. http://www.hurriyetdailynews.com/236-acquitted-in-balyoz-coup-case-80408.

Hürriyet. 2015b. 'AKP Suggests Presidential System for Turkey in Line with Erdoğan's Insistence'. *Hürriyet Daily News*, 15 April. Accessed 16 April 2015. http://www.hurriyetdailynews.com/akp-suggests-presidential-system-for-turkey-in-line-with-erdogans-insistence--81092.

Hürriyet. 2015c. 'Bülent Tezcan'dan CHP Reklamını Yayınlamayan TRT'ye Tepki'. *Hürriyet*, 4 April. Accessed 20 December 2017. http://www.hurriyet.com.tr/bulent-tezcandan-chp-reklamini-yayinlamayan-trtye-tepki-28709774.

Hürriyet. 2015d. 'President Erdoğan Puts his Stamp on AKP Congress'. *Hürriyet Daily News*, 14 September. Accessed 14 September 2015. http://www.hurriyetdailynews.com/president-erdogan-puts-his-stamp-on-akp-congress-88432.

Hürriyet. 2015e. 'Prosecutors, Judge of Turkey's Massive Graft Probe Dismissed from Profession'. *Hürriyet Daily News*, 12 May. Accessed 13 May 2015. http://www.hurriyetdailynews.com/prosecutors-judge-of-turkeys-massive-graft-probe-dismissed-from-profession-82294.

Hürriyet. 2015f. 'Secret Fund Spending Doubles in May, Erdoğan's Rallies May Be Covered by State Money: Report'. *Hürriyet Daily News*, 16 June. Accessed 17 June 2015. http://www.hurriyetdailynews.com/secret-fund-spending-doubles-in-may-erdogans-rallies-may-be-covered-by-state-money-report-84076.

Hürriyet. 2015g. 'Turkish PM Davutoğlu Accuses Court of Taking Orders from US-based Cleric Gülen'. *Hürriyet Daily News*, 26 April. Accessed 27 April 2015. http://www.hurriyetdailynews.com/turkish-pm-davutoglu-accuses-court-of-taking-orders-from-us-based-cleric-gulen--81572.

Hürriyet. 2016. 'Turkey's Ergenekon Plot Case Overturned by Top Court of Appeals'. *Hürriyet Daily News*, 21 April. Accessed 6 January 2018. http://www.hurriyetdailynews.com/turkeys-ergenekon-plot-case-overturned-by-top-court-of-appeals--98113.

Hürriyet. 2017. 'European Commission Urges Turkey to Launch "Transparent Investigations" into Referendum Results'. *Hürriyet Daily News*, 18 April. Accessed 18 April 2017. http://www.hurriyetdailynews.com/european-commission-urges-turkey-to-launch-transparent-investigations-into-referendum-results-112153.

Hürriyet. 2018a. 'Right to a Fair Trial is at Risk in Turkey: Constitutional Court Report'. *Hürriyet Daily News*, 14 February. Accessed 14 February 2018. http://www.hurriyetdailynews.com/right-to-a-fair-trial-is-at-risk-in-turkey-constitutional-court-report-127302.

Hürriyet. 2018b. 'Turkish Government Blasts Constitutional Court's Ruling on Jailed Journalists'. *Hürriyet Daily News*, 12 January. Accessed 12 January 2018. http://www.hurriyetdailynews.com/turkeys-top-court-rules-to-release-two-jailed-journalists-local-courts-refuse-125604.

Hürriyet. 2018c. 'Turkish Prosecutors Say "No Concrete Evidence of Ergenekon's Presence"'. *Hürriyet Daily News*, 1 December. Accessed 2 December 2018. http://www.hurriyetdailynews.com/turkish-prosecutors-say-no-concrete-evidence-of-ergenekons-presence-139353.

Hürtaş, Sibel. 2016. 'AKP Targets Judicial Independence in Latest Post-Coup Takedown'. *Al-Monitor: Turkey Pulse*, 9 November. Accessed 21 January 2018. http://www.al-monitor.com/pulse/originals/2016/11/turkey-silenced-critical-judges.html#ixzz54yd8eAAd.

Hürtaş, Sibel. 2017a. 'The Collapse of Turkish Academia'. *Al-Monitor: Turkey Purge*, 13 February. Accessed 21 January 2018. https://www.al-monitor.com/pulse/originals/2017/02/turkey-academics-purges-collapse-of-academia.html.

Hürtaş, Sibel. 2017b. 'Turkish Lawyers Join Clients in Prison'. *Al-Monitor: Turkey Pulse*, 22 November. Accessed 21 January 2018. https://www.al-monitor.com/pulse/originals/2017/11/turkey-lawyers-lands-in-prison.html.

İdiz, Semih. 2014. 'Erdoğan's Presidential Rivals Fight for Airtime'. *Al-Monitor: Turkey Pulse*, 5 August. Accessed 20 December 2017. https://www.al-monitor.com/pulse/originals/2014/08/idiz-presidential-elections-erdogan-fair-equal-trt-osce-akp.html.

İnal, Tuba 2015. 'Gender and Political Leadership: Turkish Experience'. *Leadership* 13(5):615–38. doi:10.1177/1742715015606512.

İnsan Hakları Ortak Platformu. 2018. *21 July 2016–20 March 2018 State of Emergency in Turkey*. Ankara: İnsan Hakları Ortak Platformu.

Isakhan, Benjamin. 2012. 'Introduction: The Complex and Contested History of Democracy'. In *The Edinburgh Companion to the History of Democracy*, edited by Benjamin Isakhan and Stephen Stockwell, 1–26. Edinburgh: Edinburgh University Press.

Işıklı, Alpaslan. 1987. 'Wage Labor and Unionization'. In *Turkey in Transition: New Perspectives*, edited by Irvin Cemil Schick and Ertugrul Ahmet Tonak, 309–32. New York: Oxford University Press.

İşleyen, Ercüment. 1999. 'Akşener: Çiller Yalancı, Güvenilmez'. *Milliyet*, 27 July: 20. Accessed 22 November 2017. https://www.milliyet.com.tr/siyaset/aksener-ciller-yalanci-guvenilmez-5243247

Jackson, James O., and Mehmet Ali Kislali. 1996. 'A Blow to Secularism'. *Time International (South Pacific Edition)* 2:16.

Jenkins, Gareth H. 2007. 'AKP Forming Closer Links with the Gulen Movemen'. *Eurasia Daily Monitor* 4: 217.

Jenkins, Gareth H. 2009a. 'Between Fact and Fantasy: Turkey's Ergenekon Investigation'. *Silk Road Paper*. Washington, DC: Central Asia-Caucasus Institute & Silk Road Studies Program.

Jenkins, Gareth H. 2009b. 'The Politics of Personality: Erdogan's Irascible Authoritarianism'. *Turkey Analyst* 2(3). Accessed 17 December 2017. https://www.turkeyanalyst.org/publications/turkey-analyst-articles/item/154-the-politics-of-personality-erdogans-irascible-authoritarianism.html

Jenkins, Gareth H. 2010. 'Waiting for Başbuğ: The Aftermath of the Sledgehammer Operation Detentions'. *Turkey Analyst* 3(4). Accessed 6 September 2017.

https://www.turkeyanalyst.org/publications/turkey-analyst-articles/item/202-waiting-for-ba%C5%9Fbu%C4%9F-the-aftermath-of-the-sledgehammer-operation-detentions.html

Jenkins, Gareth H. 2013. 'Between a Rock and a Hard Place: Turkey's Internal Power Struggle'. *Turkey Analyst* 6(3). Accessed 6 September 2017. http://www.turkey-analyst.org/publications/turkey-analyst-articles/item/26-between-a-rock-and-a-hard-place-turkeys-internal-power-struggle.html

Jenkins, Gareth H. 2014a. 'The Balyoz Retrial and the Changing Politics of Turkish Justice'. *Turkey Analyst* 7(12). Accessed 15 December 2017. https://www.turkeyanalyst.org/publications/turkey-analyst-articles/item/331-the-balyoz-retrial-and-the-changing-politics-of-turkish-justice.html

Jenkins, Gareth H. 2014b. 'The Ergenekon Releases and Prospects fro the Rule of Law in Turkey'. *Turkey Analyst* 7(5). Accessed 15 December 2017. https://www.turkeyanalyst.org/publications/turkey-analyst-articles/item/96-the-ergenekon-releases-and-prospects-for-the-rule-of-law-in-turkey.html

Jenkins, Gareth H. 2014c. 'Falling Facades: The Gülen Movement and Turkey's Escalating Power Struggle'. *Turkey Analyst* 7(1). Accessed 22 January 2018. http://turkeyanalyst.org/publications/turkey-analyst-articles/item/81

Jenkins, Gareth H. 2014d. 'Narrative Veils: Erdogan, the AKP and the Gulenist Arrests'. *Turkey Analyst* 7(23). Accessed 15 December 2017. http://www.turkeyanalyst.org/publications/turkey-analyst-articles/item/365-narrative-veils-erdogan-the-akp-and-the-

Jenkins, Gareth H. 2016a. 'Post-Putsch Narratives and Turkey's Curious Coup'. *Turkey Analyst*, 22 July. Accessed 12 December 2017. http://turkeyanalyst.org/publications/turkey-analyst-articles/item/562

Jenkins, Gareth H. 2016b. 'Power over Policy: Erdoğan's Overthrow of Davutoğlu'. *Turkey Analyst*, 11 May. Accessed 15 December 2017. https://www.turkey-analyst.org/publications/turkey-analyst-articles/item/541-power-over-policy-erdo%C4%9Fan%E2%80%99s-overthrow-of-davuto%C4%9Flu.html

Kaboğlu, İbrahim Ö. 2018. '"Beka" Yasaları Mı, "Yağma" Yasaları Mı?' *BirGün*, 6 December. Accessed 7 December 2018. https://www.birgun.net/haber/beka-yasalari-mi-yagma-yasalari-mi-239232

Kalaycıoğlu, Ersin. 1990. 'Cyclical Development, Redesign and Nascent Institutionalization of a Legislative System'. In *Parliament and Democratic Consolidation in Southern Europe: Greece, Italy, Portugal, Spain, and Turkey*, edited by Ulrike Liebert and Maurizio Cotta, 184–222. London and New York: Pinter Publishers.

Kalaycıoğlu, Ersin. 2002a. 'Elections and Governance'. In *Politics, Parties, and Elections in Turkey*, edited by Sabri Sayarı and Yılmaz Esmer, 55–72. Boulder: Lynne Rienner.

Kalaycıoğlu, Ersin. 2002b. 'The Motherland Party: The Challenge of Institutionalization in a Charismatic Leader Party'. *Turkish Studies* 3(1):41–61.

Kalaycıoğlu, Ersin. 2012. 'Kulturkampf in Turkey: The Constitutional Referendum of 12 September 2010'. *South European Society and Politics* 17(1):1–22.

Kalaycıoğlu, Ersin. 2013. 'Turkish Party System: Leaders, Vote and Institutionalization'. *Southeast European and Black Sea Studies* 13(4):483–502.

Kalaycıoğlu, Ersin. 2016. 'Personal Interview with the Author'. 19 April.

Kamer, Hatice. 2018. 'HEP'ten HDP'ye 28 Yılda Yaşananlar'. *BBC.com*, 11 February. Accessed 4 March 2018. https://www.bbc.com/turkce/haberler-turkiye-43019313

Kamrava, Mehran. 1998. 'Pseudo-Democratic Politics and Populist Possibilities: The Rise and Demise of Turkey's Refah Party'. *British Journal of Middle Eastern Studies* 25(2):275–301.

Karaveli, Halil M. 2014. 'Is Authoritarianism Forever in Turkey?' *Turkey Analyst* 7(4). Accessed 15 December 2017. http://www.turkeyanalyst.org/publications/turkey-analyst-articles/item/90-is-authoritarianism-forever-in-turkey

Karaveli, Halil M. 2017. 'Turkey's Authoritarian Legacy'. *Cairo Review of Global Affairs* 25 (Spring):62–71.

Karayalçın, Murat. 2016. 'Personal Interview with Author'. 4 May.

Karpat, Kemal H. 1972. 'Political Developments in Turkey, 1950–70'. *Middle Eastern Studies* 8(3):349–76.

Karpat, Kemal H. 2011. 'Actors and Issues in Turkish Politics, 1950–1960: Prototypes and Stereotypes'. *International Journal of Turkish Studies* 17(1–2):115–57.

Kars Kaynar, Ayşegül. 2017. 'Making of Military Tutelage in Turkey: The National Security Council in the 1961 and 1982 Constitutions'. *Turkish Studies* 19:451–81. doi: 10.1080/14683849.2017.1387055.

Kaya, Ayşe Elif. 2010. 'Demokrat Parti Döneminde Basın-İktidar İlişkileri'. *İstanbul Üniversitesi İletişim Fakültesi Hakemli Dergisi* 1(39):93–118.

Kaya, M. Kemal, and Svante E. Cornell. 2012. 'The Big Split: The Differences That Led Erdogan and the Gulen Movement to Part Ways ' *Turkey Analyst* 5(5). Accessed 8 January 2018. https://www.turkeyanalyst.org/publications/turkey-analyst-articles/item/296-the-big-split-the-differences-that-led-erdogan-and-the-gulen-movement-to-part-ways.html

Kaya, M. K. 2015a. 'Candidate Lists for the Election to Parliament Display Worrying Fault Lines'. *Turkey Analyst* 8(8). Accessed 15 December 2017. http://www.

turkeyanalyst.org/publications/turkey-analyst-articles/item/388-candidate-lists-for-the-election-to-parliament-display-worrying-fault-lines.html

Kaya, M. K. 2015b. 'The AKP's 5th Congress Showed That the Party is Deeply Split'. *Turkey Analyst*, 23 September. Accessed 9 December 2017. https://www.turkeyanalyst.org/publications/turkey-analyst-articles/item/456-the-akp%E2%80%99s-5th-congress-showed-that-the-party-is-deeply-split.html

Kayaalp, Ebru. 2015. *Remaking Politics, Markets, and Citizens in Turkey: Governing through Smoke, Suspensions: Contemporary Middle Eastern and Islamicate Thought*. London and New York: Bloomsbury.

Keane, John. 1992. 'Democracy and the Media – Without Foundations'. *Political Studies* 40(1):116–29. doi: 10.1111/j.1467-9248.1992.tb01816.x.

Keane, John. 1999. 'CSD Interview: Keeping Tabs on Power'. *CSD Bulletin* 7(1):10–12. Accessed 20 February 2018. https://www.johnkeane.net/keeping-tabs-on-power-3/

Keane, John. 2009. 'Life after Political Death: The Fate of Leaders after Leaving High Office'. In *Dispersed Democratic Leadership: Origins, Dyanmics, and Implications*, edited by John Kane, Haig Patapan and Paul 't Hart, 279–98. Oxford and New York: Oxford University Press.

Keane, John. 2020. *The New Despotism*. Cambridge, MA: Harvard University Press.

Kepel, Gilles. 2006. *Jihad: The Trail of Political Islam*. London and New York: I. B. Tauris.

Kesgin, Barış. 2012. 'Tansu Çiller's Leadership Traits and Foreign Policy'. *Perception* 17(3):29–50.

Kılıç, Ali Aslan. 2015. 'Broken Laws, Suspension of Principles of Democracy Mark Past Legislative Term'. *Today's Zaman*, 5 April. Accessed 20 May 2015. http://www.todayszaman.com/anasayfa_broken-laws-suspension-of-principles-of-democracy-mark-past-legislative-term_377063.html.

Kingsley, Patrick. 2018. 'As West Fears the Rise of Autocrats, Hungary Shows What's Possible'. *The New York Times*, 10 February. Accessed 10 February 2018. https://www.nytimes.com/2018/02/10/world/europe/hungary-orban-democracy-far-right.html?smid=tw–nytimes&smtyp=cur.

Kınıklıoğlu, Suat. 2000. 'Bülent Ecevit: The Transformation of a Politician'. *Turkish Studies* 1(2):1–20.

Kınıklıoğlu, Suat. 2002. 'The Democratic Left Party: Kapıkulu Politics Par Excellence'. In *Political Parties in Turkey*, edited by Barry Rubin and Metin Heper, 4–24. London: Cass.

Kınıklıoğlu, Suat. 2016. 'Personal Interview with Author'. 6 May.

Kinzer, Stephen. 1997a. 'Once the Hope of Secular Turks, Ex-Leader Is Now Widely Reviled'. *The New York Times*, 6 April. Accessed 16 August 2016. https://www.

nytimes.com/1997/04/06/world/once-the-hope-of-secular-turks-ex-leader-is-now-widely-reviled.html

Kinzer, Stephen. 1997b. 'Turkish Ex-Premier's Comeback Hits a Snag'. *The New York Times*, 2 July. Accessed 16 August 2016. https://www.nytimes.com/1997/07/02/world/turkish-ex-premier-s-comeback-hits-a-snag.html

Kirchheimer, Otto. 1965. 'Confining Conditions and Revolutionary Breakthroughs'. *American Political Science Review* 59(4):964–74.

Kirişci, Kemal. 2018. 'Erdoğan's War on the West Turns inward – on Turkish Academia'. *Brookings Institute*. 22 January. Accessed 22 January 2018. https://www.brookings.edu/blog/order-from-chaos/2018/01/22/erdogans-war-on-the-west-turns-inward-on-turkish-academia/

Koru, Selim. 2021. 'The Institutional Structure of "New Turkey"'. *Black Sea Strategy Papers*. Philadelphia: Foreign Policy Research Institute.

Kumbaracıbaşı, Arda Can. 2016. 'Party Institutionalization and Organizational Problems: The Case of Turkey'. 10th ECPR General Conference, Charles University, Prague, 7–10 September.

Kumbaracıbaşı, Onur. 2016. 'Personal Interview with Author'. 12 April.

Kumcu, Ercan. 2003. '32 Sayılı Karar Gidiyor'. *Hürriyet*, 21 October. Accessed 29 April 2018. http://www.hurriyet.com.tr/32-sayili-karar-gidiyor-178428.

LA Times. 1989. 'Turkish Leader, Accused of Nepotism, Fires Brother, Cousin in Cabinet Shift'. *Los Angeles Times*, 1 April. Accessed 7 March 2015. https://www.latimes.com/archives/la-xpm-1989-04-01-mn-803-story.html

Lagendijk, Joost. 2012. 'Turkey's Accession to the European Union and the Role of the Justice and Development Party'. In *Democracy, Islam, and Secularism in Turkey*, edited by Ahmet T. Kuru and Alfred Stepan, 166–88. New York: Columbia University Press.

Lancaster, Caroline. 2014. 'The Iron Law of Erdogan: The Decay from Intra-Party Democracy to Personalistic Rule'. *Third World Quarterly* 35(9):1672–90. doi: 10.1080/01436597.2014.970866.

Landau, Jacob M. 1970. 'Turkey From Election to Election'. *World Today* 26(4):156–66.

Lasswell, Harold D. 1958. *Politics: Who Gets What, When, How*. New York: Meridian Books.

Lendvai, Paul. 2017. *Orbán: Hungary's Strongman*. Oxford: Oxford University Press.

Letsch, Constanze. 2013. 'Turkish Ministers' Sons Arrested in Corruption and Bribery Investigation'. *The Guardian*, 18 December. Accessed 2 January 2018. https://www.theguardian.com/world/2013/dec/17/turkish-ministers-sons-arrested-corruption-investigation.

Levi, Avner. 1991. 'The Justice Party, 1961–1980'. In *Political Parties and Democracy in Turkey*, edited by Metin Heper and Jacob M. Landau, 134–51. London and New York: I. B. Tauris.

Levitsky, Steve, and Daniel Ziblatt. 2018a. 'How Wobbly is Our Democracy?' *New York Times*, 27 April. Accessed 3 May 2018. https://www.nytimes.com/2018/01/27/opinion/sunday/democracy-polarization.html

Levitsky, Steve, and Daniel Ziblatt. 2018b. *How Democracies Die: What History Reveals About Our Future*. London: Penguin Books

Linz, Juan J. 1990. 'Transitions to Democracy'. *Washington Quarterly* 13(3):143–64.

Linz, Juan J, and Alfred Stepan. 1989. 'Political Crafting of Democratic Consolidation or Destruction: European and South American Comparisons'. In *Democracy in the Americas: Stopping the Pendulum*, edited by Robert A. Pastor, 41–61. New York: Holmes & Meier.

Linz, Juan J., and Alfred C. Stepan. 1996. 'Toward Consolidated Democracies'. *Journal of Democracy* 7(2):14–33.

Lowry, Heath 2000. 'Betwixt and Between: Turkey's Political Structure on the Cusp of the Twenty-First Century'. In *Turkey's Transformation and American Policy*, edited by Morton Abramowitz, 23–60. New York: Century Foundation Press.

Lundberg, Craig C. 1976. 'Hypothesis Creation in Organizational Behavior Research'. *Academy of Management Review* 1(2):5–12.

Mainwaring, Scott, and Aníbal Pérez–Liñán. 2013. 'Democratic Breakdown and Survival'. *Journal of Democracy* 24(2):123–37.

Mainwaring, Scott, and Timothy Scully. 1995. *Building Democratic Institutions: Party Systems in Latin America*. Cambridge: Cambridge University Press.

Mainwaring, Scott, and Timothy R. Scully. 2010. 'Democratic Governance in Latin America: Eleven Lessons from Recent Experience'. In *Democratic Governance in Latin America*, edited by Scott Mainwaring and Timothy R. Scully, 365–404. Palo Alto: Stanford University Press.

Mainwaring, Scott, and Mariano Torcal. 2005. 'Party System Institutionalization and Party System Theory: After the Third Wave of Democratization'. 2005 Annual Meeting of the American Political Science Association, Washington, DC.

Mango, Andrew. 1996. 'Testing Time in Turkey'. *Washington Quarterly* 20(1):3.

Mango, Andrew. 2002. 'Atatürk: The Founding Father, Realist, and Visionary'. In *Political Leaders and Democracy in Turkey*, edited by Metin Heper and Sabri Sayarı, 9–24. Lanham: Lexington Books.

Mango, Andrew. 2004. *The Turks Today*. New York: Overlook Press.

Mardin, Şerif. 1966. 'Opposition and Control in Turkey'. *Government and Opposition* 1(3):375–88.

Mardin, Şerif. 1969. 'Power, Civil Society and Culture in the Ottoman Empire'. *Comparative Studies in Society and History* 11(3):258–81.

Mardin, Şerif. 1973. 'Center-Periphery Relations: A Key to Turkish Politics?' *Daedalus* 102(1):169–90.

Mardin, Şerif. 1978. 'Youth and Violence in Turkey'. *Archives Européennes de Sociologie* 19:229–54.

McLaren, Lauren M. 2008. *Constructing Democracy in Southern Europe: A Comparative Analysis of Italy, Spain, and Turkey*. London and New York: Routledge.

Mello, Brian. 2007. 'Political Process and the Development of Labor Insurgency in Turkey, 1945–80'. *Social Movement Studies* 6(3):207–25.

Mersel, Yigal. 2006. 'The Dissolution of Political Parties: The Problem of Internal Democracy'. *International Journal of Constitutional Law* 4(1):84–113.

Meyer, James H. 1997. 'Turkey's Leaders: Çiller's Scandals'. *Middle East Quarterly* 4(3):27–31.

Meyer, James H. 1998. 'Politics as Usual: Ciller, Refah and Susurluk: Turkey's Troubled Democracy'. *East European Quarterly* 32(4):489.

Milliyet. 1953. 'Demokrat Partiden İhraç Edilenler'. *Milliyet*, 29 August: 1. Accessed 6 February 2018. http://gazetearsivi.milliyet.com.tr/GununYayinlari/MQF8 kP4hIyeusQD6o7LdcQ_x3D__x3D_

Milliyet. 1954. 'Hüsnü Yaman Istanbul D. P. Müfettişi Oldu'. *Milliyet*, 3 September: 1, 3. Accessed 6 February 2018. http://gazetearsivi.milliyet.com.tr/GununYayinlari/ UfequLRQYn0yR_x2F_P1oDLqBQ_x3D__x3D_

Milliyet. 1955. '19 Demokrat Partili Mebus Haysiyet Divanına Verildi'. *Milliyet*, 13 October: 1. Accessed 6 February 2018. http://gazetearsivi.milliyet.com.tr/ GununYayinlari/sA4G2sa8_x2B_c5ZR9eIsAoo3w_x3D__x3D_

Milliyet. 1965a. 'Bursa Olayları Meclise Aksediyor: 11 Kişinin Tevkifi İstendi'. *Milliyet*, 6 July:1. Accessed 19 April 2018. http://gazetearsivi.milliyet.com.tr/ GununYayinlari/FoMJuliEGSf3xet14KZqtA_x3D__x3D_

Milliyet. 1965b. 'TİP'in Bursa Kongresi Basıldı, İl Merkezi Tahrip Olundu'. *Milliyet*, 5 July: 1. Accessed 19 April 2018. http://gazetearsivi.milliyet.com.tr/ GununYayinlari/FoMJuliEGSf3xet14KZqtA_x3D__x3D_

Milliyet. 1967a. '8'lerden Başkası Affedildi'. *Milliyet*, 30 April: 1, 7. Accessed 23 August 2017. http://gazetearsivi.milliyet.com.tr/GununYayinlari/5Mr1wvTH1 PjA3w8hP6X_x2F_Hw_x3D__x3D_

Milliyet. 1967b. 'Demirel, AP Grubunda Solculukla Suçlandı'. *Milliyet*, 14 June: 1. Accessed 18 May 2018. http://gazetearsivi.milliyet.com.tr/GununYayinlari/ 84DpldiNTVhi_x2B_TIftC_x2F_4DA_x3D__x3D_

Milliyet. 1967c. 'Ecevit: "8 Kişi Giderse 80 Bin Kişi Gelir", Dedi'. *Milliyet*, 17 April: 1, 7. Accessed 5 October 2017. http://gazetearsivi.milliyet.com.tr/GununYayinlari/ CnK4Tw75LIZRsdylx_x2F_9HNw_x3D__x3D_

Milliyet. 1967d. 'Prof Turan: "Demirel CHP ile yeni bir koalisyon hazırlıyor"'. *Milliyet*, 1 November: 1. Accessed 10 October 2017. http://gazetearsivi.milliyet. com.tr/GununYayinlari/wo8_x2B_1goFvtIMckc8uO9nzQ_x3D__x3D_

Milliyet. 1967e. 'Yeni Parti Kuruluyor: CHP'den 48 Senatör ve Mebus İstifa Etti'. *Milliyet*, 1 May: 1. Accessed 7 October 2017. http://gazetearsivi.milliyet.com. tr/GununYayinlari/dgumlz_x2B_n8WjrdZ6cKdigcg_x3D__x3D_

Milliyet. 1968. 'Ecevit: "Anayasayı AP Değiştiremez"'. *Milliyet*, 9 December: 1, 7. Accessed 12 November 2017. http://gazetearsivi.milliyet.com.tr/GununYayinlari/ DZ4Rpz_x2F_KLuaYy_x2B_y3fcETuA_x3D__x3D_

Milliyet. 1970a. '6'lar AP Genel Idare Kurulundan İstifa Etti'. *Milliyet*, 5 February: 1, 11. Accessed 24 April 2018. http://gazetearsivi.milliyet.com.tr/GununYayinlari/_ x2B_Ipdtl_x2F_HUkwRx_x2F_yMuH_x2B_0Jw_x3D__x3D_

Milliyet. 1970b. '26 AP'linin Kesin İhracı İstendi'. *Milliyet*, 25 June: 1, 11. Accessed 16 August 2017. http://gazetearsivi.milliyet.com.tr/GununYayinlari/gcKBh1a_ x2B_LJEb1jwqIXFA1Q_x3D__x3D_

Milliyet. 1970c. '72'lerin Muhtırası'. *Milliyet*, 23 January: 1, 11. Accessed 23 April 2018. http://gazetearsivi.milliyet.com.tr/GununYayinlari/_x2B_JJizCmxvwFtW0 We3DRcRg_x3D__x3D_

Milliyet. 1970d. 'Bilgiç: "AP Namuslu Teşkilât Mensuplarını Tasfiye Ediyor"'. *Milliyet*, 5 September: 9. Accessed 3 October 2017. http://gazetearsivi.milliyet.com.tr/ GununYayinlari/LYyE33jl7Ey4PGTsut7iaQ_x3D__x3D_

Milliyet. 1970e. 'Celal Kargılı CHP'den Çıkarıldı'. *Milliyet*, 22 July: 1, 9. Accessed 26 June 2017. http://gazetearsivi.milliyet.com.tr/GununYayinlari/zJubSK1tUXSAN vmrxPshig_x3D__x3D_

Milliyet. 1970f. 'Kargılı: "Ecevit CHPnin Mezarını Kazıyor" dedi'. *Milliyet*, 20 July: 1. Accessed 23 January 2018. http://gazetearsivi.milliyet.com.tr/GununYayinlari/4 39oN8vuWYdoH5bl0a1hZQ_x3D__x3D_

Milliyet. 1970g. 'Kılıçoğlu ve Önder AP'den Çıkarıldılar'. *Milliyet*, 30 January: 1, 11. Accessed 24 April 2018. http://gazetearsivi.milliyet.com.tr/GununYayinlari/ X5bXvj4Z636hsc4f5ftQhA_x3D__x3D_

Milliyet. 1970h. 'Topaloğlu: "Demirel Türkiye'yi Yönetemez"'. *Milliyet*, 31 August: 9. Accessed 19 April 2018. http://gazetearsivi.milliyet.com.tr/GununYayinlari/ P5HyAPq0XBjMLGHyIFRVOQ_x3D__x3D_

Milliyet. 1972a. 'CHP'den Ayrılan 500 Kişinin AP'ye Girdiği Açıklandı'. *Milliyet*, 31 December: 11. Accessed 25 July 2017. http://gazetearsivi.milliyet.com.tr/ GununYayinlari/36IABihUXFGHweN_x2B_c9NqMw_x3D__x3D_

Milliyet. 1972b. 'Satır CHP'den İstifa Etti'. *Millyet,* 29 July: 1, 9. Accessed 1 August 2017. http://gazetearsivi.milliyet.com.tr/GununYayinlari/36IABihUXFGHweN_x2B_c9NqMw_x3D__x3D_

Milliyet. 1973a. 'CHP Genel Sekreteri Konuştu . . . Eyüboğlu: "Beledeğimiz Oyu Alamadık" Dedi'. *Milliyet,* 16 October: 6. Accessed 24 August 2017. http://gazetearsivi.milliyet.com.tr/GununYayinlari/6OzEFn7DtEhVeIZ1A758gA_x3D__x3D_

Milliyet. 1973b. 'Kırıkoğlu (Merkez Yönetim Kuruluyla Birlikte) İstifa Etti'. *Milliyet,* 5 April: 1, 11. Accessed 25 July 2017. http://gazetearsivi.milliyet.com.tr/GununYayinlari/6OzEFn7DtEhVeIZ1A758gA_x3D__x3D_

Milliyet. 1975. 'Aksoy, Kesin İhraç Talebiyle CHP Disiplin Kurulu'na Verildi'. *Milliyet,* 20 March: 10. Accessed 29 July 2017. http://gazetearsivi.milliyet.com.tr/GununYayinlari/lvBZq47Hb2KTSvLs2uULVg_x3D__x3D_

Milliyet. 1976a. 'Demirel Yeniden AP Genel Başkanı Oldu'. *Milliyet,* 24 October: 1, 10. Accessed 24 April 2018. http://gazetearsivi.milliyet.com.tr/GununYayinlari/UpCMtQiD2SHfPFOWcl_x2F_DTw_x3D__x3D_

Milliyet. 1976b. 'Topuz: "Çankaya Kongresini Basanlar Partiden Atılacak"'. *Milliyet,* 8 June:1, 10. Accessed 20 October 2018. http://gazetearsivi.milliyet.com.tr/GununYayinlari/UpCMtQiD2SHfPFOWcl_x2F_DTw_x3D__x3D_

Milliyet. 1977. 'Dalokay ve Senatör Özer'in CHP'den İhracı İçin Temenni Kararı Alındı'. *Milliyet,* 1 August: 10. Accessed 5 September 2017. http://gazetearsivi.milliyet.com.tr/GununYayinlari/cIQroFTBey2dQ4uZSUDhcg_x3D__x3D_

Milliyet. 1977. 'Ecevit, "12'ler"le İstanbul'da Görüştü'. *Milliyet,* 22 December: 8. Accessed 11 November 2017. http://gazetearsivi.milliyet.com.tr/GununYayinlari/Mo_x2F_wfnuCDQTc7q8JjcySbQ_x3D__x3D_

Milliyet. 1979a. 'Hükümete Güvenoyu Veren Şenses CHP'den İhraç Edildi'. *Milliyet,* 6 December: 1, 12. Accessed 7 February 2018. http://gazetearsivi.milliyet.com.tr/GununYayinlari/Mo_x2F_wfnuCDQTc7q8JjcySbQ_x3D__x3D_

Milliyet. 1979b. 'Malatya Senatörü Hamdi Özer CHP'den İstifa Etti'. *Milliyet,* 20 June: 1, 9. Accessed 2 February 2018. http://gazetearsivi.milliyet.com.tr/GununYayinlari/WQJq22CJhfTiopO9SWaW9w_x3D__x3D_

Milliyet. 1980. 'Erbakan Tutuklandı'. *Milliyet,* 16 October: 1, 6. Accessed 28 May 2018. http://gazetearsivi.milliyet.com.tr/GununYayinlari/WQJq22CJhfTiopO9SWaW9w_x3D__x3D_

Milliyet. 1981. 'Partiler Kapatıldı'. *Milliyet,* 17 October: 1, 3. Accessed 28 May 2018. http://gazetearsivi.milliyet.com.tr/GununYayinlari/WQJq22CJhfTiopO9SWaW9w_x3D__x3D_

Milliyet. 1984a. 'Özal Hanedanı'. *Milliyet*, 25 July: 8. Accessed 12 October 2017. http://gazetearsivi.milliyet.com.tr/GununYayinlari/WQJq22CJhfTiopO9SWaW9w_x3D__x3D_

Milliyet. 1984b. 'Türkan Arıkan, ANAP'tan İstifa Etti'. *Milliyet*, 20 December: 7. Accessed 12 October 2017. http://gazetearsivi.milliyet.com.tr/GununYayinlari/WQJq22CJhfTiopO9SWaW9w_x3D__x3D_

Milliyet. 1985. 'Vural Arıkan İstifa Etti'. *Milliyet*, 17 May: 8. Accessed 12 October 2017. http://gazetearsivi.milliyet.com.tr/GununYayinlari/WQJq22CJhfTiopO9SWaW9w_x3D__x3D_

Milliyet. 1987. 'Keçeciler Lades Kurbanı Mı?' *Milliyet*, 3 August: 8. Accessed 12 October 2017. http://gazetearsivi.milliyet.com.tr/GununYayinlari/WQJq22CJhfTiopO9SWaW9w_x3D__x3D_

Milliyet. 1992a. 'Kalan Sağlar Bizimdir'. *Milliyet*, 2 December: 11. Accessed 2 November 2017. http://gazetearsivi.milliyet.com.tr/GununYayinlari/WQJq22CJhfTiopO9SWaW9w_x3D__x3D_

Milliyet. 1992b. 'Özal'a Yeni Parti'. *Milliyet*, 2 December: 1. Accessed 2 November 2017. http://gazetearsivi.milliyet.com.tr/GununYayinlari/WQJq22CJhfTiopO9SWaW9w_x3D__x3D_

Milliyet. 1992c. 'Semra Özal'da Ayrıldı'. *Milliyet*, 3 December: 11. Accessed 2 November 2017. http://gazetearsivi.milliyet.com.tr/GununYayinlari/WQJq22CJhfTiopO9SWaW9w_x3D__x3D_

Milliyet. 1997. 'Çiller: Çankaya Darbesi'. *Milliyet*, 21 June:18. Accessed 6 July 2018. http://gazetearsivi.milliyet.com.tr/GununYayinlari/1Qs18SrL2rljv9_x2B_yG2dnPw_x3D__x3D_

Milliyet. 1998. 'Refah Kapatıldı'. *Milliyet*, 17 January: 1. Accessed 9 April 2018. http://gazetearsivi.milliyet.com.tr/GununYayinlari/1Qs18SrL2rljv9_x2B_yG2dnPw_x3D__x3D_

Milliyet. 2005. 'AKPyi Sarsan İstifa'. *Milliyet*, 16 February. Accessed 21 December 2017. https://www.milliyet.com.tr/siyaset/akpyi-sarsan-istifa-105281

Milliyet. 2013. 'Ergenekon ve Balyoz'da Sır Dolu 12 Ölüm'. *Milliyet*, 23 October. Accessed 13 December 2017. http://www.milliyet.com.tr/ergenekon–ve–balyoz–da–sir–dolu–12/gundem/detay/1780703/default.htm.

Milliyet. 2015. 'AKP, Erdoğan Receive Many Times More Airtime'. *Milliyet*, 25 October. Accessed 20 December 2017. http://www.milliyet.com.tr/akp--erdogan-receive-many-times-more-airtimes-en-2138794/en.htm.

Morgan, Gareth, and Linda Smircich. 1980. 'The Case for Qualitative Research'. *Academy of Management Review* 5(4):491–500.

Muhsin, Öztürk. 2014. 'Turkey Now an Authoritarian Regime'. *Today's Zaman*, 27 April. Accessed 27 April 2014. http://www.todayszaman.com/national_turkey-now-an-authoritarian-regime_346188.html

Münir, Metin. 1996. 'Economic Policy: A Casualty of Party Politics?' *Euromoney*, 1 April: 158. Acccessed 27 September 2016. https://www.euromoney.com/article/b13209xygj8mt2/brighter-prospects-for-turkey

Musil, Pelin Ayan. 2011. *Authoritarian Party Structures and Democratic Political Setting in Turkey*. New York: Palgrave Macmillan.

Norris, Pippa, and Ronald Inglehart. 2019. *Cultural Backlash: Trump, Brexit, and Authoritarian Populism*. Cambridge: Cambridge University Press.

NTV. 2013. 'Erdoğan: Polis Kahramanlık Destanı Yazdı'. *NTV.com*, 24 June. Accessed 21 January 2018. https://www.ntv.com.tr/turkiye/erdogan-polis-kahramanlik-destani-yazdi,uMOX0uTl_EmkP4Ylu_2MEQ.

O'Donnell, Guillermo. 1994. 'Delegative Democracy'. *Journal of Democracy* 5(1):55–69.

O'Donnell, Guillermo. 1996. 'Illusions about Consolidation'. *Journal of Democracy* 7(2):34–51.

O'Donnell, Guillermo. 2003. 'Horizontal Accountability: The Legal Institutionalization of Mistrust'. In *Democratic Accountability in Latin America*, edited by Scott Mainwaring and Christopher Welna. New York: Oxford University Press.

O'Donnell, Guillermo, and Philippe C. Schmitter. 1986. *Transitions from Authoritarian Rule: Tentative Conclusions about Uncertain Democracies*. Baltimore: Johns Hopkins University Press.

Önal, Günsel. 1999. 'DYP'de Demirel'e Yakın İsim Kalmadı'. *Milliyet*, 5 February: 19. Accessed 30 November 2017. http://gazetearsivi.milliyet.com.tr/GununYayinlari/1Qs18SrL2rljv9_x2B_yG2dnPw_x3D__x3D_

Öniş, Ziya. 2004. 'Turgut Özal and His Economic Legacy: Turkish Neo-Liberalism in Critical Perspective'. *Middle Eastern Studies* 40(4):113–34.

Oruçoğlu, Berivan. 2015. 'Why Turkey's Mother of All Corruption Scandals Refuses to Go Away'. *Foreign Policy*, 6 January. Accessed 12 March 2015. https://foreignpolicy.com/2015/01/06/why-turkeys-mother-of-all-corruption-scandals-refuses-to-go-away/

OSCE. 2017. 'Lack of Equal Opportunities, One-Sided Media Coverage and Limitations on Fundamental Freedoms Created Unlevel Playing Field in Turkey's Constitutional Referendum, International Observers Say'. Organization for Security and Co-operation in Europe Office. *Organization for Security and Co-Operation in Europe*, 17 April. Accessed 22 March 2018. https://www.osce.org/odihr/elections/turkey/311726

Ostrogorski, Moisei. 1902. *Democracy and the Organization of Political Parties*. Vol. 2. Great Britian: Macmillan.

Özbudun, Ergun. 1993. 'State Elites and Democratic Political Culture in Turkey'. In *Political Culture and Democracy in Developing Countries*, edited by Larry Diamond, 295–316. Boulder: Lynne Rienner.

Özbudun, Ergun. 2000a. *Contemporary Turkish Politics: Challenges to Democratic Consolidation*. Boulder: Lynne Rienner.

Özbudun, Ergun. 2000b. 'The Politics of Constitution Making'. In *Contemporary Turkish Politics: Challenges to Democratic Consolidation*, edited by Ergun Özbudun, 49–72. Boulder: Lynne Rienner.

Özbudun, Ergun. 2011a. *The Constitutional System of Turkey: 1876 to the Present*. New York: Palgrave Macmillan.

Özbudun, Ergun. 2011b. 'Turkey's Constitutional Reform and the 2010 Constitutional Referendum'. *Mediterranean Politics: Turkey* 16:191–94.

Özbudun, Ergun. 2012. 'The Turkish Constitutional Court and Political Crisis'. In *Democracy, Islam and Secularism in Turkey*, edited by Ahmet T. Kuru and Alfred Stepan, 149–65. New York: Columbia University Press.

Özbudun, Ergun. 2013. *Party Politics and Social Cleavages in Turkey*. Boulder: Lynne Rienner.

Özbudun, Ergun. 2014. 'AKP at the Crossroads: Erdoğan's Majoritarian Drift'. *South European Society and Politics* 19(2):155–67.

Özbudun, Ergun. 2015. 'Turkey's Judiciary and the Drift Toward Competitive Authoritarianism'. *International Spectator* 50(2):42–55. doi: 10.1080/03932729. 2015.1020651.

Özbudun, Ergun. 2016. 'Personal Interview with Author'. 11 April.

Özbudun, Ergun, and Ömer Faruk Gençkaya. 2009. *Democratization and the Politics of Constitution-Making in Turkey*. Budapest and New York: Central European University Press.

Özdalga, Elizabeth. 2002. 'Necmettin Erbakan: Democracy for the Sake of Power'. In *Political Leaders and Democracy in Turkey*, edited by Metin Heper and Sabri Sayarı, 127–46. Lanham: Lexington Books.

Özdalga, Haluk. 2005. *Kötü Yönetilen Türkiye: Örnek Vaka DSP*. Istanbul: Kitap Yayinevi.

Özdemir, Cüneyt. 2020. 'Ali Babacan Cüneyt Özdemir'in Sorularını Yanıtlıyor'. *Cüneyt Özdemir Medya*, 26 May. Accessed 26 May 2020. https://www.youtube. com/watch?v=yRfITmbEaT8

Özen, Hayriye. 2013. 'Informal Politics in Turkey During the Özal Era (1983–1989)'. *Alternatives: Turkish Journal of International Relations* 12(4):77–91.

Özkan, Behlül. 2017. 'The Cold War-era Origins of Islamism in Turkey and its Rise to Power'. *Hudson Institute*, 5 November. Accessed 11 November 2017. https://www.hudson.org/research/13807-the-cold-war-era-origins-of-islamism-in-turkey-and-its-rise-to-power

Öztürk, Ahmet Erdil, and İştar Gözaydın. 2017. 'Turkey's Constitutional Amendments: A Critical Perspective'. *Research and Policy on Turkey* 2(2):210–24.

Panico, Christopher. 1999. 'Turkey: Violations of Free Expression in Turkey'. New York: Human Rights Watch.

Parry, Ken W. 1998. 'Grounded Theory and Social Process: A New Direction for Leadership Research'. *Leadership Quarterly* 9(1):85.

Paşa, Selda Fikret, Hayat Kabasakal and Muzaffer Bodur. 2001. 'Society, Organisations, and Leadership in Turkey'. *Applied Psychology: An International Review* 50(4):559–89.

Payaşlıoğlu, Arif T. 1964. 'Political Leadership and Political Parties'. In *Political Modernization in Japan and Turkey*, edited by Robert Edward Ward and Dankwart A. Rustow, 411–33. Princeton: Princeton University Press.

Peer, Basharat. 2017. *A Question of Order: India, Turkey, and the Return of Strongmen*. New York: Columbia Global Reports.

Pitel, Laura. 2018. 'Turkey Warned of Judicial Crisis over Jailed Journalists'. *Financial Times*, 15 January. Accessed 16 January 2018. https://www.ft.com/content/048dc200–f932–11e7–9b32–d7d59aace167.

Pope, Hugh. 1991. 'Turkish Leader Fires Defense Minister in Family Feud: Mideast: Deposed Official Was Once a Favorite Cousin, But He Disagreed with Wife of President Ozal. Nation's Gulf War Stance is Unaffected'. *Los Angeles Times*, 23 February: 27. Accessed 5 July 2015. https://www.latimes.com/archives/la-xpm-1991-02-23-mn-1539-story.html

Pope, Hugh. 1993. 'Profile: Turkey's First Female Prime Minister is No Wallflower'. *Los Angeles Times*, 22 June: 1. Accessed 5 July 2015. URLhttps://www.latimes.com/archives/la-xpm-1993-06-22-wr-5848-story.html

Post-Medya.com. 2015. '"TRT'ye Sansür Talimatını AKP Verdi": Öztunç CHP'nin Reklamının Yasaklanmasının Sebebinin AKP Olduğunu Söyledi'. *PM: Post-Medya*, 13 April. Accessed 20 December 2017. https://web.archive.org/web/20150516160856/http://www.postmedya.com/tv/trt-ye-sansur-talimatini-akp-verdi-h110043.html.

Poulton, Hugh. 1997. *Top Hat, Grey Wolf, and Crescent : Turkish Nationalism and the Turkish Republic*. New York: New York University Press.

Preston, Peter. 2013. 'Turkey's Voting for Censors'. *The Guardian*, 24 March. Accessed 20 December 2017. https://www.theguardian.com/media/2013/mar/24/turkey-voting-censors-hasan-cemal.

Pridham, Geoffrey. 2005. *Designing Democracy: EU Enlargement and Regime Change in Post-Communist Europe*. New York: Palgave Macmillan.

Przeworski, Adam. 1988. 'Democracy as a Contingent Outcome of Conflict'. In *Constitutionalism and Democracy*, edited by Jon Elster and Rune Slagsted, 59–80. Cambridge: Cambridge University Press.

Przeworski, Adam. 2003. 'Why Do Political Parties Obey Results of Elections?' In *Democracy and the Rule of Law*, edited by Jose Maria Maravall and Adam Przeworski, 114–44. Cambridge: Cambridge University Press.

Putnam, Robert D. 1976. *The Comparative Study of Political Elites*. Englewood Cliffs: Longman.

Rabasa, Angel, and F. Stephen Larrabee. 2008. *The Rise of Political Islam in Turkey*. Santa Monica: The RAND Corporation.

Radikal. 2004. 'Mesut Yılmaz Yüce Divan'da'. *Radikal*, 14 July.

Radikal. 2013. 'Polise Emri Ben Verdim'. *Radikal*, 24 June. Accessed 21 January 2018. http://www.radikal.com.tr/turkiye/polise-emri-ben-verdim-1138828/.

Rahat, Gideon, and Tamir Sheafer. 2007. 'The Personalization(s) of Politics: Israel, 1949–2003'. *Political Communication* 24(1):65–80.

Reporters Sans Frontières. 2013. *World Press Freedom Index 2013*. Paris: Reporters Sans Frontières.

Reporters Sans Frontières. 2014. *World Press Freedom Index 2014*. Paris: Reporters Sans Frontières.

Reporters Sans Frontières. 2015. *World Press Freedom Index 2015*. Paris: Reporters Sans Frontières.

Reporters Sans Frontières. 2016. *World Press Freedom Index 2016*. Paris: Reporters Sans Frontières.

Reporters Sans Frontières. 2017. *World Press Freedom Index 2017*. Paris: Reporters Sans Frontières.

Reporters Sans Frontières. 2019a. 'Business Reporters Now Being Harassed in Turkey'. Accessed 30 September 2019. https://rsf.org/en/business-reporters-now-being-harassed-turkey

Reporters Sans Frontières. 2019b. *World Press Freedom Index 2019*. Paris: Reporters Sans Frontières.

Reuters. 2016. 'Nearly 2,000 Legal Cases Opened for Insulting Turkey's Erdogan'. *Reuters*, 2 March. Accessed 9 February 2018. https://www.reuters.com/article/us-turkey-erdogan-lawsuit-idUSKCN0W42ES

Reuters, Jonathan Lyons. 1996. 'Corruption Allegations Mount Against Ciller'. *The Independent*, 10 May: 11. Accessed 9 September 2016. https://www.independent.co.uk/news/world/corruption-allegations-mount-against-ciller-1346490.html

Righter, Rosemary. 2011. 'Turkey's Military Resignations Make Erdogan Even Stronger'. *Newsweek*, 7 October. Accessed 27 November 2017. https://www.newsweek.com/turkeys-military-resignations-make-erdogan-even-stronger-67153

Rodrik, Dani. 2014. 'The Plot against the Generals'. *IAS School of Social Science* https://drodrik.scholar.harvard.edu/files/dani-rodrik/files/plot-against-the-generals.pdf

Rustow, Dankwart A. 1966. 'The Study of Elites: Who's Who, When, and How'. *World Politics* 18(04):690–717.

Rustow, Dankwart A. 1970. 'Transitions to Democracy: Toward a Dynamic Model'. *Comparative Politics* 2(3):337–63.

Şanlı, Ufuk. 2016. 'How Erdoğan Became Turkey's Biggest Media Boss'. *Al-Monitor: Turkey Pulse*, 30 June. Accessed 19 December 2017. https://www.al-monitor.com/pulse/originals/2016/06/turkey-erdogan-dictator-onslaught-press-freedom.html.

Sarı, Muhammed 2012. 'Demokrat Parti Dönemi Basınına Göre Iktidar-Muhalifet İlişkileri Açısından "Vatan Cephesi"'. In *10. Uluslararası Türk Dünyası Sosyal Bilimler Kongresi 28 August–2 September 2012,* edited by Vecdi Can and Köksal Şahin, 751–758. Istanbul: Türk Dünyası Araştırmaları Vakfı.

Sarıbay, Ali Yaşar. 1991. 'The Democratic Party 1946–1960'. In *Political Parties and Democracy in Turkey*, edited by Metin Heper and Frank Tachau, 119–33. London and New York: I. B. Tauris.

Sarılar, Süleyman. 1989. 'Vurun Kitaba'. *Cumhuriyet*, 25 February:1, 10. Accessed 24 January 2017. https://egazete.cumhuriyet.com.tr/oku/192/1989-02-25/0

Sartori, Giovanni. 1995. 'How Far Can Free Government Travel?' *Journal of Democracy* 6(3):101–11.

Sayarı, Sabri. 1978. 'The Turkish Party System in Transition'. *Government and Opposition* 13(1):39–57.

Sayarı, Sabri. 1985. *Generational Changes in Terrorist Movements: The Turkish Case.* Santa Monica: The RAND Corporation.

Sayarı, Sabri. 1990. 'Turgut Özal'. In *Political Leaders of the Contemporary Middle East and North Africa: A Biographical Dictionary*, edited by Bernard Reich, 395–401. Westport: Greenwood Press.

Sayarı, Sabri. 2002a. 'Adnan Menderes: Between Democratic and Authoritarian Populism'. In *Political Leaders and Democracy in Turkey*, edited by Metin Heper and Sabri Sayarı, 65–86. Lanham: Lexington.

Sayarı, Sabri. 2002b. 'The Changing Party System'. In *Politics, Parties and Elections in Turkey*, edited by Sabri Sayarı and Yılmaz Esmer, 9–32. Boulder: Lynne Rienner.

Sayarı, Sabri. 2010. 'Political Violence and Terrorism in Turkey, 1976–80: A Retrospective Analysis'. *Terrorism and Political Violence* 22(2):198–215.

Sayarı, Sabri. 2016. 'Personal Interview with Author'. 19 July.

Sayarı, Sabri, and Yılmaz Esmer, eds. 2002. *Politics, Parties, and Elections in Turkey.* Boulder: Lynne Rienner.

Sayarı, Sabri, Pelin Ayan Musil and Özhan Demirkol, eds. 2018. *Party Politics in Turkey: A Comparative Perspective.* London: Routledge.

Sayın, Ayşe. 2021. '"Parlamenter Demokrasi Mazi Oldu" Diyen Erdoğan'a Muhalefet Nasıl Yanıt Verdi?' *BBC Türkçe,* 2 June. Accessed 2 October 2021. https://www.bbc.com/turkce/haberler-turkiye-57335850

Schmitter, Philippe C., and Terry Lynn Karl. 1991. 'What Democracy Is . . . And Is Not'. *Journal of Democracy* 2(3):75–88.

Şener, Abdullatif. 2017. *Türkiye Gündemi.* Halk TV. Accessed 21 April 2017. https://www.youtube.com/watch?v=3HEC2_vrfbw

Sever, Ahmet. 2015. *Abdullah Gül ile 12 yıl: Yaşadım, Gördüm, Yazdım.* Istanbul: Doğan Kitap.

Shaheen, Kareem. 2018. '"Suffocating Climate of Fear" in Turkey Despite End of State of Emergency'. *The Guardian,* 19 July. Accessed 18 August 2018. https://www.theguardian.com/world/2018/jul/18/turkeys-state-of-emergency-ends-but-crackdown-continues

Shapiro, Ian. 2002. 'Problems, Methods, and Theories in the Study of Politics, or What's Wrong with Political Science and What to Do about It'. *Political Theory* 30(4):596–619.

Sherwood, W. B. 1967. 'The Rise of the Justice Party in Turkey'. *World Politics* 20(1):54–65.

Şık, Ahmet. 2016. 'Allah'ın Büyük Lütfu'. *Cumhuriyet,* 12 December. Accessed 25 January 2018. http://www.cumhuriyet.com.tr/haber/turkiye/644388/_Allah_in_buyuk_lutfu_.html.

Sinclair-Webb, Emma. 2013. 'The Turkish Trial That Fell Far Short'. *The New York Times,* 6 August. Accessed 14 December 2017. https://www.nytimes.com/2013/08/07/opinion/global/the-turkish-trial-that-fell-far-short.html

Solaker, Gülsen. 2014. 'Turkey Bans Reporting on Corruption Investigation of Ex-Ministers'. *Reuters,* 27 November. Accessed 16 January 2018. https://www.reuters.com/article/us-turkey-corruption/turkey-bans-reporting-on-corruption-investigation-of-ex-ministers-idUSKCN0JA1OR20141126.

Solaker, Gülsen. 2019. 'Cumhurbaşkanlığı Sistemiyle Geçen Bir Yılın Bilançosu'. *Deutsche Welle,* 21 June. Accessed 23 July 2019. https://www.dw.com/tr/cum

hurba%C5%9Fkanl%C4%B1%C4%9F%C4%B1-sistemiyle-ge%C3%A7en-bir-y%C4%B1l%C4%B1n-bilan%C3%A7osu/a-49265227

Soyaltın, Diğdem. 2013. 'Turkish Court of Accounts in Crisis: An Urgent Problem, Yet Not a Main Concern?' *Research Turkey* 19.

Sözcü. 2016. 'Ergenekon İçin Kim Ne Demişti?' *Sözcü*, 21 April. Accessed 17 December 2017. http://www.sozcu.com.tr/2016/gundem/ergenekon-icin-kim-ne-demisti-1195230/.

Srivastava, Mehul. 2017. 'Assets Worth $11bn Seized in Turkey Crackdown'. *Financial Times*, 7 July. Accessed 12 August 2017. https://www.ft.com/content/fed595d0-631e-11e7-8814-0ac7eb84e5f1

Stockton, Hans. 2001. 'Political Parties, Party Systems, and Democracy in East Asia: Lessons from Latin America'. *Comparative Political Studies* 34(1):94–119. doi: 10.1177/0010414001034001004.

Sunar, İlkay, and Sabri Sayarı. 1986. 'Democracy in Turkey: Problems and Prospects'. In *Transitions from Authoritarian Rule: Southern Europe*, edited by Phiippe C. Schmitter, Guillermo O'Donnell and Laurence Whitehead, 165–86. London: Johns Hopkins University Press.

Sural, Nurhan. 2007. 'A Pragmatic Analysis of Social Dialogue in Turkey'. *Middle Eastern Studies* 43(1):143–52.

Sütçü, Güliz. 2011a. 'Democratic Party and Democracy in Turkey: With Special Reference to Celal Bayar and Adnan Menderes'. Unpubl. Doctoral Diss., Department of Political Science, Bilkent University.

Sütçü, Güliz. 2011b. 'Playing the Game of Democracy through the Electoral Mechanism: The Democratic Party Experience in Turkey'. *Turkish Studies* 12(3):341–56.

Szyliowicz, Joseph S. 1975. 'Elites and Modernization in Turkey'. In *Political Elites and Political Development in the Middle East*, edited by Frank Tachau, 23–65. Cambridge, MA: Schenkman Publishing.

T24. 2018. 'AYM'den Şahin Alpay ve Mehmet Altan Hakkında Tahliye Kararı'. *T24.com*, 11 January. Accessed 11 January 2018. http://t24.com.tr/haber/aymden-sahin-alpay-ve-mehmet-altan-hakkinda-tahliye-karari,532572.

T24. 2019. 'Erdoğan: İstanbul'u Sel Götürüyor Beyefendi Tatilde, Dün Bir Bugün İki'. *T24.com*, 24 August. Accessed 29 August 2019. https://t24.com.tr/haber/erdogan-bay-kemal-sana-turk-bayragini-da-ogretecegiz,836316

Tachau, Frank. 1991. 'The Republican People's Party, 1945–1980'. In *Political Parties and Democracy in Turkey*, edited by Metin Heper and Jacob M. Landau, 99–117. London and New York: I. B. Tauris.

Tachau, Frank. 2000. 'Turkish Political Parties and Elections: Half a Century of Multiparty Democracy'. *Turkish Studies* 1(1):128–48.

Tachau, Frank. 2002. 'Bülent Ecevit: From Idealist to Pragmatist'. In *Political Leaders and Democracy in Turkey*, edited by Metin Heper and Sabri Sayarı, 107–25. Lanham: Lexington Books.

Tachau, Frank, and Metin Heper. 1983. 'The State, Politics, and the Military in Turkey' *Comparative Politics* 16(1):17–33.

Tanık, Ünal. 2009. 'Demirel'in Özal'dan Son İntikamı'. *Kanal46*, 2 November. Accessed 2 November 2017. https://www.kanal46.com/serbest-kursu/demirel-in-ozal-dan-son-intikami-h19006.html

Taşyürek, Muzaffer. 2009. *Adnan Menderes*. Istanbul: Anonim Yayıncılık.

Tekdal, Arif. 2015. 'Under Iron Grip of Erdoğan HSYK Renders Rule of Law in Turkey Obsolete'. *Today's Zaman*, 2 May.

Temelkuran, Ece. 2006. 'Genel Olarak Üç İdam'. *Milliyet*, 10 May. Accessed 11 December 2016. http://www.milliyet.com.tr/-genel-olarak--uc-idam/ece-temelkuran/guncel/yazardetayarsiv/10.05.2006/156405/default.htm.

Temelkuran, Ece. 2015. *Turkey: The Insane and the Melancholy*. Translated by Zeynep Beler. London: Zed Books.

Tepe, Sultan. 2005. 'Turkey's AKP: A Model "Muslim-Democratic" Party?' *Journal of Democracy* 16(3):69–82.

Tessler, Mark, and Ebru Altınoğlu. 2004. 'Political Culture in Turkey: Connections among Attitudes toward Democracy, the Military and Islam'. *Democratization* 11(1):21–50.

The Economist. 1968. 'Where Lies the Greater Danger?' *The Economist* 226 (6498):32–35.

Tilly, Charles. 1978. *From Mobilization to Revolution*. New York: McGraw-Hill.

Time. 1954. 'Republicans v. Democrats'. *Time* 64(22):20–21. Accessed 29 November 2015. https://discovery.ebsco.com/c/xppotz/viewer/html/c3kud2a46z

Time. 1956a. 'Afraid of Criticism'. *Time* 68(2):30. Accessed 7 September 2015. https://discovery.ebsco.com/c/xppotz/viewer/html/5xpt4mlcxj

Time. 1956b. 'Costly Joke'. *Time* 68(5):22. Accessed 30 July 2017. https://content.time.com/time/subscriber/article/0,33009,867027,00.html

Time. 1956c. 'A Scalp for the Taking'. *Time* 68(7):20. Accessed 13 August 2016. https://content.time.com/time/subscriber/article/0,33009,865429,00.html

Time. 1956d. 'Straitjacket in Turkey'. *Time* 67(24):83. Accessed 6 November 2016. https://content.time.com/time/subscriber/article/0,33009,862179,00.html

Time. 1957. 'Surrounded by Dangers'. *Time* 70(20):42. Accessed 11 November 2016. https://discovery.ebsco.com/c/xppotz/viewer/html/jw743p5x5r

Time. 1958a. 'The "Ankara Hilton"'. *Time* 72(19):72. Accessed 11 October 2016. https://content.time.com/time/subscriber/article/0,33009,938047,00.html

Time. 1958b. 'The Impatient Builder'. *Time* 71(5):20. Accessed 7 September 2015. https://content.time.com/time/subscriber/article/0,33009,865731,00.html

Time. 1958c. 'Silence, Please'. *Time* 71(7):31. Accessed 17 February 2017. https://content.time.com/time/subscriber/article/0,33009,862909,00.html

Time. 1960a. 'Children's Hour'. *Time* 75(22):22. Accessed 30 May 2015. https://content.time.com/time/subscriber/article/0,33009,939667,00.html

Time. 1960b. 'The People's Choice'. *Time* 75(23):23. Accessed 6 June 2015. https://content.time.com/time/subscriber/article/0,33009,874111,00.html

Time. 1960c. 'Slow to Anger'. *Time* 75(19):28. Accessed 5 September 2015. https://content.time.com/time/subscriber/article/0,33009,897450,00.html

Time. 1960d. 'Turkey: Premier v. Press'. *Time* 75(3):60. Accessed 18 January 2017. https://discovery.ebsco.com/c/xppotz/viewer/html/hjmavq4fzn

Time. 1965. 'Battling a Ghost'. *Time* 86(15):60. Accessed 10 August 2016. https://content.time.com/time/subscriber/article/0,33009,842174,00.html

Time. 1979a. 'Ecevit Gets a Reprieve'. *Time* 114(1):39-42. Accessed 9 October 2016. https://content.time.com/time/subscriber/article/0,33009,916831,00.html

Time. 1979b. 'A Game of Musical Chairs'. *Time* 114(18):57. Accessed 9 October 2016. https://content.time.com/time/subscriber/article/0,33009,916981,00.html

Time. 1980. 'A New Year's Warning as Terrorism Runs Wild, the Military Gets Impatient'. *Time* 115(2):40. Accessed 11 September 2016. https://time.com/vault/issue/1980-01-14/page/48/

Tisdall, Simon, and Robert Tait. 2010. 'Turkey Voters "Moving Towards Supporting Government Reforms"'. *The Guardian*, 11 September. Accessed 17 December2017.https://www.theguardian.com/world/2010/sep/10/turkey-voters-government-reforms

Tittensor, David. 2014. *The House of Service: The Gulen Movement and Islam's Third Way.* New York: Oxford University Press.

Toprak, Binnaz. 1996. 'Civil Society in Turkey'. In *Civil Society in the Middle East*, edited by Augustus Richard Norton, 87–118. Leiden: Brill.

Toptan, Köksal. 2016. 'Personal Interview with Author'. 2 February.

Tran, Mark. 2007. 'Gul Elected as Turkish President'. *The Guardian*, 29 August. Accessed 5 August 2018. https://www.theguardian.com/world/2007/aug/28/turkey.marktran1

Traynor, Ian. 2008. 'Supreme Court Threatens Islamic Party's Government in Turkey'. *The Guardian*, 1 April. Accessed 26 January 2018. https://www.theguardian.com/world/2008/apr/01/turkey.

Traynor, Ian, and Constanze Letsch. 2013. 'Turkey Divided More Than Ever by Erdoğan's Gezi Park Crackdown'. *The Guardian*, 21 June. Accessed 14 April 2018. https://www.theguardian.com/world/2013/jun/20/turkey-divided-erdogan-protests-crackdown

Turam, Berna. 2007. *Between Islam and the State: The Politics of Engagement*. Palo Alto: Stanford University Press.

Turam, Berna. 2012. 'Turkey under AKP: Are Rights and Liberties Safe?' *Journal of Democracy* 23(1):109–18.

Turan, İlter. 2007. 'Unstable Stability: Turkish Politics at the Crossroads?' *International Affairs* 83(2):319–38.

Turan, İlter. 2011. 'Türk Siyasi Partilerinde Lider Oligarşisi: Evrimi, Kurumsallaşması ve Sonuçları'. *İ. Ü. Siyasal Bilgiler Fakültesi Dergisi* 45:1–21.

Turan, İlter. 2013. 'Two Steps Forward, One Step Back: Turkey's Democratic Transformation'. In *Turkey's Democratization Process*, edited by Carmen Rodriguez, Antonio Avalos, Ana I. Planet and Hakan Yilmaz. London and New York: Routledge.

Turan, İlter. 2015. *Turkey's Difficult Journey to Democracy: Two Steps Forward, One Step Back*. Oxford: Oxford University Press.

Turan, İlter. 2016. 'Personal Interview with Author'. 19 April.

Ünlü, Mustafa, Hikmet Bila Rıdvan Akar and Ali İnandım. 1998. *12 Eylül Belgeseli*. Cine 5 Documentary.

Urbinati, Nadia. 2011. 'Representative Democracy and Its Critics'. In *The Future of Representative Democracy*, edited by Sonia Alonso, John Keane and Wolfgang Merkel, 23–49. Cambridge: Cambridge University Press.

Uyar, Hakkı. 2012. *Vatan Cephesi*. Istanbul: Büke Yayıncılık.

Waldman, Simon, and Emre Calışkan. 2017. *The New Turkey and Its Discontents*. New York: Oxford University Press.

Walker, Ignacio. 2013. *Democracy in Latin America: Between Hope and Despair*. Translated by Krystin Krause, Holly Bird and Scott Mainwaring. Notre Dame: University of Notre Dame Press.

White, Jenny B. 2013. *Muslim Nationalism and the New Turks*. Princeton: Princeton University Press.

White, Jenny B. 2015. 'The Turkish Complex: Big Man, Hero, Traitor, State'. *Campagna-Kerven 2015 Lecture on Modern Turkey*, Boston University, 15 March.

White, Jenny B. 2016. 'Personal Interview with Author'. 21 September.

White, Jenny B. 2017. 'Spindle Autocracy in the New Turkey'. *Brown Journal of World Affairs* 24(1):23–37.

Yalman, Ahmet Emin. 1970a. *Yakın Tarihte Gördüklerim ve Geçirdiklerim 2 (1922–1971)*. 2nd ed. Istanbul: Rey Yayınları.

Yalman, Ahmet Emin. 1970b. *Yakın Tarihte Gördüklerim ve Geçirdiklerim, Cilt IV (1945–1970)*. Istanbul: Rey Yayınları.

Yaşar, Beril. 2014. 'Demokrat Parti'de Parti İçi Demokrasi (1946–1960)'. *Tarih Okulu Dergisi* 7(18):503–41.

Yavuz, M. Hakan. 2013. *Toward an Islamic Enlightenment: The Gülen Movement*. Oxford: Oxford University Press.

Yavuz, M. Hakan, and Bayram Balcı. 2018. *Turkey's July 15th Coup: What Happened and Why*. Salt Lake City: University of Utah Press.

Yavuz, M. Hakan, and Rasim Koç. 2018. 'The Gülen Movement vs. Erdoğan: The Failed Coup'. In *Turkey's July 15th Coup: What Happened and Why*, edited by M. Hakan Yavuz and Bayram Balcı, 78–97. Salt Lake City: University of Utah Press.

Yayla, Ahmet S. 2017. 'Turkey's State of Emergency Horrible For Democracy'. *The Huffington Post*, 21 January. Accessed 4 January 2018. https://www.huffingtonpost.com/entry/turkeys-state-of-emergency-decrees-a-matter-of-life_us_5883b47ce4b0d96b98c1dc87.

Yeğen, Oya. 2017. 'Constitutional Changes under the AKP Government of Turkey'. *Tijdschrift voor Constitutioneel Recht* 1(1):70–84.

Yeşilada, Birol A. 2002. 'The Virtue Party'. In *Political Parties in Turkey*, edited by Barry Rubin and Metin Heper, 62–81. London: Frank Cass.

Yiğit, Ahu. 2013. 'New Faces, Old Ways: The Dynamics of Turkish Political Leadership'. *Open Democracy*, 7 August 2013. Accessed 14 April 2015. https://www.opendemocracy.net/ahu-yigit/new-faces-old-ways-dynamics-of-turkish-political-leadership.

Yıldız, Nuran. 1996. 'Demokrat Parti İktidarı (1950–1960) ve Basın'. *Ankara Üniversitesi SBF Dergisi* 51(1):481–505.

Yılmaz, Turan. 2015. 'Turkish Parliament Now Grants Secret Fund to President Erdoğan'. *Hürriyet Daily News*, 27 March. Accessed 27 April 2017. http://www.hurriyetdailynews.com/turkish-parliament-now-grants-secret-fund-to-president-erdogan-80287.

Zaman, Amberin. 2017a. 'Heads Roll at Top of Turkey's Military'. *Al-Monitor: Turkey Pulse*, 2 August. Accessed 11 January 2018. https://www.al-monitor.com/pulse/originals/2017/08/military-coup-reshuffle-gulenists.html.

Zaman, Amberin. 2017b. 'Pro-Kurdish HDP Leader Kicked out of Turkish Parliament'. *Al-Monitor: Turkey Pulse*, 21 February. Accessed 12 January 2018. https://www.al-monitor.com/pulse/originals/2017/02/turkey-unseats-figen-yuksedag-kurdish-bloc-leader.html.

Zaman, Amberin. 2017c. 'Turkey Deals Death Blow to Kurdish Leadership with DBP Conviction'. *Al-Monitor: Turkey Pulse*, 28 March. Accessed 11 January 2018. http://www.al-monitor.com/pulse/originals/2017/03/dbp-kamuran-yuksek-sentenced-eight-years-prison.html#ixzz53vWvp9pa.

Zaman, Amberin. 2017d. 'Turkish Crackdown Snares Amnesty International Chair'. *Al-Monitor: Turkey Pulse*, 13 June. Accessed 11 January 2018. https://www.al-monitor.com/pulse/originals/2017/06/turkey-targets-rights-groups.html.

Zaman, Amberin. 2019. 'Opposition Retakes Istanbul Mayor's Office to Find Powers Shrinking'. *Al-Monitor: Turkey Pulse*, 26 June. Accessed 28 June 2019. https://www.al-monitor.com/originals/2019/06/istanbul-prepares-swear-in-ekrem-imamoglu.html

Zarakolu, Ragıp. 2013. 'Sopa Mevzusu . . .' *Sendika.org*, 16 July. Accessed 14 August 2017. https://sendika.org/2013/07/sopa-mevzusu-ragip-zarakolu-ozgur-gundem-129897/

Zeldin, Wendy. 2014a. 'Turkey: Law on Internet Publications Amended'. *The Law Library of Congress*, 24 February. Accessed 1 March 2018. https://www.loc.gov/item/global-legal-monitor/2014-02-24/turkey-law-on-internet-publications-amended/

Zeldin, Wendy. 2014b. 'Turkey: New Amendments to Laws on Judiciary'. *The Law Library of Congress*, 10 March. Accessed 1 March 2018. https://www.loc.gov/item/global-legal-monitor/2014-03-10/turkey-new-amendments-to-laws-on-judiciary/

Zeyrek, Deniz 2014. 'Abdullah Gül: Bizim Cenahtan Yapılan Epeyce Saygısızlık Var'. *Hürriyet*, 20 August. Accessed 21 January 2018. http://www.hurriyet.com.tr/abdullah-gul-bizim-cenahtan-yapilan-epeyce-saygisizlik-var-27036878.

INDEX

Note: n indicates note; *t* indicates table